From
Civil Strife
to Peace
Building

Studies in International Governance is a research and policy analysis series from the Centre for International Governance Innovation (CIGI) and Wilfrid Laurier University Press. Titles in the series provide timely consideration of emerging trends and current challenges in the broad field of international governance. Representing diverse perspectives on important global issues, the series will be of interest to students and academics while serving also as a reference tool for policy-makers and experts engaged in policy discussion. To reach the greatest possible audience and ultimately shape the policy dialogue, each volume will be made available both in print through WLU Press and, twelve months after publication, online under the Creative Commons License.

From Civil Strife

Examining Private Sector Involvement in West African Reconstruction

to Peace Building

Hany Besada, editor

CIGI
The Centre for International
Governance Innovation
Centre pour l'innovation dans
la gouvernance internationale

Wilfrid Laurier University Press
WLU

Wilfrid Laurier University Press acknowledges the financial support of the Government of Canada through its Book Publishing Industry Development Program for its publishing activities. Wilfrid Laurier University Press acknowledges the financial support of the Centre for International Governance Innovation. The Centre for International Governance Innovation gratefully acknowledges support for its work program from the Government of Canada and the Government of Ontario.

Library and Archives Canada Cataloguing in Publication

From civil strife to peace building : examining private sector involvement in West African reconstruction / Hany Besada, editor.

(Studies in international governance series)
Co-published by the Centre for International Governance Innovation.
Papers originally presented at a conference held in Accra, Ghana, Dec. 6–7, 2007.
Issued also in electronic format.
Includes bibliographical references and index.
ISBN 978-1-55458-228-0

1. Economic development—Africa, West. 2. Peace-building—Africa, West. 3. Postwar reconstruction—Africa, West. 4. Africa, West—Economic conditions—1960– . 5. Conflict management—Africa, West.
I. Besada, Hany II. Centre for International Governance Innovation III. Series: Studies in international governance

JZ5584.A35F76 2009   338.966   C2008-907329-0

Library and Archives Canada Cataloguing in Publication

From civil strife to peace building [electronic resource] : examining private sector involvement in West African reconstruction / Hany Besada, editor.

(Studies in international governance series)
Co-published by the Centre for International Governance Innovation.
Papers originally presented at a conference held in Accra, Ghana, Dec. 6–7, 2007.
Includes bibliographical references and index.
Electronic edited collection in PDF, ePub, and XML formats.
Issued also in paper format.
ISBN 978-1-55458-052-1

1. Economic development—Africa, West. 2. Peace-building—Africa, West. 3. Postwar reconstruction—Africa, West. 4. Africa, West—Economic conditions—1960– . 5. Conflict management—Africa, West.
I. Besada, Hany II. Centre for International Governance Innovation III. Series: Studies in international governance

JZ5584.A35F76 2009   338.966

© 2009 The Centre for International Governance Innovation (CIGI) and Wilfrid Laurier University Press
Cover photo courtesy of iStockphoto.com. Cover design and text design by Blakeley Words+Pictures.

This book is printed on FSC recycled paper and is certified Ecologo. It is made from 100% post-consumer fibre, processed chlorine free, and manufactured using biogas energy.

Printed in Canada

Contents

List of Figures and Tables

Figures

Tables

Foreword I

Darren Schemmer

I am honoured to write a foreword for these essays, which arose from the two-day conference "From Civil Strife to Peace Building," on the theme of peacebuilding and the role of the private sector in leading reconstruction. The event was organized by the Centre for International Governance Innovation (CIGI), the Laurier Centre for Military Strategic and Disarmament Studies (LCSMDS), and the Kofi Annan International Peacekeeping Training Centre (KAIPTC). and it was held in Accra, Ghana, in December 2007. As one of the presenters at the opening session, I had the privilege to hold a dialogue with the other presenters as well as the participants. I was impressed with the quality of the discussion and with the knowledge of the subject matter that was displayed. The organizers are to be commended not only for bringing together leading international academics and respected policy-makers who have been directly involved in issues relating to peacebuilding and economic reconstruction but also for their success at attracting key decision makers to debate topical issues. The papers compiled in this book examine lessons learned in peace-building efforts currently under way in Côte d'Ivoire, Liberia, and Sierra Leone.

Continued policy and legal research to clarify the obligations of private-sector actors in zones of conflict and weak governance, as well as to raise awareness among companies regarding those obligations, is important. Clarity and predictability of obligations will benefit responsible businesses, given that the environment in which they conduct business is often unpredictable. Conferences such as this one help advance the research and knowledge base so that the private sector can play a positive and strategic role in supporting the reconstruction efforts of the region's governments and donor communities. The theme is timely. The governments of Côte d'Ivoire, Liberia, and Sierra Leone all realize that economic recovery and growth are essential to their nations' well-being. Without question, there has been increased commercial activity in these three countries over the past year. And it is not just commercial interest that is growing. For example, the Bretton Woods Institutions have taken the risky step of investing in the Côte d'Ivoire as a way of pulling that country forward. By taking the lead, they are building confidence and setting the stage for private reinvestment in Côte d'Ivoire.

In Liberia, concentrated efforts to clear debt arrears have meant that a burden is being lifted. This will enable the government to pursue more effectively its current four-pronged agenda: security, economic revitalization, governance and rule of law, and infrastructure and basic services.

Sierra Leone has just recently held elections, and the new president is calling for attitudinal change in the hope of fostering wealth and prosperity. The slashing of red tape for businesses is a presidential priority. The "democratic dividend" of the elections and the smooth transition of power from the ruling party to the former opposition should benefit the country's development.

Côte d'Ivoire, Liberia, and Sierra Leone have all been blessed and cursed by their abundance of natural resources. Much of their economic growth comes from those resources, and also much of their strife. Thus, effective action to address the peace and security challenges that so often arise when natural resources are being exploited needs to be well coordinated with broader efforts related to conflict prevention, peacebuilding, resources governance, and economic development.

Long-term peace consolidation in the Mano River Basin sub-region—which includes Guinea, Sierra Leone, and Liberia, but primarily the western frontier of Côte d'Ivoire—is closely linked to the security situation. There is an ongoing need to enhance dialogue among those countries and to promote conflict-prevention measures. Regional co-operation among the Mano River Union countries is vital to such dialogue. However, peace-consolidation efforts at the national and international levels must be supplemented by confidence-building measures among border communities, through specific dispute-resolution mechanisms and strengthened trade relations.

Several years after the conflicts have ended in Sierra Leone and Liberia, a revitalization appears to be taking place that could promote both economic growth as well as enhance security; the two are closely linked.

Despite these signs of positive change in Sierra Leone and Liberia, peace and stability remain fragile. Many of the root causes of conflict—corruption, marginalization, the disempowerment of rural communities, the lack of economic opportunities, and inadequate state capacity to deliver basic services—remain largely unaddressed. Youth unemployment and underemployment are still serious concerns, and to address these issues attention will have to focus on sustainable economic growth. Once the right conditions are created to attract investors—such as Sierra Leone is now doing by concentrating on providing energy for Freetown—business costs will decrease and more jobs will thereby be created. An educated workforce will be necessary in order to develop a diversified economy, and efforts must continue to ensure that access to education remains a priority. The UN Peacebuilding Fund, alongside key development partners, is supporting these efforts.

Notwithstanding the crisis in Côte d'Ivoire, that country remains an important economic engine for the region. Traffic at the Port of Abidjan rose by 13.5 percent in 2007 to a record 21.4 million tonnes, owing in part to recently signed agreements with Mali and Burkina Faso. With the signing of the Ouagadougou Agreement in March 2007 and the Supplementary Agreements in November, predictions are that GDP growth for Côte d'Ivoire will reach 5 percent in five years' time. It stood at only 1.5 percent for 2007.

Liberia is rich in natural resources—timber, diamonds, rubber—and the government is working hard to put the regulatory frameworks in place to ensure that these industries remain sustainable and that the benefits return to the country and are not squandered, which was what happened during the protracted war.

Private-sector investment in developing countries has the potential to bring development, greater prosperity, and an enhanced quality of life to communities around the globe. The impact of business activity is usually positive; sometimes, however, the security and well-being of people may be negatively affected. When conducting business in developing countries, companies have been known to contribute to human-rights violations or environmental degradation. In zones of conflict or weak governance, the challenges faced by business are greater and more complex, as is the potential for harm to individuals.

Canadian firms are active in the region, especially in the mining, petroleum, and environmental sectors, in which they have long experience. Over the past few years, with the return of peace and stability, they have shown increased interest in the region. And Canadian companies are not alone—others, too, have been eyeing Sierra Leone, Liberia, and Côte d'Ivoire and investing in those countries.

Civil society has an important role to play in the effective management of natural resources, and a number of Canadian and local organizations are active in monitoring the extractive industries and supporting those communities that are directly affected. Civil society can and does work collaboratively with companies in extractive industries. At the same time, they do much to promote human rights and sustainable development and to educate companies regarding both.

The natural-resources sector, if managed effectively, can contribute a great deal to conflict prevention as well as to regional peace and security. Natural-resource revenues can be a force for stability, social development, and sustained economic growth when they are reinvested in human-resource development—in education, communications, health care, and the like. Corporate social responsibility (CSR)—which companies realize is vital to their long-term growth—is taking hold in the region. International companies, including Canadian ones, are playing a leading role in this. The Canadian Department of Foreign Affairs and International Trade (DFAIT) is actively promoting CSR with the Canadian business community and civil society groups. Canada's activities are framed by internationally recognized voluntary standards, such as the OECD Guidelines for Multinational Enterprises and the UN Global Compact.

Another tool that will be effective in increasing stability and ensuring economic development is the Extractive Industries Transparency Initiative (EITI)—a multi-stakeholder initiative designed to encourage companies involved in extractive industries to disclose royalties and other payments to host governments. Governments then disclose those revenues to a wide audience. When revenues are made more transparent, opportunities for corruption are reduced, public revenues are better spent, and governments are more accountable.

Diamonds, in particular, are notorious for fuelling armed conflict. Diamonds have funded devastating conflicts in Angola, Côte d'Ivoire, the Democratic Republic of Congo, and Sierra Leone. Canada has made a strong effort to break the link between diamonds and conflict by supporting a number of UN resolutions on "conflict diamonds" and by working closely with international partners to develop the Kimberley Process Certification Scheme.

One factor that allows the development and continuation of war economies has been the access warring parties have to international markets. This enables them to sell their conflict resources or exchange them directly for arms or military equipment. One tool of multilateral diplomacy that has the potential to deny belligerents this access is targeted UN Security Council sanctions. Targeted sanctions are much more refined and discriminating than the comprehensive trade sanctions that were used in the past. Targeted sanctions as used today are directed against specific individuals or classes of goods. Such sanctions include asset freezes, travel bans, arms embargoes, and commodity boycotts. These steps place pressure on specific leaders and "abused" resources rather than whole economies.

I want to end on a positive note. While the international community has provided support, it is the resilience and perseverance of the peoples of the region that is most noteworthy, especially when viewed against the many years of hardship they have endured. The citizens of Liberia and Sierra Leone have elected new governments that are focused on fighting corruption and lawlessness and on improving the situation of their populations. Côte d'Ivoire's economy is growing and will help drive regional growth. The road ahead will not be easy, but the benefits are there for all. A better future is possible.

Darren Schemmer
High Commissioner of Canada
Accra, Ghana

Foreword II

Jonathan G. Coppel

Conflicts weaken the fabric of societies, through the tragic loss of lives and livelihoods. They also destroy the productive potential of an economy. This happens because when opponents seek military advantage, a country's infrastructure—roads, ports, railways, and so on—invariably is a strategic target. But conflict also damages an economy in much more profound ways. Once respect for the rule of law is lost and governance systems fail to function, the institutions that underpin a market economy are also severely damaged. This limits commercial exchange to basic transactions, and high risk and uncertainty deter otherwise viable investments. The end result is low or negative growth, fewer jobs, and greater poverty.

Weak economic outcomes protract conflict and can also rekindle tensions. This is why rapidly rebuilding the economic system is an important part of all post-conflict reconstruction efforts. The challenges are immense, however. The issues are weighty and go well beyond rebuilding a country's critical infrastructure. They concern the role of economic development in rebuilding a nation for a sustainable and peaceful future. How, for instance, is it possible to re-establish confidence among private investors and attract new investment when political and government institutions are still weak? To complicate matters further, in post-conflict situations, governments are under intense pressure to demonstrate tangible results quickly, to ensure against slipping into renewed conflict.

Yet when resources are scarce and implementation capacity is limited, and there are so many needs to address, where do you start? Clearly, there is a need to establish and focus on priority areas. How, then, are these priorities to be established? And can one afford to ignore the legacies of past injustices and reform the existing economic system by tackling the obstacles to investment and private sector development? Or does one need to start anew, thinking beyond policy reform and in terms of policy design that aims to address the economic causes of conflict at their source?

These were some of the issues addressed at a CIGI conference that was convened in Accra, Ghana, in December 2007 to examine the private sector's role in post-conflict economies, drawing on the experience of Sierra Leone, Côte d'Ivoire, and Liberia. This book brings together the research and policy-oriented papers from the conference. The papers by leading international academics and respected policy-makers from around the continent and elsewhere articulate the role the private sector plays in meeting the challenges of post-conflict reconstruction. They also distill the lessons learned so far in identifying what needs to be done, and how, in order to reconstruct the private sector in these three West African countries.

The three countries are geographically contiguous, yet they differ rather sharply in terms of how the conflicts they suffered came about as well as the challenges they face today in rebuilding the private sector:

- Sierra Leone emerged from a decade of civil war in 2002. That conflict was fuelled primarily by disputes over natural resources, a collapse of the state, a lack of public services, and a corrupt judicial system. While good progress has been made in rebuilding and developing political institutions, economic development is hampered by Sierra Leone's lack of economic diversification. It depends heavily on the mining industry, diamond smuggling, and a large informal economy.
- Liberia marked the end of thirteen years of civil war in 2003 with the resignation of President Charles Taylor and the signing of the Comprehensive Peace Agreement. Progress on economic reconstruction has since been made but is very slow owing to a lack of basic infrastructure, financial resources, and equipment. The peace that has been re-established is fragile, partly because the Liberian state's authority in some areas is weak.
- The conflict in Côte d'Ivoire has been less intense than in the other two countries, and the level of economic development is higher than in either. Nonetheless, stability remains precarious, and strengthening the peace will require that the citizens be encouraged to feel that they are no longer excluded from the economy. In part this will require the fostering of economic opportunities.

Clearly, then, in these three post-conflict situations a common template for private-sector development will not work. That said, sharing experiences, learning from peers, and benchmarking can help all three countries identify important factors and pinpoint what works and what does not. This approach, moreover, goes hand in hand with the fostering of dialogue—something that is crucial in post-conflict countries.

It is not possible here to survey all of the recommendations and findings from the conference. However, I would mention two points of particular importance to private-sector development in post-conflict countries that came out strongly during the conference. First, there is a need to restore a favourable image of the economy. Positive perceptions are easily lost and, once lost, take considerable time to rebuild. Doubts that peace is permanent will delay investment decisions, especially those of foreign investors, slowing the pace of reconstruction. This underscores the need for investment promotion efforts, initially targeting members of the diaspora, for it is they who tend to be the first investors to return.

Second, there is a general consensus that private investment is one of the main drivers of sustained economic growth. Since the vast majority of investment in West African economies and elsewhere is domestic, policies aimed at mobilizing investment need to concentrate on fostering conditions conducive to investment more broadly, not just foreign investment. In this context, experts at the CIGI conference stressed the importance of creating a balanced overall climate for investment, through efforts to rebuild and improve critical infrastructure, fight corruption, provide access to education, promote regional economic integration, and establish a transparent, predictable regulatory environment.

CIGI's approach to private-sector development (i.e., sharing mutual experiences) is the same one the OECD has been applying and refining for almost half a century. OECD investment co-operation programs, such as the NEPAD–OECD Africa Investment Initiative, have been applying these techniques in various development contexts. For instance, NEPAD–OECD has developed capacity-building tools such as the Policy Framework for Investment, which can be used by African governments that are interested in conducting a comprehensive assessment of their investment climate. The goal here is to build a policy reform road map that addresses obstacles and that mobilizes beneficial investment in support of development. Through such initiatives we are very pleased to have been associated with the CIGI conference in Accra in December 2007.

I am certain that those who are working on private-sector reconstruction—not just in Liberia, Côte d'Ivoire, and Sierra Leone, but in other fragile states as well—will learn from the practices, assessments, and analyses offered by the practitioners and private-sector development experts that this volume brings together.

Jonathan G. Coppel
Executive Program Manager,
NEPAD-OECD Africa Investment Initiative

Acknowledgements

This book is a compilation of insightful dissertations from those passionate about making a lasting difference in Africa. An international conference on the post-conflict and economic reconstruction efforts currently under way in the West African "fragile states" of Liberia, Sierra Leone, and Cote d'Ivoire was held December 6–7, 2007, in Accra, Ghana. The conference was a joint initiative organized by the Centre for International Governance Innovation (CIGI), the Laurier Centre for Military Strategic and Disarmament Studies (LCMSDS), and the Kofi Annan International Peacekeeping Training Centre (KAIPTC).

A CIGI conference report and this edited volume are the major compilations of the conference. The discussions focused on peacebuilding efforts and the private sector's role as a catalyst for economic growth and political stability in this historically war-ravaged region. A forum of debate and discussion brought together leading academics, respected policy-makers, and global thinkers from the international arena and across the continent to examine the way forward for the region.

Although I repeatedly put the friendship of some of my colleagues to the test at times with requests for comments on various chapters of this book, many people offered sage advice and gave liberally of their valuable time to this end. This book would not have been possible without the tireless efforts and determination of my colleague Miran Ternamian. His strategic insight and inquisitiveness encouraged me to delve deeper into the region's conflict-ridden past through the experience and expertise of our veteran scholars and practitioners. My esteemed colleague Vadim Ermakov surpassed expectations in working thoroughly on this book to explore the subtle nuances of a fragile state's transition into peace and prosperity. His knack for meticulous research and timely advice helped streamline a seemingly impossible task, ensuring the successful completion of this volume. Another indispensable member of CIGI's research team and a great source of inspiration was Erica Dybenko, who contributed selflessly.

Many other people offered their sincere encouragement and guidance during this process and gave liberally of their own valuable time. For this I am truly thankful. Lansana Gberie, senior associate and head of the Liberia Office of the International Centre for Transitional Justice (ICTJ), and Ariana Goetz, Ph.D. candidate at the Balsillie School of International Affairs, undertook the Herculean task of compiling this edited book, and their diligence was instrumental in making this work a reality.

I am especially grateful to CIGI senior management, particularly John English, Daniel Schwanen, Andy Cooper, and Max Brem, whose unwavering belief in my abilities and their endearing willingness to listen, even when it would have been easier not to, revitalized my efforts every step of the way. Without their leadership, mentorship, and encouragement this book could not have been compiled. I would also like to acknowledge CIGI's event team for their professionalism, dedication, and hard work in helping to arrange all the necessary logistics behind the conference.

Complementing the efforts of my research team were three Balsillie Fellows—Shanna Scarrow, Paul Cescon, and Ashley Heideman—to whom I am enormously indebted. Their passionate quest to better understand the complexity of the continent as it relates to international governance is indeed commendable.

Finally, without the financial, institutional, and moral support of our conference partners, namely CIGI, LCMSDS, and KAIPTC, all this would not have been possible. In particular, I would like to thank Terry Copp, Director of LCMSDS, Major General John Attipoe, Commandant of KAIPTC, and John Pokoo (formerly Opoku), Program Coordinator for the Small Arms and Light Weapons at KAIPTC, for their assistance, support, and tremendous patience in seeing this book through to completion.

It is our hope that the following pages will influence effective policy that will not only promote peace through justice in our time but also ensure a more tolerant and prosperous future for the next generation of Africans.

Hany Besada
Senior Researcher & Program Leader,
Health and Social Governance, CIGI

List of Acronyms

ACC	Anti-Corruption Commission
ACPA	Accra Comprehensive Peace Accord
ACS	American Colonization Society
AfDB	African Development Bank
AFL	Armed Forces of Liberia
AMNet	Advocacy Movement Network
APBEF	Ivoirian Banking Association
APC	All Peoples Congress
APRM	African Peer Review Mechanism
APSA	African Peace and Security Agenda
ATU	Anti-Terrorism Unit
AU	African Union
BCEAO	Central Bank of West African States
BHP	Bumbuna Hydroelectric Project
BKPS	Bo–Kenema Power Station
BOT	buy–own–transfer
BRC	Business Reform Commission
BRVM	Bourse Régionale des Valeurs Mobilières
BTU	Brigade Training Unit
CAISTAB	Caisse de Stabilisation et de Soutien des Prix des Produit Agricoles
CAS	country assistance strategy
CCA	common country assessment
CDF	comprehensive development framework
CEPICI	Ivoirian Investment Centre
CFAIT	Canadian Department of Foreign Affairs and International Trade
CIE	Compagnie Ivoirienne d'Electricité
CIGI	Centre for International Governance Innovation
CNSI	Commission Nationale de Supervision de l'Identification
CEA	Evaluation and Support Committee
CNE	National Electoral Commission
CRC	Constitutional Review Commission

CPA	Comprehensive Peace Agreement
CPC	Cadre Permanent de Concertation
CST	country support team
DDR	disarmament, demobilization, and reintegration
DFID	United Kingdom Department for International Development
DPO	development policy organization (or operation)
DRC	Democratic Republic of Congo
ECOMOG	Ceasefire Monitoring Group
ECOWAS	Economic Community of West African States
EEC	European Economic Community
EGRG	economic governance and recovery grant
EGSC	Economic Governance Steering Committee
EITI	Extractive Industries Transparency Initiative
EPCA	emergency post-conflict assistance
ERSG	Executive Representative of the Secretary-General
EUCOM	U.S. European Command
FANCI	Forces Armées Nationales de Côte d'Ivoire
FDI	foreign direct investment
FDA	Forestry Development Agency
FDS	Forces de Défense et Sécurité
FGM	female genital mutilation
FIAS	Foreign Investment Advisory Service
FN	Forces Nouvelles
FPI	Front Populaire Ivoirien
FPM	Military Provident Fund
FTO	field training officer
FTZ	free-trade zone
GAC	General Auditing Commission
GC	Governance Commission
GOSL	Government of Sierra Leone
GRC	Governance Reform Commission
HDI	Human Development Index
HIPC	heavily indebted poor country
IBC	Construction and Property International
ICC	International Criminal Court; also Integrated Command Centre
ICF	Investment Climate Facility
ICRC	International Committee of the Red Cross
ICTA	Investment Climate Team for Africa
ICTR	International Criminal Tribunal for Rwanda
ICTY	International Criminal Tribunal for the Former Yugoslavia
IDP	internally displaced persons
IEC	Independent Electoral Commission
IET	Initial Entry Training
IFC	International Finance Corporation
IGNU	Interim Government of National Unity
IMATT	International Military Advisory and Training Team

IMF	International Monetary Fund
INPFL	Independent National Patriotic Front of Liberia
INS	Institut National de la Statistique
IPP	independent power producer
IPRS	Interim Poverty Reduction Strategy
IRC	International Refugee Council
IsDB	Islamic Development Bank
ITU	International Telecommunications Union
JSDP	Justice Sector Development Program
ISU	Internal Security Unit
KAIPTC	Kofi Annan International Peacekeeping Training Centre
KPCS	Kimberley Process Certification Scheme
LAC	Liberian Agriculture Company
LBBF	Liberia Better Business Forum
LCSMDS	Laurier Centre for Strategic Military and Disarmament Studies
LEITI	Liberia Extractive Industries Transparency Initiative
LMA	Linas–Marcoussis Accord
LNP	Liberia National Police
LPPD	Liberia Public Private Sector Dialogue
LRDC	Liberian Reconstruction and Development Committee
LTV	loan-to-value
LURD	Liberians United for Reconciliation and Democracy
MDGs	millennium development goals
MDRI	Multilateral Debt Relief Initiative
MFA	Mouvement des Forces de l'Avenir
MEP	Ministry of Energy and Power
MIGA	Multilateral Investment Guarantee Agency
MJP	Mouvement pour la Justice et la Paix
MNS	Ministry of National Security
MoD	Ministry of Defense
MODEL	Movement for Democracy in Liberia
MoJ	Ministry of Justice
MPCI	Mouvement Patriotique de la Côte d'Ivoire
MPIGO	Mouvement Populaire du Grand Ouest
MRU	Mano River Union
MSU	Mechanical Services Unit
MTI	Ministry of Trade and Industry
NBI	National Bureau of Investigation
NCP	National Commission for Privatisation
NDPL	National Democratic Party of Liberia
NEPAD	New Partnership for African Development
NIC	National Investment Commission
NPA	National Port Authority; or National Power Authority
NPFL	National Patriotic Front of Liberia
NPRC	National Provisional Ruling Council
NPTA	National Police Training Academy
NRS	National Recovery Strategy

NSA	National Security Agency
NSC	National Security Council
NTGL	National Transitional Government of Liberia
ODC	Office of Defense Cooperation
OECD	Organisation for Economic Co-operation and Development
OHCHR	Office of the High Commissioner for Human Rights
ONI	Office National de l'Identification
ONS	Office of National Security
ONUCI	Opération des Nations Unies en Côte d'Ivoire
OPA	Ouagadougou Peace Accord
PA	Pretoria Accord
PAE	Pacific Architects and Engineers
PANAFU	Pan African Students Union
PAP	paper and paper board
PBC	UN Peacebuilding Commission
PCRD	Policy Framework on Post-Conflict Reconstruction and Development
PCS	Peace Consolidation Strategy
PDCI	Parti Démocratique de Côte d'Ivoire
PMDC	Peoples Movement for Democratic Change
PNP	Peoples National Party
PNRRC	Programme National de Reinsertion et de Rehabilitation Communautaire
PPO	probationary police officers
PPCC	Public Procurement and Concession Commission
PPRC	Political Parties Registration Commission
PRS	Poverty Reduction Strategy
PRSP	Poverty Reduction Strategy Paper
PSD	private-sector development
PSU	Police Support Unit
QRU	quick-response unit
RDR	Rassemblement des Republicains
RET	renewable energy technology
RHDP	Rassemblement des Houphouétistes pour la Démocratie et la Paix
RoC	Republic of Congo
PRAST	Provincial Advisory and Support
RRI	rapid results initiatives
RSLAF	Republic of Sierra Leone Armed Forces
RUF	Revolutionary United Front
SAGEM	Société d'Application Générales Electriques et Mécaniques
SDC	Swiss Agency for Development and Cooperation
SES	Senior Executive Service
SIP	Small Investment Program
SIR	Société Ivoirienne de Raffinage
SLBF	Sierra Leone Business Forum
SLET	Sierra Leone External Telecommunications

SLNTC	Sierra Leone National Telecommunications Company
SLP	Sierra Leone Police
SLPA	Sierra Leone Ports Authority
SLPA	Sierra Leone Roads Authority
SLPP	Sierra Leone People's Party
SOD	Police Special Operations Division
SOE	state-owned enterprise
SRSG	Special Representative of the UN Secretary General in Sierra Leone
SSA	Sub-Saharan Africa
SSR	security-sector reform
SSS	Special Security Services
TI-CPI	Transparency International Corruption Perception Index
TOKEN	Transfer of Knowledge through Expatriate Nationals
TRC	Truth and Reconciliation Commission
UDHR	Universal Declaration of Human Rights
ULIMO	United Liberation Movement of Liberia
UMEOA	Economic and Monetary Union of West Africa
UNAMSIL	UN Mission in Sierra Leone
UNCT	UN Country Team
UNCTAD	UN Conference on Trade and Development
UNDAF	UN Development Assistance Framework
UNDP	UN Development Programme
UNECA	UN Economic Commission for Africa
UNICEF	UN Children's Fund
UNIDO	UN Industrial Development Organization
UNIFEM	United Nations Fund for Women
UNIOSIL	UN Integrated Office in Sierra Leone
UNIPSIL	UN Integrated Peacebuilding Office in Sierra Leone
UNMIL	UN Mission in Liberia
UNOCI	UN Operation in Côte d'Ivoire
UNOWA	UN Office for West Africa
UNPBF	United Nations Peacebuilding Fund
UNSC	United Nations Security Council
UNVs	UN volunteers
UPDCI	L'Union pour la Sémocratie et la Paix en Côte d'Ivoire
USAID	U.S. Agency for International Development
UTL	Unitil
VAT	value added tax
VITIB	Village de Technologies de l'Information et de la Biotechnologie
WAEMU	West African Economic and Monetary Union
WAMCO	West African Mining Company
WB	World Bank

Peacebuilding and the Role of the Private Sector in Post-Conflict West Africa: A Conceptual Framework

Hany Besada, Vadim Ermakov, and Miran Ternamian

Peacebuilding

Peacebuilding initiatives inherently emphasize human security. Human security is usually guaranteed by the state through local ownership of peacebuilding processes that nurture efforts at reconciliation after justice has been attained. As always, peacebuilding efforts in West Africa seek to institutionalize sustainable peace and impart the responsibility for keeping that peace to each member of society. Consolidating peace within the civil-society framework promotes economic stability, human dignity, and social cohesion.

Côte d'Ivoire

In January 2003, after the peace agreement in Cote d'Ivoire collapsed during implementation, the major political parties and the Forces Nouvelles (which controlled the north of the country) signed the Linas–Marcoussis Accord, which established a framework for peace and reconciliation to be implemented by a government of national reconciliation. At that point, the UN Security Council (UNSC) stepped in to ensure progress. In November 2006, the UNSC extended the mandate of President Laurent Gbagbo and Prime Minister Charles Banny for another twelve months and postponed the presidential and legislative elections. Despite significant progress, the peace process in Côte d'Ivoire remains fragile. Political mistrust continues to run deep among the parties regarding the conflict, and more needs to be done to ensure sustainable peace.

The maintenance of peace and stability in Côte d'Ivoire after the prolonged conflict is directly linked to the success of the reconstruction process in all sectors of the economy—in the financial sphere in particular. As Addison, Le Billon, and Murshed (2001, 1) state, if broad-based peace and reconstruction is to be achieved, financial systems must be rebuilt. In this vein, the dearth of private investment has the potential to ignite further conflict. This suggests why so many post-conflict economic reconstruction plans specifically target vulnerable segments of the population—it is in order to ensure their

1

engagement and participation in economic reconstruction as the first step toward peacebuilding. Peace, if it is to take hold, requires sturdy private and civil bases. Very often the groups selected for economic reconstruction efforts include former combatants, internally displaced persons, women, minority populations, and other traditionally disenfranchised groups.

Côte d'Ivoire's government is addressing the following issues regarding peacebuilding: education; the demobilization of fighters; and the decommissioning of weapons. To achieve these, past combatants need to be reintegrated with civil society through retraining. Many join the police or find work as security guards. Reintegration has also involved offering soft loans and vocational training for ex-combatants who are returning to the agricultural sector and providing them with basic agricultural inputs. Creating new job opportunities for young people remains a challenge, one that will need to be addressed by developing private enterprise and reforming agriculture, mining, refineries, and other business and service sectors. Also needed is general education with regard to concepts such as democracy, human rights, and the rule of law. Here, the government can do much by holding free and fair elections and committing itself to equitable national development and economic transparency.

Ivoirian women face mounting economic difficulties—unemployment in particular—as well as discrimination and physical and psychological abuse. In all of these, rural women experience greater difficulties than urban women. It would be enormously helpful to peacebuilding and reconstruction if obstacles were removed in terms of their education and employment, and if there were mechanisms for extending them bank loans and other forms of credit.

The US Institute of Peace has made the following recommendations for improving the peace process:

- Explore traditional methods for resolving conflict that utilize local and religious leaders and non-governmental organizations (NGOs). Civil society should strive to become more cohesive, especially by including traditional rulers and religious leaders. Those traditional authorities must unite to establish firm positions on issues such as peacebuilding, economic development, justice, the role of the media and the empowerment of women.
- Organize national dialogue to solve smaller issues at the grassroots level. In addition, NGOs should have regular dialogue with the ministries.
- Focus on political and economic reconciliation of the sort that external actors (the UN, the African Union, etc.) can initiate and facilitate but that internal actors must carry out. Also, external entities can be urged to harmonize their policies in order to secure the trust of national actors, ensure adequate planning and the

mobilization of resources, and avert the risk of national actors exploiting divisions within the international community.

- Urge the international community to help with DDR[1] implementation and to bring to justice perpetrators of violence, perhaps through UN sanctions or the International Criminal Court (ICC).

During the present phase of development in Côte d'Ivoire, peacebuilding and economic development can be viewed as mutually reinforcing. However, the country will have to remain at peace in order to sustain progress in economic development and job creation. The major challenges on the path of peacebuilding include these: the prevailing culture of impunity and corruption; and the power wielded by the armed forces, which must be made to accept government control if peacebuilding is to work in Côte d'Ivoire.

Sierra Leone

The brutal civil war in Sierra Leone, which lasted more than a decade, brought enormous misery to a large proportion of the population. It cost many their lives and left countless others with physical and psychological scars. It also devastated the national infrastructure, which made it much more challenging to embark on peacebuilding. Despite all of this, Sierra Leone today is one of the most successful of all the post-conflict African states in terms of DDR and economic growth.[2] That said, the country faces a multitude of developmental challenges and obstacles to peacebuilding, which will have to be addressed effectively in order to ensure long-term peace and stability.

After the war, Sierra Leone's economy faced stagnation. To address this, immediately after the conflict ended, the government and the Revolutionary United Front (RUF)[3] jointly established reintegration programs for former combatants. These programs included skills training and basic education as well as monthly stipends. The purpose was to help former combatants return quickly to civilian life. In addition, RUF members were permitted to join the national armed forces and/or the police.

Women[4] and young people continue to be at an economic disadvantage in Sierra Leone. For example, women are less likely to have the same access to education and advanced skills training. Furthermore, they lack property rights and workplace protections. As a result, women are significantly less productive and secure economically, relative to men. To address these problems, the government, helped by the international community, established special economic-reconstruction programs for women and young people—including job training programs and employment seminars—while establishing credit mechanisms that would enable women to feel more secure in Sierra Leone.

According to Labonte (2004), reforms to the mining and agricultural sectors did much to encourage successful peacebuilding after the civil war. Once peacebuilding commenced with the end of the civil conflict, the government slowly strengthened its control over the country's diamond resources.[5] The revived diamond industry generated jobs that drove down unemployment. In the country's agrarian communities, poor access to resources was a serious grievance, and continues to be. Access to land, tools, seed, water, and other resources is vital to these communities' social and economic stability. External actors, including international NGOs, have helped develop a number of effective agrarian practices pertaining to the agricultural sector.

Based on the recommendation of the Technical Working Group, the Peace Building Fund (PBF)[6] Steering Committee for Sierra Leone approved in July 2008 seven new projects at a cost of $16.9 million (UN 2008). This approval brings the total amount for green-lighted PBF projects to more $32 million for Sierra Leone (African Press Organization 2008). The projects include the following: support for a Reparations Program; social reforms aimed at empowering women and children; rehabilitation of the prison system; the building of capacity for the Anti-Corruption Commission; and the promotion of initiatives to help create sustainable energy. Projects pending approval include ones that would support Parliament and civil society, establish a peacebuilding engagement committee, and help the National Commission for Democracy uphold basic human rights and freedoms.

A great deal of progress has been made in fostering peace in Sierra Leone, but it is too early to state categorically that Sierra Leone is a success story. For long-term peace to be achieved there, the government will also have to combat corruption, reform the principal income-earning industries, create more jobs, reduce poverty, promote basic democratic values, and hold itself accountable to its citizens.

Much progress has been made since the civil war ended in 2002, but Sierra Leone still faces urgent barriers to lasting peace and reconciliation. Security threats that could turn the tide on any long-term reform strategies include these two: the presence of militia command structures in the countryside; and lingering regional conflicts that could still flare as a result of fringe political uprisings. The government must address fundamental political challenges and clashing postwar social ideologies in the context of its new mandate. By addressing poverty, inequality, high unemployment, and the lack of effective governance structures and institutions, Sierra Leone's new government could help build confidence among socially alienated youth while improving accountability, battling corruption, and ushering in a renewed social contract of reform.

Liberia

The resignation of the former president of Liberia, Charles Taylor, and the signing of a comprehensive peace agreement in August 2003, marked the end of thirteen years of civil war. Since then Liberia has experienced relative peace.

Fair elections have opened the doors to more democratic reforms, economic growth, and hope for a better future. Liberia continues to be one of the UN's most expensive peacekeeping operations (IRIN 2008). Even so, in August 2007 the UN Mission in Liberia (UNMIL) was able to declare that "Liberia has become a generally stable country in a volatile sub-region" (UNPF 2008, 3).

Liberia is relatively peaceful now, but its fragility should not be underestimated. The risk of a return to lawlessness is still present; subtle evidence of this can be found across the society's political, social, and economic realms. Steps are being taken to ensure that unemployment, poor communications, shortages of basic necessities, and the weak authority of the state do not make violent outbreaks more likely to reoccur.

Liberia's task at hand might well be insurmountable without the international community's active support. President Ellen Johnson-Sirleaf's efforts to involve the global community in Liberia's political and economic future are commendable. Indeed, Liberia's new national policy is aimed at attracting and promoting bilateral and multilateral aid for the country. This shift in policy will help create a national image based on goodwill and co-operation, which will undoubtedly place Liberia and its president in a more proactive and responsible light.

DDR is a key priority. This will require the government to secure a clear mandate to establish and maintain security for the Liberian people. This in turn will allow other necessary transformations to take place, including the restoration of national pride.

The new government will fail in its mandate if it turns a blind eye to its war-ravaged citizens. The country requires national strategies aimed at recovery and development if it hopes to reinvigorate the economy. Significant numbers of Liberians were profoundly affected by the war yet either have not enrolled in new programs or are still displaced. Reintegration and rehabilitation of war-ravaged populations will be key to national revitalization; if this is not done, the social and economic recovery of communities will be harshly affected.

Democracy, rule of law, and human rights remain areas of concern for Liberia. In this regard, many reforms in the judicial sector must be viewed as encouraging. For example, a Truth and Reconciliation Commission has been established, institutions of justice are being reformed, legal professionals are being trained, and new standards are being set for human rights protections and judicial autonomy. Despite these commendable achievements, much reform remains to be implemented to ensure the proper administration of justice. Media restrictions, violence against women, and a lack of transparency and accountability with respect to suspected war criminals facing transitional justice, all remain widespread.

Restoring Liberia's infrastructure will help foster the democratic transition and ensure that civil society takes part in this process of change. The rebuilding of bridges, roads, and water and sanitation systems will be a first step in establishing community-based recovery programs. These programs will complement training and skills development, allowing Liberia's economic and institutional reconstruction to nurture the country's social fabric and become a driving force for stability and security.

Conclusion

Eradicating poverty, addressing inequality, promoting justice, and ensuring human security can all strengthen citizens' trust in government. West African leaders must understand that peace, social cohesion, economic progress, and democratic reforms can all promote to a functional society.

There is little doubt that West Africa's political, social, and economic landscape has at times been damaged by outsiders' commercial and political interference. It is clear that, far from fulfilling the hopes of West Africans, political leaders—despite their (sometimes) best intentions—have failed to create vibrant economies and durable democratic institutions.

However, this reality should not impede the international community's efforts to play a constructive role in Côte d'Ivoire, Sierra Leone, and Liberia. To encourage effective governance, the international community needs to help those countries ameliorate conditions that threaten to bring about state collapse. The challenge facing the international community is to determine which strategies will stop the violence and stimulate investment and job creation.

It is imperative to remember that peacekeeping forces on their own cannot bring about lasting stability and reconciliation. What *can* do that is co-operation among partners from all realms of society that would lead to tolerance, security, prosperity, accountable and effective governance, and—ultimately—robust and resilient institutions that nurture nascent democracies. West African states deserve no less.

Private Sector

The international community tends to believe that in many fragile African countries, a strong private sector is crucial to broad-based economic growth, a peace economy, and (it follows) poverty reduction and state reconciliation. This is especially true with regard to Liberia, Sierra Leone, and Côte d'Ivoire, which have only recently emerged from years of civil war. Crispin Grey-Johnson, The Gambia's Secretary of State for Higher Education, puts it this way: "A typical African country in conflict is poor, with a weak government and public institutions, a small private sector, high illiteracy, a narrow skills base, and limited capabilities for guaranteeing security" (Grey-Johnson 2006).

Grey-Johnson also points out that the current state of affairs "is rendered even more dire by civil strife, whose effects on the economy and the society at large are debilitating." And "the situation after the conflict is one of destruction: infrastructure destroyed; basic services, water and fuel supplies and electricity disrupted or lost; and transportation system barely functioning" (Grey-Johnson 2006).

Once this general problem is recognized, it must be addressed by stimulating growth in the domestic private sector, by attracting foreign direct investment (FDI) for reconstruction, and by establishing a "good governance" approach to peacebuilding. Communities cannot prosper unless private investment restores markets and generates employment opportunities.

Côte d'Ivoire

Unlike Liberia and Sierra Leone, which were utterly devastated by civil war, Côte d'Ivoire emerged from its conflict merely dilapidated. In kind, however, the economic legacy of that conflict has been quite similar: capital flight,[7] destroyed infrastructure, and a sharp decrease in economic production.

In the present day, insecurity and violence continue to impede reconstruction efforts, the resumption of basic services (such as electricity, water, and gas), and the re-establishment of government authority and administrative services at the local level, not to mention private and international investment. The Côte d'Ivoire government well recognizes that to attract successful private-sector development, at a minimum it will have to foster institutions capable of protecting property rights. Sustainable recovery will not occur without a flourishing private sector and political reconciliation supported by a peace economy, and for that to come about, other sectors—most important, the public sector—will have to be resurrected as strong and legitimate operations.

The strengthening of the judiciary in 2007 was a timely response to a serious bottleneck in private-sector operations. It was accomplished by supporting the Center for Legal Information, which provides information on legislation and major case law.

Key Ivoirian policy objectives that require a strong private sector include these: ensuring macroeconomic stability, generating employment, and restoring growth. To those ends the country needs to re-establish systems for managing public finances as well as develop monetary and exchange-rate policies. World Bank figures indicate that in 2006, private-sector credits and net foreign assets increased by 6 and 2 percent respectively.[8]

Significant public investment in rebuilding social and physical infrastructure is expected to encourage the development of private banking. That said, it is highly unlikely that Côte d'Ivoire will entrust infrastructure rebuilding programs to the private sector[9] in the immediate post-conflict period, especially with regard to providing credit and micro-financing. It is more prudent for the state to involve itself in restoring the infrastructure by establishing priority expenditures and by enticing foreign businesses and international organizations to participate in large projects.[10]

Indeed, one of the most urgent areas of concern for the government remains private sector development. The government's decision to divert major public funds and resources to military spending during the civil conflict left economic and social infrastructure projects in a shambles. This significantly hindered private sector development. The ramifications of this neglect were far-reaching: mounting state debt, soaring unemployment, falling FDI, and a general decline in the economy that seriously damaged investor confidence. With the onset of civil war, a number of Côte d'Ivoire's trading partners and large investors in the telecommunications, energy, transportation, and agribusiness sectors relocated to more stable neighbouring countries such as Senegal. The impacts of the conflict were felt in the deteriorating transportation system, roadblocks, and high transportation costs that served only to impede private sector development and tarnish Côte d'Ivoire's reputation as West Africa's regional hub. To re-establish conditions for sustainable economic growth and prevent a relapse into conflict, the government needs to enhance security and diversify the economy by courting new international donors and investors to rebuild its shattered infrastructure.

It is also important for the government not to neglect agriculture, which will restore thousands of livelihoods and contribute greatly to exports. To achieve this objective, the private sector will need to involve itself more in agriculture through the state's resettlement and retraining program, as well as by assisting with farming technology. Furthermore, building a strong civilian developmental administration, one capable of regulating and managing the private sector—not only agriculture but also the mining and fishing industries—should generate the confidence necessary to attract investment and foster economic growth.

The estimated real GDP growth of 1.6 percent in 2007 in Côte d'Ivoire (OECD 2008, 260), based on the ongoing reunification process,[11] a continued modest increase in private-sector confidence, and the ongoing rehabilitation of public infrastructure, is proof that private-sector development can succeed in that country. The principal challenges facing Côte d'Ivoire today remain these: macroeconomic and financial imbalances and large-scale indebtedness; an unstable currency; a shortage of skilled workers; undeveloped exports; and entrenched corruption and fraud. Necessary are structural reforms; the fostering of an economic environment conducive to private-sector activity; and the establishing of good governance in public-resource management.

Sierra Leone

By the time the civil war ended in 2002, Sierra Leone's physical and bureaucratic infrastructure was decimated and its most highly skilled citizens had fled the country. The two most urgent requirements for rebuilding the shattered economy were these: revive key government institutions such as the central bank; and establish a financial regulatory framework so that the private sector could return and start functioning again.

Certain ill-fated policy responses to external factors, as well as mismanagement of the economy by various former administrations, resulted in a general decline in economic activity and a serious deterioration of economic infrastructure. Today, Sierra Leone's short-term prospects depend on continued adherence to International Monetary Fund (IMF) and World Bank (WB) programs and continued external assistance.

The return of an efficient financial regime would make it far easier for the private sector to fund commercial ventures, make credit easier to arrange, and revive general confidence in Sierra Leone's economy. In particular, stable macroeconomic and fiscal policies would go far to attract foreign investment.

International assistance for Sierra Leone is aligned with the three pillars of the Sierra Leone Poverty Reduction Strategy (2005):

- Good Governance, Security and Peace-building
- Pro-poor Sustainable Growth for Food Security and Job Creation
- Human Development

However, for government to make substantial progress in attracting foreign investment, it needs to reduce business constraints and bottlenecks. Any unnecessarily redundant legal, bureaucratic, or financial restraint on the transfer of capital does not bode well for the business community. A more engaged private sector will help foster economic recovery and prevent the country from falling back into conflict. The government's national privatization program intends to privatize many state-owned enterprises that may well serve as a bridge for greater opportunity in spurring development of the private sector. The process represents a cornerstone of the government's strategy for national development that will lessen the burden on government coffers, stimulate the economy, and provide jobs for the unemployed.

The resurrection of the private sector is moving ahead based on existing programs in economic reform, decentralization, infrastructure development, and social welfare. Economic reform is underpinned by annual development policy operations[12] (DPOs). Support for decentralization is aimed to go beyond institutional reforms and capacity building; it is to include transferring resources to support innovative approaches to decentralized governance as well as the use of rapid results initiatives[13] (RRI) to empower local councils. To sustain high economic growth, reduce poverty, generate employment, and improve food security, the WB is supporting an integrated rural- and private-sector development initiative that targets agriculture and youth unemployment. Concurrently, the WB is continuing to support vital reforms in the power and water sectors (where there is no private-sector involvement) through investments and public–private partnerships—for example, by instituting performance-oriented management contracts for the National Power Authority (NPA) and the Guma Valley Water Corporation.

The private sector's role in addressing food security in Sierra Leone should not be ignored. In the short to medium term, agriculture,[14] mining,[15] and fishing are the country's highest-potential products. At present, farmers are suffering from insufficient access to inputs and equipment, which leads to inefficient land use and subsistence-level farming. Similarly, fishing is continuing to deteriorate because of restricted access to technology. To increase income levels and create employment in the food sector, means will have to be made available to process (i.e., add value to) food products.

Sierra Leone has done a great deal to rebuild its devastated economy, but it still faces many challenges, such as corruption and widespread poverty. Today, some 70 percent of the population lives in extreme poverty and the country has the highest maternal and infant mortality rate in the world (Government of Sweden 2009). In the 1990s and early 2000s, about 57 percent of the population lived below US$1 a day, and about 75 percent lived below US$2 a day. As stipulated in Sierra Leone's poverty reduction strategy paper (PRSP) for 2005–2007, the overall strategy is to reduce poverty levels to the levels of the 1990s (Government of Sierra Leone 2005).

The country aspires to an ambitious real economic growth rate of 8 to 9 percent per year (the country experienced growth of just over 7 percent from 2004 to 2007 [World Bank 2009]), based on increased productivity in all economic sectors. Whether it will achieve that goal depends on whether its shattered infrastructure can be rebuilt and expanded, as well as on increased involvement by the private sector—in particular, will financial reforms and privatizations of state-owned enterprises continue? The government will also have to continue to reform its judiciary, expand its macroeconomic reform program, and create an environment conducive to economic diversification through private-sector initiatives.

Liberia

Shortly after the elections of 2005, Ellen Johnson-Sirleaf, the first female African president, declared that private-sector development would be integral to Liberia's rehabilitation. Her government inherited a budget of less than US$100 million in 2006—down sharply from a pre-coup national budget of $600 million in 1980 (von Gienanth et al. 2007, 85). Most of her reforms—and the revival of the private sector in particular—would literally have to start from scratch. That is why she acknowledged the importance of the private sector in all sectors of the Liberian economy (agriculture, diamonds, mining, logging, rubber production, etc.) in terms of fostering growth, employment, and trade integration. That sector would have to provide the stepping stones to development and poverty reduction.

Private-sector–led reforms started with the judiciary. A sound legal system was established that guaranteed property rights. This sent out an important message that helped restore the confidence of domestic and foreign investors. A strengthened judiciary promised increased investment and private-sector activity in Liberia; this in turn would improve governance and reinforce the rule of law.

Since private investment was limited, another important step toward broad-based reconstruction was reform of the financial system, especially with regard to regulations and oversight. Because the Liberian post-conflict economy had weak regulatory authorities, it was necessary to build a strong institutional foundation first, in order not to exacerbate the situation with new reforms. Improved banking and fiscal policies have benefited from the private sector's performance and created opportunities for entrepreneurs to obtain loans.

Similarly, there was a need to revive the agricultural sector, bearing in mind that it is the largest private sector in Liberia, accounting for more than half the GDP and for about 70 percent of the workforce (OECD 2008, 364). Revitalizing the agricultural sector was clearly of great importance. Money would be invested in it through incentives for small and medium-size farmers. The Ministry of Agriculture's Statement of Policy Intent, issued in July 2006, highlighted the importance of private-sector development, the rehabilitation of plantations, and linkages between smallholders and commercial farmers.[16]

> According to Richard Tolbert, Chairman of the National Investment Commission of Liberia, the private sector has been playing a major role in the Herculean task of economic reconstruction in Liberia. He contends that the first step toward expanding economic empowerment in Liberia is to ensure a budgeted process of accountability and fiscal transparency, resolve the overwhelming debt issue, and increase government revenue by developing a more efficient and fair taxation system along with investor-friendly market conditions that allow the economy to operate within a regulated framework of normal fluctuations.
>
> Also vital is a satisfactory international framework. This must include international markets (such as the AGOA, ECOWAS, and the WTO); international treaties (such as double-tax treaties and framework agreements for bilateral trade); international debt relief; and proper management of foreign donor assistance to support government resources, especially in the vital area of infrastructure and basic social resources such as health, education, and housing.
>
> In addition, the restoration of the country's physical infrastructure— roads, electricity, water, seaports, airports, sanitation, telecommunica-

tions, and housing—has emerged from discussions with all economic actors as absolutely essential to economic revitalization. Parallel to the physical infrastructure, which is essential for the private sector to operate efficiently, is the institutional and legal framework for doing business. This refers in particular to good governance; the absence or at least minimization of corruption; a stable, fair, and predictable legal framework for commerce; and the reduction of regulatory and practical hurdles for doing business.

Despite strong progress, Liberia still confronts formidable reconstruction and development challenges[17] (e.g., high rates of maternal and child mortality, high illiteracy and unemployment, extreme poverty, weak governance systems, food insecurity, lack of access to basic social services, lack of skilled workers, and a debilitated infrastructure). That is why the private-sector revival is so important, and why investments in job creation (especially the support of women), infrastructure development, and education, health care, and agriculture need to take place simultaneously.[18]

Conclusion

Many years of civil war did severe damage to economic management and governance in Côte d'Ivoire, Sierra Leone, and Liberia. Deteriorated infrastructure continues to sharply constrain growth, job creation, food security, and human development. Comprehensive private-sector revival and support for institutional capacity building will be necessary to rebuild destroyed infrastructure and create hope for a more peaceful and prosperous future. These efforts need to be addressed not only by the national states but also by the international community and international organizations.

The post-conflict states' governments recognize that a thriving economy is essential to building peace. Job creation, the livelihoods jobs sustain, the opportunities they deliver, and the relationships they help build are all crucial to giving societies a stake in a non-violent future. Trade within and between countries does more than drive economic growth; it can also help establish or re-establish personal and business connections across conflict divides. The private sector has provided vital contributions to trade and economic growth in Côte d'Ivoire, Sierra Leone, and Liberia, with the benefits translating into real gains to societies.

However people evaluate the private sector's current role in the three countries, and however critical some commentators are, the economic statistics point to a general improvement in people's lives as a result of private-sector development. This leaves us with one important message: private-sector revival is essential to the stabilization of war-torn states.

The Purpose and Plan of the Book

This book examines peacebuilding efforts currently under way in Côte d'Ivoire, Sierra Leone, and Liberia and the role of the private sector in leading the reconstruction initiatives. In light of the challenges posed by the post-conflict environment and the growing realization that the private sector could play a strategic role in supporting the reconstruction efforts of donor communities and governments in the region, the book considers four important questions with regard to peacebuilding activities and the growing importance of the private sector:

1. At what stage of the peacebuilding process do Côte d'Ivoire, Sierra Leone, and Liberia find themselves at this point in time?
2. To what extent has the presence of peacebuilding initiatives and strategies succeeded in fostering more democratic and transparent institutions while, at the same time, helping to support sustainable economic growth and address poverty and inequality needed to sustain peace and security in the region?
3. What are the opportunities and, more important, the challenges facing the private sector in these West African states?
4. What policy recommendations and institutional reforms are needed to support and sustain the peacebuilding efforts in West Africa while, at the same time, strengthen the role of the private sector, which is an important player the region's economic reconstruction efforts?

The book brings together leading international academics and respected policy-makers from around the continent and elsewhere who have been directly involved in issues relating to peacebuilding efforts and economic reconstruction initiatives. In these chapters, they expand ideas and policy-related recommendations on the steps that are necessary to ensure that these fragile states do not slide back into civil strife, but rather become a catalyst in the economic growth and political stability of this historically war-ravaged region.

The volume is divided into three sections, each devoted to one of the three states. Each section critically examines peacebuilding efforts and is followed by an analysis of the private sector's role in economic reconstruction efforts and institutional capacity building.

Notes

1 Disarmament, demobilization, and reintegration.
2 Sierra Leone's national DDR program disarmed about 72,500 combatants between 1998 and 2002.
3 According to the International Crisis Group, RUF-P (the political wing of the RUF) received only 1.7 percent of the vote in the 2002 elections and has all but dissolved into separate factions.
4 Women and girls comprised between 15 and 30 percent of all combatants during the civil war.
5 In 1999, diamond exports through official channels totalled about US$1.2 million (less than

1 percent of estimated production). It is also estimated that some $138 million was generated from illicit mining. However, between October 2000 and June 2001 official exports rose to $15 million (10 percent of the annual estimated production).

6 By March 2007 the UN's newly established Peacebuilding Fund (UNPBF) allocated Sierra Leone a total of US$35 million to fund four priority areas: youth empowerment and employment, democracy and good government, justice and security, and capacity building of public administrations. The PBF itself was funded with voluntary contributions from member states and international organizations, whose goal was to support countries emerging from conflict.

7 About 60 percent of all of Côte d'Ivoire's major bank branches closed across the country.

8 Based on a spectrum of funds, including M1, savings, and small-time deposits, overnight repos at commercial banks, and non-institutional money market accounts.

9 This is the case even though the Economic and Social Council—which was established prior to the conflict—still provides a forum for dialogue between the public and private sectors.

10 For this purpose, a matching grant program was established in order to channel relatively small amounts of money directly to private exporters, so as to finance part of the costs of support services, which in turn would help develop the capacity of the local consulting industry. The program's goal is to ensure that entrepreneurs "graduate" over time and accept the costs of carrying the expert services they require. The maximum funding allowed for most enterprises is US$50,000.

11 Referring to northern Muslims with the southern Ivorians.

12 DPO is similar to developing policy lending, which is a means of rapidly disbursing policy-based financing, which the bank provides in the form of loans or grants to help a borrower address actual or anticipated developmental financing requirements that have domestic or external origins.

13 RRI is a Sierra Leone government/World Bank intervention to jump-start major change efforts and enhance the implementation capacity of the newly established local councils. The main purposes are to build confidence in the local population and get the private sector to support the councils in their developmental activities, which are geared toward the effective and efficient provision and delivery of goods and services.

14 Sierra Leone is predominantly an agricultural economy; about half its workers are subsistence farmers. Even though most Sierra Leoneans derive their livelihood from it, agriculture accounts for only 42 percent of national income.

15 Mining is controlled largely by foreign companies, which extract diamonds (the country's main source of hard currency), iron ore, gold, and so on.

16 Since Liberia is blessed with ample rainfall and has the additional advantage of being relatively close to the wealthy markets of the European Community, the agricultural industry could be tripled without much difficulty.

17 Opinion is divided regarding the current openness of the Liberian economy. The United States has harshly criticized recent privatizations in the communications and energy sectors; by contrast, the EU supports further lifting of sanctions on timber and diamonds.

18 This section is extracted from a speech by Richard Tolbert, Chairman of the National Investment Commission of Liberia. We acknowledge the use of this material and appreciate Dr. Tolbert's insight and contributions to the understanding of the role of the private sector in Liberia's peacebuilding efforts.

Cote d'Ivoire

From Linas-Marcoussis to the Ouagadougou Political Agreement
The Tortuous and Open-Ended Peace Process in Côte d'Ivoire

Gilles Yabi and Andrew Goodwin[1]

1

Introduction

In the two and a half decades following independence from France in 1960, Côte d'Ivoire was considered a bastion of stability and prosperity in an often volatile region of the world. However, it was also an undemocratic country ruled by a talented but autocratic president, Félix Houphouët-Boigny. The death of the "Father of the Nation" in 1993 led to a period of unprecedented political instability, which took a turn for the worse when a 2002 coup attempt thrust Côte d'Ivoire into a spiral of violence from which it has yet to emerge convincingly.

Several attempts by the international community to mediate an end to the crisis—including international mediation and UN Security Council (UNSC) resolutions—have halted the civil war but failed to gain peace. The most recent attempt to find peace led to the signing of the Ouagadougou Peace Accord (APO)[2] on March 4, 2007. While this agreement holds much promise, its implementation has proceeded very slowly and a successful outcome is still far from sight. Crucial issues such as the identification of the population and the disarmament, demobilization, and reintegration (DDR) of ex-combatants have yet to begin. A political tug-of-war has characterized each step of the implementation process as divergent interests vie for control. Underlying the process are the political strategies of the players involved. Laurent Gbagbo's bottom line is to retain the presidency; Guillaume Soro has had to walk a fine line between acting as an ex-rebel leader and serving as a presumably neutral prime minister. The APO serves as the basis from which peace can emerge; but it remains to be seen whether the actors involved will be able to set aside their differences and respect democratic standards and the rule of law.

A History of Peace Attempts

The peace accords of 2003 followed ten years that saw Côte d'Ivoire slide steadily toward civil war. The death of President Houphouët-Boigny in 1993 sparked a battle for succession that was won by the president of the National Assembly,

Henri Konan Bédié. Bédié maintained Houphouët's autocratic style, refused to make electoral reforms, and prevented one of his adversaries, former prime minister Alassane Ouattara,[3] from running for president on the grounds that he was not "Ivorian."[4] In 1999, growing political tensions[5] and army discontent[6] led to Côte d'Ivoire's first ever military coup, which saw Bédié replaced by General Robert Gueï. The military leader had planned to transfer power back to a civilian government but soon decided to run for president himself. Backed by the Front Populaire Ivoirien (FPI), which was led by Gbagbo and his own opportunistic supporters, Gueï ensured that both Ouattara and Bédié would be barred from contesting the presidency.[7] Both Ouattara's Rassemblement des Republicains (RDR) and Bédié's Parti Democratique de Côte d'Ivoire (PDCI-RDA) called for an election boycott, and only 37 percent of the registered electorate voted.[8] Gueï declared himself the winner of the 2000 elections despite preliminary results indicating a Gbagbo victory. After FPI street demonstrations and a bloody confrontation with the presidential guard, Gueï fled and Gbagbo declared himself president. Tensions remained high, however, especially in the northern half of the country and in the main city of Abidjan, following the chaotic elections. Ouattara demanded that new elections be called, and street violence ensued, with RDR supporters on one side battling FPI supporters and pro-Gbagbo security forces on the other. In response, the government targeted those thought to support the RDR, especially immigrants and northerners, which deepened divisions among Ivorians. Growing tensions along ethnic, regional, and political lines were mirrored in the military, where those thought to be sympathetic to Gueï or Ouattara were removed or demoted to provide space for Gbagbo's political base.

In December 2002, Côte d'Ivoire exploded into outright civil war following an attempted coup against President Gbagbo. The coup was led by former soldiers, most of them northerners who had gone into exile—mainly in Burkina Faso—before and after Gbagbo gained power. They tried to take Abidjan but were forced back toward to north. The rebel forces subsequently took Bouaké in the centre in addition to the northern towns; meanwhile, the military loyal to the government maintained control of the south, effectively dividing the country in two.

France now found itself in an awkward position. The former colonial power had a close relationship with Côte d'Ivoire during Houphouët-Boigny's rule. By this point it had a permanent military base in Abidjan as well as defence accords with the government. The French felt that the crisis was internal and political in nature and that it required a negotiated settlement, not the military solution favoured by Gbagbo, whose personal relationship with then French president Jacques Chirac was not particularly cordial. Consequently, France opted for a limited engagement, strengthening its forces to protect the expatriate population while at the same time providing logistic aid to the Ivorian military. Gbagbo later accused France of ambivalence, while the rebels accused French troops of preventing their conquest of Abidjan. Finally, in an effort to avoid a full-blown civil war while maintaining its political influence, France offered to broker a peace deal.

After initial regional mediation efforts by West African heads of state, the first international attempt to launch a comprehensive peace process was made in the Parisian suburb of Linas–Marcoussis between January 15 and 23, 2003. The peace talks were followed by a summit of heads of state, including Gbagbo and Chirac, in Paris to endorse its conclusions. The conference was tasked with reaching a compromise between President Gbagbo, who insisted that any action had to be taken within the constitutional framework, and the rebel coalition led by Guillaume Soro, who was demanding Gbagbo's immediate resignation. The compromises that resulted included, above all, a government of reconciliation with full executive powers to be established immediately; this would require the devolution of essential powers from the presidency to the office of the prime minister. Other compromises involved land reform,[9] the drafting of an electoral timetable culminating in elections in 2005, the revision of conditions of eligibility for the presidency,[10] and the reform of nationality laws.[11] The consensus government, led by a new prime minister, Seydou Diarra,[12] was mandated to implement the recommendations of the Linas–Marcoussis Accord (LMA) and to organize credible presidential elections at the end of Gbagbo's constitutional term in October 2005.

The political situation that resulted from the LMA left many in Côte d'Ivoire unsatisfied. The granting of powers to a new consensus government implied the weakening of the position of President Gbagbo. His political program was jeopardized, and he had to contend with a government that included those who had tried to overthrow him. For the rebel Forces Nouvelles (FN),[13] inclusion in the consensus government meant the acquisition of new powers and some recognition of their cause. Nevertheless, they remained suspicious of Gbagbo's desire to share real power. Consequently, despite the official endorsement of the agreement by all sides, its implementation was constantly blocked by the parties involved.[14] The resulting political impasse was not the optimal circumstance for those involved; it was, however, comfortable, and it helped ensure that the new reconciliation government would continue to be a "lame duck."[15] The belligerents—especially the government forces, which were eager to regain the territories they had lost to the rebellion—used this period to refurbish their arms stocks.

The slight progress made during 2003 and 2004 toward implementing the LMA was further impeded by a rapidly deteriorating security situation.[16] After a blatant violation of the ceasefire by government forces on November 4, 2004,[17] and the bombing of a French military camp in Bouaké on November 6,[18] South African president Thabo Mbeki, backed by the African Union (AU), offered to mediate a new agreement.[19]

Mbeki invited President Gbagbo, Prime Minister Diarra, PDCI leader Henri Konan Bédié, RDR[20] leader Alassane Ouattara, and the FN's secretary-general, Guillaume Soro, to Pretoria. The Pretoria Accord (PA), reached on April 6, 2005, was strong on paper, touching on all the major aspects of the conflict. It called for the immediate demobilization and disarmament of militias, the reinforcement of the Independent Electoral Commission (IEC) to ensure free and fair elections, the participation of the UN in the electoral process, and a new session of the National Assembly to amend legislation that did not conform to provisions set out in the LMA, such as laws on nationality and identification.

Though the PA was in principle a strong agreement, in practice it was only a partial success, owing largely to a lack of trust and political will among the signatories. First of all, Gbagbo's resort to Article 48 of the Ivorian Constitution[21] to allow all parties that signed the LMA to run in the presidential elections was welcomed and seen as a step forward; nonetheless, concerns were raised regarding that article's potential for abuse. Second, the calendar for disarmament was quickly shelved when the FN made it known that the disarmament and demobilization of its troops would be contingent on the passing of several contentious pieces of legislation related to identification and nationality, as well as the demobilization of militias close to the president, as required by the agreement.

On June 28, 2005, Mbeki stepped in again to mediate a return to the PA. On July 15, 2005, in the absence of any movement on key pieces of legislation by the National Assembly, which had failed to reach consensus, Gbagbo resorted to Article 48 to make decisions on six sensitive bills.[22] The FN complained to Mbeki about these unilateral decisions; Mbeki responded by blaming the rebels for blocking peace. The FN then accused Mbeki of siding with Gbagbo and refused the "regroupment" of its troops. This effectively killed the PA.[23]

Faced with severe political instability, which was amplified by the end of the presidential mandate on October 30, the UN intervened with UNSC Resolution 1633 on October 21. The resolution extended Gbagbo's mandate for a further twelve months and called for the appointment of a new prime minister, who was extended increased power over the entire peace process. Yet a year later, the two sides were no closer to holding elections. On November 1, 2006, the UNSC passed Resolution 1721, which built on the directives contained in Resolution 1633 and extended President Gbagbo's mandate for a "final" twelve months, until presidential elections could be organized.[24]

From the moment UNSC Resolution 1721 was signed, President Gbagbo made it clear that he would not abide by it, declaring that he would not implement aspects of the resolution that infringed on fundamental Ivorian law, including the prime minister's new authority to sign ordinances. Prime Minister Charles Konan Banny's[25] efforts to counter President Gbagbo and carry out his mandate under Resolution 1721 were neutralized by Gbagbo.[26] The UNSC, which had given the impression of being totally committed to Resolution 1721, did little in response to the neutralization of the Banny government.[27]

Both sides in the conflict were undermining international agreements, yet both—the presidential camp and the rebels—were aware that the four-year political stalemate threatened their own interests. Regional and international fatigue was growing, as was the possibility of a popular revolt that could result in both factions being rejected. Rather than risk this, President Gbagbo announced on December 19 that he had drafted a "made-in-Côte d'Ivoire" plan to solve the crisis. This would entail direct dialogue with the FN rebels to negotiate disarmament and reunification of the country, to be "facilitated" by the President of Burkina Faso and the Chair of the Economic Community of West African States (ECOWAS), Blaise Compaoré.

The Ouagadougou Peace Accord

The agreement, signed in Burkina Faso's capital, Ouagadougou, on March 4, 2007, became known as the Ouagadougou Peace Accord (APO). Much of the substance of the previous agreements remained intact; but the APO also established joint management of the agreement—primarily by President Gbagbo and FN leader Soro, with Compaoré facilitating. The APO reflected the military and political stalemate in which Gbagbo and Soro found themselves and allowed each to claim victory. With the signing of the APO, President Gbagbo had scored a political victory: he had sidelined international agreements that constrained his powers while simultaneously dividing the opposition. He had also recovered the full use of his constitutional prerogatives, and the FN leaders had agreed to recognize him as president. The price Gbagbo paid was the appointment of FN leader Soro as prime minister.

Nevertheless, the two are not equal: Soro is "Gbagbo's prime minister." Having failed to unseat Gbagbo by force, the FN needed a way forward that would not represent capitulation and that would offer them a chance to play an important political role in the future. Though there are some doubts regarding his actual power as prime minister in relation to President Gbagbo, Soro is still the head of government, which amounts to a recognition rather than a humiliation. Even so, his position remains delicate.

The APO foresees three main steps toward resolving the conflict. The first relates to voter registration. The APO recognizes that the absence of a standard identity document for Ivorians is a source of conflict. To address this, the agreement calls for (a) the deployment of audiences foraines (mobile courts) to issue birth certificates to those who were born in the country but had never been declared in the official registries, and (b) a national campaign of identification to issue simultaneously identity and voter cards to the eligible population.

The second step is to restructure the Ivorian defence and security forces. This involves reorganizing the present forces on both sides of the conflict and creating an Integrated Command Centre (ICC) to unify the current Forces de Défense et Sécurité (FDS) and FN under joint command. However, the APO remains vague on how to achieve DDR and create a new, unified army before holding long-delayed elections.

The third step toward resolving the conflict is to remove the "zone of confidence"[28] and establish joint brigades to replace the UN and French forces as providers of security in that buffer zone. The APO calls for the "zone of confidence" to be replaced by a "green line" running along its median and dotted with observation points. These posts, manned by UN forces, are to be dismantled by half every two months until none remain, at which point patrolling duties will be transferred to mixed FDS/FN brigades.[29]

The Difficulties of Implementing the Accord and Its Uncertain Future

Though the APO is a strong agreement on paper, it has faced the same problem as hindered past agreements: a lack of good faith. For a number of reasons, implementation has been slow and arduous. The first problem is political wrangling over who controls the APO's implementation. Difficulties with the mobile courts, identification procedures, and DDR processes all attest to this problem.

Though it began six months behind schedule and suffered from technical difficulties, the mobile courts can be considered a successful first step in the implementation of the APO. By the end of this stage in mid-April 2008, about half a million people had gained their legal existence.[30] However, the importance of the mobile courts to the overall peace process should not be overstated. The process for identifying and registering voters is much more crucial and politically sensitive because it has such direct consequences for the electoral lists.

Voter registration has been assigned to the IEC, which relies heavily on two institutions to carry out the technical aspects of the process. The first of these is the Institut National de la Statistique (INS),[31] which is managed by a close associate of President Gbagbo. The second is Sagem, a private firm based in France.[32]

Voter identification and registration has turned out to be the main stumbling block relating to the APO. The process decides who is an Ivorian citizen and who, it follows, has the right to vote. The difficulties negotiating this process can be explained by the political ramifications for all the Ivorian political parties. President Gbagbo worries that an increased number of electors in the north—a traditional FN and RDR stronghold—may hurt his chances of re-election. So he would like to see as few new voters identified in the north as possible. For Soro the identification of new voters is crucial, given that the recognition of northerners as Ivorians was a central plank of his rebel movement. If he does not achieve official recognition of Ivorian nationality for northerners, the FN will lose credibility. Also, northern voters will be Soro's political base should he later decide to run for office. The RDR wants to see new voters identified in the north because that is where they draw most of their support. For the PDCI, the identification of new voters in the north is not as crucial, because they draw their support mostly from the central and eastern regions. However, both the opposition parties have an interest in ensuring that Gbagbo cannot influence the identification process in his favour, as both will be competing against him for the presidency in the elections when they finally happen.

The second step in the APO's peace process relates to DDR. There have been both positive and negative results from this step. On the positive side, the level of co-operation at the operational level between the FN and the FDS can be viewed as a success. Mixed brigades have been operating under ICC command as called for by the APO, and no serious clashes between FN and FDS troops have been reported. Moreover, no serious security violations have occurred in the former "zone of confidence" since the mixed brigades took over patrolling duties.

On the negative side, the regroupment[33] of combatants has been problematic. Because the FDS are government soldiers, they found it easy to regroup at pre-existing military barracks. The situation for the FN is very different: the rebel soldiers have no barracks to regroup in. Sites assigned for their regrouping lack essential amenities such as beds, running water, and electricity, which has made FN regroupment difficult. As a result, the former rebels have largely stayed in the cities, where they continue to extort money from civilians at checkpoints. FN General Bakayoko Soumaila has repeatedly promised that the regroupment of FN soldiers will be accelerated, but his efforts have met with little success.

A more difficult issue is the merging of FDS and FN soldiers into a new, unified Ivorian army. The main difficulty is figuring out how to implement Compaoré's recommendations regarding the ranks and numbers of troops to be integrated into the new force.[34]

The difficulties inherent in integrating the recommended numbers of troops reflect divergent political interests. For Gbagbo, remaining president is fundamental. Clearly, from his perspective the existence of an ex-rebel army is a threat and its disarmament is essential. He does not want an army that might contest his re-election, whether or not the election is free and fair. On the rebel side, Soro needs to achieve a successful end to the rebellion he led. He needs to "take care of" his soldiers by integrating them into the army, the police, community projects, and the national civil service. For Soro, integration, not disarmament, is key to this part of the peace process. Disarmament would greatly weaken Soro, considering that the existence of FN soldiers is what gives him leverage in negotiations.[35] Before disarming, Soro will need assurances from Gbagbo that the agreements reached regarding the placement of FN soldiers will be honoured. Finally, many ex-rebel commanders have little interest in disarmament and reintegration, as this would spell the end of their military, political, and—most important—economic control over the north. The past year, which has seen the end of fighting without a return to real peace, has been extremely lucrative for FN commanders.

The DDR program got a boost, in theory, when the Security and Defence Working Group was established to examine the organization of a new, unified national army.[36] This group is important because in the short term it should aid the DDR of ex-combatants by working out the details regarding the ranks and numbers of FN combatants to be integrated. In the long term the working group should establish the foundations for the future Ivorian army.

Basic reform of the Ivorian Armed Forces needs to occur if a lasting peace is to take root. On its own, the DDR program cannot accomplish this. Manipulations of national identity by political leaders, as well as illegitimate elections in October and December 2000, helped trivialize political violence and armed conflict in Côte d'Ivoire. That said, also central to the outbreak of violence was the decay of the Ivorian Armed Forces. That decay was exposed during the military coup in 1999 when angry soldiers demanding higher wages ousted President Bédié. Fundamental reforms in the security sector cannot be accomplished in a few months; nonetheless, it is important to begin this task before the next presidential elections.

As a result of the removal of the "zone of confidence," a national administration is returning to the north, albeit with much difficulty. By the end of March 2008 about 75 percent of the national administrators had returned to their positions in the FN-controlled areas, according to the National Commission for Administrative Reunification.[37] These large numbers are promising, but two main problems continue to complicate redeployment. First, working and living conditions are difficult because of the dilapidated condition of government buildings; this offers little incentive for state employees to remain. Second, tax and customs unification is proving to be a highly sensitive issue. The FN replaced the state as "tax collector" when the state pulled out of the north after the 2002 coup attempt. Since then, the FN's main source of income has been exacting a "tax" for economic activities and from motorists at checkpoints.[38] Any moves to take away this source of income by centralizing revenue collection are being resisted by FN commanders. [39]

To summarize, the peace process has been slow and difficult. Adding to the difficulties is the consensus-style government favoured by Soro. Though a remarkable choice, it has had the unfortunate consequence of delaying an already slow decision-making process, since several actors must reach a compromise before a decision is reached.[40] Finally, corruption has added to the slow pace of peace; the proliferation of institutions involved in the process has created opportunities for more and more officials to benefit financially from the funding that passes through their hands.[41]

The Central Actors: Strategies and Interests

Underlying the slow and arduous implementation of the APO are the political strategies of the central actors.

Gbagbo: Holding on to Power

Since emerging as president in the controversial 2000 elections, Laurent Gbagbo has manoeuvred successfully to keep his hold on power. With the signing of the APO in March 2007, he prolonged his mandate while simultaneously gaining recognition from the FN and the political class that he is the legitimate president of Côte d'Ivoire. This has placed him in a strong position in the run-up to the next elections. He has the power to make decrees that can slow or even block the APO's implementation. As well, the identification and disarmament processes are subject to many regulations that he as president has the power to promulgate. He also has considerable financial and human resources at his disposal. Moreover, he controls the state's security and intelligence services, as the Interior Minister and the Defence Minister are his close associates.

Yet Gbagbo does not have absolute control over the transition. He still must work with his combative prime minister, Guillaume Soro, with a government that includes members of the opposition, and with an electoral commission that is numerically dominated by opposition parties.[42] As noted earlier, winning the elections is the bottom line for Gbagbo. To increase his chances he must reach out to voters beyond his traditional base. The 2000 and 2002 elections showed that Gbagbo has difficulty attracting voters from outside his traditional base of support in the south and the west. In an environment where political parties enjoy strong ethnic-based support, Gbagbo is at a disadvantage in relation to the PDCI and the RDR.

Gbagbo may be tempted to use the "security tension" strategy in the months leading up to the elections. That is, he could declare a threat to the state's security and employ repressive measures, thereby creating an environment in which free and fair elections would be difficult to conduct. It remains to be seen whether the ongoing presence of a UN peacekeeping force will be sufficient to contain possible orchestrated electoral tensions.

Soro: From Rebel Leader to Central Political Actor

With the signing of the APO in March 2007, Soro committed the FN to a position of "neutral referee" in the upcoming elections.[43] Soro has sided neither with

Gbagbo nor with the opposition. It seems that his strategy will be to maintain—at least publicly—his neutrality throughout the peace process and elections.

If Soro is remaining neutral, it is because he has an interest in doing so. If he were to join one side or the other, he would quickly lose legitimacy as a neutral arbitrator in the peace process and would find himself either in the losing camp after the elections or being accused of using his position to favour the winner. By remaining neutral he can help bring about the successful identification of the northern peoples and the reintegration of his troops, as well as reach a consensus from all political parties to hold peaceful elections. If Soro succeeds at these tasks, he could very well be chosen prime minister in the next government, or he could quit his position to pursue the presidency in future elections. Soro is only in his thirties and could have a long political career ahead of him.

That said, he may find it difficult to remain neutral. If the presidential camp begins to feel that the ex–rebel leader is too inflexible, they may be tempted to neutralize him. If that were to happen, the close relationship between Soro and Compaoré might be the only thing that could ensure the prime minister's political survival.

The June 29, 2007, rocket attack on Soro's plane revealed that he also may be in physical danger. That attack highlighted the fragile nature of the peace process. First, it showed how easily that process could be thrown into chaos. Second, it underscored that some Ivorians still have the political will and the military means to derail the peace process.[44] No one can know exactly what would have happened next had Soro been killed; but undoubtedly, the peace process launched by the APO would have ended, plunging the country into political instability. Most likely, this would have triggered spontaneous violence and revenge killings. Though tensions quickly subsided, Soro's position will remain fragile until presidential elections are held.

Bédié and Ouattara: Anticipating the Upcoming Elections

The main opposition parties, the PDCI and the RDR, have been part of successive reconciliation governments since 2003, but their influence remains limited. Though Bédié and Ouattara are both part of the Cadre Permanent de Concertation (CPC), a political dialogue framework, their influence during the transition period has depended heavily on Soro's choices and Compaoré's goodwill. The opposition parties do, however, present a credible challenge to Gbagbo in the presidential elections. In the 2001 and 2002 elections the PDCI and RDR performed strongly. In the 2001 local elections—the first in which all three main parties participated—the PDCI and RDR each received a slightly larger percentage of the popular vote than the FPI.[45] In 2002, regional elections saw the popular vote split almost evenly three ways.[46] Furthermore, on May 18, 2005, the two main opposition parties joined forces with two smaller parties[47] to create the

Rassemblement des Houphouétistes pour la Démocratie et la Paix (RHDP). The RHDP is an alliance of four signatory parties that have agreed to support whichever among them reaches the second round of the presidential elections.

Blaise Compaoré: A Pragmatic Mediator

The outcome of the peace process will depend greatly on the political strategy employed by Burkina Faso's president, Blaise Compaoré. Compaoré's involvement in the attempted coup of September 19, 2002,[48] and his close relations with the rebel forces, have provided him with particular qualities as facilitator. His relationship with both leaders offers him leverage that he can apply to keep the peace process moving forward.[49] He also wields significant power over the process as a member of both the CPC and the Evaluation and Support Committee (CEA). Finally, when there are disputes over how to interpret the APO, he is the ultimate arbitrator of the election process.

There are two main reasons why Compaoré has taken a personal interest in mediating the conflict. First, Burkina Faso has an economic, political, and social interest in the long-term stability of Côte d'Ivoire.[50] Second, ever since his past relationship with former Liberian president and warlord Charles Taylor and his support of the Ivorian rebels at the beginning of the conflict in 2002, Compaoré has fretted over his image as a meddler in other states' affairs.[51] Also, Compaoré is the second-longest serving head of state in West Africa[52] and is keen to project an image as a wise, thoughtful, and modern leader. If he succeeds as a mediator in Côte d'Ivoire after being indirectly part of the conflict there, he will appear as the master politician of the region and an influential leader on the African continent.

Conclusion

The APO has the potential to free Côte d'Ivoire from the crisis that has enveloped it since 2002, while setting the foundations for its transition to forward-looking democracy. But the end of this process is still far from sight, and much remains to be done if the country is to find a lasting peace.

Three main challenges lay ahead that the APO must overcome if it is to succeed. First, the Ivorian leaders must demonstrate that they are willing to hold free and fair elections. Getting to the elections has proved a difficult task, as the identification and disarmament processes attest. Signing an agreement is not enough. Both Gbagbo and Soro must demonstrate that they have the political will to strictly implement the APO. Compaoré must use his full powers as APO facilitator, threatening targeted sanctions if necessary, to pressure the main players to avoid shortcuts.

Second, simply holding elections will not be enough. The Ivorian leaders must not use the environment of uncertainty surrounding the elections to clamp down on opponents and consolidate their power. The elections need to be exceptionally well organized in a secure environment if they are to mark an exit from both the conflict and the political crisis. The UN and France could strengthen the security environment surrounding the elections by maintaining current ONUCI and Licorne troop levels and by giving priority to protecting civilians.

Finally, fundamental change needs to occur. The elected president must consider how power is to be wielded in a democratic era. Reforms to political institutions, the constitution, and the entire security sector are essential. Côte d'Ivoire must move away from a "winner takes all" political culture toward one that better reflects the nation's internal diversity. For this to come about, however, it must learn to view political and ethnic diversity as central to the country's richness and imagine pragmatic ways to address unavoidable conflicts of interest without recourse to violence. If these challenges are met, Côte d'Ivoire will be reborn. A successful transition to a democratic state endowed with functioning political, economic, and social institutions will have positive implications for all of West Africa.

Notes

1 When this chapter was written, Gilles Yabi was senior analyst with the West Africa Project of the International Crisis Group and Andrew Goodwin was a researcher with the same project.

2 French acronym used.

3 Trained as an economist, Alassane Ouattara was named prime minister in November 1990 in an attempt to help reverse the economic crisis that Côte d'Ivoire was then facing. When President Félix Houphouët-Boigny died in December 1993, Ouattara was interested in the presidency, but Henri Konan Bédié, as the Parliament's speaker, was the legitimate constitutional heir. Ouattara subsequently took a post with the IMF as deputy managing director. In the following years, still concerned about the challenge posed by Ouattara and the newly formed Rassemblement des Républicains (RDR), Bédié developed the divisive ideology of "Ivoirité." The political manifestations of this new concept included changes to the electoral code that reinforced conditions of origin and nationality for those who would seek the presidency. The new constitution, written during the military transition in 2000, validated the restrictive conditions for eligibility; thus Ouattara, whose father was allegedly from Burkina Faso, was barred from running for president in the October 2000 elections because of his "dubious nationality."

4 The concept of "Ivoirité" became central to Ivoirian politics and was one of the issues that led to the partitioning of the country. Southern-based politicians claimed that most northerners had foreign origins and were not real Ivoirians and, therefore, should not have the same rights as "true Ivoirians." The rebel movement was presented as an effort by a group of northerners to put an end to a state-sponsored trend toward discrimination and political marginalization.

5 Political tensions were the result of economic ruin, a slide toward authoritarianism, and the exclusion felt by many northerners.

6 Military discontent was a result of Bédié's refusal to pay back wages, deteriorating material conditions in the army, corruption, and growing authoritarianism. Promotions that favoured Bédié's own ethnic base also contributed.

7 Gueï upheld a law stating that both parents of a presidential candidate had to have been born in Côte d'Ivoire.

8 For more information, see *Cote d'Ivoire: The War Is Not Yet Over*, International Crisis Group Report no. 72, November 28, 2003, 7.

9 The LMA promised to better explain to the population the land-reform legislation passed on December 23, 1998, by the Ivoirian National Assembly.

10 A candidate for the presidency must have one parent or the other born in Côte d'Ivoire and not both parents, as was previously the case.

11 The reform of nationality laws goes to the heart of the rebellion and conflict. Among other things, the LMA proposed the suspension and revision of current national-identity operations, the reorganization and recomposition of the Independent Electoral Commission, constitutional changes regarding eligibility for the presidency, and the cancellation of residents' cards and decisions on naturalization and immigration as well as inquiries into human rights abuses.

12 Seydou Diarra had been the prime minister in 1999–2000 under General Gueï's military transition government. In December 2001 he presided over the National Reconciliation Forum, which brought together Gbagbo, Bédié, Ouattara, and Gueï.

13 The FN resulted from the amalgamation of three rebel movements: the Mouvement Patriotique de la Cote d'Ivoire (MPCI), the Mouvement Populaire du Grand Ouest (MPIGO), and the Mouvement pour la Justice et la Paix (MJP). MPIGO and MJP appeared in the western region, the homeland of the late General Gueï, in November 2002, and included Liberian and Sierra Leonean combatants associated with Charles Taylor.

14 The FN, for example, would pull out of the government of reconciliation, while militias close to President Gbagbo would openly violate the ceasefire agreement. More subtle methods of blocking the implementation included legal wrangling over such issues as nationality legislation, the formation of a new electoral commission, and the modification of the Constitution regarding presidential eligibility.

15 For more on the LMA, see *Cote d'Ivoire: The War Is Not Yet Over*, International Crisis Group Report no. 72.

16 In March 2004 a protest by the opposition was forcefully put down by Gbagbo. As a result, opposition members pulled out of the consensus government. On October 15, Gbagbo accused the rebels of not disarming; on November 4, the president launched an offensive to "forcefully disarm the rebels."

17 The Forces Armées Nationales de Cote d'Ivoire (FANCI) launched "Operation Dignité" in an effort to regain the northern half of the country. Dozens of civilians were killed.

18 FANCI aircraft attacked a French military base in Bouaké, killing nine French soldiers and one American citizen. It remains unclear who ordered this attack and their motivations.

19 On November 15, following a ceasefire breach, Security Council Resolution 1572 imposed an arms embargo on Côte d'Ivoire and threatened targeted sanctions against certain individuals.

20 The RDR, which has most of its support in the north, was formed in 1994 in a breakaway from the then ruling Parti Democratic de Côte d'Ivoire (PDCI). The RDR boycotted the 1995 presidential elections to protest Bédié's refusal to accept the electoral reforms demanded by the opposition formed by Gbagbo's FPI and RDR at that time. The RDR boycotted legislative elections in December 2000 and January 2001 to protest Ouattara's exclusion from both presidential and legislative elections.

21 Article 48 of the Ivorian Constitution allows the president to overrule any other article in "exceptional circumstances." It was invoked by Gbagbo, at the behest of Mbeki, to allow for

the inclusion of all political parties in 2005. Article 35 of the Ivoirian Constitution set conditions for participating in presidential elections that resulted in key opposition leaders being excluded from running in 2000.

22 The six pieces of legislation addressed the following: public financing of political parties and presidential candidates; population and residency permits for foreigners in Côte d'Ivoire; the National Commission on Human Rights in Côte d'Ivoire; the composition, organization, attributes, and functioning of the Independent Electoral Commission; special provisions regarding naturalization; and finally, the Nationality Code.

23 For more on the PA, see *Côte d'Ivoire: Half Measures Will Not Suffice*, International Crisis Group Africa Briefing no. 33, October 12, 2005.

24 UNSC Council Resolution 1721 of November 1, 2006.

25 Banny was governor of the Central Bank of West African States from 1993 to 2005. He served as prime minister of Côte d'Ivoire from December 5, 2005, to March 29, 2007.

26 The Banny government's poor handling of a crisis caused by the dumping of toxic waste in Abidjan contributed to his neutralization and helped erode any authority he had been given.

27 Gbagbo's lack of concern regarding UNSC repercussions was largely due to the political support he received from Mbeki and the influence the latter held in the UNSC on African issues, especially with China and Russia.

28 The "zone of confidence" is a strip of land running east to west for 600 km that separates the northern and southern halves of the country.

29 For more on the APO, see *Cote d'Ivoire: Can the Ouagadougou Agreement Bring Peace?* International Crisis Group Africa Report no. 127, June 27, 2007.

30 "Côte d'Ivoire: près de 500.000 sans-papiers identifiés en six mois (Onuci), » AFP, April 10, 2008.

31 Created in 1946, the INS is a state-run institution whose functions include ensuring on the national level the coherence, centralization, synthesis, and diffusion of all statistical information regarding the economy and demography collected by parapublic organs, as well as undertaking an annual census.

32 Sagem Sécurité was chosen by the Banny-led government to undertake voter identification. This decision was upheld by Soro in 2008. The production and delivery of the new national identity cards is to be carried out by the Office National de l'Identification (ONI) and Sagem. The entire identification process is overseen by the Commission Nationale de Supervision de l'Identification (CNSI) and the IEC.

33 The act of bringing soldiers back to military barracks where they are to reside; an initial step in the DDR process.

34 Compaoré recommended the following numbers for the reintegration of ex-rebel soldiers: 5,000 for the unified army; 4,000 for the police and gendarmerie; 20,000 for the national civil service; and 6,000 for projects with the National Reinsertion and Community Rehabilitation Programs.

35 There are signs that the FN may have kept some arms. For instance, at the "Flame of Peace" ceremony in Bouaké on July 30, 2007, only 1,606 of the intended 2,121 arms were burned, the FN having decided to keep 515 operational arms. Also, UN arms experts have often been refused permission by both sides to inspect army sites.

36 The group has three organs: a steering committee presided over by Prime Minister Soro, a scientific committee, and a technical secretariat. The group includes representatives of the president and four ministries, the commanders of ONUCI and Operation Licorne, two independent defence and security experts, and two members of civil society.

37 The number is high because the vast majority of positions in the national administration are in the education and health-care sectors. Neither is as sensitive as customs and security services. The redeployment of civil servants in those sectors would effectively end the FN's economic and political control. Fore more, see *Côte d'Ivoire: Ensuring Credible Elections*, International Crisis Group Africa Report no. 139, April 22, 2008.

38 Nevertheless, this method is increasingly unpopular with the people of the north, who see a direct link between the stagnation of the peace process and constantly having to pay a "tax" at roadblocks. The centralization of revenue collection is important, therefore, not only to fulfill the APO, but also to provide tangible results of the peace process for the northern population.

39 Also, there is no functioning judiciary in the FN-controlled half of Côte d'Ivoire. Prefects from the each region and department are present but still hold no real authority. The functions of the both the police and the judiciary are carried out by the FN leadership. This inevitably leads to extortion, which supplements FN income.

40 The government is composed of representatives from the presidential and FN camps, as well as the opposition parties PDCI, led by Bédié, and the RDR, led by Ouattara. Both men will be running for president in the upcoming election. Each important decision of the government must be agreed to by both Gbagbo and Soro, with a minimum of consent from the ministers representing the opposition parties. Compromise is difficult to achieve as the interests of the parties often clash. The position of the opposition parties is also difficult: they have to walk a fine line between supporting the government of which they are a part and criticizing a president whom they are running against.

41 As a consequence, international lenders have been slower to release badly needed funding. Also, the proliferation of *nouveaux riches* has encouraged others to demand a larger share of the wealth. Many organized professional bodies have gone on strike or threatened to do so in order to receive wage increases. In an environment where the presidential and opposition camps find themselves personally benefiting, there is little sense of urgency to hold elections.

42 The Independent Electoral Commission Bureau has twelve members: a representative of the president, a representative of the National Assembly, and one representative from each of the ten groups that took part in the LMA. These groups include PDCI, RDR, FPI, the three initial rebel movements (MPCI, MJP, and MPIGO), and four smaller political parties. Seven of the twelve participants are from the opposition parties or the FN; the remaining five are closer to Gbagbo. The IEC's president, elected from within the commission, is an opposition member.

43 Many observers wondered whether Soro and Gbagbo had secretly reached an understanding regarding how the peace process would unfold. Perhaps they reached a secret accord wherein only a portion of the population would be identified, the majority of FN soldiers would be integrated into the new Ivoirian army, and Gbagbo would be re-elected at the end of the process. However, the difficulties experienced thus far in the implementation process would suggest that this is not the case.

44 There are two theories regarding the perpetrators of the assassination attempt. The first focuses on elements within the FN who are unsatisfied with Soro. The second focuses on members of the presidential party who are not happy to have an ex-rebel soldier in the upper echelons of government. Neither of these theories can be outright excluded.

45 FPI: 25 percent, PDCI: 30 percent, RDR: 28 percent. Christian Bouquet, *Géopolitique de la Cote d'Ivoire* (Paris: Armand Colin, Paris, 2005), 103.

46 FPI: 21 percent, PDCI: 20 percent, RDR: 25 percent. Ibid.

47 L'Union pour la Démocratie et la Paix en Côte d'Ivoire (UPDCI) and the Mouvement des Forces de l'Avenir (MFA).

48 Compaoré gave refuge to military officers who participated in the coup against Bédié in December 1999. He then opposed the political ambitions of General Gueï, who initially promised to return power to a civilian government after a short military transition. After Gbagbo's disputed victory in 2000, his FPI government refused to negotiate with the exiled soldiers, who remained a threat to his power. The Ivoirian government claimed that Compaoré was harbouring two hundred deserters, though the Burkinabe government only acknowledged fifteen. Burkina Faso was also involved in arming the rebellion and providing training on its soil. Compaoré had an interest in having Gbagbo ousted from power in Abidjan, given that FPI's nationalist and increasingly xenophobic stances threatened the security and economic interests of the large Burkinabe population residing in Côte d'Ivoire (2.2 million people in 1998, according to the general census conducted that year). Had rebel forces seized Abidjan on September 19, 2002, as they almost did, Burkina Faso would have expected a policy reversal on immigration and bilateral co-operation issues.

49 Gbagbo invited Compaoré to mediate the peace accord and the subsequent peace process and has, therefore, an interest in seeing Compaoré succeed at his task. If Compaoré fails, there is nothing to fall back on. The country will remain effectively divided in two, and the UNSC will be required to take up the matter, which Gbagbo does not want. For Compaoré, peace and stability in Côte d'Ivoire is preferable, albeit not essential for his political survival at home. Compaoré's ability to walk away from the peace process, therefore, forces Gbagbo to co-operate if he wants the peace process to advance. On the rebel side, Compaoré has helped both their coup attempt and their ongoing rebellion against Gbagbo. Without the support or at least the tolerance of Compaoré, the rebel movement would not have been as effective. Meanwhile, the FN's military commanders have invested some of their savings in Burkina Faso, offering strong additional leverage to Compaoré.

50 The climate of fear in 2002 and 2003 caused a massive flight of Burkinabe nationals from Côte d'Ivoire. There were also fears that the significant migration of seasonal workers from Burkina Faso to Côte d'Ivoire would cease as a result. Furthermore, ethno-nationalist rhetoric employed by Gbagbo as part of his strategy to retain power between 1999 and 2002 was a large disappointment and then a *casus belli* for the Burkinabe president.

51 For more on Burkina Faso's interests in Côte d'Ivoire and its involvement in the conflict, see two International Crisis Group reports: *Cote d'Ivoire: Can the Ouagadougou Agreement Bring Peace?* and *The War Is Not Yet Over*.

52 After Guinean president Lansana Conté (twenty-one and twenty-four years in power, respectively). With the death of Conté in December 2008, Compaoré is now the longest-serving president in West Africa.

The Politics of Post-Conflict Elections in Côte d'Ivoire

Chrysantus Ayangafac

2

> Elections cannot settle a military conflict that
> negotiations or victory have failed to end.[1]

Introduction

The publicly paraded rationale for post-conflict elections is that by demilitarizing politics, they can end armed conflicts and usher in democracy and thus development. However, post-conflict elections in the Democratic Republic of Congo (DRC) in 2006, Republic of Congo (RoC) in 2002, and in Liberia in 1997 seem to suggest that the results of these elections merely reflect the military asymmetrics of the conflicts that preceded them. One might then wonder whether these elections are intended to legitimize a military victor or a power-sharing arrangement and in the process institutionalize wartime alliances. This might seem a naive assertion, considering there are inherent trade-offs among conflict resolution, democratization, stability, and peace.[2] Also, are elections paraded as success stories so that the international community can disengage from a conflict without losing face? And how do these elections affect interstate relations?

This chapter does not pretend to provide all the answers to the questions and polemics raised by post-conflict elections. Rather, it is an attempt to analyse the politics of elections in post-conflict societies and in so doing debunk the widely accepted view that post-conflict elections in Africa—however skewed they are—are a magic potion for conflict resolution and democratization.

Argument and Organization of Analysis

The point of departure of the chapter is that post-conflict reconstruction and development is not merely a technical process aimed at rebuilding societies. It is political venture aimed at reconstituting the distribution of power and resources in a society emerging from conflict. Thus post-conflict reconstruction and development is a political venture that in itself is conflictual with regard to managing various competing interests. Against this backdrop, there is little doubt that elections in post-conflict societies are all about power and the distribution of resources.

Using Côte d'Ivoire as a case study, the chapter contends that though the approaching presidential elections in Côte d'Ivoire may well serve as a conflict-management mechanism, thereby stabilizing the country, they will not resolve the underlying causes of the Ivorian crisis, which is the result of poor democratic governance. The chapter is premised on the thesis that the Ivorian crisis is rooted in a skewed democratization process, one that failed to manage the interests of the various competing political elites during a time of economic crisis and political liberalization. Here one must remember that the lack of indigenous capital means that to control the state is to control its economic resources. Thus, while the elections might provide some legitimacy to the eventual winner and enhance stability, democratization and sustainable peace are both contingent on a number of factors such as these: the conduct of the elections, the electoral process, the resulting political regime, and institutional governance.

The chapter begins by outlining the background of the Ivorian crisis. It moves on to examine the theoretical arguments surrounding post-conflict elections; after that it analyses Ivorian electoral politics and the roots of the country's crisis. Later, it assesses the power-sharing agreement that has provided the framework for elections. It ends by interrogating the transitional process and how it might affect on the country's political future.

Background to the Ivorian Crisis

After Félix Houphouët-Boigny died in December 1993, Côte d'Ivoire fell into a long struggle for power between President Henri Konan Bédié and Prime Minister Alassane Ouattara. Years of political instability led to a *coup d'état* in December 1999 headed by General Robert Gueï,[3] who overthrew Bédié.[4]

In the years before the coup d'état, Bédié had argued that under Article 11 of the constitution, he was Houphouët-Boigny's rightful heir. The constitution stated that in the event of the president's death, the president of the National Assembly (Bédié) was to assume the duties of the president until elections could be called. Ouattara argued that an interim president should be appointed and new elections held. Within hours of Houphouët-Boigny's death, Bédié declared himself president. Ouattara left the country and the governing party. While manoeuvring to win the 1995 presidential elections, Bédié introduced "Ivoirité," a controversial electoral law that effectively excluded Ivorians whose parents were not born in the country. The law basically stated that for someone to qualify as a presidential candidate, both parents had to be Ivorians. This disenfranchised most northerners, many of whom were descendants of people from Burkina Faso, Mali, and Guinea who had come to work on Côte d'Ivoire's cocoa and coffee plantations.[5] Ouattara attempted to run for president as the candidate for the Rally of the Republicans (RDR) but was disqualified amidst allegations that his father was Burkinabe. The RDR was a splinter group of the ruling party, the Democratic Party of Côte d'Ivoire (PDCI).

Bédié won the 1995 presidential election after the RDR and Laurent Gbagbo's Ivorian Popular Front (FPI) boycotted it.[6] Bédié was overthrown in a bloodless military coup in 1999 led by Gueï, who promised to clean up Ivorian politics and organize new elections. But Gueï harboured presidential aspirations and began to stir up ethnic tensions for his own political gain. On July 24, 2000, a referendum on a new constitution was held, and 86.5 percent of Ivorians who voted supported it. However, turnout was only 55 percent. According to Article 35 of the new constitution, a presidential candidate must be Ivorian by birth; both parents must be Ivorian by birth; and he or she must never have acquired another nationality.

Gueï also purged the army. Soldiers from the north were harassed, and Generals Palenfo and Coulibaly were dismissed after it was alleged that they had made an attempt on Gueï's life. Chief Sergeant Ibrahim Coulibaly went into exile. As it turned out, the northern soldiers who had been dismissed would be important actors in the insurgency that began in September 2002.[7]

On October 6, 2000, a controversial Supreme Court decision disqualified fourteen of the nineteen presidential candidates, including Ouattara, on citizenship grounds, as well as Bédié, the former president, for not submitting a proper medical certificate. The Supreme Court, headed by Gueï's legal adviser at the time, was widely believed to have been hand-picked by Gueï himself.[8] The October 2000 presidential election was effectively a two-horse race between Gueï and Gbagbo. Turnout was only 35 percent because of a boycott to protest Ouattara's exclusion. When preliminary results put Gbagbo in the lead, Gueï disbanded the National Electoral Commission (CNE), accusing it of fraud, and declared himself the winner.

This sparked popular protest. Official results indicated that Gbagbo had won with 59.36 percent of the vote. The RDR called for fresh elections. Gbagbo vehemently refused, which set the stage for large-scale street protests in Abidjan, Bouake, and Korhogo during which FPI and RDR supporters clashed. On October 27, 2000, a mass grave was discovered at Yopougono that contained the bodies of around fifty-seven RDR supporters from the north.[9] Despite an alleged coup attempt in January 2001, presumably by soldiers from the north, municipal elections were held in March of that year.

The municipal elections marked an important turning point for Côte d'Ivoire, as all political parties were allowed to field candidates. Ouattara's RDR party won the largest number of council seats. After the election, President Gbagbo pursued a policy of national reconciliation and sought to decentralize the state's authority by organizing provincial elections. These conciliatory moves came to an end on September 19, 2001, when about eight hundred exiled soldiers launched coordinated attacks on government and military facilities. The coup itself failed, but it morphed into a civil war that effectively divided the country between north and south.

After various attempts to resolve the crisis failed, the main belligerents— President Gbagbo and rebel leader Guillaume Soro[10]—agreed to begin direct negotiations. On March 4, 2007, they signed a power-sharing agreement— the Ouagadougou Peace Accord (APO). The two sides reaffirmed their commitment to the Lina–Marcoussis, Accra, and Pretoria Agreements and to all UN resolutions relating to Côte d'Ivoire. The APO was an attempt to address issues surrounding citizenship, voter eligibility, the electoral process, the restoration of state authority, and extension of the government to all of Côte d'Ivoire. An implementation framework was also agreed on. The document addressed the issues of peace, national reconciliation, and the free movement of people and goods, besides establishing monitoring and consultative mechanisms. It was expected that successful implementation of the APO would lead to elections that would end the crisis and place the country on the road to democracy.

Theoretical Arguments:
Post-Conflict Elections, Conflict Resolution, and Democratization

This section analyzes the theoretical relationship that exists between post-conflict elections (independent variable) and development (dependent variable), through its effect on conflict resolution and democratization (intervening variable). The relationship between post-conflict election and conflict resolution and democratization is the subject of this chapter. The relationships among peace, democratization, and development has been exhaustively debated elsewhere and will not be repeated here.[11]

Figure 2.1 shows a simple causal diagram that serves as a guideline for this chapter. Three key concepts are highlighted, with arrows showing the direction of cause and effect. If a post-conflict election impacts positively on conflict resolution and democratization, then there is a positive relationship between the post-conflict elections, conflict resolution, and development.

Post-Conflict Elections and Conflict Resolution

Elections are increasingly being viewed as conflict-resolution mechanisms. The reasoning is that elections can "manage" the security dilemmas posed by belligerents.[12] In post-conflict societies, security dilemmas are exacerbated by failures to share information and by the uncertainties surrounding peace deals (i.e., will the other side hold up its end?). All of this suggests why the parties involved are so often reluctant to abandon the military option and accept electoral results. Unless the strategic and security dilemmas are well managed during implementation, it is likely that conflicts will flare again, blocking both

Post-conflict election   →   **Conflict resolution/
democratization**   →   Development

Figure 2.1. Causal relationship between post-conflict elections, conflict resolution, democracy, and development

elections and long-term democratization. The present difficulties faced by Côte d'Ivoire in implementing demobilization and reintegration can be explained by the difficulties of ensuring the security of the belligerents.

It is also argued that elections can serve as conflict-resolution mechanisms in this sense: when constitutional and institutional reforms are carried out, and when grievances are aired, the belligerents can be herded into a framework of laws and mutual agreements, significantly reducing the possibility that conflicts will explode into violence or destabilization.[13] (The Angolan elections of 1992 suggest a different story: the election there led to a resumption of violence.) Clearly, this is an optimistic view of elections, but it is also one that the international community embraces. When power struggles hinge on structural political divisions and ancient grievances, elections may not help resolve conflict; indeed, they may create new forms of past divisions.

Post-Conflict Elections and Democracy

It is argued that political pluralism can help manage conflicts because open and fair competition for power, structured around elections, inevitably leads to democracy. The logic here is that when the electorate is the final arbiter of who achieves power, and when the candidates are accountable to that electorate, voting power will reduce the acrimony that might otherwise develop among competing political interests.

The principle at the heart of this assumption is that free individuals with equal voting power can vote their leaders and representatives into and out of power. This assumes, though, that voters have equal power and that the electoral system and its institutions are strong and functional. Empirical evidence suggests that this is not always so. The election of Charles Taylor in Liberia in 1997 did not transform that country into a democracy. Required, then, is an analysis of the variables that underpin elections, and the variables examined must include not only the electoral process itself but also the country's political economy. Elections do not exist in a vacuum: they are shaped and controlled by external variables. Furthermore, the impact of elections on a democracy can be strongly influenced by the institutional legacies of the existing order.[14] Institutions structure politics by defining who can participate in a particular political arena; by shaping the actors and their political strategies; and by influencing what those actors consider possible and desirable. Thelen and Steinmo contend that "institutions (formal such as constitution and informal such as culture) shape the goals that political actors pursue and ... structure power relations among them."[15] Linz and Stepan base their analysis of transition paths on the characteristics of the previous regime.[16] Thus, important variables such as the electoral regime inherited from the ancien régime demand critical examination.

Electoral Regimes, Conflict Management, and Resolution

A growing body of literature suggests that the electoral regime adopted by a certain polity is instrumental in either managing or instigating conflict.[17] Sisk and Reynolds (1999) argue that "electoral systems—the rules and procedures under which votes are translated into seats in parliament or the selection of executives— are a critical variable in determining whether elections can simultaneously serve the purposes of democratization and conflict management."[18] Proportional representation systems are generally regarded as more suitable in divided societies because they more often create broad, inclusive governments.[19]

Electoral Politics and the Roots of the Ivorian Crisis

Colonial Electoral Politics

During the colonial era, elections played a dual role in Côte d'Ivoire. They were a means by which the French could assimilate the emerging elites and thereby temper nationalistic tendencies; they also provided France with legitimacy with regard to how it governed the colony and in the process helped it shape decolonization when it finally arrived. For example, France manipulated the 1957 legislative elections in which the Democratic Party of Côte d'Ivoire (PDCI) won all the seats, and in so doing effectively killed "democracy and multiparty politics in the country at the eve of independence.[20] However, it should be noted that the electoral calculus of Ivorian political elite was tacitly determined by a colonial political economy that reflected a marriage of convenience between the north (labourers) and the southeast (plantation owners), the latter being the engine of the plantation economy (cocoa and coffee)—much to the chagrin of the westerners, who perceived themselves as the indigenous peoples of Côte d'Ivoire and who happened to have settled around the most productive cocoa belt in Côte d'Ivoire. The point is that on independence, Côte d'Ivoire inherited a political and electoral system that favoured a dominant role for the PDCI.

Managing Post-Independence Political Contestation

After independence on August 7, 1960, elections were meant to manage political demands and political conflicts in ways that heeded the fact that ethnic groups are at the core of Ivorian politics.[21] Ivorian politics is mainly about building coalitions of demand-bearing groups; generally, this means sustaining those coalitions by distributing rewards. How did Houphouët-Boigny manage to bring about harmony among the various ethnic groups, thereby ensuring relative political stability in the absence of political pluralism and competitive elections?

For one thing, the Ivorian economy was buoyant between 1960 and 1979,[22] and this gave Houphouët-Boigny space to apply the politics of inclusion and distribution—in local terms, "le modele houphetiste" or "le compromise houphoutiste."[23] Enough resources were available that he could meet the demands of demand-bearing groups, co-opt political adversaries, buy off the military, appease potential enemies, and keep ethnic animosities in check through regional development.[24] Also, Houphouët-Boigny was able to establish cohesion and stability in Ivorian politics through state intervention in the economy—an approach that he used to entrench patronage.[25] Notwithstanding its liberal and capitalist policies and the existence of a private sector, the Ivorian state was a key actor in the economy, in that it developed a large and dynamic public sector and established a welfare system. Boigny instituted Ivorianization[26] in response to the rising demand for it among demand-bearing groups. This meant he was able to place his cronies in important foreign companies.[27] For example, Charles Donwahi, the president of CFAO-Côte d'Ivoire from 1975 to 1991, served as parliamentarian, Minister of Agriculture, and member of the PDCI's political bureau.[28] Ivorianization also meant that Ivorian clients could hold shares in important foreign companies. For example, all of the Ivorian shares in Dafci, a leading exporter, were held by Gbon Coulibaly, political kingpin of Korhogo and long-time deputy and member of the PDCI's political bureau. Houphouët-Boigny's son Françoise presided over Etablisements Jean Abile-Gal, the nerve centre of the JAG group.[29]

Houphouët-Boigny also maintained stability through ethnic and regional balancing—that is, he attempted to balance ethnic groups within state institutions. The skillful use of ethnic quotas allowed all major groups to be represented in post-independence political institutions between 1959 and 1980, though the Akans dominated (Houphouët-Boigny was an Akan, the same as Bédié).[30] He encouraged development projects in the north, especially in the 1970s. In 1970, for example, the government launched an ambitious regional development program worth CFA 21 billion.[31]

Houphouët-Boigny succeeded in controlling the patronage system in Côte d'Ivoire by adopting a de facto single-party system. With the PDCI as the only political party, he was able to manipulate and control the various demand-bearing groups. Since membership in the party meant access to state resources, the PDCI became a mechanism for political elites to negotiate among themselves for the spoils of the state. In this context, movement within the party structure was tantamount to resource mobilization. Thus, in the absence of democratic institutions for negotiating the distribution of resources and managing conflict, Houphouët-Boigny became the mediator and adjudicator with regard to who got what, when and how.

This patronage-based system was strained to its limits after the economic crisis of the 1980s. Now there were few resources to sustain the patronage network. The severe economic crisis[32] that gripped the country led to calls for democratization. Both within the country and in the international community, the economic crisis was perceived as a result of the absence of democratization or at least political liberalization.

Political Liberalization and Electoral Politics in Côte d'Ivoire

There are sixty ethnic groups in Côte d'Ivoire, as well as five major ethnic groupings. The Akans are 42.1 percent of the population and are found mainly in the south, south-east, and centre. The Mandé are 26.5 percent of the population and are found in the north and west. The Gur or Voltaïques are 17.6 percent of the population and are in the north. The Krou are 11 percent of the population and are found in the southwest and west. The ethnic configuration of the Ivorian population is as follows: Baoulé 26 percent; Dioula 15 percent; Agni 12 percent; Bété 15 percent; Guéré 12 percent; Ébrié 8 percent; Yacouba 7 percent; Appolo 5 percent. In terms of religion, Muslims comprise 38.6 percent, Catholics 9.4 percent, Protestants 6.6 percent, and animists 11.9 percent.[33]

No single ethnic group commands an absolute majority in Côte d'Ivoire. Thus, politics is mostly about forming coalitions that are strong enough to last until the next election and that offer a shot at winning the presidency. A factor here is that Côte d'Ivoire has a first-past-the-post system. In presidential elections, if no candidate gains more than 50 percent of the votes in the first round, a second round follows in which the two leading candidates go head to head for a simple majority. Since the president holds most of the state's power, politics in Côte d'Ivoire is a zero-sum game.

With the transition to multiparty politics in the early 1990s, Houphouët-Boigny adopted a two-pronged strategy for winning the first multiparty elections in 1991. First, he assembled a coalition of the north, the centre, and the southeast. Second, he had the country adopt a single-constituency, simple-majority system in which foreigners would be allowed to vote (much to the annoyance of Gbagbo's Ivorian Popular Front; FPI).[34] This compelled the opposition to adopt identity politics; in effect, it branded itself as an ethnic party that intended to serve the narrow interests of the Bété people.[35] Houphouët-Boigny enjoyed an easy victory over his main rivals in the 1991 elections.

The PDCI's base was a coalition of northerners and southerners. After Houphouët-Boigny died, the northerners expected considerable compensation for their unwavering support. Clearly, they were dissatisfied with what the alliance had granted them so far and perceived that they ought to be rewarded with more high-ranking positions and development programs.

Their grievances were captured in the notorious Charte du Grand Nord (Great Northern Charter) in 1992, which called for fuller recognition of the Muslim Islamic religion, northern development, increased political representation, access to public jobs, and the debaoulelisation (tribalization) of the state.[36] The north's electoral clout and the political ramifications of ethnic allegiance were clear in the presidential and parliamentary elections of the 1990s. Though the PDCI won the elections, FPI—which was generally viewed as a Bété bulwark against Baoulé dominance—performed relatively well in the Bété region, specifically in the southwest. Also, the FPI gained 29 percent of the northern vote—most probably because of northerners' dissatisfaction, but also probably because several northern politicians defected from the PDCI (most notably Gbon Coulibaly).[37] The PDCI must have realized that it would be crippled politically if northern voters walked away from it.[38]

By 1995, Bédié was faced with a difficult situation with regard to the October presidential election. The economic crisis was having a severe impact on the country's social cohesion, and the RDR and FPI had formed a coalition to contest the elections. Bédié saw no option but to play the ethnic card in an attempt to strengthen his political base, which was Akan/Baoulé. It was Bédié who injected the notorious concept of Ivoirité into Ivorian legal parlance. After a 1995 amendment to the electoral code, only people with two Ivorian parents could (a) vote or (b) run for president. This disenfranchised most northerners and left them out of decisions on who was to get what, how and when, on the basis that they were "really" Burkinabe, Guinean, or Malian.

Clearly, Ivoirité was a calculated move by Bédié to exclude Ouattara from the political process. Earlier on, Gbagbo had played the ethnic card, but he had learned quickly that he could not win an election in Côte d'Ivoire insofar as his political base was restricted to the Bété region. So he joined forces with Ouattara, knowing this was his best chance to mobilize political support. Bédié was toppled in December 1999, but by then he had left an indelible mark on Ivorian politics.[39] The politics of exclusion would be sustained and practised by subsequent leaders such as Gueï.

As noted earlier, Gueï had promised to clean up Ivorian politics, but once in power he began to develop presidential ambitions and to exploit ethnicity for political gain. On July 24, 2000, a new constitution was adopted.[40] Its 35th Article disqualified fourteen of the nineteen presidential candidates, including Ouattara, on citizenship grounds.

The October 2000 election was basically a match between Gueï and Gbagbo. After the votes were counted and contested, and after a long period of infighting for the president's chair, on September 19, 2002, an attempted coup was launched that quickly descended into outright civil war. The northerners who dominated the rebellion justified themselves by declaring that they were defending northerners' voting rights. After many attempts to resolve the crisis, the two opposing sides signed the APO, which called for peace leading up to elections.

The Context of the APO and Presidential Elections

This section will analyze the APO, which is the framework on which the proposed December presidential election is anchored. The accord hinges on (a) power sharing between the rebels and the government, and (b) elections. Why was this accord possible? And how will it influence the presidential election?

The APO is the direct result of the non-implementation of previously negotiated agreements and international pronouncements on the conflict, the latest being UNSC Resolution 1721. That resolution extended the mandates of President Gbagbo and Prime Minister Banny[41] for twelve months. At the same time, it transferred some of the president's powers—especially those over security and the electoral process—to the prime minister. The resolution thus posed a threat to Gbagbo's political survival, considering that it aimed at neutralizing his influence over the electoral process and the security apparatus of the state as stipulated by the constitution.

In that context, the APO can be viewed as a strategic manoeuvre by the principal belligerents to secure their relevance, institutionalize the distribution of power, and reduce uncertainty. Direct dialogue with the rebels gave Gbagbo the manoeuvring room to seize control of the peace process, which was slipping further and frther out of his control; most important, however, it allowed him to sideline an increasingly hostile international community as well as break up the formidable alliance between the rebels and the political opposition (RDR and PDCI). The fact that Gbagbo agreed to talks with people he once vowed never to negotiate with suggests how important the accord was to his political survival.

As for the rebels, the APO offered them an escape from an untenable situation. The war had caused dire hardships to the people of the north, much of the region having been cut off from state resources. They had quickly tired of the war and were withdrawing their support from the rebels. The northern economy had collapsed, partly because of war deprivations, mismanagement, and weak infrastructure, but also because the region had been cut off from the rest of the country. The rebels had never been a homogenous group, which led to a great deal of arguing over strategy. Military force had not provided the desired results, and the stalemate could not last forever. Seccession was never an option; it would have been economically inviable and politically unsustainable. Sooner or later, the rebels would have to talk.

Also, the rebels sensed that the political opposition—specifically, Ouattara and Bédié—were exploiting the armed struggle for their own political ends. For the rebels to be relevant in the future politics of Côte d'Ivoire, they would have to distance themselves from the political opposition. Sidiki Konate, the rebels' spokesperson, argued that the rebels were not seeking the consent of the political opposition to exist as such; he added that discord between the political opposition and the rebels need not be particular problem.[42] The rebels had always wanted the position of prime minister, especially since the departure of Seydou Diarra,[43] though the political opposition vehemently opposed their getting it, for it would increase the rebels' bargaining power and grant them political influence that the politicians coveted for themselves. The APO provided the rebels the opportunity to solicit concessions from Gbagbo—concessions they could not have made in a multilateral forum. It also offered them an opportunity to influence the country's political economy in ways it never had before.

Presidential Elections and Resolving the Ivorian Crisis: Why Elections Matter

Elections are partly about economic power. Bakary Tessy argues that the development of a plantation economy led to a consensus on economic policy that is the main source of conservative politics in the country today.[44] If the APO works as intended, the coming presidential election will be a watershed event in Côte d'Ivoire and encourage the international community to re-engage with the country. That election will have the potential to dictate the rules of the game with regard to managing competing interests. In this regard, it is imperative that the winner's legitimacy be enhanced by the electoral process. Credible elections—indeed, elections of any sort—enable the international community to rally around the winner, which in turn leads to much-needed resources flowing in for post-conflict reconstruction and development. Moreover, developmental aid from international financial institutions is contingent on some degree of political stability. Also, countries—like France—have seen their influence in Africa wane over the decades; support for the electoral process can help reverse that trend.

The upcoming presidential election will do much to decide who has the political initiative in the country. The Ivorian crisis is at its base a crisis of legitimacy. For now, the regime's legitimacy hinges on the fact that the country is at war with itself. Thus, it is urgent that Gbabgo renew his mandate. That mandate effectively ended in 2005, though it has been extended once by the UNSC on the recommendation of the AU's Peace and Security Council. For now, though, he lacks a popular mandate, and he needs one if he hopes to bolster his legitimacy as he struggles to strengthen his hold on power.

There is no doubt that the APO and its supplementary accords reflect the desire of Gbagbo and his prime minister, Guillaume Soro, to seize control of the peace process, which is rapidly being hijacked by the international community. By winning an election, they will be able to ensure their political survival. There are grounds to contend that Gbagbo and Soro need the legitimacy of fair elections in order to puncture arguments that their partnership is designed to share the spoils of war.

A credible election will enable the political opposition to reassert themselves, considering that for a long time they have been overshadowed by the rebels. It will also offer them a chance to take or at least influence power. Indeed, they have a legitimate chance of doing so: if Gbagbo fails to secure a first-round victory, the opposition's combined ticket could well offer him a serious challenge. Perhaps the political opposition will be contesting the presidential election with an eye on the parliamentary elections. The country's ethnic demographics make it quite probable that the political opposition will do well in the legislative elections and in the process take the political battle to the legislature. It is against this backdrop that the various Ivorian political elites are jostling for influence over the electoral process.

Implementing Ouagadougou and the Electoral Process: What Is at Stake?

The APO is extremely important in part because its provisions will inform the decisions of competing political actors. Will they embrace the electoral process or subvert it? As Lyon points out, the choices the actors make early in the peace-implementation phase will establish precedents, norms, and institutional frameworks that will in turn structure the post-conflict political order.[45] The electoral process in Côte d'Ivoire will strongly affect how post-conflict elections are conducted in the country. Control of the transitional period and by extension the electoral process may create different interest groups and new elite coalitions, as well as—most important—determine who controls the country's wealth and governing institutions, not just in the run-up to the elections but also after the elections. In that sense, struggles for influence over the electoral process and the APO's implementation are quite simply attempts at political survival. Any Ivorian politician who helps shape the APO's implementation and the electoral process will most likely enjoy considerable influence over the country's political economy for years to come. In that context, it is a political prize to acquire control over citizen identification, voter registration, compilation of electoral lists, and disarmament and demobilization.

Identification

Identification is a core stipulation of the APO. At Ouagadougou it was decided there would be two means of identification: presentation of a birth certificate and nationality certificate, and presence on the electoral list. To accelerate matters, the electoral list was prioritized. This meant that those whose names were on the 2000 electoral list would be issued identity cards. The identification process and disarmament are to be carried out concurrently. The awarding of identification papers and nationality certificates to people who are not even listed in the civil register is a large bone of contention between the president and the prime minister. The reliance on identification papers and certificates threatens the government's electoral chances. The government has emphasized repeatedly that the awarding of these papers contravenes Ivorian law and is impeding the process. Soro insists that the slow pace of the identification process is a result of underfunding.[46] Louis Michel, EU Commissioner for Development and Humanitarian Assistance, has stated that he does not believe that underfunding was the cause of this problem.[47]

Voter Registration

Voter registration will depend heavily on success with the identification process. Like that process, voter registration was debated intensely before it was even underway. It has raised many eyebrows that the National Institute of Statistics (INS), a government agency, will be playing a key role in the elections. First, since voter registration will be based on the 2000 electoral list, the process will be inherently flawed, considering that the 2000 list excluded many Ivorians. However, the INS director, Mathieu Meleu (a member of Gbagbo's FPI), has stated that the 2000 list will serve merely as a useful template. He has admitted that the INS makes some errors when drafting electoral lists, and he has urged politicians to forget about the 2000 list, saying that such lists are a matter for technicians and that politicians should focus on political mobilization.[48] As for the political opposition, it is in their interest to increase voter registration (especially in the north), since doing so will certainly expand their constituencies, considering that so many northerners where disenfranchised during the 2000 election.

Moreover, the IEC will be supported in its work by the INS, which is under the political umbrella of the Minister of State in Charge of Planning (Paul Antoine Bohoun Bouabre, a close confidant of Gbagbo). This has raised speculation that Gbagbo is trying to influence the electoral process. When the UNSC withdrew its senior election-monitoring post on July 16, 2007, after being pressured to do so by Gbagbo, it only added fuel to the controversy. Bédié and Ouattara oppose any attempt to give the INS a chance of even slightly influencing the elections.[49] The appointment of a French company, Société d'Application Générales Electriques et Mécaniques (SAGEM), as the private technical agency that will carry out the issuance of identity cards has not gone down well with many Ivorians, especially some factions within the Forces Nouvelles (FN) and the government, because of the role France has played in the country's history and politics.[50] The Minister of the Interior, Désiré Tagro, has argued that SAGEM should report to the INS. He adds that SAGEM should be subject to the INS because of its experience with the local terrain. The FN has argued that, since the INS is under the government's political control, having SAGEM report to it might blur the transparency of the identification and electoral process.[51] Disagreement within the FN over the choice of SAGEM and its role in the electoral process could explain why Louis Dacoury-Tabley of the FN walked out of a recent Monitoring and Evaluation Committee meeting convened in December 2007 in Burkina Faso. Disagreement over SAGEM's role is animated by two divergent positions: on the one hand, there are those who argue that SAGEM should merely support the expertise of the electoral division of UN mission in Côte d'Ivoire in carrying out its mission; others argue that SAGEM should be given a free hand to make identity cards and electoral cards.[52] Soro contends that SAGEM could be retained but that its asking price of CFA 50 billion[53] is too high. President Blais Compaoré of Burkina Faso has argued that giving the contract to a new operator will delay the peace process even more.[54] In any case, SAGEM has a contract.

Disarmament, Demobilization, and Reintegration

Disarmament, demobilization, and reintegration (DDR) is a contentious issue that is delaying implementation of the APO. DDR is contentious because of the security implications. Over the past three months, attempts at DDR have sparked riots in the north by the ex-combatants, who claim that they have not been paid money owed to them. According to the national disarmament commission and the terms of a series of disarmament deals signed in 2005—the principles of which still hold, though deadlines have been repeatedly missed—the rebels have 42,564 soldiers.[55] The deals state that all of these troops are to hand in their weapons and be paid 499,500 CFA francs (£518; US$970) each. They can also benefit from loans for small business start-ups, or farming, to a maximum of 430,000 CFA (£446; US$830).[56]

At the epicentre of the blocked DDR process is the project of merging the FN with the National Armed Forces of Côte d'Ivoire (FANCI). The FN argues that the military grades obtained by its soldiers during the war should be maintained during integration and that personnel should receive the retirement benefits associated with those positions. The government seems to be proposing a lump-sum package with no offer of indemnity. Another problem relating to DDR involves raw numbers—that is, how many FN soldier will join FANCI, and which ranks? The numbers game is important in determining the amount of money each combatant will receive for disarming, as well as what they will be doing in the united army.

Conclusion

This chapter set out to show that while the upcoming elections in Côte d'Ivoire may bring some stability, they will do little to usher in and sustain democracy in the country, considering that Ivorian politics is still a zero-sum game, because of its electoral system and powerful presidency. The chapter has also shown that if the electoral process is perceived as skewed, the winner may lack legitimacy, which will heighten political tensions. The current attempts to control the electoral process will produce an election result that strengthens the present regime by giving it some international and internal legitimacy. But that same result will fail to address the basic cause of the Ivorian crisis, which is the absence of democratic means to manage elite interests in the context of economic crisis. Overall, then, the election results will not mark the end of post-conflict reconstruction and development; rather, they will turn a new page in the country's history. Perhaps then the international community will accept the role of a constructive partner.

Notes

1 Terrence Lyon, "Post-Conflict Elections: War Termination, Democratization, and Demilitarizing Politics." Working Paper no. 20, February 2002. Arlington: Institute for Conflict Analysis and Resolution, George Mason University.

2 Pauline Baker, "Conflict Resolution Versus Democratic Governance: Divergent Paths to Peace?" in *Managing Global Chaos: Sources of and Responses to International Conflict*, ed. Chester Crocker and Fen Osler Hampson with Pamela Aall (Washington: Washington: U.S. Institute of Peace Press, 1996.

3 He was dismissed in 1995 as the Army Chief of Staff for refusing to mobilize his troops to resolve a political struggle between Bédié and the opposition leader Alassane Ouattara. Though he did not take part in the 1999 coup, he was encouraged out of retirement to lead the junta. He promised to clean up Ivoirian politics.

4 Henri Konan Bédié was Côte d'Ivoire's first ambassador to the United States and Canada. He served in the government as Minister of Economy and Finance. After being elected to the National Assembly he was elected its president in December 1980; he was re-elected to that post in 1985 and 1990. As National Assembly President, he succeeded long-time President Félix Houphouët-Boigny on the latter's death in December 1993.

5 Jean-Pierre Dozon, "Economie Marchande et Structures Sociales: Le cas des Bété de Côte d'Ivoire," *Cahiers d'Etudes Africaines* 68, no. 17 (1977): 463–84.

6 Richard Crook, "Winning Coalition and Ethno-Regional Politics: The Failure of the Opposition in the 1990 and 1995 Elections in Côte d'Ivoire," *African Affairs* 96 (1997): 215–42.

7 Ousmane Dembele, "Côte d'ivoire: la fracture Communautaire," *Politique Africaine* 89 2003: 34–48.

8 Human Rights Watch, "The New Racism: The Political Manipulation of Ethnicity in Côte d'Ivoire," *HRW* 13, no. 6(A), August 2001.

9 Ibid.

10 Guillaume Soro has been Prime Minister of Côte d'Ivoire since April 4, 2007. Before that, he had led the Patriotic Movement of Côte d'Ivoire as well as the New Forces rebel group as its secretary-general.

11 Adam Przeworski, *Democracy and the Market* (New York: Cambridge University Press), 1991; Adam Przeworski and Fernando Limongi, "Political Regimes and Economic Growth" *Journal of Economic Perspectives*, Summer 1993; Adam Przeworski and Fernando Limongi, "Democracy and Development," in A. Hadenius (ed.), *Democracy's Victory and Crisis*, (Cambridge: Cambridge University Press), 157–87.

12 Lyon, "Post-Conflict Elections."

13 Cyril Obi, "Introduction: Elections and the Challenge of Post-Conflict Democratisation in West Africa," *African Journal of International Affairs* 10, nos. 1 and 2 (2007): 1–12.

14 Guillermo O'Donnell and Philippe Schmitter, *Transitions from Authoritarian Rule: Tentative Conclusions about Uncertain Democracies* (Baltimore: Johns Hopkins University Press, 1986).

15 Kathleen Thelen and Sven Steinmo, "Historical Institutionalism in Comparative Politics," in *Structuring Politics: Historical Institutionalism in Comparative Analysis*, ed. Kathleen Thelen, Sven Steinmo, and Frank Longstreth (Cambridge: Cambridge University Press, 1992), 1–32.

16 Juan J. Linz and Alfred Stepan, *Problems of Democratic Transition and Consolidation: Southern Europe, South America, and Post-Communist Europe* (Baltimore: Johns Hopkins University Press, 1996), 55.

17 See Khabele Matlosa, "Electoral Systems, Constitutionalism, and Conflict Management," *African Journal on Conflict Resolution* 4, no. 2 (2004): 11–53; Timothy D. Sisk, "Elections and Conflict Management in Africa: Conclusions and Recommendations," in *Elections and Conflict Management in Africa*, ed. Timothy Sisk and Andrew Reynolds (Washington: U.S. Institute of Peace Press, 1998), 146.

18 Ibid.

19 Ibid.

20 Coulibaly Tiemoko, "Démocratie et Surenchères Identitaires en Côte-d'Ivoire," *Politique Africaine* 58 (1995): 143–50.

21 Jean-Pierre Chauveau, "Agricultural Production and Social Formation: The Baule Region of Toumodiko Kumbo in Historical Perspective," in *Peasants in Africa*, ed. Martin A. Klein (Thousand Oaks: Sage), 143–76.

22 B. A. den Tuinder, *Ivory Coast: The Challenge of Success* (World Bank: Washington, DC, 1978).

23 Francis Akindes, "The Roots of the Military-Political Crises in Côte d'Ivoire," Research Report No. 128 (Uppsala: Nordiska Afrikainstitutet, 2004).

24 Jennifer Widner, "The 1990 Elections in Côte d'Ivoire." *Journal of Opinion* 20, no. 1 (1990): 31–40.

25 Richard Crook, "Politics, the Cocoa Crisis, and Administration in Côte d'Ivoire," *Journal of Modern African Studies* 28, no. 4 (1990): 649–69; *idem*, "Patrimonialism, Administrative Effectiveness, and Economic Development in Côte d'Ivoire," *African Affairs* 88, no. 351; Catherine Boone, "Commerce in Côte d'Ivoire: Ivorinisation without Ivoirian Traders," *Journal of Modern African Studies*. 31, no. 1 (1993): 67–92.

26 Ivoirinization basically meant that top public positions would be held by Ivoirians. It is important to note that French citizens held important posts as means to enhance and build administrative capacity in the country.

27 Catherine Boone, "Commerce in Côte d'Ivoire: Ivorinisation without Ivoirian Traders," *Journal of Modern African Studies* 3 (1997): 67–92.

28 Ibid.

29 Ibid.

30 Tessy Bakary, "Political Polarisation over Governance in Côte d'Ivoire," in *Governance as Conflict Management: Politics and Violence in West Africa*, ed. William I. Zartman (Washington: Brookings Institution, 1997).

31 Adrienne Blay Botau, "Intégration et Autonomie de Minorités en côte d'Ivoire," Université d'Abidjan. http://www.unhchr.ch/minorities/documents/2004-WP8fr.doc.

32 A. Siedou Konate, "The Politics of Identity and Violence in Côte d'Ivoire." www.west africareview.com/issue5konate.htm; Commission Nationale de coordination de Côte d'Ivoire, "Les ethnies de Côte d'Ivoire Enquête Entreprise sur le Terrain 1992–97," 275, in Adrienne Blay Botau, "Intégration et Autonomie de Minorités en côte d'Ivoire," Université d'Abidjan. http://www.unhchr.ch/minorities/documents/2004-WP8fr.doc.

33 A. Siedou Konate, "The Politics of Identity and Violence in Cote d'Ivoire," *West Africa Review*. http://www.westafricareview.com/issue5konate.htm.

34 Crook, "Winning Coalition; *idem*, "Côte d'Ivoire: Multi-Party Democracy and Political Change: Surviving the Crisis," in *Democracy and Political Change in Sub-Saharan Africa*, ed. John A. Wiseman (London: Routledge, 1995), 11–44.

35 Widner, "The 1990 Elections in Côte d'Ivoire."

36 Ibid.

37 He was a prominent supporter of the Boigny, baron of the PDCI, and a chief and businessman in the north.

38 Ibid.

39 Konate, "The Politics of Identity and Violence."

40 Armin Langer, "Horizontal Inequalities and Violent Conflict: the Case of Côte d'Ivoire." Working Paper no. 13, November 2005. Oxford Centre for Research on Inequality Human Security and Ethnicity.

41 Charles Konan Banny was Prime Minister of Côte d'Ivoire from December 7, 2005, to April 4, 2007. Before becoming prime minister he worked for the Central Bank of West African States (BCEAO). At one point he was Special Advisor to the Governor of BCEAO, Alassane Ouattara.

42 International Crisis Group, "Côte d'Ivoire: Faut-it croire a l'Accorde de Ougadougou?" in *African Report* 127, June 27, 2007.

43 Seydou Elimane Diarra was prime minister in 2000 and again from 2003 to 2005. Before joining the government, he was an ambassador to the EEC and Brazil and president of the Chamber of Commerce and Industry of Côte d'Ivoire. After the December 1999 coup, on January 4, 2000, he was appointed Minister of State for Planning, Development, and Government Co-operation under the transitional president, Robert Guéï. He was subsequently prime minister from May 2000 to October 2000.

44 Bakary, "Political Polarization over Governance."

45 Lyon, "Post-Conflict Elections."

46 Kisselminan Coulibaly, "Soro veut contrôler l'identification." Soifinfo, October 27, 2007. http://www.soirinfo.com/article.php3?id_article=4525.

47 Ibid.

48 Félix D. Bony, "Le DG de l'INS prévient: On peut être sur la liste de 2000 et absent de celle de 2008," *L'inter*, November 21, 2007. http://www.linter-ci.com/article.php3?id_article=5517.

49 Marwane Yahmed, "Gbagbo–Soro: le Divorce?" *Jeune Afrique.* http://www.jeuneafrique .com/jeune_afrique/article_jeune_afrique.asp?art_cle=LIN11117gbagbecrovi0.

50 See Jean Nanga, "A 'Civil War' That Is French and Neo-Colonial," *International Viewpoint* 4 (2005): 364.

51 Akwaba Saint Clair, "Identification: Tagro crée le clash à Ouaga: Le ministre de l'Intérieur veut substituer l'INS à Sagem," *Le Nouveau Réveil*, November 23, 2007. http://news .abidjan.net/article/?n=272684.

52 K. Kara, "Réunion du Comité d'Evaluation et d'Accompagnement de l'Accord de Ouaga Le débat coince sur les attributions de SAGEM," *Le Patriote*, November 20, 2007. http://www .lepatriote.net/lire/0c7c1856-07ee-4bbf-9f80-d77318b8f387.aspx.

53 The current exchange rate between USD and the CFA franc is around 1$=450.

54 Yahmed, "Gbagbo–Soro."

55 Fifth Progress Report of the Secretary-General on the United Nations Operation in Côte d'Ivoire, 17/6/05 (S/2005/398), para 10. http://www.un.org/Docs/sc/sgrep05.htm.

56 See UN Disarmament, Demobilisation and Reintegration website for Côte d'Ivoire: http://www.unddr.org/countryprogrammes.php?c=51. The maximum optional loan of 430,000 CFA comes from adding the following: microcredit financing at CFA 180,000 per

individual, plus a loan of CFA 150,000 for purchase of equipment, plus a loan of CFA 100,000 for agricultural projects and the purchase of seeds.

References

Akindes, F. Francis "The Roots of the Military-Political Crises in Côte d'Ivoire." Research Report No. 128. Upssala: Nordiska Afrikainstitutet, 2004.

Bakary, Tessy. 1997. "Political Polarisation over Governance in Côte d'Ivoire." In *Governance as Conflict Management: Politics and Violence in West Africa*, ed. William I. Zartman. Washington: Brookings Institution.

Baker, Pauline. "Conflict Resolution Versus Democratic Governance: Divergent Paths to Peace?" In *Managing Global Chaos: Sources of and Responses to International Conflict*, ed. Chester Crocker and Fen Osler Hampson with Pamela Aall. Washington: United States Institute for Peace .

Bony, Felix. "Le DG de l'INS prévient: On peut être sur la liste de 2000 et absent de celle de 2008." L'inter, November 21, 2007. http://www.linter-ci.com/article.php3?id_article=5517.

Boone, Catherine. "Commerce in Côte d'Ivoire: Ivorinisation without Ivoirian Traders." *Journal of Modern African Studies* 3 (1997): 67–92.

Botau, Adrienne Blay. "Intégration et Autonomie de Minorités en côte d'Ivoire." Université d'Abidjan. http://www.unhchr.ch/minorities/documents/2004-WP8fr.doc.

Chauveau, Jean-Pierre.1980. "Agricultural Production and Social Formation: The Baule Region of Toumodiko Kumbo in Historical Perspective." In *Peasants in Africa*, ed. Martin A. Klein. Thousand Oaks: Sage. 143–76.

Coulibaly, K. Kisselminan. "Soro veut contrôler l'identification." Soifinfo, October 27, 2007. http://www.soirinfo.com/article.php3?id_article=4525.

Crook, Richard. "Côte d'Ivoire: Multi-Party Democracy and Political Change: Surviving the Crisis." In *Democracy and Political Change in Sub-Saharan Africa*, ed. John A. Wiseman. London: Routledge, 1995. 11–44.

——. "Winning Coalition and Ethno-Regional Politics: The Failure of the Opposition in the 1990 and 1995 Elections in Côte d'Ivoire." *African Affairs* 96 (1997): 215–42.

Dembele, Ousmane. "Côte d'ivoire: la fracture Communautaire." *Politique Africaine* 89 2003: 34–48.

Dozon, Jean-Pierre. "Economie Marchande et Structures Sociales: Le cas des Bété de Côte d'Ivoire." *Cahiers d'Études Africaines* 68, no. 17 (1977): 463–84.

International Crisis Group. "Côte d'Ivoire: Faut-it croire a l'Accorde de Ougadougou?" In *African Report* 127, June 27, 2007.

Kara, Khristian. "Réunion du Comité d'Evaluation et d'Accompagnement de l'Accord de Ouaga Le débat coince sur les attributions de SAGEM." Le Patriote, November 20, 2007. http://www.lepatriote.net/lire/0c7c1856-07ee-4bbf-9f80-d77318b8f387.aspx.

Konate, A. Siedou. "The Politics of Identity and Violence in Côte d'Ivoire." *West Africa Review* 5 (2004). http://www.westafricareview.com/issue5/konate.htm.

Langer, Armin. "Horizontal Inequalities and Violent Conflict: the Case of Côte d'Ivoire." Working Paper no. 13, November 2005. Oxford Centre for Research on Inequality Human Security and Ethnicity.

Linz, Juan A., and Alfred Stepan. *Problems of Democratic Transition and Consolidation: Southern Europe, South America, and Post-Communist Europe*. Baltimore: Johns Hopkins University Press, 1996.

Lyon, Terrence. "Post-Conflict Elections: War Termination, Democratization, and Demilitarizing Politics." Working Paper no. 20, February 2002. Arlington: Institute for Conflict Analysis and Resolution, George Mason University.

Matlosa, K. Khabele "Electoral Systems, Constitutionalism, and Conflict Management." *African Journal on Conflict Resolution* 4, no. 2 (2004): 11–54.

Nanga, Jean. "A 'Civil War' That Is French and Neo-Colonial." *International Viewpoint* 4 (2005): 364.

Obi, Cyril "Introduction: Elections and the Challenge of Post-Conflict Democratisation in West Africa." *African Journal of International Affairs* 10, nos. 1 and 2 (2007): 1–12.

O'Donnell, Guillermo, and Philippe Schmitter. *Transitions from Authoritarian Rule: Tentative Conclusions about Uncertain Democracies*. Baltimore: Johns Hopkins University Press, 1986.

Saint Clair, Akwaba. "Identification: Tagro crée le clash à Ouaga: Le ministre de l'Intérieur veut substituer l'INS à Sagem." *Le Nouveau Réveil*, November 23, 2007. http://news.abidjan.net/article/?n=272684.

Sisk, Timothy. "Elections and Conflict Management in Africa: Conclusions and Recommendations." In *Elections and Conflict Management in Africa*, ed. Timothy Sisk and Andrew Reynolds. Washington: U.S. Institute of Peace Press, 1998.

Sisk, Timothy, and Andrew S. Reynolds. *Elections and Conflict Management in Africa*. Washington: U.S. Institute of Peace Press, 1998.

Thelen, Kathleen, and Sven Steinmo. "Historical Institutionalism in Comparative Politics." In *Structuring Politics: Historical Institutionalism in Comparative Analysis*, ed. Kathleen Thelen, Sven Steinmo, and Frank Longstreth. Cambridge: Cambridge University Press, 1992. 1–32.

Tiemoko, Coulibaly. "Démocratie et Surenchères Identitaires en Côte-d'Ivoire." *Politique Africaine* 58 (1995): 143–50.

Yahmed, Marwane Ben. "Gbagbo–Soro: le Divorce?" *Jeune Afrique*. http://www.jeuneafrique.com/jeune_afrique/article_jeune_afrique.asp?art_cle=LIN11117gbagbecrovi0.

Widner, Jennifer A. "The 1990 Elections in Côte d'Ivoire." *Journal of Opinion* 20, no. 1 (1990): 31–40.

Côte d'Ivoire
The Role of the Private Sector in Building a Peace Economy
Willene A. Johnson

3

The conference "From Civil Strife to Peace Building" took place in December 2007 at a critical juncture for peacebuilding in Côte d'Ivoire. Some months earlier the Ouagadougou Peace Agreement (APO) had established a framework for political reconciliation between the government of Côte d'Ivoire, led by President Laurent Gbagbo, and the Forces Nouvelles (FN), led by Guillaume Soro. The agreement, signed on March 4, 2007, put in place a transitional government to oversee the disarmament of militias, the integration of the army and rebel forces, and the identification and registration of voters for national elections.[1] Events in the weeks preceding the conference, including an International Monetary Fund (IMF) report[2] on Côte d'Ivoire and a Plenary Meeting of the Kimberley Process,[3] made it clear that economic issues would be a vital element in reconciliation. The conference participants learned from a representative of the Programme National de Reinsertion et de Rehabilitation Communautaire (PNRRC) that Côte d'Ivoire is carrying out the process of disarmament, demobilization, and reintegration (DDR) with a unique approach, one that emphasizes economic reintegration and community development.

This approach to DDR presumes that there will be ample opportunities for former combatants to earn incomes. If the economy of Côte d'Ivoire stagnates, the risk of renewed conflict will increase. While policy-makers and the business community recognize the importance of economic vitality as an instrument of peace, the current challenge goes beyond promoting economic growth to relieve the social and political stresses associated with a faltering economic environment. Economic growth alone will not solve the problems of Côte d'Ivoire and will not be sustainable unless it is accompanied by improved governance. In the words of Larry Diamond: "In most of the world's poor countries, the 'economy first' advocates have the causal chain backward. Without significant improvements in governance, economic growth will not take off or be sustainable. Without legal and political institutions to control corruption, punish cheating, and ensure a level economic and political playing field, pro-growth policies will be ineffective and their economic benefits will be overshadowed or erased.'[4]

This chapter examines issues of economic governance and ways in which the public and private sectors can work together to build a peace economy in Côte d'Ivoire. Economic factors played a role in fomenting and sustaining conflict in Côte d'Ivoire. Institutions must be recast and reinforced to promote economic growth that includes all regions and all ethnic groups; this will reduce the inequalities and perceived inequities that fuelled discontent and increased vulnerability to conflict. Thus, for example, while the IMF document reports that the Ivorian government made a commitment to take measures to encourage private-sector growth—including a pledge to reform the coffee, cocoa, cotton, and energy sectors[5]—these reforms will need to be designed and implemented to promote both equity and growth.

Côte d'Ivoire: Economic Hub

The conference examined the prospects for peacebuilding in the three post-conflict states of Côte d'Ivoire, Liberia, and Sierra Leone. On several issues, Côte d'Ivoire can draw lessons from both of the other countries, which are further along in the processes of reconciliation and post-conflict reconstruction. Liberia has developed a "First 150-Day Action Plan" that promulgates a framework for post-conflict reconstruction, including short-term, measurable targets and commitments to an overall, longer-term strategy of reconstruction.[6] That said, the consolidation of peace in all countries of the sub-region—especially neighboring Liberia—will depend at least in part on the progress of reconciliation and economic revitalization in Côte d'Ivoire.

Why is Côte d'Ivoire so important to the political and economic health of the sub-region? The map of the country in Figure 3.1 underscores Côte d'Ivoire's geographic importance to West Africa, which is north of the strategically important Gulf of Guinea. Côte d'Ivoire borders Liberia, Guinea, Mali, Burkina Faso, and Ghana, and it retains organizational and trade ties with all of those countries. It also plays an important role in the Economic Community of West African States (ECOWAS), a regional group of fifteen countries that was founded in 1975 to promote economic integration. ECOWAS has come to play an important role in conflict management.[7] The Ivorian economic output of $16 billion represents 40 percent of the output of the eight CFA franc countries in the West African Economic and Monetary Union.[8] Important economic links with neighbouring countries involve migration and remittances; the flows of workers from Burkina Faso, Mali, and Ghana to Côte d'Ivoire constitute three of the top six migration corridors in sub-Saharan Africa. Periods of conflict have led to reverse flows of international migrants; even so, in 2005 there were still more than 2.4 million migrants in Côte d'Ivoire, comprising 13.1 percent of that country's total population. The World Bank reports that $597 million

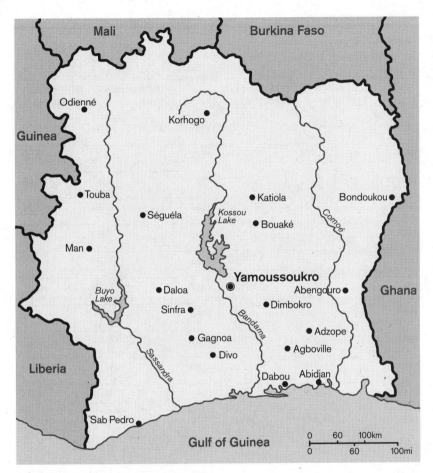

Figure 3.1 Côte d'Ivoire and the sub-region

in remittances flowed from Côte d'Ivoire in 2006 (the last date for which out-flow data are available), but that statistic includes only recorded remittances in a region where informal flows are likely to be significant.[9]

Migrants have been attracted to Côte d'Ivoire for many years and have con-tributed significantly to a large and diverse economy in which agriculture sup-ports 9 million residents—nearly half the population of more than 18 million. The major crops—cocoa, coffee, and cotton—were produced and marketed with such proficiency that Côte d'Ivoire became an export leader and an eco-nomic hub, with active ports at Abidjan and San Pedro transporting goods throughout the sub-region. Foreign workers played important roles throughout the economy. According to the 1988 census, 28 percent of the total population and 32.3 percent of the economically active population were foreigners.[10] Table 3.1, based on data from the World Bank, shows that Côte d'Ivoire benefited

Table 3.1
Economic growth in Côte d'Ivoire

Year	GDP growth (annual %)	GDP/capita (annual %)	Year	GDP growth (annual %)	GDP/capita (annual %)
1961	9.93	6.21	1981	3.50	-0.35
1962	1.23	-2.28	1982	0.20	-3.50
1963	14.49	10.43	1983	-3.90	-7.43
1964	17.61	13.34	1984	-2.70	-6.25
1965	-3.11	-6.70	1985	4.50	0.72
1966	11.58	7.38	1986	3.26	-0.43
1967	4.60	0.58	1987	-0.35	-3.87
1968	12.55	8.19	1988	1.14	-2.40
1969	9.54	5.24	1989	2.95	-0.60
1970	10.38	6.01	1990	-1.10	-4.47
1971	9.46	5.09	1991	0.04	-3.30
1972	4.24	0.06	1992	-0.24	-3.50
1973	5.94	1.71	1993	-0.19	-3.38
1974	4.33	0.18	1994	0.81	-2.34
1975	8.25	4.02	1995	7.13	3.86
1976	12.92	8.58	1996	7.73	4.61
1977	7.31	3.23	1997	5.72	2.82
1978	10.91	6.72	1998	4.75	2.04
1979	2.39	-1.46	1999	1.58	-0.89
1980	-10.96	-14.29	2000	-2.47	-4.70

Source: World Bank, World Development Indicators (WDI).

from growth averaging more than 7 percent annually in the first two decades after independence in 1960.

In his study on growth in Côte d'Ivoire, Marcel Kouadio Benie carefully dissects the economic conditions and policy actions that contributed to decades of sustained economic growth. While agriculture accounted for much of it, industrial expansion—from both import substitution and agro-industry for export—added significantly to growth and employment. The private sector's ability to prosper was enabled by government investments in infrastructure, including transportation, telecommunications, and energy. Government investment in social infrastructure—education and health—proved equally important.[11] This buoyant, export-led growth sputtered to a halt in 1980 and after that remained vulnerable to shifts in global demand and the related deterioration in the terms of trade for Côte d'Ivoire and other commodity-producing economies. The economic decline was initially propelled by the fall in commodity prices; after that, policy errors—including a heavy debt burden—contributed to economic and financial imbalances that steepened the decline. The government borrowed heavily toward the end of the 1970s, both to cover current-account deficits related to the oil-price shocks and to maintain an active program of investment associated with its programs of industrialization and modernization.[12] The deteriorating economic situation and the looming debt overhang discouraged new direct foreign investment and encouraged capital flight, thereby exacerbating the economic imbalances.

Declines in Income and Welfare

The economic stagnation experienced by Côte d'Ivoire in the 1980s and 1990s was rooted in declining export revenues. In addition, Ivorians experienced a deterioration in well-being that was more pronounced than their drop in income. Their decline in welfare contrasts with improvements in other African countries. Figure 3.2 compares the trend performance of the Human Development Index (HDI) for Côte d'Ivoire with that of the average HDI for sub-Saharan African countries. The HDI measures well-being more accurately that simple income figures do; it also allows comparisons with countries at similar income levels. The HDI for Côte d'Ivoire shows its highest value in 1985; that year, the country's poverty rate was 10 percent. Poverty tripled during the years of economic crisis, reaching 32.3 percent by 1993. Though economic growth resumed after the devaluation of the CFA franc in 1994, poverty persisted, and the poverty rate was 36.8 percent in 1995 and 38.4 percent in 2002.[13] Thus, though the initial declines in the HDI were in part a result of lower incomes, growing inequality and an increasingly precarious labour market allowed poverty to increase even while overall income was growing. The decline in well-being was also caused by governance failures; specifically, funds were diverted from their intended use and resources were insufficient to maintain investment and services at their previous levels.

Figure 3.2

Human development index

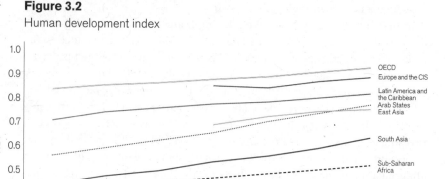

Source: Indicator Table 2 – HDR 2007/2008.

Governance: Neither Efficient nor Equitable

The decline in the quality of governance in Côte d'Ivoire is reflected in a dramatic deterioration in governance indicators, especially government effectiveness, regulatory quality, and the control of corruption. Economic policy formulation and its implementation remained in turmoil even after the economic recovery. The reduction in public investment and the freezing of government salaries, undertaken as part of structural adjustment, may have improved the fiscal accounts, but they also undermined the very foundations of the "Ivorian miracle." A review of the indicators in Figure 3.3 leads to several general observations:

- A decline in governance indicators was evident by the mid-1990s.
- Côte d'Ivoire moved from being above the African average to well below.
- Some indicators, such as government effectiveness and regulatory quality, could be linked to the government's role in creating an enabling business environment.
- Control of corruption, though a government responsibility, also related to the need for better corporate governance in the private sector.

Declines in effectiveness and probity undermined the government's credibility. Discontent also arose from the perception that government expendi-

Figure 3.3

Côte d'Ivoire governance indicators by percentile rank

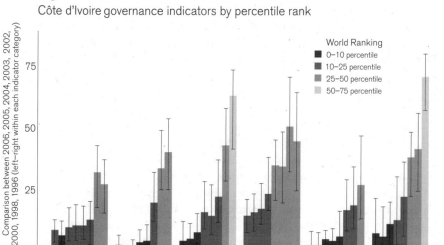

Source: World Bank, Worldwide Governance Indicators, 1996–2006. http://info.worldbank.org/governance.

tures were inequitable as well as inefficient. In a study of the role played by group inequalities in preparing the ground for violence in Côte d'Ivoire, Arnim Langer provides evidence that public investment and social expenditures were distributed unequally, with investments in education and infrastructure benefiting certain groups and regions at the expense of others. Langer notes that the first president, Félix Houphouët-Boigny, increased public investment in the country's north in an effort to counter the historic and climatic disadvantages of that region; in the 1990s, after his death, the Akan-controlled government appeared to favour its own ethnic group in expenditures on public investments such as those essential for access to electricity.[14] Langer focuses on inequalities among various groups of Ivorians, whereas Benie examines modern-sector employment, providing statistics which indicate that the vast majority of managers and technicians were non-Africans and that 46.2 percent of total modern-sector employees were Africans who were not Ivorian.[15] Given that the past two decades were a period of political liberalization that introduced multiparty elections, economic benefits may have been used to curry favour or reward supporters. These governance failures and perceived inequities stoked fires of discontent that were eventually ignited by political developments.

Since early 2007, political developments have turned positive, with the APO setting the stage for reconciliation. Political reconciliation will need to be supported by a peace economy built on a model of development that both economically and socially is more sustainable than that of the previous "miracle" economy of Côte d'Ivoire. Though the APO pledges assistance for families displaced by the war, it fails to address fundamental issues of economic inequality, leaving that challenge to the government that will take office following presidential and parliamentary elections.

The War Economy

> The lucrative cocoa trade has been at the heart of the war economy and continues to serve the interests of protagonists to the conflict, to the detriment of the Ivorian population ... The international community needs to address resource-related conflicts in a way that tackles their particular character: in other words, by proactively addressing the trade that underlies the war, as well as the war itself.[16]

Côte d'Ivoire did not suffer the dramatic and near total collapse of the economy that characterized other West African conflict zones. The conflict in Côte d'Ivoire did not rage throughout the country, forcing a flight from agriculture; nor did all of the major sources of income fall under the direct control of warlords or insurgent forces. Yet there was violence and dislocation as well as, for years, a war economy. The war economy in Côte d'Ivoire was less obvious than in Liberia or Sierra Leone but was no less insidious in how it diverted resources away from social investment toward armaments. Moreover, years of crippled public services further undermined the credibility of government.

There is ample evidence that the war economy in Côte d'Ivoire was financed by revenues from natural resources.[17] Both the government and the rebels used the cocoa sector as a key source of funding for arms purchases.[18] Some of the revenue flowed from taxes—legal or illegal—and some from outright extortion at roadblocks throughout the country. Global Witness, an NGO, published a report on how cocoa helped finance the war economy of Côte d'Ivoire: "Hot Chocolate: How Cocoa Fuelled the Conflict in Côte d'Ivoire," which describes in detail how the government and the rebels extracted funds from the cocoa sector, transforming a highly respectable endeavour—smallholder and commercial agriculture—into a revenue source for conflict and human-rights abuses.

The study by Global Witness focuses on recent misuses of revenues drawn from the cocoa and coffee sectors in Côte d'Ivoire. This misuse was facilitated by a daunting opacity that has long obscured the sources and uses of funds in the agricultural sector. The official institution that served the sector, the Caisse de Stabilisation et de Soutien des Prix des Produit Agricoles (CAISTAB), has long been known for "corrupt and patrimonial practices."[19] For several decades after independence, CAISTAB was a government-owned entity that served as the marketing board for all major agricultural exports. CAISTAB generated a sizable surplus from 1970 to 1986, with earnings that represented between 30 and 44 percent of total government revenue.[20] In 1999, reports of the embezzlement of $34.5 million of health-care assistance from the EU led the World Bank and other donors to call for a sweeping campaign against corruption in the Ivorian government. As part of this move against corrupt practices, donors urged the government to dissolve CAISTAB. Several new institutions were established during 2000–1, whose goal was to commercialize the coffee and cocoa sectors and actively involve producers in their own governance.[21] The reforms did increase commercialization and bring private firms directly into the marketing process; however, the complex array of taxes and levies and apparent variations in charges for different companies left most observers decrying the continued lack of transparency and accountability.

The goals of the five new cocoa institutions were these: ensure adequate regulation; stabilize farmers' incomes through guaranteed "farm gate" prices; and improve productivity through rural investment. Yet despite the relatively high world prices for commodities in recent years, farmers found their incomes being eroded by the higher and higher levies that the cocoa institutions were applying to fund their operations. Moreover, the government introduced both an export tax and a registration tax, both of which further eroded incomes for participants in the sector.

Some may hesitate to criticize the government for using the cocoa sector to finance its military purchases. The government of Côte d'Ivoire had a legitimate right to allocate legal revenues to finance the country's defence; that said, the lack of coherent and comprehensive budgets, combined with a lack of transparency in budget flows and various extrabudgetary receipts and expenses, made accountability impossible and undermined the government's credibility. Though any accounting can only be incomplete, Global Witness estimates that the national cocoa institutions contributed at least $20.3 million to the war effort. The contributions came in the form of cash, vehicles, and weapons, with the donations funded by cocoa levies on producers and exporters.[22] Research by Global Witness also indicates that the government diverted $38.5 million of cocoa revenues for military use. At the same time, the FN took control of cocoa produced in the zone under its control, which forced producers to export through neighbouring countries rather than through government-controlled ports on the Ivorian coast. Since 2004 the FN rebels, through various taxes and export fees, have derived considerable resources from payments related to cocoa. Global Witness estimates that the FN has gained around $30 million a year from the cocoa trade. Both the UN Panel and Global Witness have provided details on numerous "checkpoints" or "cash points" where cash is handed over to soldiers to allow passage. Taken together, taxation and extortion have wrought havoc on the agriculture sector's earnings and security. Cocoa farming, once a source of prosperity, has disintegrated into a source of uncertainty and insecurity.

Other commodities have also been a source of war funding. The UN Panel of Experts appointed by the UNSC to monitor compliance with the arms embargo and other sanctions lamented that no information on revenue and expenditures was available for the hydrocarbon sector even though that sector that has become the country's biggest export earner and represents a significant share of GDP.[23] The data may be incomplete—the current IMF program calls for improved reporting in the energy sector—but recent estimates are that in 2007, crude oil and refined products represented 33.2 percent of export earnings, compared to 28.7 of export earnings from cocoa. Output from the petroleum sector represented nearly 15 percent of nominal GDP in 2007 and is expected to grow in both absolute and relative terms for the next few years.[24]

Conflict diamonds have also been important. Illicit trade in diamonds provides considerable resources for the FN. The UN experts make note of significant diamond-mining activity in several FN-controlled areas, with persistent activity in Tortiya and Séguéla.[25] Diamond exports, though prohibited, have probably yielded the FN more than $25 million annually in recent years.[26] During the November 2007 plenary meeting of the Kimberley Process, countries in the West African sub-region committed themselves to a coordinated effort to honour the embargo on diamond exports from Côte d'Ivoire.[27] Global Witness notes that the FN controlled an area that produced 10 percent of Côte d'Ivoire's cocoa as well as the bulk of its cotton and coffee. The reports by Global Witness and the UN panel provide evidence that the FN has been managing a system of taxes and other payments to extract revenue for the war effort.

The diversion of commodity earnings for military purposes was only one aspect of the war economy. With funds being diverted from their intended uses, the deterioration of public services and infrastructure eroded productivity and earnings throughout the country. Overall, private-sector activity declined dramatically, especially trade and transport. The IMF estimates that by 2006, total output was around 35 percent below its trend level. Figure 3.4 provides snapshots of the performance of the different sectors of the economy during the period of conflict. The first panel in Figure 3.4 shows that the petroleum sector was one of the main sources of growth between 2002 and 2007. The middle section in Figure 3.5 shows the impact of the conflict on the economy—industry and trade were especially hard hit by the social unrest. Though the country resumed growth at a tepid pace in 2007, the population as a whole has gained little from the revenues generated in recent years, with real GDP per capita stagnant or declining over the past several years.[28] Indicators of health and well-being continue to decline, and the HDI rating for Côte d'Ivoire remains in the lowest category. The incidence of HIV/AIDS

Figure 3.4
Real GDP growth, Côte d'Ivoire

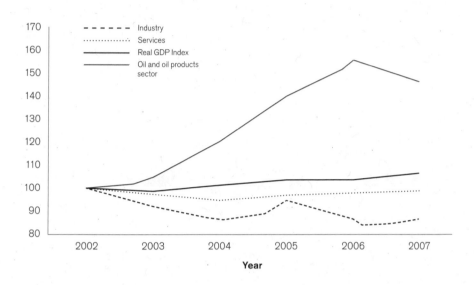

Figure 3.5
External current account, Côte d'Ivoire

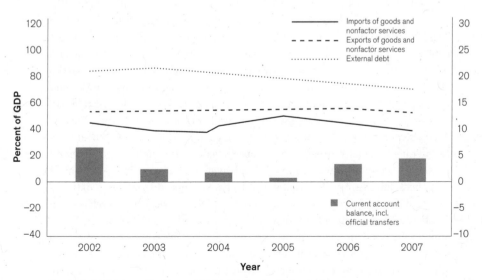

Source (both): Ivorien authorities and IMF staff estimates and projections.

Figure 3.6

Building a peace economy: Sectoral contribution to real GDP growth, 1994–2012 (percent)

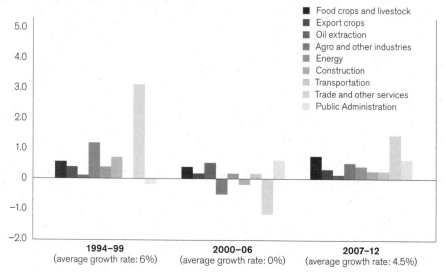

■ Food crops and livestock
■ Export crops
■ Oil extraction
■ Agro and other industries
■ Energy
■ Construction
■ Transportation
■ Trade and other services
■ Public Administration

1994–99
(average growth rate: 6%)

2000–06
(average growth rate: 0%)

2007–12
(average growth rate: 4.5%)

Source: Ivorien authorities; IMF 2008; and IMF staff estimates and projections.

remains the highest in the region (at 7.1 percent of adults), reflecting an overall deterioration of health services throughout the country.[29]

Côte d'Ivoire faces both challenges and opportunities in its efforts to rebuild its economy. The challenges are clear. The labour force has suffered because of the deterioration in education, health, and other social services; entrepreneurial capacity has withered because of a lack of training and limited access to finance; roads and railways require maintenance and extension to serve the country and the sub-region; and investment, beginning to recover, will need the support of an improved business climate. The greatest challenges relate to failures of governance—both government and corporate governance. For the private sector to flourish, both business and government will need to address these issues in a determined and deliberate fashion. Though the government has stated its commitment to support the private sector, reports of extortion at road checkpoints are still common; those checkpoints add to the cost of transportation and thus erode profit margins. The UN Experts' Report, released in October 2007, raised concerns about the lack of information regarding revenue use by both the government and the FN. The UN experts also observed illegal diamond mining in the north and northwest of the country—this, despite the ban on diamond exports. Given that the impartial observers were denied permission to inspect activities related to the arms embargo, there are concerns that revenues from diamonds, cocoa, and other natural resources are still being diverted to arms purchases. These concerns may be ill founded, but they will only be allayed when transparent reporting and strict controls become the norm.

At the same time, Côte d'Ivoire enjoys significant opportunities as it moves toward a peace economy. During the first two decades of independence, the government invested heavily in public infrastructure and made public investments in agro-industry to promote manufacturing (i.e., to convert raw commodities into finished products). This developing agro-industry has added value and employment, and though output in the sector declined sharply in 2006, it began to recover after the country was reunified under the APO. The private sector has always played an active role in this sector, but privatization of state-owned enterprises in the 1990s increased the role of that sector—both foreign multinationals and local business. The IMF reports that private investment increased in 2007 for the first time since 1999.[30]

Given the continued upward pressure on prices, oil and gas continue to bolster export earnings. Adding to refining capacity could further lift earnings. The local refinery is a public–private enterprise that is among the largest petroleum refineries in Africa. Most of the 49 percent private-sector share is held by international oil companies. Refined petroleum products are a significant source of export revenue. The share of petroleum-product value added has increased from 1.9 percent of GDP in 2003 to 3.2 percent in 2007.[31] Natural-gas-powered electricity production could expand to serve the region. Such expansion would require improved revenue collection and increased investment in the sector, both for ongoing maintenance and for higher levels of production. Payments to the independent power producers, from both the government and private consumers, have not been made in full.

The business opportunities are ample, and there are plenty of possibilities for economic growth. But the pressure to produce is great. The last panel in Figure 3.5 presents projections from the IMF and the government. The IMF estimates growth in 2007 at 1.7 percent. The forecast average growth rate between 2007 and 2012 is 4.5 percent, which suggests that growth will need to pick up to more than 5 percent in coming years if progress is to be made on poverty alleviation and sustainable economic development. And while the list of new activities and value-added extensions of existing activities is important, there is also a need to foster income and employment growth in rural areas, both by improving agricultural output and by developing a range of supportive economic activities in rural areas. Economic growth of 5 to 6 percent will require a coordinated effort, including help from external partners, so that Côte d'Ivoire can complete the process of building a peace economy. Much of the growth will come from private-sector investments and business expansion.

The following recommendations provide a framework for discussions about the changes required to build a peace economy. These recommendations have been informed by the writings of Nasser Saidi, who stresses that during the period of post-conflict reconstruction "the central issue is not reconstruction, but state building."[32] In the case of Côte d'Ivoire, however, the recommendations include specific involvements for the private sector. During the coming months the private sector must play an active role, both because of its historical importance in Côte d'Ivoire and because of the enormous potential for future private-sector-led development. Studies of recovery from conflict indicate that the private-sector development agenda must be included in initial reform efforts before new vested interests emerge to stymie reform and economic revival.[33]

Recommendations

A strategic plan for sustainable development. Designing and implementing a successful development strategy will require the private sector in Côte d'Ivoire to work with the government to develop an economic security strategy, identify critical interventions, and sequence reconstruction efforts in a way that promotes investment and growth. Three areas are critical for the early phases of recovery and reconstruction: financial management, debt relief, and banking services. We recommend the following:

Financial Management

- Economic, social, and political inequalities contributed to the conflict in Côte d'Ivoire. Thus the private sector, government, and development partners must include group equity as a goal in all policy discussions and strategic planning.[34]
- The working groups need to include the leaders of small-business associations and women's associations, which have been hit hard by the crisis. Planning for sustainable growth must include these economic actors.
- The strategy must be based on mutual accountability between the government and the private sector.
  - For the government, accountability needs to involve transparency in reporting all receipts and expenditures, with particular attention to taxes and levies in the cocoa and coffee sectors as well as fiscal accounts related to hydrocarbons, timber, and other natural resources.
    - The government has committed to conform with the Extractive Industries Transparency Initiative (EITI) and has already taken several steps to conform with the validation framework.[35]
    - The authorities have also stated their intention to clear arrears for subsidies in the cotton sector and to improve agricultural extension and marketing.

- Diamond exports from the north took place while that area was controlled by the FN. The official ban on diamond exports from Côte d'Ivoire should remain in place until a clear framework for control, sales, and exports has been established consistent with the regional implementation of the Kimberley Process.

• Accountability and transparency require that private-sector producers and exporters "publish what they pay" and establish strict internal controls to end corrupt practices.

  – The private sector has demonstrated willingness to support the candidacy of Côte d'Ivoire in EITI, and private-sector diamond firms have been active supporters of efforts to ensure compliance with restrictions on diamond sales that do not conform to the Kimberley Process.

• Mutual accountability must be enforced by the rule of law. Côte d'Ivoire will require a security-sector reform that:

  – fully integrates the security forces according to professional standards;
  – develops a system of security-sector budgeting and procurement that is open and transparent;
  – includes a reform of the judicial system to ensure independence and integrity in judicial practices; *and*
  – ensures that commercial law is respected and enforced.

• Professionalism in the security services and the end of the culture of impunity would put an end to roadblocks and other extortive practices. (The UN Experts' Report states that trucks have paid hundreds of dollars worth of fees each trip, with roadblocks and associated payments especially heavy in the cocoa-producing areas.)[36]

Debt Relief

Côte d'Ivoire is heavily in debt, with total (public and private) external debt equivalent to 71.7 percent of GDP at the end of 2007.[37] Significant progress was made in settling arrears to the World Bank and other official creditors during the early months of 2008. Nevertheless, analyses by multilateral creditors indicate that the debt-service demands are unsustainable and recommend that Côte d'Ivoire be considered for debt relief from multilateral creditors under the enhanced Heavily Indebted Poor Country (HIPC) program and Multilateral Debt Relief Initiative (MDRI). Debt relief and restructuring from bilateral official creditors under the auspices of the Paris Club will likely follow HIPC. But Côte d'Ivoire is unusual among African countries in that a significant portion of its external debt— equivalent to more than 15 percent of GDP—relates to private creditors. These private creditors, many of whom participate in the informal debt-restructuring group known as the London Club, have a responsibility to share in the burden of debt relief. Resuming normal financial relations with private-sector creditors is essential if Côte d'Ivoire is to have access to the working capital and trade credits required to revive the economy.

Banking Services

The centre, north, and west of the country were without banking services during most of the crisis that divided the country. Even in government-controlled areas, banking services and credit to small businesses were curtailed as the economic situation of these businesses declined as a result of losses of productive assets and downturns in demand. The banking industry needs to develop a strategy to address the needs of business that is consistent with prudent management. Also, microfinance institutions and other organizations must strive to provide services—savings and insurance as well as credit—to small businesses and rural producers. Growth in the new Côte d'Ivoire must be inclusive, with government services and private services reaching all parts of the country.

The scope of needed reforms in economic governance requires that international organizations and transnational corporations support and reinforce the efforts of government, civil society, and the private sector in Côte d'Ivoire. Private-sector companies will need to play an active role in rebuilding vital infrastructure and reviving access to credit and financial services throughout the country. During the coming months, Côte d'Ivoire will be involved in elections. Economic issues, including land and property rights, contract enforcement, and labour market reforms, are likely to be the focus of electoral debates and subsequent deliberations by the newly elected executive and legislature. Decisions in these areas can foster the enabling environment required for the private sector to sustain and increase the investments needed to rebuild the economy of Côte d'Ivoire, thereby allowing it to resume its role as an active economic centre in the sub-region.

Notes

1   The APO was the result of direct dialogue between Gbagbo and Soro and has been endorsed by all major international stakeholders. The transitional government, with Gbagbo as president and Soro as prime minister, took office in April 2007. Elections, originally scheduled for June 2008, were postponed until November 2008 and still have not taken place because of delays in the identification and registration of eligible voters

2   The report of progress under an IMF Emergency Post-Conflict Assistance program stated that the program aimed to overcome economic stagnation and strengthen governance and transparency. While describing a generally stable macroeconomic situation, the fund warned of rising food prices and expressed concern about the profile of spending that included large expenditures on salaries—including bonuses to the military—and insufficient expenditures on capital and recovery projects (IMF Press Release No. 07/278).

3   The Kimberly Process Certification Scheme is a joint effort by governments, industry, and civil society to stem the trade in diamonds used to finance war ("conflict diamonds"). At its November 2007 Plenary Meeting the group launched an initiative to address violations of

UN sanctions against trade in diamonds from Côte d'Ivoire, where the diamond mines were in rebel-held territory. The governments of Côte d'Ivoire and neighbouring countries took the lead in developing steps to monitor and control the diamond trade.

4 Larry Diamond, "The Democratic Rollback: The Resurgence of the Predatory State," *Foreign Affairs*, March–April 2008, 40–41.

5 IMF, "Côte d'Ivoire: Staff Report on the Use of Fund Resources—Request for Emergency Post-Conflict Assistance" (Washington, 2008), para. 34.

6 The plan detailed the "four pillars" of the reconstruction strategy—security, economic revitalization, infrastructure, and governance—and provided a list of deliverables, responsible parties, and end dates for specific projects.

7 Cf. Charles Ukeje, "From Economic Cooperation to Collective Security: ECOWAS and the Changing Imperatives of Sub-Regionalism in West Africa," in *The Crisis of the State and Regionalism in West Africa: Identity, Citizenship, and Conflict*, ed. W. Alade Fawole and Charles Ukeje (Dakar: CODESRIA, 2005).

8 IMF, Article IV, para. 5. The CFA franc zone countries share a common currency and central bank and thus have experienced considerable monetary and financial integration. The countries have taken measures to reinforce economic co-operation and prudent fiscal management. Cf. Paul Masson and Catherine Pattillo, "African Monetary Integration in Practice: CFA Franc Zone and South African CMA," in *The Monetary Geography of Africa* (Washington: Brookings Institution Press, 2005), 45–65, for an assessment of the impact of the monetary union on the economies of member countries.

9 Data on migrants and remittances are from Dilip Ratha and Zhimei Xu, *Migration and Remittances Factbook* (Washington: World Bank, March 2008). http://www.worldbank.org/prospects/migrationandremittances.

10 Marcel Kouadio Benie, "Explication de la croissance en Côte d'Ivoire," in *The Political Economy of Economic Growth in Africa, 1960–2000*, Vol. 2, ed. Benno. J. Ndulu, Stephen A. O'Connell, Jean-Paul Azam, Robert H. Bates, Augustin K. Fosu, Jan Willem Gunning, and Dominique Njinkeu (Cambridge: Cambridge University Press, 2008), Appendix to Part II, 119–66 at 140.

11 Ibid., 119–24.

12 Ibid., 125.

13 Ibid., 157.

14 Arnim Langer, "Horizontal Inequalities and Violent Conflict: The Case of Côte d'Ivoire," Centre for Research on Inequality, Human Security, and Ethnicity (CRISE), Oxford University, CRISE Working Paper no. 13 (2004), 14.

15 Benie, "Explication," 141.

16 Global Witness, 2007. "Hot Chocolate: How Cocoa Fuelled the Conflict in Côte d'Ivoire," June 2007, 59. http://www.globalwitness.org/media_library_detail.php/552/en/hot_chocolate_how_cocoa_fuelled_the_conflict_in_co.

17 The description of the financing of the war economy is based on various eyewitness reports contained in the reports by Global Witness as well as in official reports submitted by UN-appointed experts to the UNSC. See Works Cited for details of documents.

18 One of the reports by the UN Panel of experts notes: "Cocoa plays an important role in providing funds for the off-budget and extra-budgetary military procurement efforts by the government" Cf. UNSC, "Report of the Panel of Experts submitted pursuant to paragraph 7 of Security Council resolution 1584 (2005) concerning Côte d'Ivoire," July 18, 2005 (New York: 2005), paras. 28–42, for the panel's description of the cocoa sector and its role in defence expenditures of both the government and the rebel forces.

19 Global Witness, "Hot Chocolate," 46.

20 Benie, "Explication," 147.

21 For a detailed description of the five new institutions and their role in the coffee and cocoa sectors, see Global Witness, "Hot Chocolate," 60–61.

22 Global Witness, "Hot Chocolate," 3–4 and 24. http://www.globalwitness.org/media_library_detail. php/552/en/hot_chocolate_how_cocoa_fuelled_the_conflict_in_co. The three institutions were Autorité de Régulation du Café et du Cacao, Bourse du Café et Cacao, and Fonds de Développement et de Promotion des activités des Producteurs de Café et de Cacao.

23 UNSC, "Report of the Group of Experts on Côte d'Ivoire on the implementation of paragraph 2 of Security Council resolution 1971 (2006)," October 18, 2007 (New York: 2007), 15.

24 IMF (2008), "Côte d'Ivoire: Staff Report," 19 and 25.

25 UNSC, "Report of the Group of Experts," 3.

26 Global Witness, "Making It Work: Why the Kimberley Process Must Do More to Stop Conflict Diamonds," November 2005, 9, citing the Ministry of Mines and Energy in Côte d'Ivoire. http://www.globalwitness.org.

27 Kimberley Process. "2007 Kimberley Process Communiqué," 1. http://www.kimberley process.com/documents/plenary_intersessional_meeting_en.html.

28 IMF (2008), "Côte d'Ivoire: Staff Report," 18.

29 UNAIDS/WHO online database, data for 2005. http://www.who.int/globalatlas/default.asp.

30 IMF (2008), "Côte d'Ivoire: Staff Report," 38. The cumulative decline in private investment had reached 30 percent in real terms since 1999.

31 Holger Fabig, "Modeling Macro-Critical Energy Sectors in Low-Income Countries: A General Framework and an Application to Côte d'Ivoire," IMF Working Paper WP/08/156 (2008), 15–16.

32 Nasser Saidi, "Promesses Chatoyantes, Piètre Performance: Aide et Coopération dans les Pays Sortant d'un Conflit," in *Dialogue des cultures et résolution des conflits: Les horizons de la paix*, ed. by Sélim Abou and Joseph Maïla (Beirut: Presses de l'Université Saint-Joseph, 2004).

33 Rob Mills and Qimiao Fan, *The Investment Climate in Post-Conflict Situations* (Washington: World Bank, 2006).

34 Center for Research on Inequality, Human Security, and Ethnicity (CRISE), "Using Aid to Prevent Conflict: Horizontal Inequalities and Aid Policy," CRISE Policy Briefing no. 1, April 2007, 1 and 4. http://www.crise.ox.ac.uk.

35 Côte d'Ivoire was accepted as an EITI candidate country in May 2008. According to the IMF report, the country has already made the required public announcement, established a multistakeholder group that includes the government, industry, and civil society, and appointed a senior official to coordinate the activities. When implemented, EITI will involve the publication and verification of all company payments and government revenues from oil, gas, and mining.

36 The report by Global Witness actually identified the location of the checkpoints, while the 2005 report by the UN Experts Panel noted that the barriers were clustered in areas of economic activity, "underlining the economic nature of these road blocks."

37 All data on external debt are from IMF, "Côte d'Ivoire: Staff Report."

References

Benie, Marcel Kouadio. "Explication de la croissance en Côte d'Ivoire." In *The Political Economy of Economic Growth in Africa, 1960–2000*, Vol. 2, ed. Benno. J. Ndulu, Stephen A. O'Connell, Jean-Paul Azam, Robert H. Bates, Augustin K. Fosu, Jan Willem Gunning, and Dominique Njinkeu (Cambridge: Cambridge University Press, 2008), Appendix to Part II, 119–66.

Center for Research on Inequality, Human Security, and Ethnicity (CRISE), University of Oxford. "Using Aid to Prevent Conflict: Horizontal Inequalities and Aid Policy." CRISE Policy Briefing no. 1, April 2007. http://www.crise.ox.ac.uk.

Collier, Paul. 2006. "African Growth: Why a 'Big Push'?" *Journal of African Economies* 15 (2006): 188–211, AERC Supplement 2.

——. The Bottom Billion: Why the Poorest Countries Are Failing and What Can Be Done about It. Oxford: Oxford University Press, 2007.

Diamond, Larry. "The Democratic Rollback: The Resurgence of the Predatory State." *Foreign Affairs*, March–April 2008, 40–41.

Fabig, Holger. "Modeling Macro-Critical Energy Sectors in Low-Income Countries: A General Framework and an Application to Côte d'Ivoire." IMF Working Paper WP/08/156 (2008).

Global Witness. "Hot Chocolate: How Cocoa Fuelled the Conflict in Côte d'Ivoire." Report by Global Witness, June 2007. http://www.globalwitness.org/media_library_detail.php/552/en/hot_chocolate_how_cocoa_fuelled_the_conflict_in_co.

——. "Loopholes in the Kimberley Process: Illegal Trade Undermines Efforts to Combat Conflict Diamonds." Report by Global Witness, October 2007. http://www.globalwitness.org/media_library_detail.php/605/en/loopholes_in_the_kimberley_process_summary_of_trade.

——. "Making It Work: Why the Kimberley Process Must Do More to Stop Conflict Diamonds." Report by Global Witness, November 2005. http://www.globalwitness.org.

Global Witness and Partnership Africa Canada. "Illicit Diamond Flows." Note for Kimberley Process Plenary, November 2007. http://www.globalwitness.org/media_library_detail.php/604/en/illicit_diamond_flows.

IMF (International Monetary Fund). "Côte d'Ivoire: Staff Report for the 2007 Article IV Consultation and Request for Emergency Post-Conflict Assistance." Washington: 2007.

——. "Côte d'Ivoire: Staff Report on the Use of Fund Resources—Request for Emergency Post-Conflict Assistance." Washington, 2008.

Kaufmann, Daniel, Aart Kraay, and Massimo Mastruzzi. "Governance Matters VI: Governance Indicators for 1996–2006." World Bank Policy Research Working Paper no. 4280 (July 2007). http://info.worldbank.org/governance/wgi2007/home.htm.

Kimberley Process. "2007 Kimberley Process Communiqué." Official document of the Kimberley Process Certification Scheme. http://www.kimberleyprocess.com/documents/plenary_intersessional_meeting_en.html.

Langer, Arnin. "Horizontal Inequalities and Violent Conflict: The Case of Côte d'Ivoire." Centre for Research on Inequality, Human Security, and Ethnicity (CRISE), University of Oxford. CRISE Working Paper No. 13 (2004).

Liberia. "Government of Liberia 150-Day Action Plan: A Working Document for a New Liberia." Monrovia: 2006.

Masson, Paul, and Catherine Pattillo. "African Monetary Integration in Practice: CFA Franc Zone and South African CMA." Chapter 4 in *The Monetary Geography of Africa*. Washington: Brookings Institution Press, 2005.

Mills, Rob, and Qimiao Fan. "The Investment Climate in Post-Conflict Situations." World Bank Policy Research Working Paper No. 4055. Washington: World Bank, 2006.

Ratha, Dilip, and Zhimei Xu. *Migration and Remittances Factbook*. Washington: World Bank, 2008 (March). http://www.worldbank.org/prospects/migrationandremittances.

Saidi, Nasser. "Promesses Chatoyantes, Piètre Performance: Aide et Coopération dans les Pays Sortant d'un Conflit." In *Dialogue des cultures et résolution des conflits: Les horizons de la paix*, ed. Sélim Abou and Joseph Maïla. Beirut: Presses de l'Université Saint-Joseph, 2004.

Ukeje, Charles. "From Economic Cooperation to Collective Security: ECOWAS and the Changing Imperatives of Sub-Regionalism in West Africa." In *The Crisis of the State and Regionalism in West Africa: Identity, Citizenship, and Conflict*, ed. W. Alade Fawole and Charles Ukeje. Dakar: CODESRIA, 2005.

UNDP (United Nations Development Programme). *Human Development Report 2007–2008*. New York: 2007. Analysis for Côte d'Ivoire is at http://hdrstats.undp.org/countries/country_fact_sheets/cty_fs_CIV.html.

UNSC (United Nations Security Council). Letter dated March 13, 2007, from the Secretary-General addressed to the President of the Security Council, S/2007/144 [includes the "Ouagadougou Political Agreement" as Annex]. New York.

——. "Report of the Group of Experts on Côte d'Ivoire on the implementation of paragraph 2 of Security Council resolution 1971 (2006)." October 18, 2007. New York.

——. 2005. "Report of the Panel of Experts submitted pursuant to paragraph 7 of Security Council resolution 1584 (2005) concerning Côte d'Ivoire." July 18, 2005. New York.

Foreign Investors and International Donor Contributions to Côte d'Ivoire's State-Building Efforts

Lydie Boka-Mene[1] and Oren E. Whyche-Shaw

4

Background

Before the recent civil war and partition, Côte d'Ivoire enjoyed the highest standards of living in West Africa based on one of the most dynamic and productive economies in the region and was called the dragon of Africa, then the elephant of Africa. From the time of independence in 1960 until the civil war in 2002,[2] Côte d'Ivoire accounted for 40 percent of the economic output of the Economic and Monetary Union of West Africa (UMEOA), a group of mainly French-speaking countries that share the CFA Franc as their common currency.[3] Initially, Côte d'Ivoire depended mainly on its strong agricultural sector; the country was and is still the world's largest producer of cocoa and third-largest producer of coffee[4] during the first three decades after independence.[5] The mining, energy, and financial sectors were also significant and expanding. The country boasted one of the best transportation systems—land, water, and air—in the region and was a transportation hub for all of West Africa. Foreign direct investment (FDI) has always played a key role in Côte d'Ivoire, accounting for 40 to 45 percent of total capital investment in the country, averaging $300 million per year.[6] Among sub-Saharan countries and excluding oil, gas, and mining investments, Côte d'Ivoire enjoyed one of the highest levels of FDI in Africa, surpassed only by South Africa, Ghana, Nigeria, and Zambia between 1985 and 2000.[7]

Since independence, the country's most important international partner and its most important foreign investor has been France. French investments have accounted for about one-quarter of the total capital in Ivorian enterprises and for between 55 and 60 percent of total foreign investment.[8]

The devaluation of the CFA in 1994 allowed the economy to flourish by taking advantage of increased competitiveness both within the region and internationally. A privatization program was launched in 1995 to disengage the government from the productive economy—utilities, hotels, banking, telecommunications, national airlines, oil refineries, and agribusiness. This program enhanced the country's private sector's competitiveness and strengthened public finances by reducing large government subsidies in loss-making operations. Foreign investors arrived in droves, attracted by opportunities to set up profitable operations, gain concessions to operate major public works, or conduct buy–own–transfer (BOT) deals. The management of the electric company EECI was transferred to CIE, a subsidiary of the French firm Bouygues; the water company SODECI and the cotton enterprise CIDT were also privatized. FDI reached a record level of US$450 million in 1997.[9]

During this four-year period of expansion, foreign-owned assets in Côte d'Ivoire doubled from US$1.5 billion in 1995 to $3 billion in 1999.[10] Then in December 1999 a military coup toppled the "democratically elected" government of Henri Konan Bédié. The ensuing political and social instability was heightened by ethnic tensions, which political gamesmanship only made worse.[11] President Bédié had promulgated the concept of *Ivoirité* (Ivorianization) in order to exclude his rival, Alassane Ouattara, who was rumoured to be of foreign parentage, from running for president. Given that many Ivorians, especially in the north of the country, were born in other countries or had parents of Burkinabe, Malian, Senegalese, or Guinean descent, this policy excluded many people from Ivorian nationality. Relations among the various ethnic groups deteriorated.

The social and political strains resulted in delays in implementing the privatization program, and FDI flows began declining in 1999. Annual FDI investment flows decreased by 43 percent to about $240 million a year between 1999 and 2002.[12] Initial hopes of greater transparency and justice quickly vanished as the military junta turned out to be dictatorial. Growing uncertainties and increasing inefficiencies spread throughout the economy, and there were growing rumours of widespread corruption. Economic activity fell off sharply after the December 1999 coup. During elections in October 2000 in which credible candidates were barred from competing, Laurent Gbagbo was elected president. Several *coups d'état* were attempted or at least rumoured. In September 2002 a serious *coup d'état* attempt resulted in the country's partition. Surprisingly, and despite the political turmoil between 2000 and 2005, Côte d'Ivoire's FDI remained the highest in West Africa excluding Nigeria (1990–2000 average: $1.4 billion; 2002: $2 billion; 2003: $2.17 billion; 2004: $2.12 billion; 2005: $3.4 billion).[13]

Prior to the civil unrest, Côte d'Ivoire had received significant levels of financial and technical assistance from the international community.

Private–Sector and Donor Activity Prior to the Civil War

Until 1999, France was Côte d'Ivoire's principal investor and trading partner within the CFA monetary union. French companies were engaged in the telecommunications, energy, transportation, and agribusiness sectors. Between 1996 and 2000, French investors accounted for 23 percent of business registrations, compared to 7 percent for the Swiss, 5 percent for the British, and 2 percent for the Americans (and 52 percent for Ivorians).[14] Oil exploitation began in the late 1990s. Despite French predominance in almost all sectors, there was surprisingly little French investment in the oil-and-gas sector, which was dominated by American companies (Ocean Energy, Ranger Oil) and the Anglo-Dutch multinational, Shell.

Agricultural products represented 80 percent of Côte d'Ivoire's exports to France; oil, the remaining 20 percent. France sold primarily pharmaceutical products, consumer goods, and agricultural and construction equipment to Côte d'Ivoire.[15]

In November 2004 more than 240 French subsidiaries were established in Côte d'Ivoire and more than 600 French companies were active in virtually every sector of the economy: agribusiness, services, finance and industry. An estimated 68 percent of FDI came from French companies. French investment generated significant local employment. As examples, Ivorians accounted for nearly 100 percent of France Telecom's personnel (two thousand Ivorians and about twenty French nationals); and out of eight thousand employees in Bouygues' shipping business, only one hundred were expatriates.[16]

Civil War's Impact on the Ivorian Economy

Tensions started to build after the 2002 partition of the country. France sent in its military forces and began serving as a buffer between the rebels and the government forces, preventing them from attacking each other. Côte d'Ivoire demanded that France, with which it had a defence agreement, help it crush the rebels. France claimed that it could not take sides in a civil war in which there was no external aggression, yet it allowed the Ivorian air force to cross the partition line in November 2004 to bomb the rebels at their base in Bouaké. Unfortunately, the air force also bombed a French base in Bouaké, killing nine French soldiers. In retaliation, France largely destroyed the Ivorian air force. After the November 2004 bombing, angry mobs attacked French business interests.[17] As a result, small and medium-sized French businesses closed their doors and left the country. The sectors most affected by French business flight were tourism, restaurants, and a wide variety of other small and medium-scale service enterprises. The Ivorian Chamber of Commerce, representing the interests of these SME companies, requested that the government make a provision of CFA150 billion (more than EU22 million) to compensate the victims of November 2004. In March 2008 the government announced that it had earmarked US$12 million (CFA6 billion) to compensate the French companies.[18]

The regional offices of many private-sector companies relocated to more stable West African countries such as Senegal and Togo in the CFA zone, and to a lesser extent to Ghana, where English represented a language barrier for French-speaking investors. They were also deterred by inflation and the narrower market in Ghana. Air France moved its regional centre to Togo. DHL moved to Ghana. Because of transit delays and increased costs, neighbouring landlocked countries such as Mali, Burkina Faso, and Niger quickly rerouted their import and export activities through the competing ports of Dakar in Senegal, Tema in Ghana, Cotonou in Benin, and Lome in Togo.[19] Between 2004 and 2005, activity at the Port of Abidjan declined by 14.5 percent,[20] though traffic later began to return, increasing by 5 percent in 2005 (to 18.6 million tonnes, compared to 17.6 million tonnes the previous year).[21] By 2007, merchandise traffic had increased by 12 percent to 21.37 million tonnes, according the Port Authority. A total of 2,748 ships arrived at the port in 2007, compared to 2,741 in 2006.[22]

The railway company SITARAIL,[23] owned by the French business group Bolloré, had been highly profitable before the crisis, with a turnover of US$7.5 million (CFA4 billion) in 2001 and a net profit of $3.7 million (CFA2 billion). SITARAIL transported 1 million tonnes of goods and 400,000 people in 2001.[24] When the crisis began, it stopped all operations, resulting in extremely long transit delays if products were transported in the country by road. In 2004 it operated at 40 percent capacity, carrying only 400,000 tonnes of goods and 130,000 people. Operations resumed in May 2003 in Côte d'Ivoire, but only in September 2003 did operations extend into Burkina Faso with the reopening of the Côte d'Ivoire border.[25] Traffic is regularly disrupted by political instability. Bolloré is a French multinational listed on the Paris Stock Exchange that is one of the five hundred largest companies in the world and is active in diverse activities, including logistics, communications, and commodities trading.

The largest and most entrenched of the French companies held firm and remained in the country after the partition, continuing their ongoing businesses and generating new opportunities. These firms included TotalFinaElf, which distributes and markets petroleum products; France Telecom/Orange; Groupe Bolloré, and Bouygues, another French multinational listed on the Paris Stock Exchange, one of the five hundred largest companies in the world, which is active in construction, real estate, telecommunications, and television and film. All of these firms won or renewed lucrative contracts for major projects, including the construction of the Port of Abidjan extension in 2008, as well as water and electricity concessions. The contract for the Port of Abidjan stirred heated debate in the early 2000s; donors felt that it had not been awarded in a transparent manner. After a suspension of the bidding process resulting from the war, the contract was awarded to Bolloré in 2008.

International donors were also affected by the civil unrest and political instability. Many bilateral donors and development organizations moved their staff out of the country. In April 2005[26] the British Embassy moved to Accra, Ghana, because of the deteriorating political situation. One of the largest employers in the country, the African Development Bank (AfDB), relocated its entire operations to Tunis, Tunisia, in 2003.[27] It is estimated that the relocation of the AfDB led to the closing of many small businesses in Abidjan—construction and real estate firms, restaurants, retailers, and so on.[28] In addition, hundreds if not thousands of informally employed workers (gardeners, guards, drivers, etc.) found themselves out of a job as a result of the AfDB's move. Officially, the AfDB is still headquartered in Abidjan. The AfDB Board of Governors has discussed the issue of location at each of its subsequent annual meetings, but no decision to return to Abidjan has been reached.

The 1999 civil war and the partition of the country in 2002 have together taken a massive toll on the Ivorian economy. Most notably, unemployment has soared and public-sector revenues have plummeted. It is estimated that since the emergence of instability, Côte d'Ivoire has lost 20 percent of its budget as a result of uncollected taxes and diversions of cocoa,[29] cotton,[30] and rough diamonds[31] in rebel-controlled zones. In 2002 the government reported a fiscal deficit of 1.2 percent (compared to a modest surplus of 0.4 percent in 2001), the result of losses in fiscal receipts.[32]

Infrastructure deteriorated owing to a lack of public-sector investment and poor maintenance. Transportation was hit hard, a consequence of the rebels occupying three-fifths of the country, mainly in the centre and north. Suddenly, cotton could no longer be sent to the south and agricultural goods could no longer move freely to the north. According to the government and the Ivorian Chamber of Commerce, transportation declined by 30 to 60 percent, resulting in the loss of a significant number of transportation-related jobs.

Furthermore, the road network was plagued with insecurity. Police and armed militias were stopping drivers to elicit illegal rents. In 2007 the cost of those "road taxes" was estimated at US$304.8 million (CFA150 billion) in time lost and money illegally paid.[33] Côte d'Ivoire's road cost per kilometre had by then become the highest in the world, according to the president of the Ivorian Chamber of Commerce.[34] Before the civil war, it had taken about ten hours to drive the "Cotière," the 600 kilometre highway that links the west of the country to San Pedro and Abidjan. The same trip now took two or three days because of the civil conflict. Warehouses across the country were full, and transit terminals were bursting at the seams because goods could not be moved. Transportation costs soared by 50 to 100 percent. Hotel occupancy rates declined by 20 to 50 percent in Abidjan.[35] According to the Ivorian Chamber of Commerce, this too could be linked to the transportation slowdown and the decline in tourism and business. The country's status as West Africa's regional hub had been critically damaged, and related revenues declined as inland and bordering countries turned to the ports of Senegal, Ghana, Benin, and even Nigeria to import needed goods and export their products.

The Ivorian Chamber of Commerce reported that as of November 30, 2002, only two months after the attempted coup, Ivorian industries had lost 20 percent of their projected yearly revenues.[36]

Table 4.1

Impact of civil unrest on economic sectors

Sector	Evolution of Finished Goods Stocks (Unsold Goods)	Activity Loss	Impact on Employment
Mining	>5%	>30%	0%
Agribusiness	>2%	>40%	<20%
Textile	>90%	>70%	<80%
Wood	<30%	>40%	<65%
Construction	>80%	>70%	<37%
Other Miscellaneous Industrial Products	>93%	>50%	<50%

Source: Ivorian Chamber of Commerce.

The textile sector was hardest hit; firms were losing anywhere between 47 and 100 percent of their revenues depending on where they were located.[37] Companies such as UTEXI and TEXICODI lost market share almost immediately, both locally and in the export market. Ginning and weaving activities stopped, and so did cloth manufacturing.

Agriculture, for decades the foundation of Ivorian economic prosperity, suffered a sharp downturn. The cotton sector lost as much as 40 percent of its revenues within two months of the attempted coup.[38] In the north, three sugar refineries in rebel-held areas—Ferke 1, Ferke 2, and Borotou—became inaccessible as the insurgents established control over entry and movement in "their" territory, complete with a *laissez-passer* system. Lumber mills were operating at less than 60 percent capacity and recorded a 20 percent drop in revenues owing to the decline in supply, the result of transportation slow-downs and growing insecurity on the roads[39] (see Table 4.1). The domestic market for processed wood contracted. By October 2007, producers were recording inventories worth US$411,000 (CFA270 million).[40] All of this contributed to unemployment in the timber sector, which had risen as high as 62 percent by 2002, again according to the Ivorian Chamber of Commerce in its report on the crisis impact.[41]

By November 2002 the chemical industry had lost 50 percent of its revenues and 5.6 percent of related jobs (see table above). Activity in construction and public works declined by 60 percent, leading to job losses of 37 percent.[42]

According to the government, GDP growth declined from +0.1 percent in 2001 to −1.2 percent in 2002 as a result of the partition and the civil war, both of which led to disruptions in the agricultural sector, transportation, and trade. The only positive figure was the current account balance, which moved from a deficit of 0.9 percent in GDP in 2001 to a surplus of 6.1 percent in 2002 owing to higher cocoa price and a sharp drop in imports.[43]

It is estimated that during the civil war and the partition, the rebels smuggled approximately 20 percent of the country's cocoa and a significant amount of cotton across the northern border into Burkina Faso and Mali. In the mining sector, there is evidence that the rebels were smuggling diamonds and gold out of the country; however, data on those amounts are difficult to collect. In 2007, Global Witness and several other watchdog organizations reported massive smuggling of Ivorian products.[44] The "Hot Chocolate" study showed how more than US$118 million in cocoa revenues was being used to fund both sides of the conflict. The same report documented revenue mismanagement, opaque accounting practices, corruption, and political cronyism in the country's cocoa sector. Over the past year, Global Witness has been calling for greater transparency and accountability in that sector by the government and cocoa institutions, as well as by the chocolate industry itself.

To address the lack of transparency in the mining sector, Côte d'Ivoire applied for membership in the Extractive Industries Transparency Initiative (EITI). In May 2008 it was accepted as a candidate member. Over the next several years Cote d'Ivoire will have to make major improvements in the revenue management of its extractive industries in order to attain full EITI membership.[45]

In June 2008 the Ivorian Attorney General charged senior cocoa-sector officials with siphoning off funds from the national cocoa institutions— bodies that collect levies from the cocoa companies. In doing so those officials had done much to fuel the civil war, for the siphoned money had been used to finance arms purchases.[46]

Civil unrest also severely damaged the financial sector. All banks closed their branches in the country's interior and north, which resulted in cash shortages and capital flight. The central bank's branch in Bouaké, a rebel stronghold, was burglarized. Despite the climate of insecurity, cocoa purchasers were compelled to carry cash to pay cocoa farmers for their harvests. Statistics for this period are extremely scanty, but it is known that financing costs increased as well as the costs of insurance and transportation. According to the Ivorian Banking Association (APBEF),[47] the political and economic crisis resulted in a sharp reduction in credit—a drop of 11 percent in just one year, from 2002 to 2003.[48] Affected were both short-term credit (71 percent of outstanding credit) and long-term credit.[49] Banking services were interrupted in the north and west owing to the climate of insecurity. Microfinance became the only way to obtain money. Risk worsened; non-performing loans increased by 20 percent in 2003. Revenues declined and so did profits—by 10 percent in dollar terms, from US$12.8 million to $11.5 million; and by 25 percent in CFA terms, from CFA8.9 billion to 6.7 billion.[50] According to the IMF, "the share of Ivoirien banks in total WAEMU bank assets has declined from 40 percent in 2000 to around 30 percent in 2005, and private credit-to-GDP ratios in Côte d'Ivoire fell below levels in other WAEMU and SSA countries. Intermediation was also affected by the deterioration of an already weak judicial system."[51]

During the robust economic period of the 1970s and 1980s under President Félix Houphouët-Boigny, Côte d'Ivoire had welcomed workers from all over West Africa. Attracted by the available jobs, they poured in from across the region. This migration was dominated by workers from Burkina Faso (30 percent), but other West Africans were well represented: Malians, Ghanaians, Nigerians, and Guineans.[52] So many migrant workers entered Côte d'Ivoire that it was generally believed that only one-quarter of the inhabitants of Abidjan were Ivorian citizens.[53] With the civil unrest, the traditional seasonal migrations associated with coffee and cocoa harvests were sharply interrupted. Statistics here are unreliable, but it can be said that the resulting sharp decline in remittances has had a strong impact on neighbouring countries and on migrants' families.

In January 2003, Côte d'Ivoire's country risk rating was downgraded from C to D by COFACE, the leading French agency that specializes in analyzing risk, managing the French government's export guarantees, and supporting French companies in monitoring, managing, and financing accounts receivable. In December 2004, Swiss credit insurance agency GRE discontinued its coverage of Côte d'Ivoire due to the major deterioration of the political situation and the civil war risk.[54]

Corruption and fraud were not limited to the Ivorian roads and the private sector. Around the same time, the performance of Côte d'Ivoire's public institutions broadly declined—and the state ceased functioning altogether in the rebel-controlled areas of the north. In 2006 the *Probo Koala*, a Dutch ship, dumped 528 tonnes of toxic waste into Abidjan's lagoon, killing hundreds of people. The resulting scandal implicated the Transportation Ministry and the Port Authority. On February 12, 2007, the Ivorian government settled with Trafigura, the commodities trading company that had hired the ship; it agreed to pay $198 million to the Ivorian government. The money would go to establishing a compensation fund, building a waste treatment plant, and cleaning up the lagoon. In return, Côte d'Ivoire agreed to drop any present or future prosecutions or claims against Trafigura.[55] The toxic-waste scandal was generally viewed as a highly visible example of growing corruption. In October 2008, during a criminal investigation against local port authorities—which Trafigura blamed for the illegal dumping—a government lawyer insisted that even though the civil suit had been settled, the state could still prosecute Trafigura for poisoning Ivorians.[56]

In 1998, Cote d'Ivoire had a total external debt of about US$15 billion,[57] close to $800 million of it owed to the IMF and the World Bank. By then the country had been approved for exceptional assistance under the HIPC initiative.[58] Plummeting revenues drove the government to terminate its agreed-to payments of international debts. This led to an accumulation of arrears and to the suspension of the HIPC agreement. In November 2004, having fallen into arrears with the World Bank and the IMF, Côte d'Ivoire found curtailed its access to development assistance and funding from those institutions. As of year end 2004, Côte d'Ivoire also owed arrears of EU290 million to the Paris Club (bilateral donors) and EU32 million to the London Club (international commercial lenders and suppliers).[59]

Côte d'Ivoire's Pressing Need to Rebuild the Productive Economy

After the civil war, per capita GDP growth in Côte d'Ivoire fell from 6 percent in 1998 to −2.3 percent in 2001; over the same years, the population grew at 3.3 percent a year.[60] See Figure 4.1; per capita GDP fell sharply between 1999 and 2007, and Côte d'Ivoire war no longer the locomotive of the region. The economy has shown resilience. GDP growth reached an estimated 1.6 percent in 2007 and is projected to reach 2.9 percent[61] in 2008.

Despite the weak per capita GDP growth, the government's budget has been growing at 20 percent a year.[62] On average over the past five years, government revenues have represented only 10 percent of the public sector's investment budget, according to the government's own figures.[63]

As domestic resources are insufficient, the fiscal deficit has been financed mainly by the accumulation of arrears—which amounted to 14 percent of GDP in 2004 and 21 percent in 2006—and by borrowing on the financial market of the West African Economic and Monetary Union (WAEMU).[64] A bond issue of nearly CFA225 billion (or US$460 million) was floated in September 2007 to cover the costs of reconstruction and payments of domestic and external (WB and AfDB) debt arrears.[65] The clearance of IMF, WB, and AfDB arrears has opened the door for the normalization of relations with these institutions and for access to post-conflict emergency assistance.

It is widely acknowledged that to broadly decrease poverty, developing countries require an average annual growth rate of 6 percent as well as yearly investments of 25 percent of GDP. Côte d'Ivoire requires significant investment not only to recapture the level of pre-civil-war investment but also to address the country's growing needs. In 2007 the transitional government's macroeconomic policies focused on three priorities: the promotion of peace, security, and national reconciliation; reunification of the country; and economic revival and poverty reduction. These priorities formed the basis for negotiations with

Figure 4.1

Decline in per capita GDP, 1999–2007

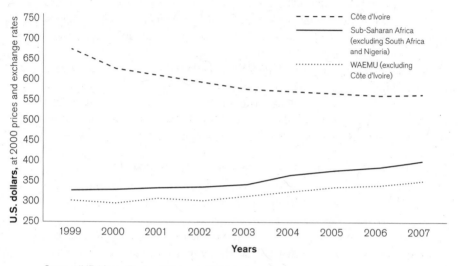

Source: IMF, African Regional Economic Outlook.

the IMF over an emergency post-conflict assistance (EPCA) program, which was approved by the IMF's Executive Board on August 3, 2007.[66]

Côte d'Ivoire will need investment in virtually all sectors of the economy to recapture its productive base, regain its competitive stance in the region, create jobs, and feed its growing population. The need is all the more critical given the population pressures the country faces. According to the UNDP 2007/2008 Human Development Report, between 1975 and 2005 the country had an annual population growth rate of 3.5 percent; it is projected that between 2005 and 2015 that rate will average 1.8 percent.[67] According to government sources, in 2002 an estimated 4 million Ivorians were unemployed—about 22 percent of the population—and 70 percent of them were young people.[68] And while there will be a slight decrease in the percentage of Ivorians under the age of fifteen, from 41.7 percent in 2005 to 37.9 percent in 2015, the government will still face enormous pressure to create jobs.[69] Especially in the north, there is critical need to expand infrastructure and provide adequate social services.

As if those pressures were not enough, the global food crisis has sent clear signals to Côte d'Ivoire that it will have to invest significantly in agriculture not only to regain its position as a major agricultural exporter but also to ensure sufficient food production to feed its growing population. During the first quarter of 2008 the prices for meat shot up by 35 to 50 percent, for fuel by

35 percent, and for staple foods by 25 to 50 percent.[70] In March 2008, food riots gripped the capital, Abidjan, brought on by dramatic hikes in prices for food and fuel; in only three days, the price of beef had risen from $1.68 to $2.16 per kilogram, the price of gasoline from $1.44 to $2.04 per litre.[71] In the third quarter of 2008, government health officials and aid agencies launched an emergency feeding and nutritional-training program in the north in response to what experts called "alarming" malnutrition levels caused by "poor agricultural production, livestock disease, lack of access to a variety of nutritious foods and global food price hikes."[72]

With the peace accord in place, the Ivorian government's budget in 2007 was approximately CFA2,100 billion,[73] or US$6.7 billion. Difficulties in securing external resources to fill the budget gap resulted in delays in parliamentary approval of the budget. When finally approved, it called for investments in construction and infrastructure rebuilding. Specifically targeted were water and sanitation, the road network, and rural electrification. There was also money to rehabilitate social services (health and education). The budget also earmarked funds to build public-administration facilities and to transfer the capital from Abidjan to Yamoussoukro. Finally, the government announced plans for major agriculture, food-security, and nutrition initiatives, some in conjunction with international development organizations. For example, CFA18 billion was earmarked for rice production; the goal here was for Côte d'Ivoire to become a net exporter by 2012.[74]

Donors Are Back

Outside development aid has begun to flow again, to finance the demobilization and disarmament of ex-combatants. Broadly speaking, donor support is targeting institutional rebuilding and governance, infrastructure, social services (especially for those populations most affected by the civil war), and the re-establishing of conditions for economic growth.

In April 2008 the IMF approved about US$66 million of emergency post-conflict assistance (EPCA) for Côte d'Ivoire to support the country's efforts to foster sustained recovery. The EPCA funding was intended to strengthen the government's institutional capacity. The IMF expects economic growth in the country to rebound to 3 percent in 2008 from 1.5 percent in 2007.[75] The program's main objectives for 2008 are two: to bring Côte d'Ivoire to its pre-crisis growth rate, and to relaunch a poverty reduction strategy. The program seeks to achieve peace dividends in several ways: by mobilizing revenue in the whole country, in particular through the redeployment of tax administrators; by combating tax evasion and corruption; and by reducing non-priority spending to create space to meet education, health, and basic infrastructure needs. The program also calls for "considerable contributions" to the budget from the state oil company. According to the U.S. Energy Information Admin-

Figure 4.2
FDI flows to Côte d'Ivoire

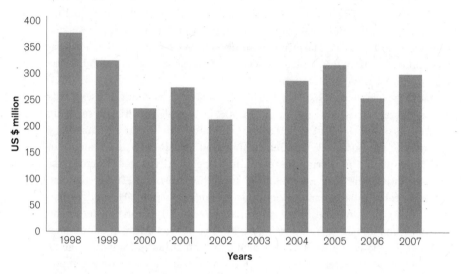

Source: UNCTAD, IMF, Government.

istration, as of 2007 Côte d'Ivoire was producing 537,000 barrels of oil per day and had proven reserves of about 100 million barrels.[76]

For its part, the World Bank has resumed assistance to Côte d'Ivoire through an economic governance and recovery grant (EGRG) totalling US$308 million.[77] The EGRG focuses on three strategic areas: stabilization of the crisis, in part by addressing its causes; aid to war-affected populations; and economic reform and recovery. The general goals touch on economic governance and growth, institution building, and the rebuilding of civil society.[78]

The World Bank's assistance package includes a number of project components that address public financial management and anti-corruption efforts. These components relate to public-expenditure management reforms, enhanced governance and transparency in the energy sector, and adherence to the EITI. The Ivorian government has agreed to an audit of the cocoa and oil sectors. In June 2008, this increased transparency resulted in the investigation and arrest of the twenty-three cocoa- and coffee-sector managers, who were accused of embezzling funds, at least some of which were used to finance the civil war.[79]

The World Bank also is financing a program that supports national identification cards and provides basic services for those affected by the conflict. Citizenship cards are at the root of the country's instability; many northerners believe they have been marginalized by a government controlled by southerners. Most northerners are Muslims and bear the same names as Malian, Burkinabe, Senegalese, and Guinean nationals. Thus they are often mistaken for foreigners in their own country and are deprived of Ivorian citizenship. The rebel movement has made it a precondition for peace that the handing out of identity papers be conducted in a professional manner that clearly determines who is Ivorian and thus eligible to vote and to run for office.

Beyond fiscal year 2008–2009, a country assistance strategy (CAS) will be aligned with the Poverty Reduction Strategy Paper (PRSP) currently being prepared by the government. Also, a donors' forum is being planned during which a collective longer-term strategy for financing reconstruction will be agreed on.

In December 2007 the AfDB approved a US$31.4 million[80] grant for a post-crisis multisector institutional-support project that will help restore public services in education, health, and rural development in central, western, and northern Côte d'Ivoire. The goal is to reinforce public entities and strengthen civil society.[81] Specifically, this program will train about 12,500 government agents and about 260 co-operatives and grassroots organizations. In April 2008 the AfDB approved a $1.8 million grant to the San Pedro Port Authority to finance preparatory studies as part of a regional project that will link Côte d'Ivoire with Mali, Guinea, and Liberia by road.[82]

For the period 2008–13 the European Community has approved about EU218 million for program assistance to Côte d'Ivoire as well as an additional EU36.7 million for emergency assistance.[83] Part of the 2008–13 funding was approved to support preparations for the upcoming Ivorian elections. This program includes, but is not limited to, building local NGO and community capacity, preparing ballots, and assisting with voter registration.

Non-traditional development institutions are also assisting in rebuilding the country. In July 2008, Arab donors—including the Islamic Development Bank, the Arab Development Bank, the Arab Bank for Economic Development in Africa, the OPEC Fund, and FSP Kuwait—met in Abidjan and pledged a total of US$440 million (CFA191.9 billion)[84] to help fund infrastructure, water, energy, agriculture, and education. Examples of 2008 projects being undertaken include the OPEC Fund's $8 million Singrobo–Yamoussoukoro Road project[85] and the Islamic Development Bank's $22.9 million upgrading and expansion of the freight terminal at Abidjan International Airport.[86]

Current State of Foreign Direct Investment

It would be an understatement to suggest that Côte d'Ivoire's recent history has been mixed. The country appears trying to put behind it the political turmoil it experienced at the turn of the twenty-first century, but the risks to political and economic stability are still significant. Though the troubles of recent years damaged investor confidence, the government is determined to forge ahead with economic diversification and to attract investment in industries earmarked as ripe for development, such as telecommunications, banking, financial services, minerals, and oil and gas, while continuing to build on its traditional role as an exporter of agricultural products. There have also been sizable investments in offshore oil and gas exploration and production, petroleum-product distribution, and the cocoa, coffee, shipping, and banking sectors. As a result, oil exports are becoming the country's largest foreign exchange earner.

In 2007, France was Côte d'Ivoire's main investor (31 percent of FDI), closely followed by the United States (nearly 28 percent) and Britain (23 percent).[87] France remains the country's main economic and trading partner. According to the French Embassy in Abidjan, France accounts for about 20 percent of foreign investment in the country. Trade with France is on the rise.[88] The French Embassy notes that in 2006 bilateral trade totalled EU1.1 billion, and that trade grew by 17 percent in 2007. From Côte d'Ivoire, France buys agricultural products (bananas, cocoa, pineapples, rubber, processed wood, and canned fish) as well as crude and refined oil.

France Telecom is the main operator in Côte d'Ivoire's telecommunications sector, holding 45.9 percent of Côte d'Ivoire Telecom[89] and 84 percent of Orange (a mobile-phone company). TotalFinaElf controls 38 percent of fuel distribution and is seeking to increase its 25 percent participation in the refining company Société Ivoirienne de Raffinage (SIR). Saur (Bouygues) is the main shareholder of the utility company Compagnie Ivoirienne d'Electricité (CIE) and of SODECI, the water company. Bolloré is active in the transportation sector, and Air France recently bought 51 percent of Air Ivoire, the national airline. The Ivorian government holds 10.5 percent of the airline's shares; the remainder are publicly owned. At present, cocoa and oil together account for about 60 percent of Côte d'Ivoire's exports. In 2007, oil exports accounted for 28 percent of government revenues, surpassing cocoa and coffee exports for the first time.

A number of foreign companies—Addax, Canadian Natural Resources, Dana Petroleum, Energy Africa, ENI-Agip, ExxonMobil, Gentry, Gulf Canada, Mondoil, Afren Energy, PanCanadian Petroleum, Pluspetrol, Shell, Santa Fe Snyder, Stratic Energy, Total, Tullow, and Vanco Energy—are participating in the Ivorian oil industry. As of May 2008, Côte d'Ivoire became a candidate country for the EITI. It has two years to comply with EITI criteria and undergo validation. Membership could further boost foreign investment in the oil, natural-gas, and mining sectors.

Côte d'Ivoire has been trying to diversify its trading partners and sources of investment by "looking East" toward China, India, and even Iran. China, for example, is building the new Parliament in Yamoussoukro, the largest in Africa, at a cost estimated at EU152 million. Trade between China and Côte d'Ivoire is currently estimated at US$300 million.

Côte d'Ivoire is also seeking to strengthen its relations with the United States and Britain. It is currently the 124th largest export market for American

Figure 4.3

Cocoa exporters in March 2008 (%)

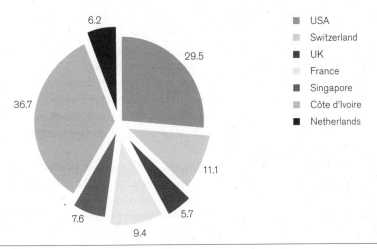

▓	USA
▓	Switzerland
■	UK
▒	France
■	Singapore
▒	Côte d'Ivoire
■	Netherlands

Source: StrategiCo., Ivorian Customs, Reuters.

goods. American FDI in Côte d'Ivoire was estimated at US$298 million in 2006 (down from $304 million in 2005).[90]

French investors have not re-engaged at former levels, and American companies now are the largest foreign buyers of Ivorian cocoa. Cargill represents about 17 percent of American purchases of Ivorian cocoa.[91]

Côte d'Ivoire has received substantial investments from the United States, China, India, South Africa, and the EU countries, as well as some neighbouring countries. Recent investors include the construction firm Construction and Property International (IBC); the telecommunications firm Unitil (UTL), which established a presence in the country in 2007 and is operating UTL Africa out of Côte d'Ivoire; the Indian construction company Shapoorji Pallonji; the UAE telecoms firm Etisalat; the South African telecoms firm MTN; and the Chinese biotech company Huassen Investment.

UTL's involvement in Côte d'Ivoire started when it worked on the design and building of the Mahatma Gandhi IT and Biotech Park for Village de Technologies de l'Information et de la Biotechnologie (VITIB), a free-trade zone for biotechnology, information technology, and telecommunications companies.

An increasing share of investment in Côte d'Ivoire is by African businesses and entrepreneurs. While most of this investment involves neighbouring countries such as Ghana, Burkina Faso, and Nigeria, investors from as far away as South Africa are also looking for opportunities there, albeit cautiously. And it should not be forgotten that the Ivorian private sector accounted for over 57 percent of the US$1.5 billion (CFA737 billion) invested between 2002 and 2007, according to the Ivorian Investment Centre (CEPICI).[92] Ivorians and foreign Africans have been investing in telecommunications, mining, energy, and transportation.

Encouraged by reunification and by the modest uptick in investment, the economy registered a modest recovery in 2007 and is set for stronger growth in 2008. Continued growth during the recovery phase will come from enhanced security, renewed private-sector confidence and investment, the rehabilitation of public infrastructure, and the redeployment of government services in the centre, north, and west. All of this will enable improved utilization of existing capacity, especially in industry and services. Longer-term growth will come from continued investment, helped along by anticipated reforms in the cocoa, energy, and financial sectors.[93]

Côte d'Ivoire holds a distinct advantage in West Africa when it comes to financial markets. Abidjan's Bourse Régionale des Valeurs Mobilières (BRVM) is the only regional stock exchange in West Africa and serves the markets of the seven Francophone countries of the region as well as Guinea-Bissau.[94] Despite the Ivorian crisis, the regional stock market's capitalization has more than quadrupled since 2005, from US$2.327 billion to $10 billion.[95] The increase in capitalization was due mainly to an Ivorian bond issue. BRVM lists thirty-eight WAEMU companies. It is widely acknowledged that the stock exchange would have played a more important role had there not been a crisis in Côte d'Ivoire. BRVM could play an important part in Côte d'Ivoire's development by providing local firms with more efficient sources of financing. It would also offer foreign investors an alternative entry into the Ivorian market.

Investment Promotion Efforts in Key Sectors

The government recognizes the importance of foreign investment and has enacted laws to attract more of it. Key sectors for private investment include these:

- building and construction equipment and materials—new, used, and remanufactured
- auto parts—new, used, and remanufactured
- plastic materials and resins
- oil and gas field equipment and services
- agricultural products and services
- medical equipment and products
- telecommunication services and equipment
- paper and paper board (PAP)

There have been a number of recent changes to the country's business regulations. Goods/services that are manufactured/conducted in the free-trade zone (FTZ) are now exempt from all import and export duties. Taxes in the FTZ are extremely low, with numerous rebates based on local employment and reinvestment. Foreign and local investors are now exempt from value added tax (VAT) on electricity, water, and petroleum consumption; they are also protected by law from nationalization, and they face no restrictions on ownership.

About six hundred French companies now operate in Côte d'Ivoire, compared to more than one thousand before the crisis.[96] There is a general feeling that the French companies that left because of the crisis will return, and indeed some are. However, many of the companies that left are waiting for the results of the upcoming elections before deciding whether to return. Meanwhile, new companies are entering the market. Of the French companies that remained in Côte d'Ivoire during the crisis, nine out of ten anticipate higher revenues in 2008. In March 2008 the country's finance minister urged French investors to consider entering the agribusiness, tourism, energy, and retail sectors.

In June 2008, during a G77 meeting of developing countries[97] with China in Côte d'Ivoire, Ivorian president Laurent Gbagbo called for a regional investment bank, to be funded through a commodity tax on raw-materials exports. He also advocates a commodity stabilization fund. This initiative is similar to Venezuelan president Hugo Chávez's proposal for a "southern bank."

A round table was held in July 2008 to discuss a third bridge (Riviera–Marcory) as well as a toll road between Abidjan and Bassam. The Islamic Development Bank (IsDB), the Ivorian banks SGBCI and BIAO, the West African Development Bank, the Caisse Nationale de Prévoyance Sociale or Retirement Fund (CNPS), the Ecobank, and the Military Provident Fund (FPM) have announced that they will co-finance the projects, which are expected to cost EU200 million (CFA130 billion for the bridge, CFA40 billion for the road).[98] Financing will be secured by December 2008; work will start in early 2009.

China Exim Bank will provide CFA12 billion to develop the VITIB technology park in Grand Bassam. Côte d'Ivoire's IT and Biotechnology Law provides for the sale of at least 51 percent of VITIB's shares to foreign investors. The park, whose opening is not yet scheduled, will enjoy a state-of-the-art communications infrastructure and is expected to create hundreds of jobs for young Ivorians.

The government has announced plans to produce an extra 200,000 tonnes of white rice per year. Ivorians consume 1.6 million tonnes per year, only 700,000 of which are grown in the country.

Finally, negotiations are underway to increase Petroci's refining capacity by 60,000 barrels a day. Petroci, the Côte d'Ivoire National Petroleum Company, engages in exploration, extraction, and refining. Côte d'Ivoire currently refines 70,000 barrels a day.[99]

Outlook and Challenges for Future FDI

Though the fighting has stopped, Cote d'Ivoire is still tense and divided. With the continuing uncertainty surrounding the upcoming elections, Côte d'Ivoire has not attracted as much FDI as it would in normal circumstances. Despite the OPA/APO, many issues remain thorny, not the least of these being how to disarm and disband the rebel militias and merge some of their soldiers with FANCI. The elections were initially scheduled for November 30, 2008. The elections, however, have been postponed for technical reasons and because disagreements remain over sequencing. The government wants the rebels to disarm before the elections; the rebels themselves want the reverse. In addition, the rebels awarded themselves ranks during the war, and now that they are about to merge with the national army, they want to keep the ranks they awarded themselves. There will be painful adjustments and compromises as integration progresses, and the two sides don't yet trust each other. As of mid-September 2008, President Gbagbo was expressing hope that the elections could be held on December 15, 2008. They have now been set for 29 November 2009.

The Ivorian population has been growing at 2.5 percent a year, and 40 percent of Ivorians are under fifteen.[100] Before the war, about 50 percent the population lived in urban areas (40 percent just in Abidjan).[101] The impact of the partition and civil war has resulted in growing poverty with slightly under half of Côte d'Ivoire's 20 million people are now below the poverty threshold, living on less than about US$1.25 per day—up from 38.4 percent in 2000 and the highest in twenty years, according to results released by the National Statistics Institute (INS) in November 2008.[102]

During the partition, people fled rebel-controlled zones for the south, placing considerable pressure on Abidjan's resources. By 2015, 61 percent of Ivorians will be living in urban areas, and this will raise challenges in terms of housing, employment, water, and sanitation as well as food. The informal sector has been flourishing, especially since the war. While there are no current statistics, the high youth-unemployment rate represents a threat to peace and stability in a region that is still licking its wounds from the bloody civil wars in Liberia and Sierra Leone and that is still fragile. (Guinea may be the next country to experience severe turbulence.)

The presence of new players such as China has greatly changed the picture. China seems blasé about the political situation and is hard at work building the new Parliament building in Yamoussoukro. Russia is also entering the scene. Lukoïl Overseas, which has been in the country since 2006, will be investing more than $250 million in oil exploration. Its first drillings (blocks CI-205, CI-101, and CI-401) will begin in 2009.[103]

With the recent election of President Nicolas Sarkozy, France has redefined its foreign policy in Africa, placing greater emphasis on business development. In 2008, Sarkozy declared that France will be competing hard with China and other investors for a larger market share in Africa.[104] Only by committing to a future of broad-based economic growth, inclusiveness, and transparent government and public finance, and by embracing private-sector development, will the country be able to overcome the significant challenges it faces.

Because of the country's political fragility, it is likely that the presidential election will experience successive delays. The November 30 election date has been postponed and it is possible that elections won't be held until 2009 or 2010. Côte d'Ivoire faces several huge tasks before the election can take place. The voters' lists alone will take six to twelve months to compile. Around 9 million voters need to be registered in a country where the free circulation of goods and people is not yet a consistent reality; as of December 2008, only about two million have been registered to vote. Second, the rebels and the government distrust each other, and the APO has not put a stop to weapons caching. The rebels do not want to stop collecting taxes in their zone, nor do they want to merge with the regular army, where they would lose whatever prestige they have and be placed on the government payroll. Third, judging from Gbagbo's manoeuvrings, he will not now allow elections to be held until he is certain he will win them.

Until political uncertainty is resolved, long-term investment is likely to stagnate around present levels as investors maintain a wait-and-see attitude.

Donors are helping facilitate the transition and are encouraging progress toward social stability by addressing some of the economic and developmental needs facing the country—for fiscal transparency, for rehabilitated infrastructure, for increased food production and food security, for a resumption of social services. Success at these will foster an environment in which the private sector can generate broad-based economic development. Meanwhile, absent of political will to break the impasse, Côte d'Ivoire has to resign itself to a waiting game.

Notes

1 Manager, StrategiCo. Country Risk Analysis, Africa and the Middle East. http://www.strategico.org.

2 WAEMU, Central Bank BCEAO, Government statistics.

3 The CFA franc was established in 1945 when France ratified the Bretton Woods agreements. Originally the acronym signified "Franc des Colonies françaises d'Afrique" (franc of the French colonies in Africa). It is now the currency of eight countries in West Africa: Benin, Burkina Faso, Côte d'Ivoire, Guinea-Bissau, Mali, Niger, Senegal, and Togo. FCFA means signifies "franc de la Communauté Financière d'Afrique."

4 http://www.unido.org/index.php?id=550.

5 CIA, https://www.cia.gov/library/publications/the-world-factbook/geos/iv.html; Cargill, http://www.cargill.com/news/issues/cocoa_westafrica.htm; International Cocoa Organization, http://www.icco.org/about/growing.aspx.

6 UNCTAD, Government, French Ministry of Co-operation. http://www.izf.net/pages/c%C3%B4te-d-ivoire/4981, StrategiCo.

7 UNCTAD FDI and calculations from "IMF Foreign Direct Investment in Africa—Some Case Studies 2002." http://www.imf.org/external/pubs/ft/wp/2002/wp0261.pdf.

8 French Co-operation, IZF. http://www.izf.net/pages/c%C3%B4te-d-ivoire/4981.

9 Encyclopedia of Nations, Africa, Côte d'Ivoire. http://www.nationsencyclopedia.com/Africa/C-te-D-ivoire-FOREIGN-INVESTMENT.html.

10 French Co-operation, IZF. Côte d'Ivoire Investissements Directs Etrangers. http://www.izf.net/pages/c%C3%B4te-d-ivoire/4981.

11 Encyclopedia of Nations, Africa, Côte d'Ivoire. http://www.nationsencyclopedia.com/Africa/C-te-D-ivoire-FOREIGN-INVESTMENT.html.

12 Calculations from FDI data (UNCTAD).

13 http://www.unctad.org/sections/dite_dir/docs/wir06_fs_ng_en.pdf.

14 Investir en Zone Franc. http://www.izf.net/pages/c%C3%B4te-d-ivoire/4981.

15 French customs, Ivorian Government and French Cooperation in Abidjan. http://www.izf.net/affiche_oscar.php?num_page=4977.

16 Company's website: http://www.bouygues.com; and Investir en Zone Franc. http://www.izf.net/pages/c%C3%B4te-d-ivoire/4981.

17 UNHCR, Human Rights Watch World Report 2005—Côte d'Ivoire. http://www.unhcr.org/refworld/country,,HRW,,CIV,,421da30f30,0.html.

18 Chamber of Commerce data. http://www.chamco-ci.org/pdf/impactcrise.htm.

19 Republic of Côte d'Ivoire—Briefs. http://businessafrica.net/africabiz/countries/cote_ivoire.php.

20 Abidjan Port Authority. Quoted by Otal.

21 OTAL.com. http://www.otal.com/cotedivoire/0.

22 Port authorities quoted by OTAL: http://www.otal.com/cotedivoire.

23 Société Internationale de Transport Interafricain par Rail.

24 SITARAIL CEO Thiam, in Le Fasozine, September 10, 2004. http://www.lefaso.net/spip.php?article3922.

25 http://www.lefaso.net/spip.php?article23.

26 http://www.fco.gov.uk/en/about-the-fco/country-profiles/sub-saharan-africa/ivory-coast?profile=intRelations&pg=4.

27 African Development Bank. http://www.afdb.org/portal/page?_pageid=473,968629&_dad=portal&_schema=PORTAL.

28 StrategiCo, "Côte d'Ivoire," April 30, 2005 (in French).

29 Ploughshares. http://www.ploughshares.ca/libraries/ACRBriefs/ACRBrief-CotedIvoire.htm.

30 IRIN News. http://www.globalsecurity.org/military/library/news/2005/01/mil-050127-irin04.htm.

31 AllBusiness.com. http://www.allbusiness.com/retail-trade/miscellaneous-retail-miscellaneous/4222397-1.html.

32 "IMF concludes 2003 Article IV Consultation with Cote d'Ivoire." http://www.imf.org/external/np/sec/pn/2004/pn0442.htm.

33 Ivorian Chamber of Commerce.

34 Le Nouveau Réveil, August 20, 2008. http://fr.allafrica.com/stories/200808210141.html?page=2.

35 Chamber of Commerce, "Impact of the Crisis."

36 Ivorian Chamber of Commerce. http://www.chamco-ci.org/pdf/impactcrise.htm.

37 Ivoirian Chamber of Commerce. http://www.chamco-ci.org/pdf/impactcrise.

38 Ibid.

39 Ibid.

40 Ibid.

41 Ibid.

42 Ibid.

43 http://www.bceao.int/internet/bcweb.nsf/pages/pr004.

44 Global Witness, "Hot Chocolate: How Cocoa Fuelled the Conflict in Côte d'Ivoire." Report by Global Witness, June 2007. http://www.globalwitness.org/media_library_detail.php/552/en/hot_chocolate_how_cocoa_fuelled_the_conflict_in_co.

45 Extractive Industries Transparency Initiative. http://eitransparency.org/node/364.

46 http://www.globalwitness.org/media_library_detail.php/650/en/cote_divoire_cocoa_indictments_key_players_escape.

47 *Jeune Afrique*, October 29, 2006.

48 APBEF quoted in *Jeune Afrique*, October 29, 2006.

49 Ibid.

50 Ibid.

51 http://www.imf.org/external/pubs/ft/scr/2007/cr07312.pdf.

52 http://en.wikipedia.org/wiki/Demographics_of_Côte_d'Ivoire.

53 New World Encyclopedia. http://www.newworldencyclopedia.org/entry/Abidjan.

54 http://www.risques-internationaux.com/presentation/actuassurancecredit/actuassde.pdf.

55 Business and Human Rights Resource Centre. http://www.business-humanrights.org/Categories/Lawlawsuits/Lawsuitsregulatoryaction/LawsuitsSelectedcases/Trafigura lawsuitsreCtedIvoire.

56 UN Office for the Coordination of Humanitarian Affairs, Humanitarian News and Analysis. http://www.irinnews.org/report.aspx?ReportId=80710.

57 African Forum and Network on Debt and Development. http://www.afrodad.org/index.php?option=com_content&task=view&id=31&Itemid=73.

58 http://www.imf.org/external/np/sec/PR/1998/PR9806.HTM.

59 http://www.oecd.org/dataoecd/26/32/38562750.pdf.

60 Executive Board of the UNDP and UNPF. http://64.233.169.104/search?q=cache:N0GNdlb5-ZAJ:www.unfpa.org/exbrd/2002/final/dpfpaciv5.doc+Cote+d%27Ivoire+economic+data+1998+2007&hl=en&ct=clnk&cd=9&gl=us&client=safari.

61 http://www.imf.org/external/pubs/ft/scr/2008/cr08142.pdf.

62 Calculations based on the government's published budgets every year.

63 Ministry of Finance, Côte d'Ivoire.

64 OECD 2008 Country Report on Côte d'Ivoire. http://www.oecd.org/dataoecd/13/38/40577266.pdf.

65 Ibid.

66 Ibid.

67 UNDP 2007/2008 Human Development Report. http://hdrstats.undp.org/indicators/39.html.

68 Fraternité Mating July 29, 2008, quoting Jeannette Koudou. http://www.educarriere.info/actualites/news_emplois.php?actu=220.

69 UNDP 2007/2008 Human Development Report. http://hdrstats.undp.org/countries/data_sheets/cty_ds_CIV.html.

70 AFP French news agency. http://news.abidjan.net/article/?n=292215.

71 *Nouveau Réveil*, March 26, 2008. http://fr.allafrica.com/stories/200803260277.html.

72 http://allafrica.com/stories/200810250025.html.

73 OECD African Economic Outlook 2008. http://www.oecd.org/dataoecd/13/38/40577266.pdf.

74 UN Humanitarian News and Analysis. http://www.irinnews.org/Report.aspx?ReportId=78895.

75 IMF, Statement of an IMF Mission at the conclusion of a staff visit to Côte d'Ivoire. http://www.imf.org/external/np/sec/pr/2008/pr08144.htm.

76 Energy Information Administration, Official Energy Statistics. http://tonto.eia.doe.gov/country/country_energy_data.cfm?fips=IV.

77 World Bank office in Abidjan. http://www.worldbank.org/ci.

78 World Bank. http://web.worldbank.org/WBSITE/EXTERNAL/COUNTRIES/AFRICAEXT/CD IVOIREEXTN/0,,menuPK:382613~pagePK:141159~piPK:141110~theSitePK:382607,00.html.

79 European Commission audit quoted in *Le Patriote*. http://www.africatime.com/ci/nouvelle .asp?no_nouvelle=408761.

80 African Development Bank. http://appablog.wordpress.com/2007/12/05/cote-d%E2% 80%99ivoire-31-millions-de-dollars-pour-le-projet-d%E2%80%99appui-institutionnel -multisectoriel-a-la-sortie-de-crise-cote-d%E2%80%99ivoire-us31-million-grant-for-post -crisis-multi-sect.

81 African Development Bank. http://www.afdb.org/portal/page?_pageid=293,174339&_dad =portal&_schema=PORTAL&press_item=29462395&press_lang=us.

82 African Development Bank. http://www.afdb.org/portal/page?_pageid=293,174339&_dad =portal&_schema=PORTAL&press_item=30723704&press_lang=us.

83 http://ec.europa.eu/development/geographical/regionscountries/countries/country_ profile.cfm?cid=ci&type=short&lng=en.

84 PANA 07/02/2008. http://www.africanmanager.com/articles/117535.html.

85 OPEC Fund. http://www.opecfund.org/projects_operations/commitments_2008.aspx.

86 Islamic Development Bank Member Country Profile—Côte d'Ivoire. http://www.gouv.ci/ declaration_print.php?recordID=72.

87 http://www.state.gov/e/eeb/ifd/2006/61972.htm.

88 French Ambassador to Abidjan André Janier, quoted by AFP, October 15, 2008. http://www. izf.net/pages/actualite-politique-et-economique-de-la-c%F4te-d-ivoire/3175.

89 http://www.nationsencyclopedia.com/economies/Africa/C-te-D-ivoire-INFRASTRUCTURE -POWER-AND-COMMUNICATIONS.html.

90 http://www.ustr.gov/assets/Document_Library/Reports_Publications.

91 See accompanying graph, "Cocoa Exporters March 2008," and Reuters, June 29, 2007.

92 CEPICI. Director in "Les Afriques." http://www.lesafriques.com/actualite/tendance- nouvelle-les-ivoiriens-investissent-dans-leur-eco.html?Itemid=89?article=4674.

93 World Bank. http://web.worldbank.org/WBSITE/EXTERNAL/COUNTRIES/AFRICAEXT/CD IVOIREEXTN/0,,menuPK:382617~pagePK:141132~piPK:141107~theSitePK:382607,00.html.

94 Wikipedia. http://en.wikipedia.org/wiki/BRVM.

95 Website of the regional stock exchange—Bourse Régionale des Valeurs Mobilières BRVM. http://www.brvm.org/fr/presentation/marche.htm.

96 French Embassy, Chamber of Commerce.

97 http://www.g77.org.

98 http://www.abidjan-info.com/mapage/index.html.

99 Calculations based on IMF, Government, and U.S, Department of Energy data.

100 UNDP HDI. http://hdr.undp.org/en/media/hdr_20072008_fr_indictables.pdf; CIA, http:// www.cia.gov.

101 Government statistics.

102 AllAfrica.com, December 3, 2008.

103 *African Manager*, June 6, 2008. http://www.africanmanager.com/articles/117074.html.

104 Following the declaration by French Secretary of State for Cooperation Alain Joyandet. In ejdd.fr, "On veut aider les Africains, mais il faut que cela nous rapporte" (*Libération*, June 24, 2008).

Sierra Leone

Breaking with the Past
Transitional Justice in Sierra Leone
Ozonnia Ojielo

5

Introduction

When a period of authoritarian rule or civil war ends, a state, and its people, stand at a crossroads. What should be done with a recent history full of victims, perpetrators, secretly buried bodies, pervasive fear, and official denial? Should this past be exhumed, reserved, acknowledged, apologized for? How can a nation of enemies be reunited, former opponents reconciled, in the context of such a violent history and often bitter, festering wounds? What should be done with tens of thousands of perpetrators still walking free? And how can a new government prevent such atrocities from being repeated in the future?

International humanitarian law does not distinguish among the reasons underlying acts of violence. It looks at the participants in an armed conflict without regard to whether their cause is just or legitimate. International humanitarian law considers the legality of the means and methods of warfare and the protection of vulnerable, groups, especially civilians. It is immaterial whether the combat formation is composed of rebels or government forces. No actor in an armed conflict can use the justice of its cause as a defence when perpetrating human-rights violations and abuses.

The Universal Declaration of Human Rights (UDHR) acknowledges in its pre-amble the need for human-rights protection under the rule of law as a means to avoid rebellion against tyranny and oppression. Some have interpreted this as meaning that the declaration accepts the right of rebellion in some cases. What *is* clear is that human-rights law does not encourage rebellion. It assumes that rights will be pursued using legal means and under the rule of law.

International human-rights law also acknowledges the right of states to restrict or suspend certain fundamental rights when certain conditions exist, such as public emergencies that threaten the nation's existence. At the same time, international human-rights law insists that certain fundamental rights and freedoms cannot be suspended even in times of war. These rights, which are deemed sacrosanct, include the right to life, the prohibition of torture and other cruel, inhumane, or degrading treatment, and the right to protection against discrimination. No protection is available to a government or its allies when they violate any of these rights.

All international human-rights treaties require governments to investigate violations and provide effective remedies. Conventions dealing with crimes against humanity and war crimes consistently require legal action to be taken against suspects. The UN Convention Against Torture of 1985 requires state parties to ensure the prompt and impartial investigation of torture allegations. The Genocide Convention imposes an obligation to punish whether perpetrators are "constitutionally responsible rulers, public officials or private individuals." Under the Geneva Conventions of 1949, states are required to search for war criminals and either bring them before their own courts (whatever their nationality) or extradite them for trial in another jurisdiction.

In light of the jurisprudential foundations established above for punishing human-rights violations, it may be surprising that criminal prosecution was rejected in the peace accords that ended the civil war in Sierra Leone. This paper reviews the causes of the conflict, the political settlement that was eventually arrived at to bring the conflict to an end, and the nature of the justice mechanisms that were implemented, along with their implications for sustainable peace in the country.

Past political repression can generate emotional and practical burdens, ones that often affect a country's stability. How can a transitional society peacefully question former officials who were associated with a past of repression? How can it return both victims and perpetrators to the fold? And how can an emerging democracy respond to the demands of some that their legitimate grievances be redressed without creating new injustices for others? Sierra Leone has been asking these questions for the past seven years, since the end of its civil war.

Background to the Conflict

The Sierra Leone Truth and Reconciliation Commission (TRC) was established in 2002 to create an impartial historical record of violations and abuses of human rights and international humanitarian law related to the armed conflict in the country, from the beginning of the conflict in 1991 to the signing of the Lomé Peace Agreement in 1999. It was further tasked with addressing impunity, with responding to the needs of victims, with promoting healing and reconciliation, and with preventing a repetition of the violations and abuses suffered.[1] The commission identified four distinct phases in Sierra Leone's history. It regarded these as crucial to understanding the conflict's causes and the country's present-day challenges. Those phases were as follows: (a) the colony and the protectorate, (b) the era of party politics, (c) the Sierra Leone People's Party (SLPP) in power, and (d) the 1967 elections and its aftermath.[2]

The Colony and the Protectorate

Sierra Leone's problems have their roots in the duality that marked the political, administrative, and historical experiences of the major constituent groups. The colonial capital, Freetown, known as the Colony, and the much larger area beyond it, known as the Protectorate, were ruled as separate entities with distinct legal and political regimes for much of the period leading to independence. The repercussions of this duality carried forward well into the post-colonial period.

The British government implemented a deeply divisive social-engineering strategy. The Colony and the Protectorate were developed separately and unequally. Using commerce, Christianity, and notions of "civilization" as their tools, the British manipulated the relations among the indigenous peoples. In doing so they sowed distrust, competition, and intransigence.[3]

The separate and unequal treatment of the Colony and the Protectorate was most obvious in the legal systems operated by the British. In the Colony, English common law prevailed; in the Protectorate, different legal doctrines were combined with a three-tier court system. These tiers were the Court of Native Chiefs, which dealt with issues relating to land and factional fights but had no criminal jurisdiction; the Court of the District Commissioner, which had original jurisdiction over all offences; and the Court of the District Commissioner and Native Chiefs, on which both parties sat to try criminal cases. This last court had the power to impose the death penalty.

Common law was practised consistently in the Colony, whereas in the Protectorate the legal system was mixed and was applied in an inconsistent and irrational manner. Common law was to supersede customary law in the event of a conflict between the two. In reality, most disputes were decided by the whim of the adjudicator—most often the chief. Common law was codified, whereas the customary law applied in the Protectorate became increasingly susceptible to arbitrary interpretation, varying from chiefdom to chiefdom as well as from ethnic group to ethnic group. As a result, people were treated differently for the same types of behaviour. Resentment against the chiefs intensified in the Protectorate, exacerbated by the people's sense that they were being treated as second-class relative to the Krio. The Krios are composed of four distinct groups: the black poor shipped from England; labourers from Nova Scotia; the Maroons; and recaptured slaves from slave ships on the Atlantic Ocean. They were all deposited on the Western Peninsula of Freetown and over time developed a distinct identity. Krio or Creole is a unique form of corrupted English that incorporates words and phrases used in popular dialect by the freed slaves. Sierra Leone's ethnic mix includes Temnes and Mendes (the two majority groups, with approximately 30 percent each of the population), as well as Limba (20 percent). Other minority groups include Susu, Koranko, Yalunka, Vai, Krim, Sherbro, Kono, Kissi, and Gola. Scattered among theses groups are the Fulla and Mandingo.[4]

Local governance in the Colony differed from what was practised in the Protectorate. In the Colony, a municipality had been established for Freetown by 1895, which was managed by an elected council based on limited suffrage. In the Protectorate, there were native administrations, which became town councils in the 1950s. The chiefs managed the native administrations, and this enabled them to strengthen their power and influence over their subjects.[5] This was in effect a continuation of indirect rule, which served the colonial authorities very well. Among the British authorities, there was no motivation to change it. In the Protectorate, this deepened pervasive feelings of alienation, especially among the young, who were in effect encouraged to view the "system" as anti-youth—a view that years later would be a recurring theme of the civil war.[6]

In terms of resources, the Colony and the Protectorate were unequally endowed. The Protectorate held all the mineral and agricultural wealth that could have transformed Sierra Leone into a well-developed country— iron ore, rutile, bauxite, diamonds, cocoa, and coffee. The Colony had no minerals but did have a highly educated workforce, whose members held all the key positions in the civil service. This educated class made sure that all of the Protectorate's resources were channelled into the development of the Colony's infrastructure. The Protectorate was left in abject poverty and with an underdeveloped infrastructure.

But the more serious impediment to the development of a Sierra Leonean identity related to citizenship. In the early twentieth century, new waves of arrivals from the Middle East—mostly Lebanese and Syrians—presented the British with new collaborators and enabled them to call the bluff of the Krio-educated elite,[7] who had been pressuring the authorities for increased participation in governance. The colonial administration began practising a deliberate policy to separate the Krio from the "natives," and this helped heighten the perception that different peoples were living in the same country. Laws were enacted that excluded the Krio from the hinterland. They were required to pay "stranger fees" to the local chief before being granted entry into any community; and they were not entitled to own land in the Protectorate.[8]

As "foreigners" in the hinterland communities, they had no rights except those extended by the local chief. The chief could arbitrarily recover any land that had been sold to a non-native. This law persisted well into the post-colonial era and partly explains the lack of development in the hinterland, given that most of the people with resources to invest there were non-natives—that is, Krio or other settler groups. As a result, in spite of the huge agricultural potential in the Protectorate, the only investments were in mining or trading.

The Era of Party Politics

The impact of separate development of the Colony and the Protectorate, and of the divide-and-conquer strategy practised by the British, became clear with the onset of party politics. By 1947 the Colony and the Protectorate had been merged following the Stevens Constitution of 1946, which proposed a single Legislative Council. Once the council had been established, the numerical strength of the Protectorate began to count, and representatives of the two sides found themselves in a bitter struggle to control the state's resources. The chiefs were the key representatives of the Protectorate, and they united with other elites to meet the challenges posed by the Krio. Together they formed a political party, the Sierra Leone People's Party (SLPP). This marriage of convenience was to prove enduring; the SLPP held power for the first five years following independence. The SLPP was anchored in the traditional practices and powers of the chiefs and had no reformist program. As a consequence, it was largely alienated from the Protectorate's working class. The chiefs would continue to be the SLPP's power base. Resentment grew over the "marriage" between the new national elite represented by the SLPP and the chiefs, who were able to retain their power and control. A critical opportunity to reform the governance system was in this way lost in the early post-colonial years. The consequences became apparent when the chiefs and other symbols of traditional authority were targeted during the conflict.

The SLPP's lack of an ideological foundation led to an internal split in 1957, with each faction in the party led by one of the Margai brothers—Albert and Milton. The party prevailed on Albert—who had been elected party leader—to allow Milton to become leader and lead the party to national independence. Yet Albert and his supporters were denied ministerial posts in the first post-colonial cabinet, which alienated the large wing of the party loyal to Albert. That wing responded by forming a new party, the Peoples National Party (PNP). Among the leaders of this new party was the trade-union leader, Siaka Stevens. The political system was further fragmented when, in 1960, Milton purged the cabinet of people from the Temne ethnic group. Exploiting popular disenchantment with Milton's policies, Stevens established the All Peoples Congress (APC). The APC was ideologically different from the SLPP. It espoused socialist ideals and called for the democratization of the institution of chieftaincy.[9]

The politics of the independence years were defined largely by the rivalry between the APC and the SLPP. The APC appealed to the masses with its socialist credentials. Most of its leaders were from the north. This served the APC well when it came to mobilizing that part of the country. The SLPP relied on support from the middle class and the chieftaincy elite, which was dominated by the ruling families of the south and southeast. Party politics would supplant the Colony–Protectorate divisions, but the resulting alliances would continue to mirror past cleavages. This zero-sum approach to politics promoted hostilities that eventually turned to violence.

The SLPP in Power

Almost immediately after independence, Sierra Leone faced several challenges. On the eve of independence in 1961, opposition leaders led by Siaka Stevens were accused of plotting to overthrow the government by force and imprisoned by the prime minister, Sir Milton Margai.[10] A year later, the 1962 elections became a benchmark for measuring the level of ethnic and regional polarization that now gripped the country and for gauging the ideological platforms of the parties (or lack thereof). The SLPP and the APC won in their respective "tribal or affiliated areas" of Mendeland and Temneland. The parties increasingly began to look and act like "ethnic champions."

The 1967 General Elections and Their Aftermath

The 1967 elections made it clear that the country was sharply divided along ethnic and regional lines. This was partly a consequence of Sir Albert Margai's policies and partly due to the APC's mobilization strategies. To stave off electoral defeat, Albert Margai attempted to establish a one-party state. This was vehemently resisted by the opposition as well as by civic groups. Having failed at this, Margai claimed that there had been an attempted *coup d'état* and arrested some leading Krio as the conspirators. He also arrested several military officers of northern origin, including the Deputy Commander of the Sierra Leone Army. These arrests fuelled accusations that opposition supporters were victims of ethnic targeting.[11]

Even within his party, Albert Margai was battling dissent. Those who opposed him were denied use of the party symbol, which was the official acknowledgment that the candidate would represent the party at the elections.

The outcome of the elections was predictable. Once again, the SLPP won in the largely Mende areas of the south and east, while the APC won overwhelmingly in the north. With the support of the Krio, the APC also won all the seats in the west (Freetown and environs). Out of 66 seats in Parliament, the SLPP won 28, the APC 32. The other 4 went to independents who had deserted the SLPP and had declared publicly that they would not support Sir Albert Margai for prime minister.[12] In accordance with the constitution, 12 paramount chiefs also entered Parliament. They were by tradition expected to support the party with the largest number of seats. The electoral commissioner declared that since the 4 independent MPs were former members of the SLPP, he would allocate their seats to the SLPP; thus, both parties were considered to have won 32 seats. On that basis, the commissioner further declared that the chiefs would be supporting the SLPP. In this way the SLPP was named winner of the election.

This led to tensions and stalemate throughout the country. On the basis of a letter written by the four independent candidates that they would not rejoin the SLPP as long as Sir Albert remained prime minister, the Governor General concluded that the APC had won the majority of seats in Parliament and invited the APC leader Siaka Stevens to form a government. On the day Stevens was to be sworn in as prime minister, elements in the army loyal to Sir Albert, led by Lieutenant Hinga Norman, the aide-de-camp to the Governor General, disrupted the ceremony and announced a formal takeover of power by the army on the orders of the Force Commander, Brigadier Lansana. Twenty-four hours later a counter-coup was organized by another group of soldiers calling themselves the National Reformation Council. The army had thrust itself into Sierra Leone's politics.

The four periods discussed are important in the political history of Sierra Leone because they show how British colonial policies laid the foundations for national division and sowed the seeds of distrust. As a consequence, the political elite was unable to construct a sense of national identity. Those same periods also highlight the crass self-centredness of the political elite, who were so intent on protecting individual and group privileges that they missed excellent opportunities to bridge divisions. When stresses arose in the political life of the country, sufficient goodwill did not exist anywhere in the polity to guarantee workable political solutions. Furthermore, ethnic "outbidding" and mobilizations of support based on ethnicity by the early leaders stunted the development of national political parties. Because of the parochial agendas of all the parties, none had sufficient clout and acceptance all over the country. The result was that politics became a zero-sum game anchored in what spoils could be acquired for oneself and for one's ethnic group. Advantage was calculated in terms of how much damage could be done to the other side. This led to an unnecessary focus on the security of the individual and the regime, with the cost paid in terms of the state's security. People were hauled into prison on the slightest excuse, the easiest pretext being that they were planning a coup.

Following the rejection of the results of the 1967 elections and the several coups that followed thereafter, when Siaka Stevens finally came to power, the overwhelming focus was placed on regime security to the detriment of everything else. Sadly, Sierra Leone's history is a catalogue of ifs. What if the colonial legacy had been different? What if the country had had more enlightened and dedicated political leaders? What if the SLPP had accepted defeat in 1967 and gone into opposition? Would history have been kinder to the nation and spared it the agonies of civil war?

The APC and the Politics of Attrition

The APC and Siaka Stevens assumed power in 1968. This came about as a result of what has been called the "Non-Commissioned Officers' coup" of the same year, when the army's junior ranks rebelled, overthrew the military government of Andrew Juxton-Smith, and invited Stevens to form a new government.

Stevens's immediate task was to consolidate power. His fears about the regime's security, and his own personal security, were so strong that he brought all of the state's institutions under his own direct control as prime minister. This continued even after 1971, when he declared himself president and the country a republic.[13] Unsure of the army's loyalty, Stevens also created the dreaded Internal Security Unit (ISU), whose mandate was to support the police to ensure law and order. However, its members were chosen from loyal party youth and members of his own ethnic group, and it evolved into a paramilitary force for the protection of the regime.

By most accounts, the APC's strategy was one of divide, conquer, or eliminate.[14] In front of the TRC, witnesses described how APC stalwarts would bring water pipes, roofing sheets, electric poles, and construction equipment to a village on the eve of an election as evidence of the government's intention to bring development there.[15] If the APC lost the election within the village, those things would all be taken away. The next time around, the thoroughly deprived communities would know which party to support; the alternative was continued marginalization and denial of development. Stevens's hold on power was so absolute that most of the SLPP's stalwarts felt compelled to join the APC.

Every single institution of the state was targeted in this way. Through gerrymandering and other illegitimate methods, Stevens ensured that his party retained absolute control of Parliament. The TRC heard testimony that opposition candidates were kidnapped on the eve of elections.[16] When they could not show up at the election stations to certify their candidacy, the APC candidates were declared as elected unopposed.

Through control of the judiciary's budget and by reserving the right to appoint or suspend judges, and to extend their tenure after the mandatory retirement age, Stevens ensured that the judiciary remained compliant. Parliament became a rubber-stamp institution. The APC party constitution gave Stevens the power to reject candidates for Parliament. Any attempts at independence among party members were immediately squelched by threats of isolation and imprisonment. Not surprisingly, Parliament in 1970 endorsed the closing of the railways, which were the only secure means of transport between the hinterland and the main cities. Parliament also supported the dissolution in 1972 of elected local government in favour of direct rule from the centre. Service delivery to the hinterland collapsed. Then in 1978 Parliament endorsed the imposition of a one-party state. The tool for this was the One-Party Constitution, which specifically referred to Stevens as Sierra Leone's president. In this way the office was personalized.[17]

The One-Party Constitution destroyed all pretense of participatory democracy. Dissent and public criticism were met with violence by the thuggish ISU or bands of armed youths. The 1982 general elections were noteworthy more for state terrorism than for the opportunity to choose the country's leaders.

Those candidates whose loyalties were in doubt either were not issued with party symbols or had to watch helplessly as roaming bands of armed APC members descended on their communities to frighten people out of voting. Those who did try to vote risked detention.[18]

There were attempts at resistance in many parts of the country. These were viciously crushed. The most serious of these attempts, now remembered as the Ndorgboryosoi Rebellion,[19] was a harbinger of the 1991 conflict. It flared in Pujehun district in the Mende-speaking south of the country, whose political loyalties lay with the SLPP. There, Stevens's vice-president, Solomon Demby, sought to show that he was the area's new strongman. He was stoutly resisted. Many of those who participated in this rebellion surfaced again ten years later when the Revolutionary United Front (RUF) arrived in the district. They became the initial mobilizers for the RUF and led the military campaigns against the APC government.[20]

By 1984 all legitimate opposition in the country had been silenced. According to the ombudsman, the ISU "was the instrument of tyranny in this country. It was used to cow opposition leaders; it was used to cow the press, the citizens, students and people who tried to protest. It was used for killing people, maiming and to some extent armed robbery. But everybody kept silent because of the fact that we were scared that they could seek their revenge [if people spoke out]."[21]

The state was in decay and in decline. Because of Stevens's[22] oppressive rule, most Sierra Leoneans became convinced that reform was impossible through democratic means.[23] The state would have to be confronted violently if peace and development were to be achieved. Stevens's undoing was the poor state of the economy. He had bled the country dry through his personal control of state resources—in particular, its mineral resources—and by offering concessions to his friends, including Jamil Said Mohammed, a Lebanese businessman who became highly influential in the diamond industry through his Precious Mineral Mining Company. Jamil Mohammed actually lent money to the country to pay the salaries of public servants.[24] In 1985, Stevens handed over power to the army commander, Joseph Momoh, whom he had chosen as his successor.

Momoh was grossly unprepared for the tasks he faced. His attempts at reform were half-hearted and too little, too late. State finances were in deficit. It was impossible to finance the importation of essential items. Local manufacturing had all but collapsed as a result of the rent-seeking orientation of the APC government. Public officials were awarding major public-works and infrastructure contracts to their friends, who in turn paid rents to them. Overall, Stevens established a system whereby he controlled the diamond industry through a network of partners without having to engage the government apparatus.[25] Momoh imposed a state of economic emergency in 1987, designed to arrest the freefall of the currency and to stabilize the economy through price controls and state intervention, but implementation of this was a disaster, for it only provided more opportunities for rent seeking, extortion, and seizures of private property by overzealous state officials. Rice, the national staple, was in extremely short supply. Imported rice was highly coveted and became a powerful political weapon in the hands of party officials, who supplied rice to communities that supported them and withheld supplies from those that did not. Only the army was guaranteed its rice ration, and senior officials used their official allocations to undercut quotas to the rank and file and to skim off huge profits for themselves.[26]

The Beginning of a Rebellion

Every opportunity for dissent having been stifled, there was no space for constructive discussion of the challenges facing Sierra Leone as it entered the last decade of the twentieth century. People could only congregate in informal settings. Only university students, journalists, and high school graduates found enough spirit to gather and discuss the state of their country.

Veterans of several student revolts—especially the 1985 revolt led by the students of Fourah Bay University—provided leadership in "ideological"[27] discussions of the country's state of affairs and of how to bring about change. These discussions took place in local taverns, backcountry huts, private residences, and newspaper offices, beyond the watchful eye of the dreaded ISU. In these hidden precincts was born the idea of a revolution that would dramatically redirect Sierra Leone's path by the close of the century. At the University of Sierra Leone, several clubs and social groups became hotbeds for these discussions. The most famous of these groups were the Gardeners Club and the Pan African Students Union (PANAFU). These were among the first organized opposition cells in Freetown and Bo, and they gradually extended themselves into the broader Sierra Leonean community.

One book that was widely read on university campuses was the Green Book, in which Libyan leader Mu'Ammar Qadhafi outlined his socialist ideology, which called for democratic and revolutionary forces to take responsibility for their country's independence, and which called for self-determination, autonomy, and democratic socialism. A Green Book Club was formed in which students discussed Qadhafi's writings. The Green Book was popular among the student radicals, who were looking for alternative forms of resistance to the APC regime and for ideas for reforming the state and introducing responsive governance. The student radicals quickly established contact with the Libyan mission in Ghana, and many of them participated in political workshops and training programs in Tripoli and other Libyan cities.[28]

After forty-one students and three lecturers were expelled from Fourah Bay College in the wake of the 1985 students' revolt, ideological discussions gave way to concrete planning for a revolution. The student radicals approached the Libyan authorities for military training.[29] In August 1987, four Sierra Leoneans left for Libya to receive that training. The student organizers hoped this group would form the nucleus of a body of Libyan-trained revolutionaries. Libya's own objective in this was to establish an Africa-wide "Green Army" to confront the global hegemony of the United States.

There are several accounts of how revolutionary change in Sierra Leone fell into the hands of Foday Saybana Sankoh—a man with no revolutionary credentials whatsoever.[30] The most authoritative account of what transpired has been distilled by the TRC. The student radicals belonged to various contingents that travelled to Libya for military training. One of the candidates for military training, Sankoh, belonged to a cell managed by one of the original four trainees—Victor Reider. According to Reider and others, Sankoh did not evidence any revolutionary zeal.[31] He did not understand any of the competing ideological issues. He seemed consumed by the simple idea of "changing the system," and he spoke very little at cell meetings.[32] To his advantage, however, he was an army veteran and so had basic military knowledge.

The would-be revolutionaries fell out while in Libya, and most of their leaders abandoned the idea of military training and revolution. Some returned to Sierra Leone and resumed civilian life, while others immigrated to the United States. Because of his age and military background, Sankoh quickly assumed control of the remaining group and led the movement, the Revolutionary United Front (RUF), which finally entered Sierra Leone on March 23, 1991. This signalled the onset of a bloody conflict that lacked ideological foundations and was rooted only in the simplistic idea of system change.[33] It is the tragedy of Sierra Leone that the man who came to symbolize the people's resistance to the APC's oppression—at least in the early days of the conflict—was the one who least understood the process and mechanics of revolution. According to the TRC report, the war was a dark page in the country's history. It was marked by brutality and the targeting of civilians, especially women and children. A multitude of human-rights violations were committed by the respective factions: murders, amputations, abductions, sexual slavery, looting, and disembowelment, among others.[34] Access to the diamond mines of Sierra Leone enabled the RUF to prolong the war for nine years. Institutions of the state and community infrastructures were destroyed.

After the devastating attack on Freetown in January 1999 by the RUF and elements of the former national army, the international community intervened by sending forces to shore up the Economic Community of West African States Monitoring Group (ECOMOG), which had been in the country since 1997 and had failed to entirely neutralize the RUF. Combining their forces, ECOMOG and British troops quickly repulsed the RUF fighters, driving them out of Freetown to districts bordering Liberia and Guinea. It became obvious to the government and the RUF that neither could win the war by military means. After intense diplomatic negotiations, in July 1999 the government and the RUF met in Lomé, where a peace agreement was finally signed.

Background to the TRC and the Special Court

Between January and July 1999, Sierra Leonean political discourse was more open to reaching an accommodation with the RUF, more so than it had been before the invasion of Freetown in January. It was perceived that the RUF was strong and resilient and that ECOMOG did not have the capacity to defeat it militarily. Also, there was a general belief among Sierra Leoneans that no international force such as a UN military mission would be established. Indeed, most members of the international community encouraged the government to seek accommodation with the RUF. The U.S. government began organizing capacity-building programs for the RUF to enable them to participate in peace talks; the British government stated that continued military aid to the government was conditional on a peace agreement with the RUF.[35]

A national consultative conference was held in April 1999, attended by political leaders, traditional leaders, and civil-society representatives. There, the terms of a peace settlement were outlined based on the Abidjan Peace Agreement. The settlement was to include a cessation of hostilities; recognition by the RUF of the government's legitimacy; limited power sharing leading up to general elections; amnesty for the combatants; and the establishment of a truth-and-reconciliation commission (TRC).[36]

All of the signatories viewed the TRC as an alternative process for accountability, as a means to ensure that the human-rights violations that had taken place during the fighting would not recur. While the peace talks were under way in Lomé, the UN High Commissioner for Human Rights, Mary Robinson, visited Freetown. She drew attention to the large number of human-rights abuses and the need for justice and accountability. The UN, the government, and civil society adopted a human-rights manifesto during her visit. At that time, she committed her office to support the founding of a TRC in the country.[37]

According to the Lomé Peace Agreement, the TRC was to be established within ninety days of the agreement's signing. Despite the agreement, however, the fighting did not end. Not until November of that year, with the signing of the Abuja Ceasefire Agreement, could the process begin for founding the TRC. The commission was to be the sole mechanism for ensuring accountability for the human-rights violations that had arisen during the conflict.

Then in May 2000 a series of events unfolded that dramatically affected the process. The end result would be the establishment of the Special Court. The DDR process was proceeding very slowly, and the RUF and the government forces were both violating the peace agreement. RUF combatants continued to obstruct UN peacekeepers in the performance of their duties; they were also abducting journalists, missionaries, and others. It seemed that the RUF was fracturing. The situation continued to deteriorate in 1999 and 2000.

In May 2000, RUF commanders in Makeni, Augustine Gbao, and Morris Kallon laid siege to a UNAMSIL compound, insisting on the return of ten RUF combatants who had surrendered to UNAMSIL as the disarmament and demobilization program began to take hold.[38] When the UN peacekeepers refused to return the combatants, the RUF commanders attacked the compound, killing some and taking several Kenyan peacekeepers hostage. Later, a contingent of Zambian peacekeepers sent from Freetown to relieve their beleaguered colleagues were arrested. UN peacekeepers became targets of arrest all over the country—in the end, around five hundred were abducted.[39] Rumours spread quickly that RUF combatants were marching on Freetown from other parts of the country to finally take over the government.

Concerned about the apparent breakdown of the peace agreement, a coalition of civil-society leaders organized a protest march to Sankoh's residence in Freetown. This march fell in with other plans by the government and the Civil Defence Forces (CDF) to provoke a fight with Sankoh and finally deal with him.[40] The protest led to gunfire from Sankoh's residence, which was then attacked by elements of the army as well as by the Kamajor and other militias allied to the government. More than forty people were killed, and Sankoh escaped into the bush.[41] All over the city, RUF leaders and members were attacked, and scores of them were killed. Sankoh was arrested after a few days and hauled into detention.

Following this incident, the president of Sierra Leone wrote to the UN Secretary General, asking the UNSC to establish a court to "try and bring to credible justice those members of the RUF and their accomplices responsible for committing crimes against the people of Sierra Leone and for the taking of UN peacekeepers as hostages."[42] The president explained that "with regard to the magnitude and extent of the crimes committed, Sierra Leone does not have the resources or expertise to conduct trials for such crimes."[43] The government hoped that the court would break the "command structure of the criminal organisation responsible for the violence."[44]

The letter was well received by the UNSC, which mandated the Secretary-General to prepare a report on the founding of such a court.[45] The UNSC, however, felt that the target for such a court could not be just the RUF, as the president's letter had proposed—it would have to include anyone who had held a command position during the conflict and who had participated in violations of international humanitarian law. The Secretary-General's report proposed the establishment of a court, not by a Security Council Resolution, but by agreement between the UN and the Government of Sierra Leone. This court would comprise Sierra Leonean and non–Sierra Leonean judges and would have three offices: the Chambers (of judges), the Office of the Prosecutor, and the Registry.[46] These proposals were broadly welcomed by Sierra Leone's human-rights community.

The UN and the Government of Sierra Leone agreed to a Special Court whose task would be prosecute "persons who bear the greatest responsibility for serious violations of international humanitarian law and Sierra Leonean law committed in the territory of Sierra Leone since 30 November 1996."[47] The court was to function in accordance with a statute enacted by the Parliament of Sierra Leone.[48] The Special Court was formally established in January 2002 by the Government of Sierra Leone following passage of the relevant act by Parliament.[49] The Special Court Act declared that amnesty (meaning the Lomé amnesty) should not be a bar to prosecutions for the international crimes referred to in the act.

Sierra Leone's TRC was created by Article 2(1) of the Truth and Reconciliation Commission Act, 2000. It was to comprise seven members: four Sierra Leoneans and three international members. The country's civil society insisted that no Sierra Leonean had escaped being touched by the conflict and doubted that a commission staffed entirely by Sierra Leoneans could be sufficiently detached to carry out the TRC's mandate. It was hoped that the inclusion of international commissioners will give the commission the independence and integrity it needed to elicit the participation of all Sierra Leoneans.[50] The commissioners were to be appointed by the president following a selection procedure to be coordinated by the Special Representative of the UN Secretary General in Sierra Leone (SRSG).

The act enjoined the commission's members to be persons of integrity and credibility who would be impartial in the performance of their functions and who would enjoy the confidence of the people of Sierra Leone. Also, they would be of high standing or competence as lawyers, social scientists, religious leaders, psychologists, and other disciplines relevant to the TRC's functions.[51]

The TRC's Mandate

The Truth and Reconciliation Commission Act sets out the objects of the Commission:

6(1) The object for which the Commission is established is to create an impartial historical record of violations and abuses of human rights and international humanitarian law related to the armed conflict in Sierra Leone, from the beginning of the conflict in 1991 to the signing of the Lomé Peace Agreement, to address impunity, to respond to the needs of the victims, to promote healing and reconciliation and to prevent a repetition of the violations and abuses suffered.

(2) Without prejudice to the generality of subsection (1), it shall be the function of the Commission

(a) to investigate and report on the causes, nature and extent of the violations and abuses referred to in sub section (1) to the fullest degree possible, including their antecedents, the context in which the violations and abuses occurred, the question of, whether those violations and abuses were the result of deliberate planning, policy or authorisation by any government, group or individual, and the role of both internal and external factors in the conflict.

(b) to work to help restore the human dignity of victims and promote reconciliation by providing an opportunity for victims to give an account of the violations and abuses suffered and for perpetrators to relate their experiences, and by creating a climate which fosters constructive interchange between victims and perpetrators, giving special attention to the subject of sexual abuses and to the experiences of children within the armed conflict.

(c) to do all such things as may contribute to the fulfilment of the object of the Commission.[52]

Among other functions, the commission was to undertake investigations and research into key events and their causes, patterns of abuse, and violations, as well as the parties responsible; to conduct hearings, which might be open or closed to the public; to take individual statements and gather additional information with regard to the causes and patterns of the conflict; and to promote reconciliation.[53]

The act further empowered the commission to seek assistance from traditional and religious leaders to facilitate its public sessions; and to resolve local conflicts arising from past violations or in support of healing and reconciliation.[54]

Part V of the act, dealing with the report and recommendations, charged the commission to "make recommendations concerning the reforms and other measures, whether legal, political, administrative or otherwise, needed to achieve the object of the Commission, namely, the object of providing [an] impartial historical record, preventing the repetition of the violations and abuses suffered, addressing impunity, responding to the needs of victims and promoting healing and reconciliation."[55]

In constructing its mandate, in order to clarify the intentions of Parliament at the time the bill was enacted, the commission referred to the Memorandum of Objects and Reasons that had been attached to the bill creating the TRC. The memorandum referred to the commission's proceedings as "a catharsis for constructive interchange between the victims and perpetrators of human rights violations and abuses"[56] and stated that the commission should compile a clear picture of the past. There was also a reference that the commission's main function was to develop an impartial historical record of events as the basis for preventing their recurrence.[57]

When the commission was inaugurated, the president interpreted its mandate as follows:

> The Commission will investigate and report on the causes, nature and extent of the violations and abuses of human rights and international humanitarian law during the conflict. Of course it will create an impartial historical record of the atrocities perpetrated against innocent civilians during a ten-year period of the war. However, it is absolutely necessary that we look beyond those functions, and see the work of the TRC as a therapeutic process. It was a brutal war. It caused grievous physical and emotional damage for thousands of our compatriots. It also created divisions between families, and among neighbours and friends. To a large extent the conflict also fractured the body politic of the nation. Well, the guns may be silent, but the trauma of the war lingers on. We have a great deal of healing to do. This is why the TRC is, and should be seen, as an instrument of national reconciliation, and another means of strengthening the peace.[58]

The commission defined its mandate as having five distinct elements, which it clustered into two groups. The first group consisted of one element: "to create an impartial historical record of violations and abuses of human rights and international humanitarian law related to the armed conflict in Sierra Leone, from the beginning of the conflict in 1991 to the signing of the Lomé Peace Agreement."[59] The second group consisted of four elements: to address impunity, to respond to the needs of the victims, to promote healing and reconciliation, and to prevent a repetition of the violations and abuses suffered. The commission did not see any ranking or hierarchy among the five elements. However, based on the Statement of Objects and Reasons, it concluded that the development of an impartial historical record was at the core of its mandate.[60]

The Lomé Peace Agreement had proposed the following as the commission's mandate: "to address impunity, break the cycle of violence, provide a forum for both the victims and perpetrators of human rights violations to tell their story, get a clear picture of the past in order to facilitate genuine healing and reconciliation."[61] From the TRC Act, it is obvious that the Parliament of Sierra Leone wanted a historical record to be a key result of the commission's work.

The act specified that the historical record would need to be impartial. The commission, for its part, noted that "historical truth"—indeed, any truth— by definition is impartial. A "partial" truth is no truth at all; it is merely a distorted version of events tailored to suit a given party. The commission viewed the process of selecting the commissioners as one step in uncovering the historical truth.[62]

The commission argued that the concept of violations and abuses lay at the core of its mandate. After all, several sections of the act referred to "violations and abuses—[for example], investigate and report on the causes, nature and extent of the violations and abuses [and] investigation and research into key events, causes, patterns of abuses or violation and the parties responsible."[63]

The act did not define "violations and abuses." Those terms lack recognized technical meanings in human-rights law and international humanitarian law. The commission therefore ascribed only literal meanings to those terms. Under international human-rights law, the term "abuse" is usually applied in reference to acts committed by individuals against other individuals rather than by states.[64] In human-rights and international humanitarian law, the terms "breaches," "grave breaches," and "serious violations" and "gross violations" are used more generally to describe certain types of violations or abuses.

International humanitarian law refers to "violation" of the Geneva Conventions, which prohibit the targeting of civilians and unarmed populations in armed conflict. Human-rights law and international humanitarian law bind states to certain obligations. The assumption here is that an individual cannot violate the human rights of another person. However, some violations of international humanitarian law, such as war crimes, are applicable to individuals.

A state may sometimes be held responsible for acts or omissions that constitute violations or abuses when those acts or omissions are committed by individuals or groups under the control of the state or for whom the state bears some responsibility. Furthermore, it is increasingly possible to attribute violations and abuses of human-rights and international humanitarian law to non-state actors, even when those actors are not parties to human-rights and international humanitarian law treaties. The commission concluded that this was strictly the intention of the TRC Act when it referred to "perpetrators of human rights violations and abuses" in the Memorandum of Objects and Reasons.[65] The reference in the act to child perpetrators of abuses and violations strengthened this conclusion; so did the charge to the commission to determine whether the violations and abuses were a result of deliberate planning, policy, or authorization of any government, group, or individual.

The act limited the collation of the impartial historical record to violations and abuses that occurred during the "armed conflict in Sierra Leone."[66] However, the act also enjoined the commission to consider the role of internal *and* external actors in the conflict. The commission decided that violations and abuses committed outside Sierra Leone were relevant to its work to the extent that those violations and abuses were related to the armed conflict in Sierra Leone. In trying to understand the violations that occurred during the conflict, the commission considered how the RUF had gone about recruiting its earliest members inside Liberia. The forced recruitments and the terrible initiation and training programs contributed to these members' dehumanization and turned them into animals with scant regard for human life.

The act also provided a time frame for the commission's work. In this regard it referred to the beginning of the conflict in 1991 and to the signing of the Lomé Peace Agreement. The commission interpreted this section quite broadly. In its view there was nothing in the act to prevent it from looking deeper into the past (i.e., prior to 1991) or beyond Lomé. The commission believed that if it was to prevent a repetition of the violations and abuses, it would have to go back to the colonial period to understand what led the country to 1991, and it could not remain blind to the events that had transpired since Lomé.

With regard to the aspect of the mandate dealing with impunity, the commission adopted the Joinet Principles,[67] which have three components: the victim's right to know, the victim's right to justice, and the victim's right to reparations.

According to Joinet, the right to know means "the inalienable right to the truth": "Every people has the inalienable right to know the truth about past events and about the circumstances and reasons which led, through the consistent pattern of gross violations of human rights, to the perpetration of aberrant crimes. Full and effective exercise of the right to the truth is essential to avoid any recurrence of such acts in the future."[68]

This "right to the truth" also includes a duty to remember. Knowledge of the history of oppression is part of a people's heritage and should be preserved through appropriate measures as part of the state's duty to remember. This will preserve the collective memory from extinction and guard against the development of revisionist and negationist arguments. Joinet also contends that victims have a right to know. Also, families and dear ones have the right to know the circumstances of violations and, if death or disappearance is the result, the fate of the victims.[69]

Joinet also describes "extrajudicial commissions of inquiry" such as truth commissions as having a special role to play in facilitating the right to the truth.[70] In confronting impunity, therefore, truth commissions are better equipped than other approaches because they are better at responding to the need for truth seeking.

Regarding the second category, 'the right to justice," Joinet argues that this implies that any victim can assert his rights and receive a fair and effective remedy, including obtaining reparations and seeing that his oppressor stands trial.[71] There can be no just and lasting reconciliation without an effective response to the need for justice; as a factor in reconciliation, forgiveness—a private act—implies that the victim must know the perpetrator of the violations and that the latter has shown repentance. For forgiveness to be granted, it must first have been sought.[72]

As the commission observed on this issue, there are post-conflict societies in which victims have been denied access to traditional justice yet in which reconciliation is still quite possible. Examples include Namibia and Mozambique. Following the civil wars in these countries, the state did not establish any accountability mechanisms to respond to the human-rights violations that had taken place. Rather, these countries moved to establish constitutional frameworks in which such violations would no longer be permissible. By focusing on and constructing a future based on a constitutional order, all these states sought to draw a line between a past marked by human-rights violations and other atrocities and a future guaranteeing full protections to the citizenry. When the perpetrators of violence are dead, justice cannot be a reliable option. Sankoh and his chief lieutenant, Sam Bockarie—alias Mosquito or "Maskita"—both died before they could face justice. Applying Joinet's principle, does this mean that there can be no reconciliation in Sierra Leone? The commission appropriately departed from him on this point. Joinet's argument raises the further issue of the nature and timing of justice. Whose responsibility is it to determine the nature of the justice a society should impose? What is appropriate in a given context: retributive or restorative justice? In what circumstance can either or both of these be implemented? What factors enable a state to choose an approach? Sierra Leone did not have the luxury of choice, as the decision had been made for it by those members of the international community which provided the funding for the transitional justice mechanisms. The preferences of ordinary Sierra Leoneans did not count, given their national experience and conflict-resolution processes. More important for the commission was that in many cases it was impossible to determine who the perpetrators were. Bands of combatants had moved through communities committing atrocities against civilians. Most of the victims found it difficult to identify individual perpetrators—all they could do was guess their affiliation. So the community had no choice but to move on. This meant that the search for justice had to follow restorative processes without rendering individual apologies or offering forgiveness.

Joinet sees the third category, the "right to reparation," as having several elements. These include restitution (seeking to restore the victim to his or her previous situation), compensation for physical or mental injury (including lost opportunities, physical damage, defamation, and legal costs), and rehabilitation (medical care, including psychosocial and psychiatric treatment).[73]

In accordance with the TRC Act, the commission was to provide information or make recommendations to or regarding the Special Fund for War Victims provided for in the Lomé Peace Agreement and to assist that fund in any manner it deemed appropriate.[74] The act also required the commission to make recommendations on reforms and other measures—legal, political, administrative, or otherwise—that might be required in order to achieve the commission's object—namely, "the object of providing impartial historical record, preventing the repetition of the violations and abuses suffered, addressing impunity, responding to the needs of victims and promoting healing and reconciliation."[75]

In responding to the mandate to promote healing and reconciliation, the commission believed that its principal activities—taking statements and conducting hearings—provided people with a forum for private and public acts of reconciliation. The commission facilitated private and public exchanges between victims and their perpetrators; these resulted in various expressions of remorse and a desire among the parties to reconcile. By establishing district support committees and partnering with the Inter-Religious Council of Sierra Leone, the commission hoped to lay the foundations for lasting reconciliation in the country.

The TRC Act did not refer to reparations. However, the Lomé agreement required the commission to "recommend measures to be taken for the rehabilitation of victims of human rights violations."[76] The commission in its report made some recommendations for reparations in fulfillment of the mandate to promote healing and reconciliation.

On the aspect of the mandate that required the commission to prevent a repetition of violations and abuses, the commission interpreted this as a mandate to look into the future and make proposals on governance. The commission believed that it had discharged this aspect of the mandate with its recommendations on institutional and other reforms. The TRC Act charged the government to move expeditiously on the commission's recommendations. The use of the word "shall" in the act strongly suggested to the commission that Parliament envisaged that its recommendations would be binding. However, the commission did not want to saddle the government with all kinds of recommendations. So it established three categories of recommendations. Some were imperative—that is, they were *binding* on the government—and the commission hoped that they would be implemented as quickly as possible. These particular recommendations would establish and uphold human rights and values.

The second category encompassed recommendations that the government *should work toward* fulfilling, such as to amend the customary laws that are embedded in the constitution, many of which offend the human-rights protections offered by the same constitution and also violate the state's international obligations. Regarding this category the government was expected to take steps that would allow these recommendations to be met eventually. Such recommendations might require in-depth planning and a marshalling of resources. No time frame was set for their implementation. The final category included recommendations that the government *should seriously consider*. Here the government was expected to thoroughly evaluate the recommendations but was under no obligation to implement them. The commission acknowledged that the funds and skills available in the country to implement this third category were limited. In addition, the commission made several recommendations directed at bodies that were not part of the government, such as NGOs and members of the international community. The commission's recommendations could not bind these bodies, so instead it "called on" them to implement the respective recommendations.[77]

The commission believed that preventing repetition must also involve an attitudinal change at the individual and collective levels. The commission established a project called "National Vision for Sierra Leone." This was an attempt to provide Sierra Leoneans with a platform for ongoing reflection and dialogue on the conflict and on the kind of society they wanted for their children, in the hope that they would be able to mobilize their resources and energies to work toward that vision. The National Vision campaign provided a fillip to the development of a transformational and economic development agenda for the country titled "Sweet Salone: Vision 20202 Agenda" (2005).

The Special Court

International criminal tribunals are important means for dealing with the past. They may differ in basic ways in terms of design and mandate, but they share the same purpose: to help foster peace by dispensing justice and re-establishing the rule of law. International criminal tribunals contribute to transitional justice in a country in a number of ways, including these:

By establishing the facts and the truth. A society can only develop lasting peace if it addresses its past effectively. Establishing the past is an important step toward finding the truth. Facts, once they come to light, prevent the creation of legends and rumours, lies and myths, heroes and martyrs, that could be exploited in the future. International criminal tribunals are similar to truth commissions: they help establish the objective facts of some of the terrible crimes that were committed during the period under investigation. In this way they enable societies to reflect on their past so as to construct a better future.

By individualizing guilt. Crimes are not committed by unknown entities. They are committed by individuals who are personally responsible for their conduct. When a conflict was driven by national, ethnic, or religious motives, it is even more important to acknowledge that the ultimate responsibility for crimes, however serious, is not with a group—rather, it rests with individuals. Criminal procedures establish the guilt or otherwise of individuals. In this way a sense of collective guilt is avoided that might otherwise threaten the development of a peaceful society.

By fostering a culture of accountability. When terrible atrocities are committed, it is usually while a climate of impunity exists. The perpetrators are likely to commit more violence when they believe their behaviour will not be punished or sanctioned. And in such a climate, the targets of violence may feel justified in resorting to violence themselves in order to exact revenge. Impunity undermines societies by encouraging further violence. The activities of international criminal tribunals help break this cycle.

By restoring confidence and restating the law. Societies facing a legacy of past abuses are often characterized by a loss of confidence in authorities and institutions. It follows that the transition from war to peace or from despotism to democracy—as well as the reconstruction of the state, which is often necessary at such times—is a difficult undertaking. An international criminal tribunal can support such processes by sending several strong messages. It can show that the international community is interested in what is happening in the country. It can also make it clear that the law still stands and will be applied. Furthermore, messages like these indicate that the law will be applied without discrimination and in accordance with an orderly procedure that is fair to everyone involved.

By restoring the dignity of both victims and perpetrators. War accompanied by violations of human rights can be traumatizing. International criminal tribunals do not offer an encompassing therapy. However, they do give victims the opportunity to be recognized, and this can help restore their dignity and humanity. Perpetrators also need to see their dignity restored. This is especially the case for child soldiers who have committed war crimes. There may be other categories of perpetrators who were also victims. International criminal tribunals usually focus on those who bear the greatest responsibility and do not deal directly with the "perpetrator-victims." By revealing some of the underlying mechanisms of violence in a particular conflict, the tribunals can help low-level perpetrators address their own role and responsibility more successfully. Where this process fails, perpetrators tend to blame their victims, thereby adding to their victimization.

By preventing violence. It has not been established—it can only be speculated—that international criminal tribunals prevent the recurrence of violence. Preventive effects work indirectly. International criminal tribunals may contribute to a climate of accountability in which violence is no longer an attractive approach to resolving conflicts.

It is debatable whether President Kabbah considered all of the above when he sent his letter to the UNSC on June 12, 2000, requesting that the council establish a court to try the RUF and its minions who had endangered the peace process.

What *was* obvious was that by the end of the war, Sierra Leone's judiciary lacked the capacity to hold perpetrators accountable for the crimes they had committed. The country's judiciary had long been plagued by corruption and political manipulation. Criminal suspects were detained for long periods, many of them without the due process guarantees laid out in the

Sierra Leonean constitution. There were not enough judges, magistrates, and prosecutors. Courtrooms and police stations had been destroyed during the war, and few Sierra Leonean families had come out of the war unscathed. So there was general concern about the judiciary's capacity to handle criminal trials of the RUF combatants.

President Kabbah therefore wanted a court along the lines of the International Criminal Tribunal for the former Yugoslavia (ICTY) and the International Criminal Tribunal for Rwanda (ICTR). Such a court would have been a creation of the UNSC—in other words, an international court; this in turn would have meant that all UN member countries would be obliged to respect and act on its summonses. The UNSC demurred, opting instead for a court to be established by treaty between the UN and the Government of Sierra Leone. The treaty was formalized by the Parliament through the Special Court Agreement 2002 (Ratification) Act 2002.

The Special Court is quite different from the ICTY and the ICTR. Its design reflects an attempt to draw lessons from the experiences of the ICTY and ICTR, which were established in 1993 and 1994 respectively. Those two tribunals have been criticized for their slow pace, prosecution strategies, high operating costs, and lack of connection to the societies in which the crimes were committed.[78]

Mandate of the Court

According to the Statute of the Court, the Special Court has the power to prosecute persons who bear the greatest responsibility for serious violations of international humanitarian law and Sierra Leonean law committed in the territory of Sierra Leone since 30 November 1996 [when the Abidjan peace agreement was signed], including those leaders who, in committing such crimes, have threatened the establishment of and implementation of the peace process in Sierra Leone.[79]

The crimes for which persons can be prosecuted include the following:

- Crimes committed as part of a widespread systematic attack against any civilian population, such as murder, extermination, enslavement, deportation, imprisonment, torture, rape, enforced pregnancy (and any other form of sexual slavery), and other inhumane acts.[80]
- Violations of Article 3 Common to the Geneva Conventions and of Additional Protocol 11. These include violence to life, including murder and cruel treatment such as torture, mutilation, or any form of corporal punishment; collective punishments; the taking of hostages and acts of terrorism; and—finally—the passing of sentences and carrying out of executions without judgment having been pronounced by a regularly constituted court affording all the judicial guarantees that are recognized as indispensable by civilized peoples.[81]

- Other serious violations of international humanitarian law, such as intentionally directing attacks against civilian populations (which also encompasses individual civilians who are not taking direct part in hostilities); intentionally directing attacks against personnel, installations, material, units, or vehicles involved in humanitarian assistance or a peacekeeping mission in accordance with the UN Charter; conscripting or enlisting children under the age of fifteen into armed forces or groups or using them to participate actively in hostilities.[82]
- Crimes against Sierra Leonean law, such as offences relating to the abuse of girls; abusing a girl under thirteen years of age; abducting a girl for immoral purposes; offences relating to the wanton destruction of property, such as setting fire to dwelling houses and persons therein; and setting fire to public buildings or to other buildings.[83]

The indictments issued by the court were the clearest evidence of prosecutorial strategy. By November 2003, thirteen had been issued and ten of the indictees were already in the court's custody: Foday Sankoh, the founder and former leader of the RUF; Issa Sesay, who had replaced Sankoh as RUF leader; Augustine Gbao and Morris Kallon, senior RUF commanders; Alex Tamba Brima, Ibrahim "Bazzy" Kamara, and Santigie Kanu, senior members of the Armed Forces Revolutionary Council (AFRC); Sam Hinga Norman, national coordinator of the CDF and Minister of Internal Affairs and National Security at the time of his arrest; Moinina Fofanah, Director of War for the CDF; and Allieu Kondewa, Chief Initiator and High Priest of the Kamajors. Three other indictees were still at large: Sam "Mosquito" Bockarie, former Battlefield Commander of the RUF, had been killed in Liberia in 2004; Johnny Paul Koroma, head of the AFRC, is still at large; and Charles Taylor, former President of Liberia, is standing trial in The Hague.

All were charged with war crimes, crimes against humanity, and other serious violations of international humanitarian law. The crimes charged included murder, rape, extermination, acts of terror, enslavement, looting and burning, sexual slavery, conscription of children into an armed force, and attacks on peacekeepers and humanitarian workers.[84]

The indictments focused on the leaders of the three main armed groups that had fought in the civil war. The prosecutor has alluded repeatedly to the financiers who pulled the strings behind the war but has not issued any other indictments since the thirteen listed above.

The prosecutor quickly doused speculation that he would be indicting children who had committed violations of human rights and have them tried by the court—an issue that had generated intense debate within the country and in human-rights circles. No children were subsequently indicted. And on Human Rights Day in 2002 he declared that he would not be seeking any evidence from the TRC[85]—an inflammatory issue that had long been agitating commentators on Sierra Leone's transitional justice process. The fear that testimony from the TRC would be handed over to the court was one of many challenges the TRC encountered as a result of the contemporaneous existence of both institutions. Ex-combatants were afraid that testimony given before the TRC would be used by the Special Court to prosecute their former commanders and comrades. The prosecutor's statement was timely but did not end the confusion surrounding the relationship between the court and the commission.

Dispensing Justice

There has been criticism of the court's interpretation of its mandate.[86] The court's statute states that individuals may be found responsible for crimes under the authority of the court where they either:

6(1) planned, instigated, ordered, committed or otherwise aided and
abetted in the planning, preparation or execution of a crime, or
(2) knew or had reason to know that a subordinate was about to commit
such acts or had done so and the superior had failed to take the
necessary and reasonable measures to prevent such acts or to punish
the perpetrators thereof.[87]

Responsibility under 6(2) is referred to as "command responsibility." However, persons who are individually responsible may only be prosecuted if they also bear the "greatest responsibility" for the crimes indicated in Article 1 of the statute.

Those indicted by the court have been characterized as the highest-level commanders in the CDF, the AFRC, and the RUF—that is, the ones who directed the various factions in the war. They therefore "knew or had reason to know" that crimes were being committed and may even have participated directly in atrocities.

Human Rights Watch has argued that these indictments reflect an excessively narrow interpretation of the mandate to prosecute "those who bear the greatest responsibility."[88] That group contends that the mandate should be interpreted to include regional or mid-level commanders who stood out among their colleagues of similar rank for the exceedingly brutal terrorist acts they committed against civilians.[89]

Staff of the court have resisted a broadened interpretation of the mandate so as to prosecute regional and mid-level commanders. Early in the life of the court, the widely held view was that it should try no more than twenty-five to thirty people. The court is now entering its seventh year and has concluded only three sets of trials. In part this is because it has consolidated the cases against the leaders of the RUF, the AFRC, and the CDF into group trials. There is no likelihood that it will issue further indictments. A large majority of the perpetrators—many of whom have been identified in the TRC report—are unlikely to face prosecution, as no other indictments have been issued by the court, which is now in the process of winding down its activities.

An important innovation in criminal justice pioneered by the court is the establishment of the Defence Office. It provides initial legal advice through duty counsel; legal assistance if the accused does not have sufficient means to pay for it or as the interests of justice may require; and facilities for counsel to prepare the defence. The office was created partly in response to difficulties encountered during the ad hoc tribunals, including issues of overpayment of defence counsel and fee splitting between the accused and the defence. At present, all of the indictees are being defended by counsel paid for by the court. The defence teams have repeatedly complained about the lack of logistical support and other resources; they allege that this has constrained their ability to mount a vigorous defence for their clients. Specific issues include the lack of suitable investigators, the use of inexperienced staff by the defence office, the lack of equipment and storage facilities, limited office space, limited opportunity to receive additional compensation for necessary work, and the limited training offered to defence teams. While efforts have been made to address some of these concerns, they have not been resolved to the satisfaction of the defence teams.[90]

The court has also been criticized for being slow to rule on motions, especially as those motions relate to the rights of the accused. In one instance, a decision denying bail was handed down almost four months after the initial application.[91] In another, a decision on a request to modify the conditions of detention took about four months to resolve.[92] Criminal prosecution is still time consuming, in part because the courts guarantee the right of accused persons to exhaust all available remedies. According to Human Rights Watch, judges in the Appeals Chamber took eight to nine months (from June 2003 to March 2004) to rule on three motions challenging the court's jurisdiction on the basis of the Lomé Peace Agreement, lack of judicial independence, and lack of constitutionality.[93]

Other criticisms centred on the treatment of witnesses and courtroom management. Judges are alleged to have made disparaging remarks about the "degree of intelligence of a witness"; to have laughed at the illiteracy of a witness; to have requested that a witness whose arms had been amputated raise them to demonstrate; and to have stated the name of a child witness in open court. Also, trials have been scheduled in ways that do not reflect efficient use of time and resources.[94] Sittings do not last for full days, and opportunities to consolidate motions are not explored.

The trials have now mostly been concluded, except for Charles Taylor's trial, which is taking place in The Hague. So it is possible to begin examining how the court has contributed to reconciliation and sustainable peace in Sierra Leone.

A trenchant criticism of the court comes from a Sierra Leonean historian, Lansana Gberie, who has questioned the system of justice that prosecutes "and persecutes" heroes as an intellectually slovenly contrivance. He contends that the Special Court, by prosecuting people like Hinga Norman, has profaned the very concept of international humanitarian justice. He notes that the most "important" indictees (Sankoh, Bockarie, Koroma, Norman) have died or disappeared and that the remaining eight in custody "are virtually politically unknown, and their fate of very little concern to the wider public in Sierra Leone. The idea that their trial would have any valence with respect to impunity, in other words, is totally moot, indeed highly unlikely."[95] This criticism reflects the frustration and anger that many Sierra Leoneans feel regarding the indictment of Hinga Norman, whom they perceive as a war hero and a liberator. Also, they have noted that the same treatment is being meted out to villains *and* heroes.

Conclusion

The contribution that criminal tribunals make to reconciliation has not been proven. They offer justice to victims and may contribute to victims' willingness to put the past behind them. The assumption is that once the perpetrator has been punished, the victim may feel restored and thus more inclined to participate in reconciliation.

It is not clear how reconciliation is linked to trials before criminal tribunals. Criminal prosecutions are suffused with uncertainty. Thirteen indictments were issued by the Special Court. The most important indictees and actors during the conflict are dead or have disappeared. Sierra Leoneans argue that those facing trial are the "second eleven," not those who bear the greatest responsibility for the violations and abuses that occurred. With the deaths of these people, the full truth about what happened during the conflict may never be known. So it is risky to assume that reconciliation can be achieved based on the successful conclusion of criminal prosecution.

Restorative processes such as truth commissions allow the possibility of broader inquiry into the violations and abuses that occurred. The Sierra Leone TRC was effective in catalyzing dialogue in many communities and laying the foundations for healing and reconciliation in the country. TRC's are expensive processes and unless well funded may be unable to meet their full potential. Transitional justice in Sierra Leone was shaped and affected by the determination of some key countries in the international community to demonstrate that Special Courts are better suited than other international tribunals to punish crimes against humanity and other international crimes.

In addition, there was a clear effort to arrest armed insurrection and civil war in West Africa by apprehending and prosecuting Charles Taylor. This subregional focus affected transitional justice in Sierra Leone through haphazard funding for the TRC and a focus on the Special Court as the more important mechanism. In this respect, the TRC is unfinished business. The Special Court and the TRC have provided some accountability for the violations and abuses that occurred during the civil war in that country. In that context, they have made some contribution toward consolidating peace, security, and rule of law in the country. The real journey to reconciliation and healing in Sierra Leone will need to be taken up by the government and civil society with more vigour and commitment so that the outstanding issues contained in the recommendations of the TRC can be substantively dealt with. Only then will we be able conclude that Sierra Leone is on the path toward sustainable peace and development.

Notes

1 Section 6, Truth and Reconciliation Commission Act of Sierra Leone (2000).
2 "Historical Antecedents," *Witness to Truth: Report of the Sierra Leone Truth and Reconciliation Commission*, vol. 3A (Accra: Graphic Packaging Company, 2004), 5.
3 *Witness to Truth*: vol. 3A, 6.
4 See generally C. Fyfe, C.; *A Short History of Sierra Leone* (London: Longman, 1962).
5 "Historical Antecedents," *Witness to Truth*, vol. 3A, 12.
6 Ibid.
7 Ibid., 13.
8 Ibid. See also J.D. Kandeh, "Politicisation of Ethnic Identities in Sierra Leone," *African Studies Review* (1992): 7.
9 Ibid., 18. See also J.R. Cartwright, *Politics in Sierra Leone* 1947–1967 (Toronto: University of Toronto Press, 1970).
10 Ibid., 136.
11 E. Conteh-Morgan and M. Dixon-Fyle, *Sierra Leone at the End of the Twentieth Century: History, Politics, and Society* (New York: Peter Lang, 1999), 69.
12 Ibid., 24.
13 See "Submission by the All Peoples Party to the TRC," April 2003. Copy in author's possession.
14 Conteh-Morgan and Dixon-Fyle, *Sierra Leone at the End of the Twentieth Century*, 79–83.
15 Submission to the Truth and Reconciliation Commission by the Sierra Leone People's Party (SLPP), April 2003.
16 Alhaji Daramy Rogers, former minister of the APC government. Interview with the TRC, October 24–29, 2003. See also Francis Garbidon, ombudsman, testimony before the TRC, June 2003.
17 See Chapter 111, Section 21(4), of the 1978 Constitution of the Republic of Sierra Leone.
18 "Historical Antecedents," *Witness to Truth*, vol. 3A, 57.
19 Ibid., 29–30.
20 Ibid., 57.
21 Garbiddon, submission to the TRC, June 2003, in ibid., 68.
22 Siaka Stevens, a Limba from the North, rose to prominence as a labour leader. He exploited this relationship to build a formidable political party with strong ties to proletarian groups

such as market men and women, teachers, clerks, the unemployed, and artisans. The Krio found in him a willing ally in fending off Mende domination of the politics of the country. This coalition of forces was sufficient to give his party, the APC, the majority in the 1967 general elections.

23 Most Sierra Leonean writers on the conflict agree that Stevens's virulent despotism made peaceful change impossible. See for example, Joe Alie, Lansana Gberie, and Ibrahim Abdulla.

24 A Lebanese businessman, Jamil Said Mohammed, whose Precious Mineral Mining Company had been given a large diamond concession by Siaka Stevens, and who controlled a large part of Sierra Leone's mining industry.

25 For more details on the rent-seeking orientation of the APC government, see W. Reno, *Corruption and State Politics in Sierra Leone* (Cambridge: Cambridge University Press, 1995), 57.

26 The TRC report cites several witnesses who testified that Momoh's APC government used rice as a political weapon.

27 Pan-Africanist ideas and writings and the songs of Bob Marley—accompanied by generous doses of Indian hemp—provided the intellectual foundations for these discussions.

28 *Witness to Truth*, vol. 3A, 93.

29 Ibid.

30 Ibid.

31 V.I. Reider, testimony before the TRC. See *Witness to Truth*, Vol. 3A, 94.

32 Ibid., 94–95.

33 See *Witness to Truth*, vol. 3B, Chapter 3, for a full discussion of the conflict's political history.

34 Ibid., Chapter 2, for a full discussion of the nature of the conflict.

35 Address of the British High Commissioner, Peter Penfold, to the April 1999 National Consultative Conference, reported in *The Road to Peace: Report of National Consultative Conference on the Peace Process in Sierra Leone* (Freetown: National Commission for Democracy and Human Rights, April 1999), 5–54.

36 Ibid.

37 Michael O'Flaherty, "Sierra Leone's Peace Process: The Role of the Human Rights Community," unpublished manuscript in possession of the present author.

38 "Military and Political History of the Conflict," *Witness to Truth*, vol. 3A, 356.

39 Ibid., 358.

40 The TRC report comprehensively captures the intrigues by the government and its allied militia groups to confront Sankoh. They took advantage of this protest to start a gunfight. Sankoh was later blamed for ordering his troops to shoot at the protesters. See TRC, *Witness to Truth*, vol. 3A, pp. 364–420.

41 Ibid.

42 Letter dated June 12, 2000. A copy of letter is in the possession of the present author.

43 Ibid.

44 Letter dated August 9, 2000, from the Permanent Representative of Sierra Leone to the United Nations, addressed to the President of the Security Council, Annex, UN Doc. S/2000/786.

45 See UN Doc.S/RES/1315 (2000).

46 See "Report of the Secretary General on the establishment of a Special Court for Sierra Leone," UN Doc. A/2000/915.

47 Section 1(1) of the Statute of the Special Court 2002.

48 Agreement dated December 27, 2001. A copy is in the possession of the present author. The agreement dealt with issues such as the composition of the court and the appointment of the judges; the appointment of the prosecutor, deputy prosecutor, and registrar; the court premises and its expenses; and the seat of the court and its juridical capacity.

49 See the Special Court (Ratification and Enforcement) Act, 2002.

50 M. O'Flagherty, "Sierra Leone's Peace Process: The Role of the Human Rights Community," unpublished manuscript in possession of the author.

51 See ss. 3(1) and (2) of the TRC Act.

52 Section 6, TRC Act 2000.

53 See s. 7(1) of the TRC Act.

54 See s. 7(2) of the TRC Act.

55 Section 15(2), TRC Act 2000.

56 See "Memorandum of Objects and Reasons," TRC Act 2000.

57 See Memorandum of Objects and Reasons attached to the act.

58 Speech by Alhaji Dr. Ahmad Tejan Kabbah, President of Sierra Leone, at the inauguration of the commission, July 5, 2002, Freetown.

59 "Mandate," *Witness to Truth*, vol. 1, 31.

60 TRC, *Witness to Truth*, vol. 1, 30.

61 See Article XXVI(1).

62 Ibid.

63 See ss. 6 and 7 of the act. See also the Memorandum of Objects and Reasons.

64 See the Protocol to the African Charter of Human and Peoples' Rights on the Rights of Women in Africa, adopted in July 2003, which uses the term in several provisions.

65 "Mandate," *Witness to Truth*, vol. 1, 36.

66 See s. 6(1).

67 Louis Joinet, Special Rappatteur of the UN Sub-Commission for the Promotion and Protection of Human Rights, *Question of the Impunity of Perpetrators of Human Rights Violations (Civil and Political)*, final report prepared pursuant to Sub-Commission Decision 1996/119, UN Doc. E/CN.4/Sub.2/1997/20.

68 Ibid.

69 "Mandate," *Witness to Truth*, vol. 1, 44.

70 Louis Joinet, in ibid.

71 Ibid.

72 Ibid.

73 Ibid.

74 See s. 7(6) of the act and Article XXIV of the Lomé Peace Agreement.

75 See s. 15(2) of the act.

76 See Lome Peace Agreement Between the Government of Sierra Leone and the Revolutionary United Front, Article XXIV; see also Section 15(2) of the TRC Act.

77 TRC, Witness to Truth, vol. 2, 119–21.

78 International Centre for Transitional Justice, The Special Court for Sierra Leone: *The First Eighteen Months*, Case Study Series, New York, March 2004, 8.

79 Article 1, Statute of the Special Court for Sierra Leone 2002.

80 See Article 2 of the Statute.

81 Ibid.

82 Ibid.

83 See Articles 1, 2, 3, 4, and 5 of the Statute of the Special Court.

84 http://www.sc-sl.org.

85 See Statement by Prosecutor on the Occasion of the Joint Appearance with the Chairman of the TRC on Human Rights Day, Freetown, December 12, 2002. A copy of the statement is in the possession of the present author.

86 Human Rights Watch, "Bringing Justice: The Special Court for Sierra Leone—Accomplishments, Shortcomings, and Needed Support," vol. 16 (September 2004), 19–21.

87 See Article 6 of the Statute of the Special Court.

88 Human Rights Watch, "Bringing Justice," 20.

89 Ibid.

90 Interview with a member of the defence team of Augustine Gbao, Freetown, February 14, 2007.

91 Decision on the Motion by Morris Kallon for Bail (Sesay, Kallon, Gbao) (Trial Chamber), February 24, 2004.

92 Decision on Motion for Modification of the Conditions of detention (Norman) (Trial Chamber), November 26, 2004.

93 Human Rights Watch, "Bringing Justice," 14.

94 Ibid., 17.

95 Lansana Gberie, "Norman's Death and the Legacy of the Special Court." http://www.the patrioticvanguard.com/article.php3?id_article=1090, accessed on March 26, 2007.

Post-Conflict Peacebuilding
The Role of the UN Integrated Office in Sierra Leone (UNIOSIL)
Sunday Abogonye Ochoche

6

The UN Charter states that one of the organization's purposes is to maintain international peace and security. To that end, its mandate includes taking "effective collective measures for the prevention and removal of threats to the peace, and for the suppression of acts of aggression or other breaches of the peace" (Article 1). Also under the charter, primary responsibility for maintaining international peace and security rests with the UN Security Council. Over the years, the UN has adopted diverse strategies, including peacekeeping, to achieve its mandate to promote international peace and security. In Sierra Leone the UN deployed a large peacekeeping operation but then followed it up with the first-ever peacebuilding mission. This chapter reviews the contribution of the peacebuilding mission to peace and stability in Sierra Leone. It concludes that despite persistent challenges to the peacebuilding process, overall the mission has succeeded and will likely be a model for future missions.

UN Intervention in Sierra Leone

Sierra Leone suffered a civil conflict between March 1991 and January 2002. It was a vicious one even by the standards of a region notorious for conflicts, insecurity, and instability. It took the initial intervention of the Economic Community of West African States (ECOWAS) Ceasefire Monitoring Group (ECOMOG) and, later, the deployment of the UN Mission in Sierra Leone (UNAMSIL) to bring it to an end. UNSC Resolution 1270 (1999), which established UNAMSIL, had provided for a maximum of 6,000 troops, yet by October 2000 the actual numbers on the ground had reached 12,510.[1] By September 2001 the authorized strength was 17,500, with 16,664 deployed[2]—the largest UN peacekeeping operation in history.

Adebajo[3] has noted that based on a UN assessment mission sent to Sierra Leone in June 2000, UNAMSIL faced problems such as managerial deficiencies, lack of proper training and equipment, and a lack of common understanding of the mandate and rules of engagement. UNAMSIL also faced problems meeting some key targets, including the schedules for the critical task of disarmament. Adebajo adds, however, that on the whole, as a result of UNAMSIL's intervention, "by the end of June 2001, there appeared some glimmers of hope that peace might yet come to Sierra Leone ... Disarmament of the factions was completed by January 2002. Parliamentary and presidential elections are planned for May 2002. But ... the security situation ... still remains fragile."[4]

Lessons learned from past UN peacekeeping missions made it clear that an end to hostilities did not necessarily mean that a conflict had been resolved or that peace had been achieved. Indeed, the UN secretary-general's twenty-sixth report on UNAMSIL stated as much. While commending UNAMSIL's success, the report noted that "many root causes of the conflict in Sierra Leone are yet to be addressed. The long-term sustainability of the gains achieved so far will require sustained international involvement and support, especially through joint effort by the United Nations and the donor community."[5] Accordingly, the Security Council, by Resolution 1620 (2005)—later extended by Resolutions 1734 (2006) and 1793 (2007)—established the UN Integrated Office in Sierra Leone (UNIOSIL) to help the Government of Sierra Leone address the root causes of the conflict and help build and consolidate the peace.

Among others steps, Resolution 1620 mandated UNIOSIL to assist the national government in doing the following: build the capacity of state institutions to address further the root causes of the conflict; build the capacity of the National Electoral Commission (NEC) to conduct free, fair, and credible elections in 2007; enhance good governance, transparency, and accountability of public institutions; develop a national action plan for human rights and establish a national human rights commission; strengthen the rule of law; strengthen the security sector; promote a culture of peace, dialogue, and participation regarding critical national issues; and develop initiatives to protect youth, women, and children and promote their well-being.

In implementing its mandate, UNIOSIL has been guided mainly by, and has drawn from, overlapping and mutually reinforcing frameworks developed through inclusive and participatory processes of engagement with the Government of Sierra Leone and other stakeholders, which include civil society, international partners, and the private sector. These processes have included the Peace Consolidation Strategy (PCS),[6] adopted primarily to guide reconstruction and peacebuilding; the Poverty Reduction Strategy Paper (PRSP);[7] and the UN Development Assistance Framework (UNDAF).[8] Meanwhile, the Peacebuilding Commission (PBC) continues to provide an important platform for the government's engagement with international partners on peacebuilding.

The PCS is a joint effort of the Government of Sierra Leone and the UN. It involved extensive nationwide consultations in October and November 2005. This strategy reflects the key priorities outlined in UNSC Resolution 1620.

The PCS calls for support to build Sierra Leone's national capacities for preventing, managing, and resolving potentially violent threats. It also promotes national reconciliation and trust building through effective communication, dialogue, and attitudinal change in the hope of strengthening the resolve of Sierra Leoneans to continue to choose peace. The PCS groups the threats facing Sierra Leone into six categories: (1) continuing challenges to internal security, as well as insecurity emanating from a still turbulent sub-region; (2) challenges to a national dynamic of reconciliation; (3) lack of momentum for accountability; (4) weak respect for human rights and the rule of law; (5) a widespread sense of economic disempowerment; and (6) lack of a national infrastructure for peace.

The PRSP, adopted in June 2005 after extensive nationwide consultations, was the government's response to the threats that extreme poverty was posing to peace and security in Sierra Leone. It was built on three main pillars: (1) good governance, peace, and security; (2) food security, job creation, and growth; and (3) human development. There are strong linkages between the PCS and the PRSP: the PRSP provides the framework and guidelines for attaining poverty reduction and sustainable development; while the PCS aims to create conditions for implementing the PRSP—namely, by consolidating and sustaining peace and stability and by building and strengthening national institutions of democratic governance.

The UNDAF is the UN Country Team's (UNCT's) framework to support Sierra Leone's national effort to improve the lives of (especially) its most vulnerable citizens. The government itself is to lead this effort. In particular, taking into account all of the millennium development goals (MDGs), the UNDAF has developed five priorities: (1) governance and human rights; (2) shared growth, food security, and livelihoods; (3) maternal and child health care; (4) primary education, with special emphasis on girls' education; and (5) HIV/AIDS, tuberculosis, malaria, and related diseases.

The aim of the PBC's Sierra Leone Peacebuilding Framework is to "ensur[e] sustained attention of the international community in providing additional political, financial and technical support to the country's peace consolidation efforts."[9] That framework identifies the commitments made by both Sierra Leone and the PBC, "based on three main criteria: they are critical to avoiding relapse into conflict, they are short-to-medium-term in duration, and they require mutual action from the Government and other national stakeholders and Sierra Leone's international partners."[10]

UNIOSIL has been in place for about two-and-a-half years and has been highly praised by the international community and the Sierra Leone government for its work thus far. UNIOSIL's work in Sierra Leone is an example of best practices; its success stories need to be told. Enormous challenges remain—including poverty, corruption, high unemployment, and weak infrastructure and judiciary, to name just a few—but on the whole, political and democratization processes are taking hold, security-sector reforms are being consolidated, and human rights are being promoted and protected through processes of continued engagement with the government and people of Sierra Leone. Throughout the process, the international community has provided coordinated support.

The Security Situation

Sierra Leone has been stabilized, though the peace is still fragile. UNAMSIL has helped rebuild the Sierra Leone Police (SLP) and the Republic of Sierra Leone Armed Forces (RSLAF). As a result, it was possible to complete the transfer of primary responsibility for security to the Government of Sierra Leone as of September 23, 2004.[11]

The country continues to benefit from the peace-consolidation process in Liberia and from political progress in Guinea and Côte d'Ivoire. In Liberia in 2005 there was a highly successful election; since then the new government of President Ellen Johnson-Sirleaf, in concert with the international community, has been working quickly to consolidate peace in her country. This is of particular significance for Sierra Leone when one recalls how its armed conflict was first ignited: In March 1991 a little-known group calling itself the Revolutionary United Front (RUF), consisting of Sierra Leonean fighters and elements of the National Patriotic Front of Liberia (NPFL), attacked southeastern Sierra Leone from Liberia. A second rebel incursion, also from Liberia, was launched into Guinea in May and September 1999.[12] Given the close political, historical, and cultural ties among the countries of the Mano River Union (MRU), developments in one country can easily and quickly cross the border to other countries. This means that peace, too, can cross borders, which seems to be happening.

Internally, Sierra Leone is benefiting from a further strengthening of security-sector institutions, especially the SLP and the RSLAF, and from enhanced co-operation between those forces. This is encouraging; however, high levels of poverty and youth unemployment remain key challenges to Sierra Leone's fragile stability. Acknowledging this, the Government of Sierra Leone's PRSP states that "poverty ... became more pervasive and intensified during the 1990s ... About 82 percent of the population lived below the poverty line ... Since 1996, Sierra Leone has been ranked among the least developed in the UNDP Human Development Index, and is ranked bottom in the 2004 Index. The poverty situation is worsened by the rising incidence of HIV/AIDS, typhoid, malaria and communicable diseases, including tuberculosis."[13]

UNIOSIL's support for strengthened security has focused on capacity building through advice, mentoring, and training. The same program has provided basic logistics to the SLP, the RSLAF, and the Office of National Security (ONS), a new office tasked with overseeing and coordinating all of the country's security agencies. Between November 2006 and February 2007, UNIOSIL, the British Department for International Development (DFID), and the SLP together developed a national-security plan to ensure effective policing and security for voter registration and for the general elections of July 2007. During the same period, with the assistance of UNIOSIL and DFID, the SLP trained 2,200 police in crowd control and public-order management.[14] These trained police were deployed in urban areas identified as high-threat spots.[15] In collaboration with DFID and the PBF, UNIOSIL helped the SLP acquire crowd control equipment so that they would be ready for the elections. These initiatives contributed to the highly civil manner in which the SLP policed the 2007 elections.

UNIOSIL, in co-operation with the UN Development Programme (UNDP) and the British-led Justice Sector Development Program (JSDP),[16] organized training for the police on the basics of community policing; the goal here was to establish trust and co-operation between the police and the population in the context of the 2007 general elections. Today, UNIOSIL police advisers also provide strategic policy advice on skills development training in various specialized policing fields—beat patrolling, duty-officer supervision, intelligence gathering, crime management, human resources development, and the like. Most police advisers are deployed within the Provincial Advisory and Support (PRAST) framework in the Western Area and Lungi Airport as well as in Makeni, Bo, and Kenema, the headquarters of the northern, southern, and eastern areas, respectively.

The RSLAF is continuing to review its structure with support from DFID as well as the International Military Advisory and Training Team (IMATT), a British group that has been engaged to restructure and reform the armed forces. The review's task is to determine a structure for the armed forces that will be affordable in the long term, given the country's limited resources, while still allowing the country to defend itself. Ideally, the restructuring will lead to a further reduction of the armed forces, to be achieved through attrition and buyouts. The hope is to scale down from 10,300 to approximately 8,500 military personnel by 2010.[17] The ONS has been established to coordinate the workings of the security sector.

UNIOSIL liaises with the Sierra Leonean security sector. It reports on the security situation and makes recommendations concerning external and internal threats. UNIOSIL consults on security matters with IMATT as well as the UN missions in Liberia (UNMIL), Côte d'Ivoire (UNOCI), and, more generally, West Africa (UNOWA). One positive outcome of these collaborative efforts has been joint border patrols between the armed forces and security agencies of Sierra Leone and Liberia. A goal of these joint patrols is to strengthen co-operation between the security agencies of the two countries and to deter cross-border crimes.

The 2007 General Elections

The 2007 presidential and parliamentary elections were a watershed for the peace consolidation efforts in Sierra Leone. The elections faced many challenges: (1) they would be the first to be conducted by the national authorities since the end of the conflict; (2) the principal responsibility rested with two new commissions—the NEC and the Political Parties Registration Commission (PPRC); (3) the parliamentary election would be the first constituency-based one in more than two decades; (4) the elections would be held at the height of the rainy season, compounding the logistical problems; and (5) the SLP was inexperienced at providing the necessary level of security.

The first round of elections was held on August 11, 2007. It saw the All Peoples Congress (APC) winning a majority: 59 of the 112 seats in Parliament. The then ruling Sierra Leone Peoples Party (SLPP) won 43 seats, with the new entrant, the Peoples Movement for Democratic Change (PMDC), winning the remaining 10. Seven candidates participated in the presidential contest. Because none met the constitutional requirement of 55 percent of the vote to win outright, a runoff election was held on September 8 between the two leading candidates after the first round: Ernest Bai Koroma of the APC and Solomon Berewa of the SLPP. Koroma won, and was sworn in on September 17, 2007. The elections were judged by national and international independent observers to be among the most transparent and credible ever held in Africa. This will be the first smooth transition of leadership from one civilian president to another since Sierra Leone gained independence in April 1961.

UNIOSIL and the UNCT worked closely with the relevant agencies on all aspects of the election. With the support of UNIOSIL and the UNDP, the NEC carried out a boundary-delimitation exercise. This involved drawing the boundaries of the 112 parliamentary seats, applying the criteria of population and land mass, among others. On November 30, 2006, Parliament approved the report of the boundary-delimitation exercise. The registration of voters for the elections commenced on February 26, 2007, and was completed on March 18, on schedule. The UN provided the NEC with considerable policy, technical, and financial support for this exercise. For example, the UN expanded its electoral advisory team substantially; that team had reached its complete strength by early January 2007. The number of advisers to NEC headquarters rose to nineteen: fourteen technical advisers and five UN volunteers (UNVs).[18] These were complemented by twenty-eight UNVs deployed throughout the country to support local electoral offices. For all its complexity—including considerable logistical challenges and the NEC's limited operational capacity—the registration was a remarkable success: in all, 2.6 million eligible voters (91 percent) were registered. Women accounted for 48 percent of registered voters; 56 percent of registered voters were under the age of thirty-two.[19]

The PPRC was the newest and weakest of the election-administration agencies. It seems that there was limited understanding of and commitment to its role in the electoral process. Established in part to register, oversee, and manage relations among political parties, it suffered from a shortage of human and material resources. The staff went for months without salaries because of delays in the release of government funding. The PPRC also lacked the logistic support to travel outside Freetown to inspect party offices. UNIOSIL, the UNDP, and the U.S. Agency for International Development (USAID) provided the commission with considerable technical and financial assistance. The UNDP provided it with a full-time technical adviser. With support from UNIOSIL, the PPRC facilitated the development and signing, on 23 November 2006, by all the major political parties, of the Political Parties Code of Conduct. Therein the parties agreed to adhere to conditions conducive to the conduct of free, fair, and democratic elections in a climate of democratic tolerance, without fear of coercion, intimidation, or reprisals. Given the history of political violence and the level of political intolerance leading up to the 2007 elections, this was a significant development.

The NEC focused on monitoring the implementation of the Code of Conduct. In part, this entailed training and working with district committees, mediating disputes between political players, sensitizing paramount chiefs regarding their role in ensuring credible elections, and sensitizing political parties on the need to encourage women's participation in the elections. The commission established a Code Monitoring Committee with representatives from all stakeholders in order to monitor adherence to the code. To provide national coverage, district sub-committees were set up in April 2007. With support from UNIOSIL and the UNDP, all committee members were given training in mediation and conflict mitigation. The UN also supported the commission's engagement with the country's paramount chiefs, who were significant actors in the electoral process and who were a potential threat to free and credible elections, since they involved themselves in the electoral process, seeking to compel voters in their chiefdoms to align with their political preferences. Political parties complained several times that paramount chiefs were refusing to grant permission for rallies because they were not the chief's party of choice.

In a similar vein, on March 17, 2007, the Sierra Leone Association of Journalists, with the support of UNIOSIL and the UNDP, concluded a Media Code of Conduct under which the major national media agreed to self-restraint and monitoring of their performance by an independent panel. The media's adherence to this code was weaker than that of the political parties to their own, partly because the signing of it came much closer to the election and the self-regulatory mechanisms were not as developed and efficient. Indeed, the media's conduct so raised the political temperature that on September 1, 2007, the ONS and the PPRC convened a national consultative meeting regarding the media's impact on peace, security, and development. This conference was meant to help dampen the inflammatory messages being broadcast on radio stations, especially stations affiliated with the political parties. In general terms, the Codes of Conduct for both the media and the political parties served as critical frameworks that helped promote peace and reduce levels of violence during the election campaign. Also, UNIOSIL and the UNCT provided senior staff of the major political parties with training in conflict management and the dispute resolution. This helped the parties manage intra- and inter-party disputes in a less violent manner.

The campaign preceding the elections witnessed intense political activity, including frequent violent clashes between supporters of the SLPP and the APC/PMDC. Tensions were especially high in the east and south of the country, traditionally controlled by the SLPP, in those places where the APC and its electoral ally the PMDC were conducting their campaigns. UNIOSIL played a key role in facilitating dialogue and mediating differences among key political actors. The Executive Representative of the Secretary-General (ERSG) held several breakfast interparty dialogue sessions; these were attended by all registered political parties and did much to reduce tensions. On August 29, 2007, the ERSG arranged a meeting between the Advocacy Movement Network (AMNet), a coalition of key national and international civil-society organizations, and the APC and SLPP to discuss how to promote political tolerance. Also, on September 6 the ERSG facilitated separate meetings between the diplomatic community and the presidential candidates of the SLPP and APC during which the latter two recommitted themselves to peaceful elections. On 27 August, former president Kabbah, worried about the intensity of the clashes and sensing a danger to peace and security, threatened to impose a state of emergency in order to bring the situation under control. It is worth noting that despite the political tensions and violent clashes, not a single person died. Similarly, for a country just recovering from a major armed conflict, there were almost no cases of gunplay. This suggests that the disarmament process had succeeded and that the SLP handled the situation in a professional manner.

UNIOSIL coordinated the mobilization of international funding for the elections, which came to over 70 percent of the budget of approximately US$24.6 million and was managed by the UNDP through a basket fund.[20] Contributors to the fund included the EU (EU8 million), Japan (US$2.8 million), Denmark (DKr5 million), Ireland (EU1 million), and Britain (2.5 million sterling).[21] The government was able to meet only half its commitment of the balance of 30 percent. The shortfall of 15 percent was met from funds provided by the newly created UN Peace Building Fund.

Human Rights and Rule of Law and Gender Equality

In the areas of human rights and rule of law, UNIOSIL has worked hard to implement the recommendations of the Truth and Reconciliation Commission (TRC). With support from the Office of the High Commissioner for Human Rights (OHCHR) and UNIOSIL, Sierra Leone established a national Human Rights Commission in 2006.[22] The OHCHR and UNIOSIL provided technical assistance for the drafting of the law to establish the commission as well as for the naming of commissioners; they are also providing comprehensive training for the commission.

Through the advocacy of the UN Children's Fund (UNICEF), in December 2006 Sierra Leone launched a National Child Justice Strategy, which provides a framework for protecting the rights of children in the criminal justice system. To facilitate judiciary reforms, UNIOSIL embarked on a more structured engagement with all key partners in the justice sector. Accordingly, a Justice Sector Coordination Committee was established in February 2007, comprising the Justice Sector Development Program (JSDP), UNIOSIL, the UNDP, UNICEF, the International Committee of the Red Cross (ICRC), the UN Fund for Women (UNIFEM), and three key donors: DFID, the World Bank, and Irish Aid. This forum will coordinate activities in the justice sector to prevent any overlapping and duplication of interventions.

In 2006 UNIOSIL conducted a nationwide survey of the corrections system, including a review of the 1960 and 1961 National Prison laws, and made recommendations that are now being implemented. Among other things, those recommendations call for better training for corrections officers and for a review of laws considered out of date. UNIOSIL is also providing technical assistance to both the Constitutional Review Process and the Law Reform Commission on issues pertaining to human rights and rule of law.

The UN as a whole has prioritized gender equality by advocating actively for women's empowerment. In this regard, it has focused on greater participation by women in the electoral process; on the promotion of women's rights—including legislation to address sexual and gender-based violence; on support for the enforcement of legislation related to sexual and gender-based violence (in Sierra Leone, this includes building the capacity of the SLP's Family Support Unit); and on the promotion of women's economic empowerment.

UNIOSIL has been advocating for a more central role for women in the decision-making process. During the voter-registration process, UNIOSIL worked closely with the NEC to deliver specific messages aimed at women. UN Radio, in close collaboration with community radio stations, was utilized to enhance women's confidence and capacity to participate in the political process and to sensitize the population. Three regional workshops organized by the PPRC in Bo, Kenema, and Makeni, with technical and financial support from UNIOSIL and the UNDP, formulated a comprehensive strategy for increasing women's representation in key governance institutions, including Parliament and local councils. Participants included representatives of political parties, civil-society organizations, and women's advocacy groups.

The high registration of women during the voter-registration process was in part a result of these initiatives. It raised hopes that more women would participate in the democratic process. Unfortunately, at the end of the exercise, only 64 women out of 556 candidates won their party nominations, and there was no female presidential candidate. This contributed directly to a decrease in the number of elected women; only 16 out of 112 elected parliamentarians were women (compared to 18 in the previous Parliament).[23] In the same vein, only three out of twenty cabinet members are women. Women remain badly underrepresented in the state's political and decision-making processes. This circumstance has cultural, social, historical, and (in particular) economic causes; addressing those causes will require sustained efforts from all stakeholders.

Future Challenges

Despite the progress made since the end of the conflict in 2002 and UN support for development, Sierra Leone remains fragile. Tangible economic and social progress has been evasive. This is attributable in part to the collapse of public infrastructure, especially communications and energy; the weakness of the private sector, which has slowed down job creation; human-capital flight that accompanied the conflict; high-level corruption; and low foreign investment. Poverty remains entrenched, and socio-economic indicators remain among the lowest in Africa. According to the 2007 UNDP country report for Sierra Leone, "looking at the trends in global human development computed by UNDP every year since 1990, it is evident that despite its massive potential wealth, Sierra Leone is one of the poorest countries in the world. Since 1996, it has been ranked among the lowest in the UNDP Human Development Index. The 2006 UNDP Human Development Report ranks Sierra Leone 176 out of 177. Life expectancy at birth was 41 years in 2004 and adult literacy was estimated at 35%."[24]

Corruption remains an impediment to efficient and effective public services and has reduced the credibility of the political system. The country's ability to attract foreign investment—which is crucial to economic growth—hinges on progress in the fight against this menace. The government must do more to address this problem. The Transparency International Corruption Perception Index (TI-CPI),[25] which ranks countries in terms of the degree to which corruption is perceived to exist among public officials and politicians, scored Sierra Leone at 2.3 and 2.4 in 2004 and 2005 respectively. The country's performance deteriorated to 2.1 in both 2006 and 2007.[26] Put simply, Sierra Leone is among the most corrupt countries in the world.

The government of President Koroma has prioritized the fight against corruption. It has made some positive preliminary moves—for example, it has placed before Parliament the final audit reports for 2002, 2003, and 2004. Also, the government has approved a new national anticorruption strategy and promised to review the existing legislation with a view to ensuring the independence of the Anti-Corruption Commission (ACC). The revised anticorruption strategy has adopted a combination of measures in the fight against corruption. These include "prevention centered around public education on the forms and ills of corruption in our society … confrontation which includes exposure, investigation and prosecution of corrupt practices and delivering just punishment for proven offences of corruption; strengthening the Anti-Corruption Commission (ACC) so that it is effective in providing leadership in the fight against corruption; and cross-cutting institutional capacity strengthening as highlighted in the various public sector and civil service reforms."[27]

At the political level, considerable successes have been achieved so far. Even so, the political intolerance that reared its head during the 2007 election, and the violence of the recent past, suggest that the situation remains fragile and that more must be done to promote reconciliation as well as political rapprochement at the uppermost levels in the new government. In many ways the 2007 elections reignited a number of old regional and ethnic divides in Sierra Leone.

The conduct of peaceful and credible local-council elections on July 5, 2008, by the government, with strong support from the UN, will do much to strengthen local democracy, governance, and development. Just as during the 2007 general elections, UNIOSIL coordinated the mobilization of funds, which were managed by the UNDP through a basket fund. The UN also provided an electoral-assistance team to support the NEC; and UNIOSIL supported the security agencies in their efforts to provide effective security. The government urgently needs to address a series of related challenges—for example, it needs to defuse persisting tensions in some parts of the country (especially in the Mende-speaking areas of the south and east) so as to establish a safe and peaceful environment. It is hoped that the political parties and the government will use the elections to redress the acute gender imbalance in the political system and some of the challenges of power decentralization.

The report of the TRC is perhaps the most comprehensive assessment of the conflict in Sierra Leone. Its recommendations are valuable, and their implementation will be key to the achievement of sustainable peace in the country. Some samples of its findings:

> The central cause of the war was endemic greed, corruption and nepotism … Successive political elites plundered the nation's assets, including its mineral riches … Government accountability was non-existent … Many Sierra Leoneans, particularly the youth, lost all sense of hope in the future … The Sierra Leone civil war was characterized by indiscriminate

violence. It ... tore apart the very fabric of society ... Forced displace-
ments, abductions, arbitrary detentions and killings were the most common violations ... Successive governments abused the death penalty to
eliminate political opponents.[28]

The recommendations touch on all aspects of the conflict, from the protection of human rights, to reforming the security services, promoting good
governance, and fighting corruption, to reparations, reconciliation, and a national vision for Sierra Leone. Implementation has been slow so far and must
be accelerated. Some recommendations, such as the payment of reparations
to the war affected, have perhaps been blocked by the government's straitened
circumstances; but others, such as a strong campaign against corruption, have
perhaps been blocked because the political will is not there.

The Constitutional Review Commission (CRC) submitted its report to
President Koroma on January 10, 2008. So far the review has been selective,
even though the Lomé Peace Agreement of July 7, 1999—which provided
the framework for ending the conflict and launching the TRC—called for a
new constitution. The old constitution (1991) was generally viewed as not
reflecting the common aspirations of the people and as non-participatory in its
formulation process. In this regard, a number of the TRC's recommendations,
such as the abolition of the death penalty, have not been included in the
amendments proposed.

Sierra Leone remains one of the world's poorest countries. After years of
conflict and underdevelopment, most people are poor, the infrastructure is
weak, and opportunities are few. Five years after the formal end of the war
and the mounting of successful elections, Sierra Leoneans are beginning to
demand the dividends of peace and democracy. Expectations are high, and
the government is being pressured to make a concrete difference in people's
lives. However good its intentions, the government has a limited capacity to
meet its people's expectations.

UNIOSIL was the first UN post-conflict integrated office, and thus was in
itself an experimental project. There has been little past experience for it to go
by. The ERSG is the head of the mission and reports to the UN Secretary-General
through the Undersecretary-General of the Department of Peacekeeping; but
he is also the UN Resident Coordinator and UNDP Resident Representative.
He therefore is responsible for guiding the activities of the entire UN system
in the country and for coordinating the UN's work in an integrated manner to
achieve the organization's objectives in Sierra Leone. Considering that most of
the related agencies predated UNIOSIL and will outlive it in Sierra Leone, it
has sometimes been difficult for UNIOSIL to achieve horizontal collaboration
within the country team. After all, most of those agencies have been used to
vertical links with their headquarters.

But the greater challenges for UNIOSIL come from the state. Resolution 1620 called for UNIOSIL to support, not lead, in the areas with which it had been tasked. UNIOSIL was aware that leadership and ownership of the process belonged to the government. As it then turned out, a number of things were affected by government's weakened capacity. For example, as already mentioned, the two main electoral administration institutions, the NEC and the PPRC, took some time to find their feet because of their limited resources. UNIOSIL and other international partners had to mobilize to accelerate their work. The devolution of power to the local authorities—also an important recommendation of the TRC—has been considerably slowed by a lack of capacity at the level of local councils.

Political will is a factor in all of this. For example, the TRC found that "endemic corruption was a central factor that produced the dire conditions that made the civil war inevitable."[29] It further asserted that "real economic development is not possible, when corruption and bad governance are the order of the day."[30] Among other things, it recommended that public officials be made to declare their assets and that the ACC be given powers to prosecute corruption. These recommendations were not implemented. The powers of prosecution remained with the Attorney General, who showed no interest in taking on his political colleagues or any high-ranking officer. Also, the SLPP government saddled the ACC with a very ineffective leadership. Indeed, one of the major international partners of the government in the area of anti-corruption had to suspend its support to the ACC owing to lack of confidence in the leadership. And yet the ACC remained unreformed until the new APC government took power.

Great improvements have been made in human rights; that said, gender-based violence—including female genital mutilation (FGM)—remains a major problem. UNIOSIL has campaigned hard against this practice, but not much has changed, largely because no government has found the courage to address a culturally sensitive and politically suicidal issue. Indeed, during the 2007 electoral campaigns, some major political parties actually promoted FGM for their political gains.

Conclusion

UNIOSIL, the UN's first integrated peacebuilding mission, has overall been a great success. It has worked collaboratively with national and international entities to help address the root causes of the devastating conflict that Sierra Leone suffered. The political and security situation in the country is now reasonably stable. The conduct of the 2007 general elections indicated that Sierra Leone has come a long way and that democracy has a promising future there. But there remain key challenges that will require the ongoing support of the UN and other international partners. These include promoting sustainable democratic governance; strengthening national security; protecting the human rights of vulnerable groups; creating jobs (especially for youth); increasing the country's capacity to manage development and tackle human and income poverty; broadening political participation to include marginalized groups such as women and youth; accelerating the pace of social advancement; and reducing the heavy dependence on external development assistance.

Sierra Leone will need the continued support of the UN and international partners for a while longer in order to achieve lasting stability. The founding of UNIOSIL was in itself an acknowledgment of this need for sustained engagement. The mission winds down on September 30, 2008. As noted, there will still be a number of critical challenges left to address. Accordingly, the UN will be establishing a follow-on mission to succeed UNIOSIL. In October 2008 a new mission—the UN Integrated Peacebuilding Office in Sierra Leone (UNIPSIL)—will be formed. Among other things, UNIPSIL will be assigned the responsibility of "carrying forward the peacebuilding process, mobilizing international donor support, supporting the work of the Peacebuilding Commission and Fund, and completing any residual tasks left over from UNIO-SIL mandate, in particular promoting national reconciliation and supporting the constitutional reform process."[31] This is a further demonstration of the commitment of the UN and the international community to the peace, development, and stability of Sierra Leone. But this framework is not a Sierra Leone–specific initiative. It is also an indication of the UN's new approach to conflict management—one that emphasizes sustainable peacebuilding and the promotion of reconciliation in post-conflict societies.

Notes

1. UN Security Council S/RES/1270 (1999), October 22, 1999, 3.
2. Eleventh Report of the Secretary-General on the UN Mission in Sierra Leone, S/2001/857/Add.1, September 10, 2001, 1–2.
3. Adekeye Adebajo, "Building Peace in West Africa: Liberia, Sierra Leone, and Guinea-Bissau," International Peace Academy Occasional Paper (Boulder: Lynne Rienner, 2002), 100–1.
4. Ibid., 103.
5. Twenty-Sixth Report of the Secretary-General on the UN Mission in Sierra Leone, S/2005/596, September 20, 2005, 9.
6. "Harnessing Hope: Catalyzing Efforts for Accountability, Participation, and Reconciliation in Sierra Leone—A Peace Consolidation Strategy (PCS)," 2006, Freetown.
7. Government of Sierra Leone, "Poverty Reduction Strategy Paper—A National Programme for Food Security, Job Creation, and Good Governance (2005–2007)," March 2005, Abidjan.
8. UN Country Team, "UN Development Assistance Framework, Sierra Leone, 2008–2010," February 2007, New York.
9. UN Peacebuilding Commission, "Sierra Leone Peacebuilding Cooperation Framework," PBC/2/SLE/1, December 12, 2007, 3.
10. Ibid.

11 Twenty-Fourth Report of the Secretary-General on UN Mission in Sierra Leone, S/2004/965, December 10, 2004.

12 See Anatole Ayissi and Robin Edward Poulton, eds., *Bound to Cooperate: Conflict, Peace, and People in Sierra Leone* (New York: UN Institute for Disarmament Research, 2006); Adebajo, "Building Peace in West Africa."

13 Government of Sierra Leone, PRSP, 1.

14 Fourth Report of the Secretary-General on UNIOSIL, S/2007/257, May 7, 2007, 3.

15 Ibid.

16 The JSDP is a DFID-funded and British Council–managed program to build the capacity of the justice sector in Sierra Leone.

17 Sixth report of the Secretary-General on UNIOSIL, S/2008/281, April 29, 2008, 4.

18 Fourth Report of the Secretary General on UNIOSIL, 5.

19 Ibid., 1.

20 Ibid., 5.

21 Ibid.

22 Ibid., 8.

23 Fifth Report of the Secretary General on UNIOSIL S/2007/704, December 4, 2007, 1.

24 UNDP, Sierra Leone Human Development Report 2007, 7.

25 Scores range from 10 (highly clean) to zero (highly corrupt). TI considers a score of 5.0 as the border separating countries that do and do not have a serious problem of corruption.

26 Government of Sierra Leone, "National Anti-Corruption Strategy, 2008–2013," Freetown.

27 Government of Sierra Leone, "National Anti-Corruption Strategy, 2008–2013," 2.

28 "Witness to Truth: Report of the Sierra Leone Truth and Reconciliation Commission," Vol. 2 (2004), 27–29.

29 Ibid., 159.

30 Ibid.

31 Sixth Report of the Secretary-General on UNIOSIL, 12.

The Role of the Private Sector in Sierra Leone's Post-Conflict Reconstruction Efforts

Emmanuel Nnadozie and Siham Abdulmelik[1]

7

Introduction

Despite impressive growth of 7.3 percent in 2006 and 6.5 percent in 2007,[2] most of it mineral-induced, Sierra Leone's economy has not performed optimally when it comes to supporting human development goals set forth by its government. The private sector was largely devastated by a decade of civil war, which ended officially on January 18, 2002. Six years later, in 2008, much remains to be done in terms of strengthening the private sector's role in the national economy. Doing business in Sierra Leone remains an uphill battle for many local and foreign investors. In 2005 the UN estimated the unemployment rate at 40 percent, which is alarmingly high, and bearing the brunt of it are the young, many of whom were caught up in the civil war.[3] Infrastructure—especially water and electricity—is still inadequate, especially in rural areas. This strongly indicates that the private sector is not fully playing its proper role in the economy. This chapter focuses on the role of the private sector in Sierra Leone's economic recovery and answers the following questions: What can the private sector do to promote economic recovery in Sierra Leone? How can it play this role? And what is needed for the private sector to play this role?

This chapter argues that the private sector has a critical role to play in Sierra Leone's post-conflict economic recovery, not just in the conventional sense but also in dealing with the impact of the conflict and addressing its causes. For example, Sierra Leone's private sector can generate economic growth, create decent jobs, help diversify the economy, promote value-added exports, and contribute to reducing both poverty and inequality. Given the unique challenges and special needs facing post-conflict Sierra Leone, the private sector's role will need to extend beyond the conventional in both the short and the long term. Either independently or in partnership with the public sector, the private sector must engage itself in the key challenges facing the country in its post-conflict reconstruction efforts, especially when it comes to developing critical infrastructure, building capacity, and providing social services.

The challenges are simply too large for the government to confront on its own. Those challenges offer an opportunity for all stakeholders—the private sector, civil society, and community groups—to address the conflict factors so as to prevent a relapse.

This chapter is organized as follows. Following the introduction, Section 2 describes Sierra Leone's post-conflict economy in order to illustrate the challenging nature of the recovery. Section 3 discusses the role the private sector can play in the country's economic recovery and the opportunities for this to occur. Section 4 focuses on the policy framework that will be necessary if the private sector is to play a key role in the reconstruction effort, while Section 5 concludes the paper.

Sierra Leone's Post-Conflict Economy and the Private Sector

Background to the Economy

Post-conflict Sierra Leone has not recovered from ten years of civil war, which destroyed the country's infrastructure and left it, in 2008, at the very bottom of the UN Human Development Index,[4] ranked 179th out of 179. The conflict had a devastating impact on all facets of society, and the worst affected were the country's women and children.[5] The massive raping of girls and women and the mutilation and psychological harm done to boys abducted into the army and militias has left a terrible scar on the country's social fabric. The impact included the following:

- Over 50,000 deaths.[6]
- Displacement of 50 percent of the total population to neighbouring countries.
- Destruction of social, economic, and physical infrastructure and social services.
- Destruction of business and economic activities, including farming, the livelihood of the large majority of Sierra Leoneans.
- Mass violence against girls and women.
- Violence against children, including abduction, forced recruitment, sexual slavery, amputation, displacement, and torture.[7]
- An increase in HIV/AIDs. Official HIV rates were estimated as 0.2 percent before the civil war. According to UNICEF and UNAIDS, in 2005 prevalence rates for ages 15 to 49 had risen to 1.6 percent.[8]
- Weakening of national institutions, in particular the judiciary and other institutions of accountability, as well as those that provide public services.

Like many low-income conflict countries, Sierra Leone is overwhelmingly dependent on commodity exports for its revenues. The country's excessive dependence on diamond exports did more than fuel the conflict; it also created economic management problems because of the volatility of world prices, which caused strong "booms and busts" in government revenues.[9] Conflict commodities, including "blood diamonds," have funded and fuelled civil conflicts, including Sierra Leone's, and are now a focus of international action.[10] Even so, there remain significant problems at the production end of the diamond chain. Up to half of Sierra Leone's gemstones are still smuggled out of the country.[11]

Over the past several years the Sierra Leonean government has done much to stabilize the economy through prudent macroeconomic management. It has also reformed tax administration, strengthened the capacity of government ministries, departments, and agencies, improved service delivery, restructured public enterprises, reformed the civil service, strengthened the financial sector, and upgraded expenditure systems. Progress has been made on many fronts; but in many ways, post-conflict Sierra Leone has yet to deal with the conflict's aftermath—in particular, with the deep social, political, and psychological scars that have been left on a population that lived for years in a state of conflict.[12] One result is that, in addition to the aforementioned problems and their legacies, the post-conflict economy of Sierra Leone is characterized by extremely high levels of poverty, especially in rural areas, where it is as high as 79 percent.[13] Inflation remains high even though it stabilized between 2006 and 2008. It now hovers at 12 percent and is showing signs of moving into single digits.[14]

The country's needs are many. The basic infrastructure—including roads, schools, hospitals, factories, homes, communication networks, and trade links—has all been destroyed.[15] Financial, governmental, and legal institutions are weak or dysfunctional; the resulting corruption, poor governance, and lack of public services has complicated recovery efforts. In the postwar era, "high expectations for improved governance and socioeconomic conditions as well as redress of human rights issues could be conflict-producing if not met."[16]

The Investment Climate

Because of the difficulties facing post-conflict Sierra Leone, doing business in the country remains a challenge (see Table 7.1). The country is ranked 158th out of 181 economies in 2008 World Bank's Doing Business survey—an improvement over its rank of 163th of 175 in 2007 with regard to ease of doing business and regulations directly affecting businesses.[17]

In almost all indicators of ease of doing business, Sierra Leone does not fare well, even compared with its neighbours. This is especially so when it comes to arranging licences, employing workers, registering property, getting credit, paying taxes, trading across borders, enforcing contracts, and closing a business, in all of which the country is ranked 100th or worse.[18] The number of procedures (nine) involved in starting a business in Sierra Leone has not changed in the past

Figure 7.1

Sierra Leone's ten economic freedoms

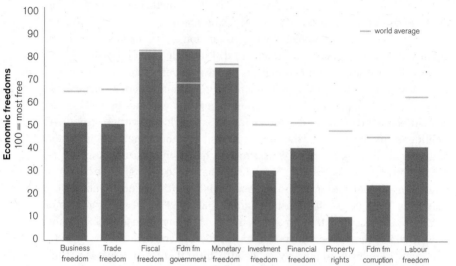

Source: James Dean and Tim Kane, *Index of Economic Freedom*, 2007.

three years (2005–2007), nor has how long it takes to do so (twenty-six days). Table 7.1 shows that in absolute terms and relative to other countries in West Africa, the cost of setting up and closing a business is extremely high. This discourages entrepreneurship and thus hampers the growth of the private sector.

As shown in Table 7.1, growth is constrained by a number of factors: the macroeconomic environment, the availability of skilled labour, governance issues, and the condition of infrastructure. Good governance is vital to poverty reduction. Though governance is improving in Sierra Leone, much remains to be done, especially with regard to accountability, the rule of law, social and ethnic inclusion, a corruption-free environment, creating a business-friendly environment for domestic and foreign investors, and sensible investment priorities. The 2007 Index of Economic Freedom compiled by the Heritage Foundation (see Figure 7.1)[19] links economic opportunity with prosperity; this highlights the challenges of property-rights protection and corruption in Sierra Leone. The country still has weak capacity to carry out its basic functions, and it has made insufficient investments in education and health, which are the main ingredients for human-capital formation. However, its overall score is 1.3 percentage points higher than the previous year, reflecting moderate improvement in five of the ten economic freedoms.

According to Chukwuma Obidegwu, postwar economic and social recovery will require stepped-up humanitarian assistance, more aggressive economic

Table 7.1

Indicators of investment climate in Sierra Leone and West Africa

	Sierra Leone	Ghana	Cape Verde	Nigeria	Senegal	Guinea-Bissau	Benin
Macroeconomic Environment							
GDP Growth	7.5	5.6	5.8	7.4	6.4	2.4	5
Inflation rate	8.5	14.5	0.4	14.8	1.6	3	3
Openness (imports plus exports, as % of GDP)	66.7	80	96.6	88.4	—	92.1	39.6
Populations (millions)	5.525	22.710	507	133.400	11.658	1.586	8.439
Inputs							
Labour force education (Literacy rate 15 to 24) 2003	35	92.7	89.6	89.4	54	62.2	56.7
Primary school completion rate (%) 2004	n/a	72	n/a	75	45	n/a	49
Governance Issues (%)							
Political stability	30.7	50.5	77.4	47	42	30.2	57.5
Regulatory quality	17.8	49.5	48	16.3	43.1	13.4	30.2
Rule of law	12.1	48.3	58	5.8	47.3	6.3	35.7
Control of corruption	17.2	45.3	61.6	6.4	52.2	12.3	16.3
Infrastructure							
Access to electricity (% of population) 2000	5[†]	45	n/a	40	30.1	n/a	22
Telephone lines in largest city (per 1000 people) 2002	5[††]	83	n/a	12	71	n/a	n/a
Personal computers (per 1000 people) 2003	12[†††]	3.8	n/a	7.1	21.2	n/a	3.7
Paved roads (% of total) 1997–2002	8	18.4	n/a	30.9	29.3	10.3	20
Entry/Exits and Operations							
Number of business start-up procedures	9	12	12	9	10	17	7
Time required to start business (days)	26	81	52	43	58	233	32
Cost (% of GNI per capita)	1194.5[**]	49.6	45.6	54.4	112.6	261.2	173.3

Source: World Development Indicators database, World Bank 2005.

[*] These indicators are not exhaustive; they are intended to be indicative.

[**] Among the costliest in the world, according to recent research.

[†] This figure is from "National Investment Brief: Sierra Leone," high-level conference on Water for Agriculture and Energy in Africa: The Challenges of Climate Change, Sirte, Libyan Arab Jamahiriya, 15–17 December 2008.

[††] The figure is from the website The Commonwealth@60. Sierra Leone–Society: Key Facts 2005, http://www.thecommonwealth.org/YearbookInternal/139288/society/.

[†††] The figure is from 2004 data. Kofi Mangesi, "Survey of ICT and Education in Africa: Sierra Leone Country Report" (Info-Dev, 2007).

reform policies, and political reforms. He identifies the following priorities for rapid postwar recovery: stabilization of the economy, a revival of agriculture and small-scale private-sector activities; the restoration of social services; and more thorough economic reforms.[20] The newly elected government of President Ernest Koroma has been installed and is enacting a number of reforms, but much remains to be done in the area of humanitarian assistance and economic reforms. The latter especially include institutional reforms—for example, to the judiciary (e.g., building its capacity) and to public finances. Also urgently needed are decentralization, community development, and a zero-tolerance policy on corruption,

Main Arguments and Key Questions

In this chapter it is argued that given post-conflict Sierra Leone's unique challenges and needs, all stakeholders must engage in addressing key challenges facing the country. It is also argued that the private sector has a critical role to play in post-conflict Sierra Leone—a role that must extend beyond the conventional. Given these basic arguments, the natural questions that come to mind are as follows: Why should the private sector play a role in the economic recovery of post-conflict Sierra Leone? What should its role be in this regard? How can it play that role? And what is needed for the private sector to play that role? The rest of this essay answers those questions.

The Role of the Private Sector

The private sector can contribute to the economy in a variety of ways, especially through its core functions of generating economic growth, providing jobs, and creating wealth. When the private sector plays its proper role as an engine of growth, it provides opportunity, which leads to poverty reduction. Unfortunately, the private sector is not playing its full role in Sierra Leone's reconstruction efforts, for a number of reasons. These include lack of awareness and understanding of its potential role among private sector operators; lack of a collective and unified approach owing to the private sector's diverse interests and agendas; reluctance among members of the private sector to involve themselves in what they perceive to be political matters; and, most important, the overall weakness of the private sector as a result of the prolonged conflict. All of this could be overcome through better coordination among members of the private sector and with support from the public sector and development partners.

The question to ask is this: Why should the private sector play this role in post-conflict Sierra Leone? To begin with, in many cases the private sector is not a neutral player in conflict, given that conflicts are very often driven or sustained by economic agendas.[21] This was the case in Sierra Leone, where diamonds financed the civil war. Put another way, diamonds fuelled the conflict in Sierra Leone, mainly because diamond traders struck bargains with foreign private-security companies, which offered military assistance in exchange for diamond concessions.[22]

Also, businesses often reinforce conflict by exacerbating and prolonging hostilities and, later on, making relapse into conflict more likely.[23] The private sector can generate conflict in any number of ways—another reason for encouraging it to play a constructive role. Conflict actively benefits *some* businesses; but more are harmed by it, because it stifles business growth and job creation. All the more reason, then, why the private sector ought to be motivated to help with peacebuilding. The fact is that economic recovery cannot happen without the active involvement of the private sector.

Admittedly, economic recovery is largely the purview of the public sector. Even so, the private sector has much to contribute through its economic influence, political contacts, financial resources, skilled labour, access to global markets, transportation and communication chains, capacity to drive balanced development, and connections at all levels of society. The specific role the private sector can play is a function of its resources, interests, and skills.[24]

It is possible to recruit the private sector as a bridge between economic and peace-oriented interventions in conflict-prone societies.[25] However, international interventions have not yet harnessed the skills and resources of the private sector in a strategic and systematic manner. In some places, the private sector has contributed significantly to post-conflict reconstruction and recovery—for example, in South Africa, Northern Ireland, and Sri Lanka—but so far there has been no concerted effort to adapt and transfer these experiences to other countries.[26]

The private sector can contribute to economic recovery in the following distinct and overlapping areas. In the economic sphere, businesses have the potential to address the economic root causes of conflict such as the socio-economic exclusion of one or more groups, especially minority groups. They can also have a positive impact on governance issues that perpetuate such dynamics. Businesses can tackle the economic factors that sustain or drive conflict, such as unemployment and underemployment, especially among youth; and they can address the economic impacts of conflict by rebuilding infrastructure and by raising awareness and disseminating information about the costs of conflict. Businesses can also play a meaningful role in reconciliation and serve as change agents as they conduct business across the conflict divide, finding common ground as economic players through dialogues that bring together business leaders from opposing sides. With regard to security, businesses can contribute to disarmament, demobilization, and reintegration (DDR), weapons-collection programs, and early-warning and community-level security arrangements through community outreach and development programs.[27]

What Can the Private Sector Do in
Sierra Leone's Post-Conflict Reconstruction Efforts?

The role the private sector can and must play in post-conflict situations differs from its conventional role as described earlier. The key issue in post-conflict Sierra Leone is economic recovery and post-conflict reconstruction. Economic recovery, in this context, is at least partly a matter of overcoming the legacy of conflict and reducing the potential for relapse, the goal being to generate socio-economic development and put the country back on a trajectory of normal development.[28] The private sector's role in Sierra Leone must extend beyond simple economics to encompass conflict prevention, employment generation, poverty reduction, and wealth creation.

Before delving into the specific role of the private sector, we must define that sector as it relates to Sierra Leone. The country is characterized by an active private sector that is heavily skewed toward trade, with a handful of large firms dominated by foreign owners in the mining and service sectors. The country is also home to many sizable small and medium-sized enterprises, as well as a large informal sector involved mainly in petty cross-border trade. Women are overrepresented in this latter sector, a result of their traditional role in the society and their low labour-force participation rate. For the purposes of this chapter, the private sector includes both local and international firms—large, medium, and small—as well as the agricultural and informal sectors.

Where, then, are the points of intervention for the private sector? Besides serving as engines of fast, sustained growth and creating meaningful employment opportunities, and reducing the country's massive unemployment and high rates of poverty, private firms can help expand economic opportunities and improve economic security. They can do these things in any number of ways, including these: managing their own core operations effectively; undertaking social investment in ways that address development and social issues; initiating policy dialogue; influencing policy-making and institution building; and addressing the root causes of conflict.

Sierra Leone's private firms need to develop sound internal policies and standards within their own sphere, starting with their own operations and behaviour. Having done so, they will be in a position to carry out their social responsibilities and help build peace. Many of the principles of responsible business double as principles of peacebuilding—combating corruption, for example, and addressing discriminatory employment practices through affirmative action or quota systems. The private sector can participate actively in preventing a resurgence of conflict by supporting national development and small-enterprise development, as well as by protecting cultural and ethnic diversity through hiring practices.

Private firms can also help strengthen the social fabric of the communities in which they operate by offering philanthropic support for public advocacy, local development, multi-ethnic understanding, civic education, youth development programs, and so on. And the private sector can help ameliorate the ravages of war by offering humanitarian assistance, rehabilitation efforts, and investments in critical areas. Businesses should also launch initiatives to provide jobs for ex-combatants by engaging both formally and informally in DDR-type programs.[29]

Likewise, there is much that the private sector can do to support education and health programs and local enterprise development in ways that target issues relevant to the conflict. Given Sierra Leone's shortage of skilled labour and high illiteracy, the business community needs to mobilize itself to support education and training colleges so that the country's skills and employment needs will eventually be met. The private sector can help fund areas that meet its needs by providing monetary incentives to retain teachers and by setting up scholarships, grants, and awards.

Finally, the private sector must use its clout to influence policy-makers to address the fundamental challenges facing Sierra Leone's post-conflict economy, such as corruption and lack of transparency and accountability, given that these determine the environment in which businesses operate. Firms can collectively promote better governance by lobbying policy-makers to create the conditions for growth and to remove obstacles to private-sector development and thereby improve the investment climate.

In particular, the private sector can tackle—alone or in partnership with the public sector and NGOs—some of the strategic challenges confronting post-conflict reconstruction and development in Sierra Leone. For example, it can:

- support the development of a comprehensive strategic framework to guide post-conflict recovery activities, which at this writing are highly fragmented;
- support efforts to ensure that the root causes and consequences of conflict are resolved effectively, along with issues such as state security, DDR, and emergency humanitarian assistance; *and*
- support the development of institutional and human-resource capacity and the implementation of development programs.

The private sector's role must extend to dealing with conflict factors. According to the World Bank, Sierra Leone's key conflict factors include these: overcentralization of control over resources and political power, which has caused disaffection in provincial areas; lack of accountability and capacity of governance structures; exclusion of youth from national and community politics; economic degeneration and extreme poverty; and reverberations from political instability throughout the Mano River Basin of West Africa.[30]

Sierra Leone's private sector has already started to play a role in addressing these factors. For instance, the Sierra Leonean branch of the diaspora-based mobile phone company Celtel,[31] in partnership with an international NGO, Search for Common Ground, is using the launch of its mobile network to hold a radio-broadcast debate on the importance of national reconciliation and the role of communications in creating a neutral platform for frank public dialogue. The role that women entrepreneurs can play in post-conflict recovery is being recognized; with the support of an American NGO, the Sierra Leonean Market Women's Association is providing market women with micro-financing and training to strengthen their livelihoods as well as their contributions to the post-conflict economy.[32] Similarly, the UN Industrial Development Organization's (UNIDO) Integrated Program for SMEs is addressing capacity building for small to medium-sized enterprise (SME) development; the goal here is to create opportunities for self-employment and income generation, especially among youth.[33]

For the private sector in Sierra Leone to deal proactively and concretely with these problems, whether alone or through public–private partnerships (PPPs), it will need to be developed and supported. This will require strong support from the public sector and the international community, both of which need to recognize the private sector's potential to galvanize peacebuilding. The private sector's impact will be limited unless it is supported by a wide range of actors and unless it is perceived positively by the general public. Collective action will play a significant role in generating and sustaining private-sector intervention.[34]

Opportunities: The Growth–Employment–Poverty Reduction Linkage

To understand where opportunities exist, we need to examine the growth–employment–poverty reduction nexus. In a country like Sierra Leone, growth can reduce poverty in two ways. First, by providing the resources and capacity for social spending to attack poverty directly (i.e., through health, education, and other services). Second, by creating jobs that will lift people out of poverty— provided that the growth occurs in sectors in which the poor are concentrated, such as agriculture. There is a relationship between employment and poverty just as there is between growth and employment. The main causes of poverty are rapid labour-force growth fuelled by rapid population growth (2.28 percent),[35] poor access to employment opportunities (especially for women and youth), and low productivity. In post-conflict Sierra Leone the poor include those who have jobs but are underemployed (i.e., the working poor), those who have low productivity, and those who receive low wages or incomes, as well as those who are unemployed. To reduce poverty, it follows, the incomes of the working poor must rise above the poverty line and the unemployed poor must be able to find work that produces incomes high enough to lift them out of poverty, be it in rural areas or the informal sector.

If strong economic growth occurs in labour-intensive sectors such as agriculture, light manufacturing, construction, textiles, and services, the associated rise in employment will have a positive impact on the working poor and their dependants, as well as on the unemployed poor, who will be able to find work or start their own businesses. How growth affects poverty in Sierra Leone will depend on the extent to which (a) growth increases opportunities for employment and (b) the poor can "join" the economy and benefit from the improved situation. Education, skills, and access to capital and productive assets are important variables; so is social spending on health, education, and training, which will enable the poor to benefit from the more rewarding employment opportunities generated by growth. There is plenty of opportunity in all of this for the private sector.

Certain drivers must be in place for growth to occur at high and sustained levels. The two most important are human capital and technology. Investment in human capital through education (especially for women) stimulates growth both directly and indirectly (i.e., through spillover effects). Through optimal education policies, the Government of Sierra Leone could raise its citizens' education levels, thereby increasing human capital, thereby creating a virtuous cycle that enables the economy to increase its capacity to produce new ideas. But sustainable growth does not depend solely on the efficient use of productive resources and growth drivers. Countries such as South Korea and Taiwan have grown rapidly by fostering an environment marked by peace and security, quality institutions, infrastructure, and support for the private sector. Good governance and macroeconomic stability are especially important.

For poor people to participate in growth and to share in its benefits, the Government of Sierra Leone needs to recognize and support the entrepreneurial spirit of its people, especially those who work in agriculture and in small- and medium-sized enterprises (SMEs), which constitute the bulk of domestic private-sector activity in Sierra Leone. The government has a significant role to play in addressing constraints, which include inadequate irrigation and transportation for farmers; the serious difficulties that farmers and SMEs face in accessing finance; and the shortage of information and vital skills.

In education, the curriculum could be reformed so that it is more relevant to industry. Educational institutions would benefit from career centres where students can seek information about available jobs. Those career centres would need to offer counselling services such as resumé workshops and interview training, as well as internship placement; they would also need to help businesses recruit on-campus. Centres like these have been a big success in India, where leading domestic companies like WIPRO, Infosys, and Tata, and prominent multinationals like IBM, Oracle, and General Electric, are now recruiting recent graduates through on-campus channels.

In Sierra Leone—indeed, in many African countries—growth and investment opportunities are hampered because most businesses find it difficult to arrange financing—in particular, risk capital. Recently, the Central Bank of

Sierra Leone has established a number of programs with the support of organizations such as the World Bank and UNIDO, which are designed to facilitate access to finance and expertise for SMEs. ProCredit Bank Sierra Leone, which is part of the worldwide ProCredit group, is one example of a newly established bank that offers ordinary people access to banking services and that provides loans to small and medium-sized enterprises.[36]

The Special Role of Agriculture

Agriculture has direct and indirect effects on employment and food security. It also provides the surest foundation for sustainable growth, through its linkages with the industrial and service sectors. That sector is Sierra Leone's largest employer—52 percent of the population is involved in subsistence agriculture.[37] So it makes sense to modernize that sector through mechanization as a means to increase both incomes and employment opportunities. The successful experience of East Asia shows that when farm incomes increase, so does demand for agricultural and non-agricultural goods, which in turn boosts aggregate demand, output, and employment. Growth in rural agricultural and tertiary sectors has a strong impact on poverty; note, however, that in the long run the agricultural strategy may *increase* poverty if a country does not diversify. In Asia, agricultural modernization and the resulting productivity gains fuelled growth in the manufacturing sector. The private sector can do much to make Sierra Leone's agriculture more competitive by transforming it from a low -input, low-investment, subsistence-oriented system into a more competitive, market-oriented system. This shift will need to involve seeking out and adopting both conventional technologies and new ones (such as high-yielding pest-resistant seeds) in order to increase productivity, reduce unit-production, processing, and distribution costs, and enable low-income producers to compete effectively in domestic, regional, and global markets.

Education, Public Health, and Water and Sanitation

Despite recent commendable efforts, Sierra Leone still suffers from a very low literacy rate (35.1 percent).[38] According to UNICEF, between 2000 and 2006 the literacy rate for boys between 15 and 24 was as high as 60 percent, and for girls 15 to 24 it was 37 percent.[39] This calls for an urgent effort to increase literacy, especially in terms of building capacity, reforming the curriculum, and providing educational infrastructure. The private sector needs to help address the education system's weaknesses by complementing the efforts of the public sector and non-profit groups, be it alone or through partnerships, especially public–private partnerships. For example, firms could establish private schools or form partnerships with existing public schools to improve the quality of education. They could also support the expansion of education at all levels; and they could improve the quality of instruction and support manpower development by providing training, capacity development, and skills upgrading. Companies could also provide vocational training, either directly or in co-operation with the public system, to prepare young people for the workforce; in particular, they could make scientific, technical, and vocational education available to girls. Finally, private firms could offer continuous training in the workplace to assist employees adapt to technological change.

Sierra Leone's health-care system suffers from too few medical profession-als, too many untrained practitioners, a lack of health-care facilities, and shortfalls in operating funds. Other problems include weak managerial and institutional capacity.[40] The private sector could play a key role in training medical professionals, building institutional and managerial capacity, and providing its own health-care services to complement public services.

Sierra Leone's systems of sanitation and water supply are in dire straits. Less than half the country's people have access to safe water and sanitation; 20,000 children under five die each year from water-borne illnesses.[41] Given the health implications of inadequate water supply and sanitation—especially in rural areas—the private sector has a role to play in providing waste-disposal systems and safe drinking water.

Apart from agriculture and social infrastructure other recognized areas of strong possibility for opportunities are ICT, tourism, fishery, and financial services.[42]

The Policy Framework for Getting Back on Track

Sierra Leone still has a chance to improve its economy, increase human welfare, and achieve its MDGs[43] as well as NEPAD's objectives.[44] An assessment of needs and capacity reveals that with sustained effort and adequate resources, the coun-try is likely to achieve some of its MDG targets—specifically, universal primary education, gender equality, and the containment of diseases such as HIV/AIDS and malaria. But it is unlikely to attain other MDGs. Quite possibly, the country could achieve much-needed economic recovery by rapidly adopting a radical approach and taking bold action to involve the private sector. That said, strate-gies targeting the private sector are no substitute for government policies to foster broader social and economic development; what private-sector policies can do is harness global partnerships to encourage solid and sustainable growth as part of a broader development agenda. Which summons these questions: What is the appropriate policy framework for private-sector–driven post-conflict economic recovery in Sierra Leone? What does Sierra Leone's private sector need to contrib-ute to the post-conflict economic recovery? And, finally, what conditions must the government create to make all of this happen? Clearly, a multidimensional strategy will be necessary in order to address the political, socio-economic, and institutional challenges facing the country. This will involve setting priorities in light of the country's multiple and competing needs. The first step, which is already being taken, is to develop a homegrown strategy that will address the constraints the country is facing even while boosting key sectors.

A Sierra Leone–Specific Growth Strategy

The countries that have succeeded best at reducing poverty over the past two decades (China, India, Botswana, Vietnam) have all enjoyed rapid economic growth; the same can be said of the countries that reduced poverty rapidly *before* the MDGs were launched (Korea, Taiwan, Thailand, Malaysia, Indonesia).[45] All of these countries pursued country-specific strategies—confirmation that there are no generic formulas. However, certain common elements can be traced, such as these: context-specific planning; macroeconomic stability; striking a balance between government intervention and market autonomy; application of technology to production; investment-friendly conditions (in particular, the reduction of risks and provision of access to credit on reasonable terms); and a minimum level of effective governance and capacity building.

So it is fair to suggest that economic recovery and significant poverty reduction in Sierra Leone will require a homegrown, country-specific strategy—one that is innovative, courageous, and ambitious. Given that the drivers of growth vary widely among countries, the appropriate strategy for Sierra Leone will depend on factors such as the importance of mineral extraction relative to agriculture and services (such as tourism); the opportunities for trade provided by the global and regional economies; the amount of effort required to stimulate private domestic investment and to attract foreign direct investment (FDI); and continued liberalization of the economy. All of these things will be heavily influenced by macroeconomic reform programs. Sierra Leone will have to take into account the private sector's profile and its own economic circumstances in order to determine the best points of intervention for maximum effectiveness.

The Sierra Leone–specific strategy should be based on a long-term vision that takes into account the factors that caused the civil conflict, in the context of (a) strategies that can be linked to sources of growth and (b) measures to improve the investment climate and infrastructure, coupled with (c) intra- and inter-sectoral diversification to reduce dependence on diamonds as well as vulnerability to external shocks. The current privatization program—which emphasizes the agricultural sector and an institutional capacity to promote expanded private-sector investment in agriculture, agro-industry, manufacturing, and support services—should, if properly implemented, help diversify the economy. For a mineral-rich country like Sierra Leone, transparency and good governance in the mineral sector, accompanied by redistributive fiscal policies and encouragement of backward linkages, will be important, if earnings are not to become drivers of corruption and conflict rather than growth and development. On October 20, 2003, Sierra Leone joined the Kimberley Process, which led to a dramatic increase in legal exports of diamonds. The government also created a mining community development fund, which returns a portion of diamond-export taxes to diamond-mining communities, thereby raising the local communities' stake in the legal diamond trade.

Given Sierra Leone's specific needs for growth, poverty reduction, and overall development, and given the government's limited resources, it is fair to suggest that the following approaches would go far to develop the country.

Modernize the Agricultural Sector

With the agricultural sector contributing significantly to GDP, the emphasis should be on higher productivity and better market access.[46] Sierra Leone needs to exploit its membership in regional groups such as ECOWAS in order to promote its exports and seek new markets. The private sector could take measures to increase output—for example, it could develop high-yielding crop varieties, better production techniques and practices, diversification, irrigation, post-harvest infrastructure, research, and innovation, as well as markets.

Support and Address Challenges Facing the SMEs

Given the profile of private sector, the government needs to focus on SMEs.[47] In this regard, it needs to design industrial policies that favour SMEs' competitiveness and that foster entry and growth opportunities; develop a holistic approach to broadening SMEs' access to finance by enhancing banks' capacity for micro-lending; promote financial-sector development to diversify sources of funds; broaden the range of financial instruments to serve various segments of the economy; and create institutional mechanisms to support SME development.

Take Urgent Action to Address Youth Unemployment

A youth employment strategy needs to be crafted, and it must encompass a number of elements. First, it must combine self-employment opportunities (which means offering vocational education) with micro-financing services, while also encouraging wage-earning jobs and voluntary service activities. Second, it must ensure that a significant number of young people are employed; that means fostering an economy that generates more jobs for young people and enhances their employability. Finally, it must provide relevant education and skills training to match the demand for labour. As part of the post-conflict reintegration process, the government negotiated a deal with several Sierra Leonean institutions and companies in which those sponsors agreed to pay school fees and other educational expenses for ex-combatants and to provide employment opportunities for them.

Intervention can mean two things: creating a national policy environment that is conducive to the hiring of young people, and providing youth with relevant education and skills. A demand for young workers can be created in several ways. Critical to all of them is identifying sectors (such as agriculture and the fishery) that have strong income-generating potential for youth. The emphasis should be on production and on storage, processing, and distribution; this will ensure that a large number of people are employed. Infrastructure development/redevelopment is crucial in Sierra Leone, and this is another sector where youth can find work. However, policies have to be in place to ensure that young people are in fact hired to build/rebuild roads, hospitals, and schools. Providing differentiated education, skills training, and income-generating opportunities will go a long way to alleviating the long-term problem of youth unemployment. Mentoring programs, skills upgrading programs for entrepreneurs and credit-access policies are also crucial here. Those who are oriented toward wage-earning jobs need access to relevant education and/or training. Formal education needs to be examined in terms of its relevance and quality so that public- and private-sector demands can be met. It is possible to arrange mentoring, internships, and on-the-job training with private firms so that youth acquire skills and, perhaps, jobs once they have been trained. Career guidance and job counselling are other important means to help young people make career choices and find work. Finally, special efforts must be made to target youth who have become despondent and unwilling to help themselves.

Deal with the Gender Dimensions of Inequality and Poverty

Gender inequality is both an economic issue and a social one. Increased gender equality could be a potent force for accelerated poverty reduction in Sierra Leone. In that sense, gender is a missing link in achieving sustained growth and reducing poverty. The Government of Sierra Leone and other partners and stakeholders, including the private sector, must explore all opportunities to address gender inequality if the country is to significantly reduce poverty and meet the MDGs. There has been increased recognition of the gender dimensions of poverty, but much remains to be done to address the economic gap between women and men, especially in terms of incomes. Rural women's deepening poverty and their unequal access to health, education, financial, and other essential resources remains a serious concern. So it is important to take measures to improve the status of women in Sierra Leone. This will require that women's empowerment be injected into business practices, that women's education be supported, and that micro-credit and other financing instruments be extended to women. These steps will strengthen women's capacity engage with the economy.

Improve the Overall Investment Climate:
Property Rights, Commercial Law, and Capital Flight

Any credible strategy to accelerate development in Sierra Leone must include promoting trade and investment, which includes building and strengthening institutions to support the market economy.[48] This will require (a) an efficient legal system that protects property rights and enforces contracts, (b) infrastructure to reduce transaction costs, and (c) a regulatory framework that promotes healthy competition.

A number of projects to support Sierra Leone's private-sector development are currently underway, financed in part by the international community and development partners of the MTI. The World Bank has assigned US$30 million to a Rural Development and Private Sector Development project. That project aims to improve efficiencies along the value chain of agricultural commodities; if it works, higher benefits will flow to the producers, domestic distribution channels can be improved, the necessary tools and services will be provided for promoting agricultural exports, and farmers' access to agricultural technology and practices will be increased. The same project is underwriting the development of policy regulations. DFID, too, is involved in activities to improve the investment climate and encourage privatization. In particular, it is supporting the government's medium-term private-sector development (PSD) program by providing expert advice and implementation support to the MTI, by drafting appropriate legislation to support PSD, and by offering "institution strengthening" for the MTI and other public- and private-sector stakeholders. The Sierra Leone Business Forum (SLBF), an IFC-supported program,[49] has been established to foster government-to-business dialogue and to provide a non-partisan platform for policy advocacy that will promote investment-friendly reforms and encourage effective service delivery by government institutions.[50] In addition, a number of studies have been undertaken by the Foreign Investment Advisory Service (FIAS)[51] to identify administrative barriers to investment in the private sector and to provide the government with concrete recommendations. In addition, the government needs to explore the possibility of public–private partnerships (PPPs) in different post-conflict initiatives and facilitate the establishment of effective working relationships with the private sector.

Aggressively Target FDI (not debt, not ODA), Especially the Diaspora Human and Financial Resources

The government needs to find ways to attract FDI, which would have a strong positive impact on the post-conflict economic recovery by bringing in much-needed capital, technology, and skills, as well as by stimulating local industries. The government could make use of the Investment Climate Facility (ICF) and the Multilateral Investment Guarantee Agency (MIGA),[52] both of which have played a critical role in encouraging FDI back into post-conflict countries. Through an innovative new program, MIGA is encouraging smaller investors to consider projects in Sierra Leone by providing a standardized package of political-risk insurance that protects against transfer restriction, expropriation, and war and civil unrest. Known as the Small Investment Program (SIP), this program streamlines and expedites the agency's underwriting process, making it quicker and easier for smaller firms to apply for coverage.[53]

The government also needs to take action to exploit its diaspora community, since remittance flows can be an important source of FDI. In particular, measures need to be taken to mobilize steady flows of remittances, especially through official channels.[54]

Financial liberalization—especially foreign-exchange liberalization—should be encouraged, as this could induce migrants to transfer more of their savings into Sierra Leone. In this vein, the government now allows foreign-currency–denominated accounts. Offering relatively higher interest rates on these types of accounts could entice migrants to remit their wages. The government should also consider providing incentives to import machinery and equipment at reduced tariffs as a way of attracting more investment. The provision of special incentives such as settlement grants could be used to encourage return migration, especially of skilled and professional migrants. Where long-term return migration is not possible, short-term and virtual return should also be encouraged, in order to facilitate the diffusion of scientific and technical knowledge.[55]

Address Informality

As in many African countries, the informal economy accounts for a sizable proportion of output, employment (estimated at 60 to 70 percent of urban employment), and job creation in Sierra Leone.[56]

Informality is a result of economic, social, and political processes that interact with and reinforce one another. For this reason, it must be addressed in a holistic and comprehensive manner. In many ways, to address informality is to address poverty, create opportunity, empower people, and provide economic and social security.

If opportunities are to be created, market reforms must be targeted at the informal sector. This means eliminating or simplifying the regulations affecting micro-enterprises and small- and medium-sized firms. It also means strengthening land registries to allow small producers to use land as collateral, and developing policies that make insurance possible for micro-firms. The government has enacted policies that have reduced barriers to investment and that have simplified operating procedures. In particular, these policies have reduced the tax burden—a burden that has long encouraged informality. By providing basic social services (complemented by civil society and the private sector), the state helps mitigate the risks and vulnerabilities associated with informality. This sort of security reduces the vulnerability of people in the informal sector to risks such as economic shocks and natural disasters and helps them cope with adverse shocks when they do occur.

The Government of Sierra Leone needs to recognize that the informal economy can no longer be viewed as a temporary phenomenon. It needs to recognize that the informal economy is a significant generator of jobs and incomes and that its existence offers poor consumers low-priced goods and services. The informal economy needs to be better understood both by governments and by other stakeholders. This means doing the following:

- Mainstreaming informal-sector development strategy into private-sector development strategies and into the overall national-development strategy.
- Addressing the perennial urban-biased development strategies of African countries and the rural neglect associated with them.
- Tackling the specific issue of the overrepresentation of women in the informal economy, which is characterized by lower wages and higher wage gaps between men and women.
- Addressing the challenge of coordinating efforts and programs to address informality in particular and private-sector development in general, working in close partnership with all stakeholders.
- Moving from declarations and plans to the implementation of decisions and strategies. This will require measurable and time-bound outcomes. It will need to be indicated clearly who will implement projects, how and with what resources, and which stakeholders will monitor implementation.

Finally, informality must be reduced because of its high economic and social costs. In this respect, the Government of Sierra Leone needs to broaden its reforms in order to ensure an environment that encourages private investment through sound macroeconomic and microeconomic policies, control of corruption, and infrastructure development. The private sector should participate in and contribute to the reform process to ensure that its issues and concerns are adequately addressed.

Conclusion

The civil war has had a devastating impact on Sierra Leone. Almost six years on, the situation has not improved much and the country is still a difficult place to do business. Despite recent impressive growth, Sierra Leone's economy is not doing well, especially in terms of human and social development, and the business environment continues to suffer from the devastation left behind by the ten-year conflict. The private sector has a critical role to play in post-conflict Sierra Leone—a role that extends beyond its conventional one. The private sector was closely linked to the conflict and must be part of the solution. Businesses reinforce and mirror conflict dynamics through their behaviour, and conflict is bad for business in that it stifles growth and job creation—which is all the more reason to involve the private sector in peacebuilding and post-conflict reconstruction. More important than this, economic recovery cannot happen without the active involvement of the private sector as the engine of growth.

The private sector can continue to play its traditional role—generating economic growth, providing jobs, and creating wealth—but the key issue in the case of Sierra Leone is that post-conflict economic recovery must be approached in the context of preventing more conflict, generating employment, reducing poverty, and creating wealth. It must be seen in terms of overcoming the legacy of the conflict and reducing the potential for relapse. The private sector has much to contribute to the economy, to reconciliation efforts, and to different dimensions of security.

In particular, the private sector can support the development of a comprehensive and strategic framework to replace the fragmented post-conflict recovery activities that are currently in place. It can also support efforts to address and resolve the war's root causes as well as its present-day consequences—for example, by helping provide state security, DDR, and emergency humanitarian assistance. The private sector could support public-sector efforts in skills training, education, and employment, and provide income-generating opportunities for returnees and internally displaced persons. Furthermore, it could help the country to develop its institutional and human-resource capacity and to implement development programs. And the private sector must help the country diversify its exports and break its dependence on a handful of commodities. Possibilities for this exist in agriculture (especially rice production), education, public health, and water and sanitation. Other strong possibilities are tourism, the fishery, and financial services.

At the same time, the private sector in Sierra Leone needs to be developed, promoted, and strongly supported by the public sector and the international community through concerted action; otherwise, its impact will be limited. Given the profile of private sector, government needs to design industrial policies that encourage SMEs' competitiveness and growth, that widen their access to micro-financing, and that create institutional mechanisms to support SME development.

Tackling informality is also important. Doing so will help address poverty and will require reforming the market so as to eliminate or simplify regulations affecting micro-enterprises and small and medium-sized firms. The informal sector needs to be mainstreamed into overall national development strategies.

In sum, economic recovery cannot happen without the active involvement of the private sector. Furthermore, there is plenty of scope for utilizing the private sector as a "bridge" between social and economic questions in a conflict-prone country such as Sierra Leone. That said, the private sector's local characteristics will have a great deal to say about the precise role it will need to play in Sierra Leone's recovery. In addition, the private sector is not monolithic and does not have a uniform agenda. Its interests are varied, and this points to both opportunities and challenges in identifying its potential contributions to peacebuilding and post-conflict reconstruction. Though the private sector can play the roles that have been identified so far, either alone or in partnership with other stakeholders, its success in driving post-conflict economic recovery in Sierra Leone will ultimately be determined by the leadership, capacity, and political will of the country's national and local actors. Sierra Leone's agreement to participate in the APRM should encourage it to fully harness the private sector's potential to generate a more stable and prosperous Sierra Leone.

Notes

1 Presented at the conference "From Civil Strife to Peace Building: Examining Private Sector Involvement in West African Reconstruction," Accra, Ghana, December 6 and 7, 2007. This paper should not be viewed as representing the views of the UN Economic Commission for Africa (UNECA). The views expressed are those of the authors and do not necessarily represent those of the UNECA or UNECA policy.

2 The figures are from UNECA official data. The growth rates in Sierra Leone were 17.9, 27.5, and 9.3 percent, respectively, in 2001, 2002, and 2003, and the economy continued to grow at a rate in excess of 7 percent in real terms. See Andrew Lawson, "DFID Budget Support to Sierra Leone, 2004–2007: Achievements and Lessons for the Future" (London: August 2007).

3 Elizabeth Schreinemacher, "Sierra Leone War-Crimes Court Running Out of Money," Mail and Guardian Online, October 6, 2005.

4 The Human Development Index (HDI) is a summary measure of human development published by the UN Development Programme (UNDP). The HDI provides an alternative to the common practice of evaluating a country's progress in development based on per capita GDP. The criteria for calculating rankings include life expectancy, educational attainment, and adjusted real income.

5 Fighting had begun in 1991, when rural youth frustrated with socio-economic and political stagnation were mobilized by the Revolutionary United Front (RUF). The RUF's aim was to topple the government, which had ruled for twenty-four years. Sierra Leone's war ended in January 2002, following intervention by the UN Mission to Sierra Leone (UNAMSIL) and British troops.

6 http://www.globalsecurity.org/military/world/war/sierra_leone.htm.

7 Sexual violence, especially against girls, is widespread. The U.S. State Department reported that at a Freetown sexual-assault centre, 83 percent of the patients were between six and fifteen years old and children as young as three months had been raped. Physicians for Human Rights reports that internally displaced women and girls in Sierra Leone suffered extraordinary levels of rape, sexual violence, and other gross human-rights violations during their country's civil war. Half of those who said they came into contact with RUF forces reported sexual violence. See Physicians for Human Rights, "War-Related Sexual Violence in Sierra Leone: A Population-Based Assessment" (Washington: 2002).

8 http://www.unaids.org/en/KnowledgeCentre/HIVData/Epidemiology/latestEpiData.asp.

9 UNCTAD, cited in Tony Adison, "Post-Conflict Recovery: Does the Global Economy Work for Peace?", United Nations University World Institute for Development Economic Research (UNU-WIDER), Helsinki 2004.

10 The main international initiative to deal with the problem of blood diamonds is the Kimberley Process Certification Scheme (KPCS), which has been in operation since January 1, 2003, and has a membership of fifty diamond producing, trading and polishing countries. The participating countries have agreed to import and export only diamonds that have the KPCS certificate. In effect, the KPCS aims to create a two-tier market in which illegitimate diamonds sell at a discount relative to legitimate (i.e., certified) diamonds, thereby cutting the value of conflict diamonds to sellers (Collier and Hoeffler 2004).

11 Diamonds and Human Security Project (2004), cited in Tony Addison, "Post-Conflict Recovery: Does the Global Economy Work for Peace?" United Nations University World Institute for Development Economic Research, Helsinki 2005, 4–5.

12 World Bank, "Toward a Conflict-Sensitive Poverty Reduction Strategy: Lessons from a Retrospective Analysis," Report no. 32587, June 30, 2005, Washington; Standard Times Press, "Promoting Private Sector Development, Trade, and Investment for Poverty Reduction," May 14, 2007.

13 IMF, "Sierra Leone: Poverty Reduction Strategy Paper Preparation Status Report," Country Report no. 05/201, June 2005.

14 Katrina Mason, "Democratic Feat Bodes Well," *African Business*, November 2007; World Bank Group "Economic and Financial Indicators for Sierra Leone Development," Economics LDB database, 2007; Central Intelligence Agency, *CIA Factbook: Sierra Leone* (Washington: 2008).

15 Mason, "Democratic Feat Bodes Well."

16 World Bank, "Toward a Conflict-Sensitive Poverty Reduction Strategy."

17 http://www.doingbusiness.org/EconomyRankings.

18 World Bank and International Finance Corporation, *Doing Business 2008* (Washington: 2007).

19 James Dean and Tim Kane, *Index of Economic Freedom: The Link Between Economic Opportunity and Prosperity* (Washington: Heritage Foundation, 2007).

20 Chukwuma Obidegwu, "Post-Conflict Peace Building in Africa: The Challenges of Socio-Economic Recovery and Development," Africa Region Working Paper no. 73 (Washington: World Bank, 2004).

21 Paul Collier and Anke Hoeffler, "The Challenge of Reducing the Global Incidence of Civil War," paper prepared for the Copenhagen Consensus 2004, March 26 (http://www .copenhagenconsensus.com); Jane Nelson (2000), "The Business of Peace: Private Sector as a Partner in Conflict Prevention and Resolution," Prince of Wales Business Leaders Forum, International Alert, Council on Economic Priorities (London: September 2000); Nick Killick, V.S. Srikantha, and Canan Gunduz, "The Role of Local Business in Peacebuilding," Berghof Research Center for Constructive Conflict Management (Berlin: 2005).

22 Nicholas Shaxson, "Transparency in the International Diamond Trade," in *Global Corruption Report 2001* (Cambridge: Cambridge University Press, 2001).

23 International Alert, "Local Business, Local Peace: The Peacebuilding Potential of the Domestic Private Sector" (London: 2006).

24 Killick et al., "The Role of Local Business in Peacebuilding"; Nelson, "The Business of Peace."

25 Killick et al., "The Role of Local Business in Peacebuilding"; International Alert, "Local Business, Local Peace"; Nelson, "The Business of Peace"; Allan Gerson, "The Private Sector and Peace," *Brown Journal of World Affairs* 7, no. 2 (2000): 141–45.

26 International Alert, "Local Business, Local Peace."

27 Ibid.

28 It is a return to the "steady state," where a country has re-established the capability to make and implement economic decisions and priorities as part of a largely self-sustaining process of economic governance. See UNDP (UN Development Programme), "Sustaining Post-Conflict Economic Recovery: Lessons and Challenges," BCPR Occasional Paper no. 1, October 2005.

29 International Alert, "Local Business, Local Peace"; Killick et al., "The Role of Local Business in Peacebuilding."

30 World Bank, "Sierra Leone–Country Brief" (Washington: 2007). The Mano River sub-region is the most volatile in West Africa. All three of its countries (Guinea, Liberia, and Sierra Leone) have been affected by conflict, insecurity, and constant population movements. Cross-border conflicts have affected this region tremendously, leading to death, mutilation, and the displacement of millions of people as well as sabotaging development in countries emerging from conflict.

31 The company began operating in 1998. In 2006, Celtel launched One Network, the world's first borderless network, across East Africa, later extending it to Central Africa. It now spans more than fifteen African countries, with over $750 million in investments and 20 million subscribers.

32 International Alert, "Local Business, Local Peace."

33 http://www.mtisl.org.

34 Killick et al., "The Role of Local Business in Peacebuilding."

35 CIA, *CIA Factbook: Sierra Leone.*

36 Abu S. Tarawalie, "Sierra Leone: Creating Access to Financial Services." Standard Times Press News, December 2, 2008. http://business.africanpath.com/article.cfm?articleID=48255.

37 CIA, World *Factbook 2000: Sierra Leone.*

38 Mariama Kandeh, "Sierra Leone: 500,000 Job Seekers in Country," *Concord Times*, April 19, 2008.

39 http://www.unicef.org/infobycountry/sierraleone_statistics.html#46.

40 Government of Sierra Leone, "Millennium Development Goals Report for Sierra Leone" (2005). http://planipolis.iiep.unesco.org/upload/Sierra%20Leone/Sierra_Leone_MDG_Report.pdf.

41 DFID (Department for International Development), "UK Helps Sierra Leone Turn On the Taps for Clean Water: £32 million Support for Water and Sanitation to Save Thousands of Lives," February 23 (London: 2008). http://www.unicef.org/infobycountry/sierraleone_statistics.html#44.

42 World Bank and International Finance Corporation, *Doing Business 2008*; U.S. Department of State, Doing Business in Sierra Leone: *A Country Commercial Guide for U.S. Companies* (Washington: 2005); Standard Times Press, "Promoting Private Sector Development, Trade, and Investment for Poverty Reduction," May 14 (Freetown: 2007).

43 The Millennium Development Goals (MDGs) are measurable and time-bound targets designed to address poverty in all its forms. The eight goals are as follows: eradicate extreme poverty and hunger; achieve universal primary education; promote gender equality and empower women; reduce child mortality; improve maternal health; combat HIV/AIDS, malaria, and other diseases; ensure environmental sustainability; and develop global partnership for development.

44 The New Partnership for African Development (NEPAD) is a comprehensive strategic framework for the socio-economic development of Africa. The initiative is premised on good governance and democracy and on Africa's ownership, leadership, and management of the plan. The long-term objectives of NEPAD are to eradicate poverty, spearhead sustainable development, integrate Africa at regional and global levels, and empower women. The framework's three key areas of focus are these: establishing the conditions for sustainable development; fostering policy reform and investment in priority sectors; and mobilizing resources.

45 Steven Radelet, Jeffrey Sachs, and Jong-Wha Lee, "Economic Growth in Asia," background paper for the Asian Development Bank's study Emerging Asia: Changes and Challenges, July 1997.

46 CIA, *Factbook: Sierra Leone.*

47 World Bank, Sierra Leone-Country Brief (Washington: 2007); DFID, "Sierra Leone Private Sector Development Support to the Ministry of Trade and Industries for a Programme to Develop and Implement a National Private Sector Development Strategy" (London: 2005).

48 For a discussion of the role that the African Peer Review Mechanism (APRM) can play in improving the investment climate, see, for example, Emmanuel Nnadozie, Kavezuea Katjomuise, and Ralf Krüger, "NEPAD's African Peer Review Mechanism and Investment Climate in Africa," in *Unlocking Africa's Potential: The Role of Corporate South Africa in Strengthening Africa's Private Sector*, ed. Neuma Grobbelar and Hany Besada (South Africa: University of Witswatersrand, 2008), 169–200.

49 The International Finance Corporation (IFC) fosters sustainable growth in developing countries by financing private-sector projects, mobilizing capital in the international financial markets, and providing advisory and risk-management services to businesses and governments.

50 http://www.publicprivatedialogue.org/workshop%202007/SLBF%20PPD%20Note.doc.

51 FIAS is a multi-donor service of the IFC, the private-sector arm of the World Bank Group, the Multilateral Investment Guarantee Agency (MIGA), and the World Bank. FIAS advises governments of developing and transition countries on how to improve their investment climate for domestic and foreign investors. FIAS focuses on regulatory simplification, industry-specific investment-climate issues, and investment policy and promotion.

52 MIGA has supported fifty-six projects with guarantee in sixteen post-conflict countries (including Mozambique, for instance), amounting to US$1.5 billion. The development benefits have been far-reaching: cash flows have been restored, financial sectors have been put back on their feet, governments have been able to allocate funds to social sectors, and the private-sector confidence to invest in the reconstruction has been renewed.

53 World Bank Group Multilateral Investment Guarantee Agency, "Managing Country Risk in Frontier Markets," September (Washington: 2007).

54 UNECA (UN Economic Commission for Africa), "Maximizing the Contributions of the African Diaspora to Private Sector Development," in *Unleashing Private Sector in Africa* (New York: 2005).

55 Refer to ibid. for a full discussion of the diaspora's role in the development of the private sector in Africa.

56 Department of Public Information, "'Jobless Growth' Shifts to Informal Economies, and Need for Stronger Protection for Workers Among Issues, as Social and Development Commission Opens Session," Commission for Social Development, 46th Session, 2nd & 3rd Meetings, February 6, 2008. http://www.un.org/News/Press/docs/2008/soc4737.doc.htm.

The Role of the Privatization Program as a Catalyst for Economic Reform in Sierra Leone

Andrew K. Keili[1]

8

Introduction

Sierra Leone emerged from a decade of civil war in 2002.[2] Despite the country's successes in maintaining peace and holding two successful presidential elections—in May 2002 and August and September 2007—it remains a challenge to address human development and rebuild the economy and infrastructure.

According to the UN Development Programme's (UNDP) Human Development Report, Sierra Leone is the lowest-ranked country on the Human Development Index (HDI) and seventh lowest on the Human Poverty Index (HPI). State intervention in the rebuilding effort was necessary soon after the conflict; since then, the private sector has been assigned an important role in the post-conflict economic recovery. In November 2002 the Government of Sierra Leone embarked on a privatization program by passing the National Privatization Act, which encompassed the operations of several state-owned enterprises (SOEs).

> This paper examines the role of the privatization program as a catalyst for economic reform in Sierra Leone. It explores the links between the government's privatization program and private-sector development initiatives undertaken directly by government and the donor community. It also examines the mandate of the privatization program, discussing the opportunities it presents, the challenges it faces, and the government's efforts to address these. Relevant conclusions are drawn that will help address the problems of privatization and private-sector development in Sierra Leone. As infrastructure development is so essential for economic revitalization, particular emphasis is placed on the infrastructure sectors.

Since 2000 the international community—the UN in particular—has played a critical role in sustaining the peace. Between 2000 and 2002 the focus was on the return and resettlement of displaced people, as well as the extension of state authority, including both line ministries and traditional authorities.[3] Most of the country's infrastructure had been destroyed and the economy was in a precarious state. To improve social and economic services in the immediate post-conflict period, in 2002 the government prepared a National Recovery Strategy (NRS). This listed four priorities: the restoration of state authority; the rebuilding of communities;[4] peacebuilding and human rights; and the restoration of the economy. State infrastructure, which was in a poor state even before the civil conflict began in 1991, had been severely damaged. The unreliability and sparse coverage of infrastructure services, especially electricity, was recognized as a major barrier to sustainable economic growth and poverty reduction.

> The government, under the Sierra Leone Peoples Party (SLPP), was cog-
> nizant of the failures and inefficiencies of the public sector, and it real-
> ized that the private sector would need to play a leading role in economic
> revitalization. One of the main ways in which this could be achieved was
> by privatizing many of the SOEs that had become a burden on govern-
> ment but that were nevertheless vital in rebuilding the financial, infra-
> structural, and other sectors. In 2002 an Act of Parliament was passed to
> establish a National Commission for Privatisation (NCP). Under the NCP
> Act the commission was to serve as the policy- and decision-making
> body with regard to the reform and divestiture of public enterprises.
> Management of all such enterprises was to be transferred to the commis-
> sion, and this would end interference by the ministries in the operations
> of public enterprises. This in turn would ensure transparency and cor-
> porate governance, besides reducing conflicts of interest.

In the early 1990s there were forty-four public enterprises engaged in a va-
riety of economic sectors. Though the 1993 Public Enterprise Reform Act[5] had divested fourteen of these, the largest of them remained under government control. Those enterprises that could easily be divested—including the smaller ones—were on the list of divested enterprises. In September 2003 the Gov-
ernment of Sierra Leone (GOSL) relaunched its privatization program with the publication of a Strategic Plan for the Divestiture of Public Enterprises. That plan addressed four broad sectors—finance, utilities, commerce, and transportation. The Strategic Plan set out an implementation program for the period 2003 to 2006. It was envisaged that during this time twenty-four public enterprises would be restructured and divested in some manner. Apart from some of the enterprises in the financial sector such as formal banks, almost all of the enterprises were operating at a loss, were carrying excessive debt, and were overstaffed. Management problems, lack of capitalization, operating inefficiencies, and poor corporate governance by government-appointed boards were the main reasons for their poor financial performance. Many of the en-

terprises were operating in sectors in which the policy, legal, and regulatory framework was outdated, unclear, or completely non-existent.

With the implementation of the Sierra Leone Poverty Reduction Strategy early in 2005, the country began a transition from the post-conflict emergency to a poverty-reduction–based development framework.[6] The Poverty Reduction Strategy Paper (PRSP) prioritized progress toward the millennium development goal (MDG) of reducing poverty across the country. To achieve this, the government adopted a comprehensive development framework (CDF) under which diagnoses were to be systematically linked to public actions to address poverty. The PRSP had three pillars: (1) promoting good governance, security, and peace; (2) promoting pro–poor sustainable growth for food security and job creation; and (3) promoting human development.

After the GOSL adopted the PRSP as the basis for economic development, the NCP Strategic Plan (2003–2006)—which touched on the timing of divestitures, strategies for divestiture, and funding and other issues—was updated in January 2005. Once again, emphasis was placed on harnessing the private sector as the engine for economic growth and prosperity. The time frame reflected a number of constraints. Privatization would help achieve macroeconomic stability in the medium to long term and facilitate private-sector development.

Overview of the Economy

Sierra Leone's economy has suffered prolonged deterioration, mainly because of the decade-long civil war. One result has been a low standard of living despite the country's significant resource endowments.

The economy today is characterized by narrow production and export bases and chronic structural rigidities. In the 1990s and until 2002, despite macroeconomic reforms and support from development partners such as Britain, the economy contracted by 4.6 percent annually.[7] After the civil conflict ended, the economic situation improved sharply—real GDP grew at around 5.9 percent per annum from 2002 to 2004.[8] Macroeconomic stability was maintained while the peace process was consolidated. Growth was generated through the recovery of the agricultural sector, especially rice (paddy), cassava, maize, sweet potatoes, and groundnuts.[9] Also contributing was expansion in the mining sector—especially diamonds, rutile, bauxite, gold, and ilmenite. There was also modest growth in manufacturing and construction.

Sierra Leone's dependence on mining is reflected in that sector's high contribution to GDP (20 percent) and registered exports (90 percent) throughout most of the 1990s.[10] Fiscal revenues peaked at about 8 percent of GDP in 1990 before declining to less than 2 percent[11] in 1994 after two large-scale mines were closed: Sierra Rutile Ltd. and SIEROMCO, mining rutile and bauxite respectively, in Bonthe and Moyamba Districts. Mining is currently Sierra

Leone's second most important sector, after agriculture. Exports of rutile and bauxite recommenced in 2006, with exports of US$31 million for the former and $24 million for the latter.[12] Diamond production has improved gradually since the end of the war, with production in 2007 at about $150 million. Production rose steadily from an export value of about $26 million in 2001 to $125.3 million in 2006. Privately owned mines have been at the forefront of this resuscitation. It is estimated that within a decade the successful realization of the country's large-scale mineral potential could lead to several new mines being opened in the northern, southern, and eastern provinces and that annual production could easily top $370 million.[13]

The manufacturing base is still narrow, with a concentration on a few commodities: beverages, plastics, paints, and cement. The manufacturing sector has been recovering since the war, though it has recorded inconsistent outputs over the past three years.

The government has attempted to increase and sustain growth rates, largely by establishing a liberalized trade regime. Fundamental to this is private-sector development, and the government recognizes that it has a role to play in creating an enabling environment for business.

Sierra Leone is still a poor country. It relies on development aid for 44 percent of its budget. Most of its foreign exchange flows in through grants and concessional loans, since exports of goods and services are very low.[14] Clearly, the government will have to generate more domestic revenue.

The Sierra Leonean economy witnessed an overall good performance in 2006: real GDP growth was estimated at 7.8 percent, following 7.3 percent growth in 2005. This growth was the outcome of a revitalized mining sector, sustained agricultural output, and service delivery. This economic momentum was also facilitated by strong support from the country's development partners for economic programs and by the government's continued emphasis on macroeconomic stability and good governance as the bases for socio-economic development.[15]

Though the economy continued to grow in 2007, the rate was lower than had been achieved in 2006 and also below the projected rate of 7.4 percent in 2007. The causes were protracted shortages of electricity, reduced government spending, and rising oil prices. On the good side, exports grew in 2007, reflecting improved performance in mineral and agricultural output.

The Government and the Private Sector After the War

The government intends for the private sector to take the lead in developing the postwar economy. It is fully committed to supporting private-sector development (PSD), and it fully realizes that that sector is vital to economic growth, income generation, job creation, and poverty reduction.

Since 2000 the GOSL has been promoting a pro-business policy environment. The *Doing Business* survey of 2008, published by the World Bank, ranks

Sierra Leone 160th out of 178 countries with regard to ease of doing business. This compares unfavourably with The Gambia and Ghana, which rank 131st and 87th respectively. Sierra Leone is rated poorly for registering companies and properties, for licensing procedures, and for enforcement of contracts and labour laws.[16] Programs are in place to address myriad issues: growth, competition, PSD, public-service reform, capacity building, infrastructure development, poverty reduction, good governance, primary health care, sanitation, food self-sufficiency, and so on. Also in place are a decentralization program whose aim is to devolve power to local governance units; an HIV/AIDS Secretariat (the National AIDS Secretariat); and several education programs— for example, to increase school enrolment and encourage girls' education.

Despite the government's good intentions, however, the private sector's problems persist. Domestic constraints to private-sector growth include legal impediments, an unyielding bureaucracy, poor access to capital, a financial system that is largely insensitive to the business community, lack of support services (i.e., infrastructure), a poor macroeconomic environment, and, more generally, attitudinal problems. The latter were evident in the past and have hardly gone away.

According to the Minister of Finance, the new government (APC) is committed to reforms that will strengthen the investment climate. The government will continue to implement the recommendations of the Study on Administrative Barriers to Trade and Investment as those relate to business registration, regulatory costs, investment, and export promotion.[17]

The Privatization Process

In addressing the private sector's problems, the government has placed particular emphasis on sorting out the problems of SOEs through the NCP so that those enterprises will be able to contribute more meaningfully to revamping the economy. This is being spearheaded by the NCP. The enterprises slated for privatization are listed in Appendix 8.1.

Objectives and Functions of the NCP

The NCP was established to serve as the policy- and decision-making body with respect to the divestiture and reform of public enterprises. The management of all public enterprises would be transferred to the commission, thus ending interference in them by the line ministries and ensuring transparency and good corporate governance. Acting as a prudent shareholder, the commission would manage all public enterprises while preparing them for divestiture. It would be expected to deal with donors for all projects in the divestiture process and to approve the appointments of advisers and consultants.[18] The commission's objectives are these:

- To enable the public sector to focus on the efficient delivery of basic services to the poor, especially in the rural areas.
- To allow broader private-sector participation and thereby enhance economic opportunities, increase economic growth, and create jobs.
- To remove the fiscal burden imposed by non-performing public enterprises on the government budget.

Privatization will stimulate domestic and foreign investment. It will also strengthen the quality and coverage of infrastructural and financial services and help refocus government resources. A secondary effect will be to increase the scope and scale of private-sector activities and thereby generate employment through business growth.[19] The commission's functions are as follows:

- To act as a prudent shareholder, heeding the distinction between shareholders and management, and delivering efficient services while preparing public enterprises for divestiture.
- To approve policies for divestiture.
- To approve guidelines and criteria for the valuation of public enterprises for divestiture, and to choose strategic investors wisely.
- To recommend to the government the legal and regulatory framework for public enterprises that are to be divested.
- To determine whether the shares of a public enterprise should be offered through public or private issues or otherwise.
- To determine when a public enterprise is to be divested.
- To approve the prices for shares or assets of public enterprises offered for sale.
- To act as interlocutor with the World Bank and other donors with regard to public enterprises as well as all projects in the divestiture process.
- To review from time to time the socioeconomic impact of the divestiture program and decide on appropriate remedies.

The Divestiture Process

The divestiture process for loss-taking enterprises engaged in production will involve outright sale without further capitalization. Performing enterprises will initially be run by management contracts until such time as full divestiture takes place. For commercial banks, the divestiture will involve a withdrawal by government in order to increase the participation of such private investors as will enhance the efficiency of the financial sector.

The divestiture will take one or a combination of many forms. These include the following:[20]

- The sale of the business to a private-sector investor or investors, or the sale of the assets of the business in part or in whole.
- A joint venture between the state and a private-sector investor.
- Management contracts—with a single company or a consortium of companies—relating to all or part of the public enterprise.
- Performance contracts.
- Liquidation of the public enterprise.
- Sale to other shareholders in the company, with the government owning some part of the shares.
- Leases, in the case of hotels.
- Employee or management buyouts so as to broaden local participation.

Making the NCP Operational

The task of the NCP Secretariat is to manage the overall privatization program. This includes the following:

- Determining the appropriate timing and sequencing of restructuring and divestiture activities for enterprises and sectors.
- Ensuring that company accounts are up to date, and commissioning audits where needed.
- Restructuring operations, organization, and management where the current situation is an impediment to private investment.
- Determining the need for independent regulation and appropriate legislation to enable private investment in an enterprise/sector.
- Financial restructuring of enterprises where financial liabilities are a barrier to new investment.
- Commissioning independent valuations of businesses (or assets, in the case of non-trading entities).
- Determining optimal divestiture routes for business units and enterprises and ensuring alignment with overall program objectives.
- Marketing investment opportunities to domestic and international investors.
- Managing the transaction process from bidder evaluation through to negotiations and deal close.

Many of these activities require the services of professional advisers. Capacity (both institutional and human) within the NCP is weak. The NCP Secretariat's role is to draw up terms of reference, contract these advisers, coordinate their activities, and ensure that the quality of their work meets appropriate professional standards. The NCP also has a large role to play in coordinating the line and functional activities of key ministries.

Major enterprises and those in the infrastructure sectors will be managed as discrete projects. The teams of advisers engaged for these projects will include sector specialists, economists, financial advisers, regulatory specialists, legal advisers, accountants, and engineering consultants, depending on need.

Progress of the Divestiture Process

The NCP Strategic Plan set out an implementation program for the years 2003 to 2006. It was envisaged that during those years, twenty-four public enterprises would be restructured and divested in some form. Notable successes included these:

- The National Power Authority (NPA) was restructured (ongoing as of this writing), and the Bumbuna Hydroelectric Project was launched. Power-sector reforms also underway include the drafting of an electricity law and the design of a regulatory body. This work is being undertaken by a World Bank team funded by a World Bank Power and Water Project credit (US$7.8 million).
- Work began on restructuring and rehabilitating the Guma Valley Water Authority, also with a World Bank credit.
- Work began on restructuring the Sierra Leone Ports Authority. This involved the development of a framework port strategy and the designation of core and non-core activities. This work continues to be supported by a World Bank credit.
- The national workshops were divested to a group of Chinese investors. This project was implemented by the Ministry of Trade and Industry as an investment-promotion initiative.
- Some preparatory work was done to verify accounts and valuate the assets and liabilities of a number of small, non-performing commercial enterprises.
- Internal NCP technical and procedures manuals were developed with the assistance of a DFID-funded part-time adviser.[21]

The NCP has been receiving donor assistance since November 2006, under the auspices of DFID. This support is part of DFID's broader PSD program. PricewaterhouseCoopers Associates Africa Limited (PwC) has been contracted to provide technical advisory services in support of the NCP and its secretariat until November 2008.[22] PwC has provided six long-term sector advisers and one senior adviser, who work alongside counterparts at the NCP. There is also a provision for short-term advisers for specific areas of input—for example, to address legal, labour, and communication issues.

Progress on Some Privatization Activities

NCP's privatization activities are affecting key infrastructural sectors. Activities in some of these sectors undertaken between 2003 and 2007 are described below.[23] The power sector is treated separately and in greater detail as the new government views this sector as a top priority.

Sierra Leone Ports Authority (SLPA)

The Sierra Leone Ports Authority (SLPA) is a semi-autonomous enterprise and was established by the Ports Act, 1964 (amended in 1991). At its inception it was charged with the following tasks:

- Regulatory control of all port and maritime activities in Sierra Leone.
- Operation of the Port of Freetown.
- Overseeing the Ports of Nitti and Pepel, which were operated by private mining companies and which handled mostly the bulk export of bauxite, rutile, and iron ore.

According to the Government Budget and Statement of Economic Financial Policies (2008), the SLPA suffered a loss of Le 433 million in 2006.[24] Total turnover for the first half of 2007 was Le 16.9 billion with an operating profit of Le 1.08 billion. In 2008 the Ports Authority plans to invest in various projects including civil works, plant, and machinery as well as stevedoring gear to be financed by the World Bank. There are plans to make the operation leaner and more efficient by transforming the port from a service port into a landlord port. The SLPA has suffered from weak management and extremely limited capacity.[25] However, an experienced general manager has been recruited from Ghana. The restructuring of the SLPA as a landlord port will entail private-sector participation in the core activities. This will involve (1) the concession of the container terminal; (2) licensing to service providers for shore handling of break bulk cargo; and (3) definition of the economic and technical regulatory functions associated with the revised SLPA structure, which will require new legislation. As part of the restructuring of the SLPA's operations, the ferry services are now overseen by management contractors. Advertisements are pending for the management-services contracts of the non-core ferry services and slipway.

Sierra Leone Roads Authority (SLRA)

The state-owned Sierra Leone Roads Authority (SLRA) constructs, operates, and maintains the country's roads. Sierra Leone has about 11,000 kilometres of public roads. Maintenance of that network is financed through the Road Fund, whose budget comes from a user levy attached to the price of fuel (this provides more than half the fund's resources) and from fees collected by the Roads Transport Authority through vehicle registrations and driver's licences.[26] The SLRA has been managing the country's public roads since it was established by an Act of Parliament in 1992. The act provides for the SLRA to delegate its responsibilities for certain roads to local governments.[27] The quality of the infrastructure and service delivery is poor, and this poses a major barrier to economic growth. The civil war decimated an infrastructure that was already decrepit following decades of underinvestment.

The challenges faced by the SLRA include an underdeveloped local capacity to plan, design, and operate roads, and an absence of reliable data that could be used to apply modern management techniques. The country's transportation sector continues to be characterized by a dilapidated infrastructure, inefficient services, administrative barriers (e.g., inappropriate and obsolete rules and regulations), and cumbersome procedures. These deficiencies are manifested in poor traffic flows.[28]

The semi-autonomous Mechanical Services Unit (MSU) of the SLRA hires out road-making plant and machinery to the SLRA and the private sector. This enables the SLRA to focus on its core functions; it also enables private companies to embark on feeder-road projects and other infrastructure projects. There are plans (embryonic at this point) to divest the MSU as a commercial firm under private-sector ownership.

Sierra Leone Telecommunications Company (Sierratel)

In April 1995 the Sierra Leone Telecommunications Company (Sierratel) was formed by merging Sierra Leone External Telecommunications (SLET) with the Sierra Leone National Telecommunications Company (SLNTC). The main objectives of this merger were to harmonize and coordinate internal and external telecommunication services, to rationalize investment in telecommunications development, and to provide accessible, efficient, and affordable services. Sierratel is currently the sole fixed-line telephone provider in the country, with exchanges in Freetown, Bo, and Kenema. Freetown represents 96 percent of the coverage of the fixed lines; in other words, the rest of the country is virtually ignored by Sierratel. Telephone penetration remains low, at about 1 telephone line per 440 inhabitants; this is well below the target of 1 per 100 recommended by the International Telecommunications Union (ITU) for developing countries. The quality of service is largely unsatisfactory—that is, unreliable, congested, expensive, and customer unfriendly.[29] Rural areas all over the country are basically cut off from telecommunications. Almost all the transmission lines and switches were destroyed during the war, and most of these have not been repaired, especially in the provincial towns.

The liberalization of the telecoms sector in 2003 enabled the expansion of mobile cellular telephone services. At this writing, five competitors are providing mobile services. The combined mobile subscriber base is estimated at almost 500,000.[30]

The Telecommunications Act, passed in 2006, established the National Telecommunications Commission as an independent regulatory authority. It also introduced a telecommunications licensing and regulatory regime based on promotion of competition and universal access.

The Guma Valley Water Company

The Guma Valley Water Company was founded in 1961 by the Guma Valley Water Act to manage the provision of water to Freetown. At inception it had the capacity to provide water for 350,000 inhabitants. This number has since more than tripled. According to the Sierra Leone Integrated Household Survey (2004) as cited in the Sierra Leone Human Development Report (2007), 74 percent and 46 percent of the urban and rural populations respectively have access to safe drinking water.

With donor assistance, a review of technical, commercial, and financial practices is being undertaken. Private-sector participation will be encouraged in areas such as drilling, storage, security, and support services.[31]

The company faces problems such as insufficient water production, poor distribution, high loss rates, and poor billing and revenue-collection practices. Funding is lacking for major investments in infrastructure expansion and for other improvements in the system, though donor funding is available.[32] It is envisaged that the Guma Valley Water Company will continue under government ownership.

Historical Perspective of the Power Sector

The power sector in Sierra Leone is in dire straits. Only about 7 percent of Sierra Leoneans have access to electricity, and only Freetown, Bo, and Kenema are connected to the grid. Power for Freetown and the rest of the western area is supplied by the National Power Authority (NPA); for Bo and Kenema it is supplied by a semi-autonomous body, the Bo–Kenema Power Station (BKPS). The power stations in other provincial towns were destroyed during the war. Mining companies in the south and east of the country provide their own power. The total installed power of the national utilities and these companies is less than 100 MW. Installed capacity at the NPA power station is about 38 MW, with 8 MW in operation and the rest of the units needing major repairs. BKPS operates a dual hydro/thermal scheme at various times of the year. The thermal power station has a capacity of 5 MW, and the hydro scheme has recently been upgraded to 6 MW.

It is estimated that an investment of US$470 million—equivalent to $880 million in 2007 dollars—has been made in the power sector since 1964 from donor funds.[33] Of this total, 65 percent is for the Bumbuna Hydroelectric Project (BHP) (Bumbuna is in Tonkolili District in the north), 30 percent for NPA-related projects, and 5 percent for BKPS-related projects. In the short term, Bumbuna is expected to serve the capital, Freetown, but coverage will eventually extend to parts of the Bombali and Tonkolili Districts.

This significant investment has not had any impact on electricity consumption or access in the country: consumption is still low, at less than 10 kWh per capita in 2006.[34] The GOSL has always focused on providing power to Freetown and the big provincial towns; it has paid little attention to rural electrification. All of the provincial power stations and their infrastructures (except for Bo and Kenema) were damaged during the war. Electricity supplies were declining even before the war began in 1991; the conflict only accelerated this.

The country faces difficulties with commercial energy supply, especially electricity supply. Freetown is supplied with electricity from the oil-fired King Tom generating station; most areas in the interior, except for Bo and Kenema, are largely without power supplies. Freetown faces problems with extremely intermittent power supply. The available electricity generation capacity is grossly inadequate, and load shedding is constantly in force. Sierra Leone imports all of its petroleum fuel. The country depends on petroleum products to satisfy most of its modern energy needs, especially for transportation and electricity production.[35]

Rationale for Reform

Reforms to the Sierra Leone power sector are necessary for the following reasons:

Capital crisis. The NPA's financial performance is very poor as a result of high transmission and distribution losses, low bill-collection rates, and inefficiencies in generation. There is little scope for the NPA to generate its own capital to finance expansion. The money needed to maintain current operations is not within the government's reach. Traditional funding agencies have generally been too slow in providing such funds.

Performance crisis. The NPA is plagued with a serious performance crisis arising from inadequate availability of supply and weaknesses in the distribution system. These weaknesses are attributable to the NPA's deteriorating financial position, poor accountability, poor management, lack of capitalization, and operating inefficiencies.

Access crisis. Private-sector participation would make electricity more available to the rural population. In this vein, the government's energy policy calls for several measures: establishing a rural electrification scheme operated by a Rural Electricity Board; reducing duties on renewable energy technology (RET) equipment; and using the Bumbuna transmission line as the backbone of a new national grid that would serve other areas of the country. These projects are still, however, at the planning stage.

Cost burden to government. Privatization would do much to ease the government's considerable financial burden.

A study of electricity reform carried out by Electricity Africa under the World Bank's supervision ("Reform of Sierra Leone's Electricity Sector," 2002) made these recommendations:

- *Efficiency.* The sector should produce, transmit, distribute, and market electricity, and be more effective at recovering reasonably incurred costs from electricity users.
- *Sustainability.* The sector should become financially self-supporting. This would involve establishing sufficient credit-worthiness to access long-term funding at competitive rates.
- *Improved access.* The reach of electricity supply, the security of supply, and the level of service should be extended within the financial means of the sector, supported by appropriate cross-subsidization within the sector and by targeted subsidies to the sector.

Recommended Reform Measures

The following are the main reform measures contemplated as recommended by the Consultants for the Reform of the Power Sector, Electricity Africa, and as adopted by the GOSL:[36]

- The Ministry of Energy and Power (MEP) will focus on crafting electricity policy. In-house technical expertise will support this mandate. There is very little capacity, and funds will be sought to expand it.
- An independent regulator from the private sector will oversee entry into the electricity sector, technical and safety performance of sector operations, and tariff adjustments. A new electricity policy will be promulgated and the existing act revised.
- The existing NPA will be transformed into a corporatized, self-funding utility. It will mainly be a transmission and distribution company and will act as an electricity producer of last resort. Independent power producers (IPPs) will be allowed to produce power and sell it to the NPA, whose operations will be considerably shored up and made more efficient. BKPS[37] will continue as a non-grid operation until reached by the national grid. Provincial stations will be connected to the national grid. Some isolated stations will require technical and financial support.
- The NPA will be managed for a few years through a performance-based management contract. During those years the operation will be considerably strengthened by the infusion of capital into appropriate areas.
- The BHP[38] will be operated as an IPP. A private operator will be given a concession to operate Bumbuna and its transmission line as an

IPP, selling power to NPA, which will in turn distribute and sell the power. The sector regulator will regulate the tariff to ensure a level playing field with other IPP operators.

A technical wing has been established within the Ministry of Energy and Power, and a study has been conducted on setting up the regulatory agency. The 1982 NPA Act was amended in 2006 (NPA (Amendment) Act, 2006) to accommodate a special-purpose company for Bumbuna and to allow other players to enter the generation market. Several projects are now being funded or about to be funded by several donors. Relevant bid documents have been prepared and are being reviewed. A resettlement plan for Bumbuna has been completed, and people affected by the project have been compensated. The GOSL is planning to form the Bumbuna Trust to manage environmental and socio-economic issues associated with the project and to recruit a management contractor, using funds from the World Bank.

Challenges and New Opportunities

The NCP has made slow progress with privatization. The challenges here are enormous. A major one is arranging funding to run the organization and to hire consultants. Because privatization is, obviously, a key component of the private-sector development program, many of the problems affecting the private sector also apply to that program. The major challenges are described below.[39]

Availability of Funds to Employ Outside Advisers

Most divestitures require the support of outside institutions—for example, accountants to audit financial statements and to value real estate. Sierra Leone does not possess a great depth of such supporting institutions, and the cost of employing outside consultants can be prohibitive.

Time Needed to Procure Advisers

When donor funds—and, therefore, procurement rules—are involved, procurement can take a great deal of time. For example, the author worked under contract on an NPA team, helping manage the procurement of goods and services needed to refurbish NPA generators. It took nine months, as the procurement rules required separate bidding processes and contracts for assessing the problems, purchasing parts, and installing and commissioning those parts—all as required by the World Bank. The whole process would have taken three months at most, had it been contracted to one reputable private-sector group.

Time Needed to Consult All Relevant Stakeholders

Stakeholders must be brought on board. Yet ensuring that all stakeholders are satisfied with the consultation process can take a considerably long time.

Time Needed for Any Legislative Change

It usually takes about twelve months for the country's Parliament to change a law, but it can also take as long as three years. For example, the Telecommunications Act took two years to move from the planning stage to final ratification by Parliament.

Market Capacity for the Transactions Planned

Because Sierra Leone has a relatively underdeveloped private sector, the appetite for participating in transactions can be lacking. This touches on a number of transactions, including management contracts, share purchases, and buyouts of divested firms.

Lack of a Social Action Program to Deal with Employees Made Redundant by Privatization

Many enterprises lack the funds to make redundancy payments. This makes restructuring harder. This problem could be remedied with government or donor funds. However, the government is strapped for cash. Donors are the most likely source of funds for redundancy payments, but they would require some sign that the government is serious about carrying on with reforms and would need to see comprehensive plans.

Excessive Debts Owed by Enterprises

Many enterprises to be divested are highly indebted. As a consequence, private-sector participation can be difficult to attract. Most of the debts are held by the government (either the donor funds have been lent forward to the enterprise by the Finance Ministry, or the government owes the debt directly). A number of enterprises may also owe debts to other parastatals.

Lack of Capacity at the NCP Secretariat

The secretariat is understaffed to handle the range of projects they are tasked with.

Legal, Regulatory, and Institutional Framework to Facilitate Reform

A number of bills required for sector reforms, including those to establish regulatory frameworks (especially in the utilities sector), will be required before a number of privatizations can proceed.

Absorptive Capacity of the Market

It is unclear whether the small, underdeveloped capital market will be able to absorb the number of pending transactions in the time frame envisioned, especially with regard to private-sector participation in financial institutions.

Problems with Communications and Competing Agendas

A present problem with communications is that they are reactive rather than proactive. Poor communications can lead to confusion among stakeholders. In a privatization program, those stakeholders may have different objectives and, it follows, competing agendas. Also, the public may resist the divestiture of enterprises and the rising costs of services that can result. This was the case with the bungled initial attempt to bring aboard a strategic partner for the Rokel Commercial Bank, in which the government held a 51 percent share and local shareholders 49 percent. Local shareholders organized themselves and succeeded in having the project aborted.

Ability to Attract Domestic and International Investors

Privatization programs often find it difficult to attract appropriate domestic and international investors.

With help from the government and the donor community, the NCP is responding to these challenges. In 2006 it revised its divestiture program to take many of the above constraints into account. The program's duration was reconfigured by PriceWaterhouseCoopers (PwC) under the current technical assistance being provided by DFID. The cost of implementing the divestiture and reform program over the next two to three years has been estimated as $8.4 million. Part of this cost has been funded by donors, but there is still a shortfall of some $2.8 million. Since November 2006, funding has been provided by DFID as part of its broader program for private-sector development. Technical services provided by PwC will last until the end of 2008. These services will support the NCP in order to ensure the timely and effective implementation of the GOSL's strategy for restructuring and privatizing SOEs. The project will provide technical assistance to four branches of the NCP:

- The office of the NCP Secretariat.
- The sector specialists in the NCP Secretariat. There are six key sectors: power, water, transportation (including ports), telecommunications, financial services, and general/commercial/manufacturing.
- The NCP's legal department.
- Communications, public relations, training, specialist legal-advisory services, and various other departments.

Notwithstanding this assistance, the NCP still faces considerable financial problems. Unfunded employee liabilities could amount to as much as $30 million.[40] In addition, the government is finding it difficult to meet the annual operating budget of US$1 million.

The new capital market, the rising number of banking institutions, and the introduction of more varied financial instruments could create further opportunities to improve the performance of the private sector and thus the NCP. Parallel reforms of the private sector will be essential to the overall success of the privatization scheme.

Complementary Private-Sector Development Initiatives

Since 2005, with assistance from donors, the government has launched complementary reforms.

Initiatives by the Ministry of Trade and Industry (MTI) and Donors

The privatization program needs to be implemented in the context of broader PSD objectives. New private investments in SOEs will grow Sierra Leone's private sector and boost its productivity. The privatization program can be viewed as a catalyst for economic reforms. Support for private-sector development is reflected in the revised objectives of NCP's revised privatization strategy.

DFID's Private Sector Development Program calls for the removal of administrative barriers to investment. That program covers three broad areas:[41]

- National PSD strategy. Led by the Ministry of Trade and Industry (MTI), a comprehensive strategy will be developed to promote domestic and foreign investment in trade and industry.
- Commercial law reform. The legal and regulatory framework governing business and commerce will be modernized.
- Program implementation. Programs identified and prioritized in the PSD strategy will be designed and delivered. These programs will encompass investment-promotion initiatives, the alignment of GOSL policies and statutes with relevant international conventions, and institutional development to ensure capacity to deliver these programs.

The MTI has launched several initiatives that will aid private-sector development. Several programs are envisioned to foster the development of small and medium-sized enterprises. A Trade Policy Review has been undertaken with the support of the WTO. The investment climate has been largely deregulated in order to boost investment and private-sector development. The government's capacity in trade negotiations is being enhanced through technical assistance to the MTI. Laws to support implementation of the trade policy are gradually being passed, under the stewardship of the Law Reform Commission. A Partnership Law has been drafted, and a review of commercial land use has been completed. The government also intends to develop policies and laws on competition and intellectual property rights.

PSD opportunities will increase as restraints on business are removed. The government is committed to improving the effectiveness, stability, and efficiency

of the financial sector, streamlining bureaucratic procedures for business registration, and improving and reviewing the legal and regulatory framework.

Post-Election Thrust

Free and fair elections in September 2007 ushered in a new government and bol-
stered Sierra Leone's democratic credentials. The new government has indicated
its desire to continue with the private-sector development initiatives undertaken
by the previous government. It is committed to providing emergency power
to Freetown while waiting for Bumbuna to come on line (slated for the end of
2008).[42] Bumbuna has a capacity of 50 MW; however, capacity will drop to 25
MW during the dry season. To address this serious problem, the government, with
International Development Association (IDA) support, is pursuing a competitive
procurement process, on an accelerated timetable, for the emergency rental of 15
MW of power-generation capacity. This emergency capacity is proposed to be installed in Freetown by the end of the year and to be operational for at least twelve
months while other, longer-term and lower-cost generation solutions are implemented. It will be subsidized at first; the government justifies this by pointing out
that the costs in lost production, lost jobs, and lost competitiveness as a result of
not having power would be much higher than whatever subsidy is provided.

The government is committed to supporting the NCP's work and speeding
up privatization. It will be known in a few months whether it has succeeded.

Conclusion

Sierra Leone has made considerable strides in governance, having held successful
elections and improved its economic performance. The privatization program
has gone slowly because of the several factors mentioned, the main ones being
weak capacity at the local level and within the NCP Secretariat; the high cost
of employing outside advisers; the time needed to change laws; the market's
weak capacity to absorb the transactions being planned; excessive debt held by
enterprises; the lack of social programs to deal with employees made redundant
by privatizations; difficulty attracting international investors; a weak legal,
regulatory, and institutional regime to facilitate reform; and communication
problems.

The challenges are enormous, and the government, with donors' help,
has been addressing them. Significant improvements have been made with
the implementation of the private-sector development program. Both the
government and the donors have been highly supportive of that program.
For example, administrative barriers to doing business have been removed
through legislation and a trade policy review, and procedures for business
registration have been streamlined. The government is especially committed
to reforming the country's infrastructure sector. As Sierra Leone's economic
performance continues to improve, this will boost the privatization program.

That said, many of the key issues facing the NCP have yet to be addressed—for example, funding shortfalls and the social costs of privatization. There are a number of steps in the offing that will improve the performance of the private sector and, it follows, the NCP. These include establishing a new capital market, increasing the number of banking institutions, introducing more varied financial instruments, making other reforms to the financial sphere, and removing still more administrative barriers to doing business. For all of that to happen, the government will have to make a determined effort to find the money to accelerate the pace of divestitures and other reforms. Only then will the NCP have its desired impact in the near future.

Notes

1 Mr. Keili, a consulting engineer, is Managing Director of CEMMATS Group Ltd., a leading multidisciplinary engineering and project management consulting practice in Sierra Leone. He studied Mining Engineering at the University of Newcastle upon Tyne. Over the past thirty years he has held positions of increasing responsibility in the private mining industry, in parastatals, and in consultancy work in Sierra Leone. He is currently Chairman of the National Social and Insurance Trust and is also on the boards or councils of several private-sector firms in Sierra Leone. He has extensive experience of Sierra Leone's business sector.

2 The war in Sierra Leone lasted from 1991 to 2002. It involved some 70,000 casualties and the displacement of 2.6 million people from their homes. The war was characterized by widespread atrocities, including the abduction of children and systematic rape. The conditions that led to the war included a repressive predatory state, dependence on mineral rents, the impact of structural adjustment, a large and excluded youth population, the availability of small arms after the end of the Cold War, and interference from regional neighbours. Human security has improved because the conflict is over, though the state is still very weak despite extension of state security.

3 SL-PRSP-2002-2007.

4 Community structures such as court barries (traditional court buildings), clinics, schools, markets, community centres, churches, mosques, and dwelling houses were destroyed or completely razed. Some villages were completely burned down. Basic infrastructure had to be rebuilt before displaced persons could be repatriated to their communities.

5 This act to divest state-owned enterprises was passed by the National Provisional Ruling Council (NPRC) government in 1993.

6 SL-PRSP-2002-2007.

7 WTO (World Trade Organization), Report by Secretariat, *Sierra Leone Trade Policy Review* (Washington: 2005).

8 Sierra Leone, National Programme for Food Security, Job Creation, and Good Governance, *Poverty Reduction Strategy Paper* (2005-2007) (Freetown: 2005).

9 Production of rice (paddy) in 2006 was 1,062,320 metric tonnes (mt), compared to 422,065 mt in 2002. Cassava was 2,973,100 mt in 2006 compared to 895,817 mt in 2002 (Ministry of Agriculture and Food Security, as cited in BSL 2006 Annual Report and Statement of Account, 2007).

10 Government of Sierra Leone, "Ministry of Mineral Resources Annual Report" (Freetown: 2006).

11 Bank of Sierra Leone, "Annual Report and Statement of Accounts for the Financial Year Ending 2007" (Freetown: 2008).

12 Government of Sierra Leone, *Ministry of Mineral Resources Annual Report* (Freetown: 2006).

13 PREM (Poverty Reduction and Economic Management Sector Unit), Africa Region, "Sierra Leone: Tapping the Mineral Wealth for Human Progress—A Break with the Past," Report no. 26141-SL (Washington: World Bank, 2004).

14 Government of Sierra Leone, "Government Budget and Statement of Economic and Financial Policies for the Financial Year 2008," speech delivered by the Minister of Finance and Economic Development (Freetown: 2007).

15 Bank of Sierra Leone, "Annual Report."

16 World Bank and International Finance Corporation, *Doing Business* (Washington: 2008).

17 Government of Sierra Leone, "Government Budget, 2008."

18 NCP (National Commission for Privatisation), "Strategic Plan for the Divesture of Public Enterprises" (Freetown: 2003–2006).

19 Ibid.

20 Ibid.

21 DFID, "Sierra Leone Private Sector Development: Support to the National Commission for Privatization (NCP) Secretariat for Implementation of Privatization Strategy, 2005–2019," Project Memorandum and Framework, February (London: 2005).

22 Ibid.

23 Victor Strasser-King, "Report on Current Privatisation Status—National Commission for Privatization," Report for Sierra Leone Institution of Engineers (Freetown: 2007); DFID, "Sierra Leone Private Sector Development."

24 US$1 is equivalent to Le2,970.

25 Sierra Leone, *Poverty Reduction Strategy Paper* (2005).

26 WTO, *Sierra Leone Trade Policy Review* (Washington: 2005).

27 Sierra Leone, "National Transport Strategy and Investment Plan" (unpublished).

28 Sierra Leone, *Poverty Reduction Strategy Paper.*

29 Sierra Leone, *Poverty Reduction Strategy Paper.*

30 Sierra Leone Institution of Engineers, "Power Sector in Sierra Leone—Current Status, Challenges, and the Way Forward" (Freetown: 2007).

31 Strasser–King, "Report."

32 Ibid.

33 Sierra Leone Institution of Engineers, "The Power Sector in Sierra Leone."

34 Ibid.

35 CEMMATS Group, "Energy Policy for Sierra Leone—Summary for Policy Makers 2004."

36 Miscellaneous sources: Report by the World Bank Consultant, *aides-mémoiré*, and power-sector–related reports.

37 BKPS, the Bo Kenema Power Services, is a semi-autonomous part of the NPA and supplies power to the townships of Bo and Kenema.

38 Bumbuna is a 50 MW hydroelectric project in the north of the country slated to come on stream at the end of 2008.

39 DFID (Department for International Development). "Technical Assistance to the National Commission for Privatisation: Sierra Leone Inception Report" (London: 2007).

40 Strasser-King, "Report."

41 DFID, "Technical Assistance."

42 The new president has made pronouncements on this issue in several speeches since his election.

References

Bank of Sierra Leone. "Annual Report and Statement of Accounts for the Financial Year Ending 2007." Freetown: 2008.

Bank of Sierra Leone, Research Department. "Monthly Economic Review." Freetown: March 2008.

Child, Andrew. "Attractive Sweeteners Are Needed to Underwrite Corporate Risk-Privatisation." *Financial Times* (London), February 14, 2005.

DFID (Department for International Development). "Technical Assistance to the National Commission for Privatisation: Sierra Leone Inception Report." London: 2007.

——— . "Sierra Leone Private Sector Development: Support to the National Commission for Privatization (NCP) Secretariat for Implementation of Privatization Strategy, 2005–2019." Project Memorandum and Framework. Freetown: February 2005.

FIAS (Foreign Investment Advisory Service). "Sierra Leone-Diagnostic Study of the Investment Climate and the Investment Code. Freetown: May 2004.

GOSL (Government of Sierra Leone). "Government Budget and Statement of Economic and Financial Policies for the Financial Year 2008." Speech by Minister of Finance and Economic Development. Freetown: 2007.

——— . "Ministry of Agriculture and Food Security Annual Report." Freetown: 2006.

——— . "Ministry of Mineral Resources Annual Report." Freetown: 2006.

——— . National Commission for Privatisation Act. Freetown: 2002.

——— . "National Programme for Food Security, Job Creation, and Good Governance." Poverty Reduction Strategy Paper, 2005–2007. Freetown: 2005.

——— . (2006) NPA Amendment Act. Freetown: 2006.

——— . "Private Sector Development: Support to the National Commission for Privatisation Secretariat for the Implementation of the Privatisation Strategy 2005–2010." London: DFID, 2005.

GOSL, Ministry of Trade and Industry. "Private Sector Development Policy and Strategy Framework for Poverty Reduction—Making the Private Sector Work." Freetown: 2004.

GOSL, National Commission for Privatisation. "Strategic Plan for the Divesture of Public Enterprises—Implementation Programme, 2003–2006." Freetown: 2003.

GOSL and UNAMSIL. "National Recovery Strategy, Sierra Leone, 2002–2003." Freetown: 2002.

GOSL and WTO (World Trade Organization). "Trade Policy Review." Freetown and Geneva: 2004.

PREM (Poverty Reduction and Economic Management Sector Unit), Africa Region. "Sierra Leone: Tapping the Mineral Wealth for Human Progress—A Break with the Past." Report no. 26141-SL. Washington: World Bank, 2004.

Sierra Leone Human Development Report. "Empowering Local Government for Sustainable Human Development and Poverty Reduction: The District Focus Approach to Development." Freetown: 2007.

Sierra Leone Institution of Engineers. "Power Sector in Sierra Leone—Current Status, Challenges, and the Way Forward." Proceedings of the Public Lecture on the Power Sector in Sierra Leone. Freetown: 2007.

Strasser-King, Victor. "Report on Current Privatisation Status—National Commission for Privatization." Report for Sierra Leone Institution of Engineers. Freetown: 2007.

World Bank and the International Finance Corporation. *Doing Business*. Washington: 2008.

WTO (World Trade Organization). *Sierra Leone Trade Policy Review*, Report by Secretariat. Geneva: 2005.

Appendix 8.1

First Schedule (Public Enterprises for Divestiture)

1. Sierra Leone Housing Corporation
2. Sierra Leone Produce Marketing Board
3. Mining and General Services Limited
4. Sierra Leone Road Transport Corporation
5. Sierra Leone Postal Services Limited
6. Sierra Leone Airlines
7. Sierra Leone Telecommunications Company Limited
8. Sierra Leone Airport Authority
9. National Power Authority
10. Sierra Leone Port Authority
11. Guma Valley Water Company
12. Sierra Leone National Shipping Company Limited
13. Forest Industries Corporation
14. National Insurance Company Limited
15. Sierra Leone State Lottery Company Limited
16. Sierra Leone Commercial Bank Limited
17. National Development Bank Limited
18. Sierra Leone Roads Authority
19. Rokel Commercial Bank Limited
20. Seaboard West Africa
21. Sierra Leone Daily Mail
22. National Workshop
23. Government Printing Department
24. Sierra Leone Broadcasting Service

Liberia

State-Building Efforts in Post-Conflict Liberia

Sunny Nyemah[1]

9

Introduction

Sanity has been restored to Liberia since the signing of the Comprehensive Peace Agreement (CPA)[2] in 2003 and the deployment of UN peacekeepers. There is now a semblance of peace, and significant efforts have been made to sustain that peace so that Liberia can rebuild itself. But full recovery is distant because of factors such as these: food insecurity, inadequate price controls, a poorly functioning justice system, lack of land reform, a dilapidated health care system, and limited institutional capacity.

For all these challenges, the people of Liberia and their government are also blessed with opportunities. Development is beginning to happen: Mittal Steel is investing in job-creating facilities, micro-credit programs are being funded, and small and medium-sized enterprises (SMEs) are finding financing. The question is, how will Liberians and their government maximize these opportunities? The goodwill and generous contributions of the international donors can be thanked for much of this. Other factors are the influx of international investors as a result of the "Ellen factor"[3] and the president's efforts to reduce the country's debt.

Developmental consultants agree that Liberia is at a crossroads and that the current regime, with the continued support of the international community, has an opportunity to rebuild Liberia and improve the lives of its people.

A History of the Conflict

One cannot understand the peace without understanding how the civil war started. The civil strife in Liberia, which destroyed the state, was the result of a convergence of social, cultural, economic, and political factors.

Liberia fell into turmoil in 1989. There were two broad phases to this civil unrest: between 1989 and 1997, Charles Taylor[4] led an uprising against Samuel Doe's[5] government. Doe was assassinated in 1990. There was an interim government between 1990 and 1997. Then between 1999 and 2003, two rebel groups—Liberians United for Reconciliation and Democracy (LURD)[6] and the Movement for Democracy in Liberia (MODEL)[7]—fought to overthrow the Taylor-led government. As a result of these conflicts, in 2005 Liberia ranked 142nd out of 159 countries on 2005 Transparency International Corruption Perception Index and had a per capita GDP of $163—a significant drop from 1990, when according to the World Bank (Statistics 1983–89) that figure was $1,200.

According to the Liberian finance ministry's External Debt Report, the country's external debt exceeded US$3.2 billion. Around the same time, the World Bank estimated unemployment at 75 percent.

The years preceding these events were marked by strong discontent among "Indigenous Liberians,"[8] who felt marginalized by the "Americo-Liberians."[9] This discontent deeply affected Liberian development and impeded efforts to make one nation out of the two groups. To begin with, Indigenous Liberians had for decades been trying to wrest control of their land from their Americo-Liberian leaders in Monrovia, especially when those controls limited their slave-trading activities. Also, British and European merchants, with the support of their governments, refused to treat Liberia as a sovereign state. The European powers enacted import and export duties for the sole reason that Liberia was the only African nation run by blacks. For many years the Liberian government had little control of the country's hinterland, which was surrounded by French and British protectorates (Guinea, Ivory Coast, Sierra Leone). This led the Liberian government in 1864 to limit access to the country by enacting the Ports of Entry Law. A final factor: Monrovia burdened itself with unfair concessions with Western corporations such as the Firestone, Uniroyal, Goodrich, Republic Steel, and Bethlehem Steel. An example: according to "Liberia Past and Present," an online media on Liberia:

> Under pressure of the US State Department, the Liberian Government, represented by its Secretary of State Edwin Barclay, continued the negotiations which eventually lead to the 1926 Firestone Concession Agreement and two additional agreements Harvey Firestone had won. He obtained a one million acre concession for a 99-year period, was granted the exclusive rights (!) upon the lands selected, and became—with only few, small, exceptions—exempted of all present and future taxes.

> Thus, Firestone acquired virtually unlimited rights over an area equal to 4 per cent of the country's territory and nearly 10 per cent of what was considered the arable land in the country. Moreover, Firestone lent $5 million to the Liberian Government through a wholly-owned and especially for this purpose created subsidiary, the Finance Corporation of Liberia. The $ 5 million Loan put Liberia virtually under control of US administrators and supervisors. An American Financial Advisor

appointed by the US Government controlled the Republic's finance and had to approve the country's budget every year. But the most striking and important consequence of this Loan was that the Liberian Government was now forbidden to contract new loans without the written consent of the Finance Corporation of America, i.e. Firestone.[10]

As a result of all this, and because power rested firmly in the hands of the Americo-Liberians in Monrovia, there was almost no integration between the two groups of Liberians. Then in 1944, William V.S. Tubman,[11] leader of the True Whig Party,[12] became president and launched a program of social, economic, and political reforms. He introduced or expanded the Unification Policy and the Open Door Policy.[13] The Unification Policy[14] brought about some level of social and political integration between Americo-Liberians and Indigenous Liberians. The Open Door Policy stimulated the economy and helped attract foreign direct investment (FDI). Tubman succeeded in opening up Liberia's hinterland and bringing powerful tribal leaders into his government; but at the same time, he was a political maverick who dominated the country through a patronage system.

Unfortunately, economic development was impeded by the country's heavy reliance on extractive sectors such as iron ore, rubber, and timber. So the boom did not greatly benefit most Liberians,[15] and severe inequalities persisted, especially with regard to education and employment opportunities.

William R. Tolbert, Jr.,[16] the nineteenth president of Liberia, was a visionary leader. Under his rule, changes began to accelerate. One of his innovative programs was "Mat to Mattress," through which he intended to elevate the common people. Its core principles were mass education, agricultural development, and social empowerment. A related program was "Total Involvement for Higher Heights," whose goal was to narrow the gap between haves and have-nots by resorting to "Humanistic Capitalism."[17] Tolbert was one of the few presidents before Doe who spoke an indigenous language (Kpelle).[18]

These monumental changes were intended to encourage a one-state, one-citizenship mentality among all Liberians. But Tolbert's dream was short-circuited by political pressures: Liberia's progressives[19] were calling for multi-party democracy; the "old guard"[20] was insisting that a one-party state be continued. One can argue that Tolbert's dream of multi-party democracy, of forging a unified society out of Indigenous and Americo-Liberians, never had a chance, given the rivalry between the old guard and the progressives. One result of that rivalry was an end to Liberia's long-standing stability. In addition, the Tolbert government could not evade the world economic crisis of the 1970s, which caused the price of rice—Liberia's staple food—to soar. Inflation and political instability led to the 1979 rice riots. The government responded by arresting the alleged instigators[21] of the riots. Samuel Doe responded by launching a *coup d'état* and installing himself as president.

On April 12, 1980, Doe led a band of eighteen ordinary soldiers, who assassinated President Tolbert and overthrew his government. As the highest-ranking non-commissioned officer, Doe became chairman of the People's Redemption Council. Political parties and activities were immediately banned. On April 12, 1981, Doe announced the formation of a Constitution Review Commission and appointed Dr. Amos Sawyer to head it. (Nine years later, in 1990, Sawyer would be appointed interim president after Doe left the country.)

It can be argued that Liberia enjoyed some infrastructure development and social cohesion during Doe's tenure. For example, government buildings were constructed, highways were paved, and more Indigenous Liberians began attending university.

In fact, during Doe's reign, Liberia enjoyed one of the highest per capita GDPs in Africa (US$1,200) and had one of the most vibrant middle classes (World Bank Statistics, 1983–1989). Four years into his rule, Doe lifted the ban on political parties and immediately formed his own, the National Democratic Party of Liberia (NDPL). Around this time, however, a series of events unfolded: the razing of Sawyer's residence after he refused to be Doe's vice-presidential candidate; the suppression of a student demonstration at the national university; and, on August 22, 1984, a raid by the army on the university campus, at Doe's command. During the latter event, several students were beaten, raped, and murdered. In the aftermath, political opponents were jailed without due process, the 1985 election was rigged, and an attempted invasion by former Commanding General Thomas Quiwonkpa led to Quiwonkpa's execution.

By 1989, Liberians in the diaspora and at home were beginning to raise serious concerns about Doe's actions. They accused him of fostering corruption, abusing power, violating human rights, and jailing opponents without due process. The U.S. government slashed its financial support for Doe's government pending efforts on his part to curb corruption and promote good governance. Pressure began to mount from his opponents in the diaspora. The climax of all this was Charles Taylor's invasion of December 1989, which enjoyed considerable popular support.

It has been alleged that Taylor's invasion was masterminded by a group of influential Liberians. The story is that Doe's opponents lobbied for Taylor's "escape" from a Massachusetts prison and that the U.S. government arranged this in a way that would minimize its embarrassment for having associated itself with Doe.

Taylor had been a friend of Quinwonkpa, and now he leveraged that friendship, tricking the people of Nimba into believing that only through him could they avenge themselves on Doe for the atrocities he had committed against them.

In December 1989, Taylor invaded Liberia through Côte d'Ivoire under the banner of the NPFL. Midway through the invasion, a breakaway group led by one of Taylor's generals, Prince Y. Johnson, formed the Independent National Patriotic Front of Liberia (INPFL). Johnson marshalled his more disciplined forces toward Monrovia, where he captured the country's only commercial port. At this point the international community and the West African regional association dispatched a peacekeeping mission styled the Economic Community Monitoring Group (ECOMOG). With the arrival of ECOMOG, a buffer zone was established between Doe's forces and those of Prince Johnson, and between Johnson's and Taylor's. In the midst of these buffer zones, Doe was captured and murdered by Johnson. The INPFL visited the port at the invitation of ECOMOG's commander, General Quinoo. Now a new player was injected into the crisis: Sawyer, who was appointed to head an interim government, which controlled about one-quarter of the country.

By 1993 a new group had been formed calling itself the United Liberation Movement of Liberia (ULIMO), headed by Raleigh Seekie. This group was a merger of Krahn soldiers of the Armed Forces of Liberia and some Mandingo-speaking Liberians, who felt marginalized in Liberia and who saw the crisis as an opportunity to be fully accepted as Liberians. A series of peace accords resulted in the weakening of Taylor's base; at that point, Taylor agreed to join a five-man power-sharing government that would include a representative of the Interim Government of National Unity (IGNU), Kromah of ULIMO, and Boley of the LPC; this group would be headed by Wilton Sankawulo (who died in late 2008). On July 19, 1997, Taylor won a quickly arranged election that was declared free and fair by international observers.

Six years after Taylor achieved the Liberian presidency, his government still had not improved the lives of Liberians. During this tenure, Liberia suffered 75 percent unemployment and its per capita GDP fell to $162.22 FDI was elusive because of political instability and because Taylor made no real effort to curb corruption. This did not make a stable environment for foreign investment. Also, the United States and Great Britain did not trust Taylor, especially after it was alleged that he was encouraging the civil war in neighbouring Sierra Leone. The issue of Sierra Leone led the UN to place an embargo on Liberia and (later) to ban the export of diamonds and timber from that country.

By now, armed groups such as LURD and MODEL, comprised mainly of old enemies of Taylor in the previous civil war, were beginning to challenge Taylor's rule. After these groups conquered several major towns, the Economic Community of West African States (ECOWAS) arranged a peace conference for June 4, 2003. Around this time the Chief Prosecutor of the Special Court of Sierra Leone announced that a sealed indictment against Taylor had been opened. That indictment accused him of committing atrocities in Sierra Leone.

In July 2003 a ceasefire agreement was signed among the factions (the Government of Liberia, LURD, and MODEL). Unfortunately, all parties failed to honour it; as a result, brutal fighting erupted in central Monrovia in July and August 2003. This caused a massive humanitarian crisis. On August 11, 2003, under intense American and international pressure, Charles Taylor resigned and went into exile in Nigeria.

On August 18, 2003, with Taylor out of the way, the factions signed the CPA. The signatories included Taylor's government, LURD, MODEL, the Liberian political parties, and civil-society organizations. From this process arose the two-year National Transitional Government of Liberia (NTGL). A first contingent of 3,600 peacekeepers under ECOWAS was dispatched to Liberia. In October 2003, the UN assumed the peacekeeping role by absorbing ECOMIL into a larger peacekeeping force (13,000 troops, 1,194 police) under the UN Mission in Liberia (UNMIL).[23]

The second round of the presidential election took place on November 8, 2005. Ellen Johnson-Sirleaf emerged as winner, defeating soccer legend George Weah.

Gains and Interventions

Ellen Johnson-Sirleaf is Africa's first female president. In her ascendancy can be found hope for Liberia's future. For one thing, she is a Harvard-educated public administrator, a former Citibank and World Bank executive, and a former assistant administrator of the United Nations Development Programme (UNDP).

An observer of Liberian events would notice that under Johnson-Sirleaf's stewardship, the economy has improved spectacularly in less than three years. According to the CIA's *World Factbook*, Liberia's per capita GDP increased from $162 in 2005 to about $500 (based on purchasing parity) in 2007 and unemployment fell from 85 to 80 percent. The government of Liberia, however, insists that the CIA's data are estimates. The Ministry of Finance (http://www.mofliberia.org) indicates 80 percent unemployment. Furthermore, a more responsible, disciplined, and transparent economic and financial management system has taken root. The government is taking back control of the economy by implementing programs such as the Government Economic Management Assistance Program (GEMAP), the Public Procurement and Concession Commission (PPCC), and the General Auditing Commission (GAC). It has suspended all forestry concessions and is reviewing concessions in other sectors. With a grant from the U.S. government, the country has disbanded its armed forces (the army, the police, paramilitaries) and is rebuilding them almost from scratch.

At the international level, the country's relationship with its trading and commercial partners has markedly improved. Debt reduction has been fast-tracked, evidenced by the fact that Liberia achieved status as a heavily indebted poor country (HIPC) in March 2008. FDI has surged with the signing of a US$1.5 billion concession with Arcelor Mittal, the solicitation of two further mining concessions, and the resumption of logging as well as diamond- and gold-mining operations. Johnson-Sirleaf has appointed some of the country's brightest lights to manage key ministries and agencies (e.g., Antoinette Saryeh as finance minister and Richard Tolbert as head of the National Investment Commission). She is establishing sound fiscal management; for example, she has promulgated Executive Orders nos. 1 and 2, which call for the centralization of all government revenues connected, and she has implemented GEMAP.

These important developments, coupled with the security established by a 15,000-man multinational force and the restructuring of Liberia's security apparatus (2,000 AFL soldiers have been trained under her tenure), have created an enabling environment for rebuilding Liberia.[24]

But have these gains and interventions improved people's lives? The president is focusing on three priorities in her project of rebuilding and developing the country. First, she has fast-tracked debt reduction; in this regard she has made significant gains—for example, she has negotiated the waiver of more than US$890 million by the World Bank and the IMF, as well as the waiver of more than $394 million by the U.S. government.[25]

Second, in terms of "rebranding" Liberia, she has largely succeeded in erasing perceptions that Liberia is a nation in permanent violent turmoil. She has done so through committed and prudent leadership in spite of the corruption malaise hanging over the government. To this end, she has utilized her personal networks at Harvard University, the UNDP, and the World Bank. She has leveraged her friendship with people like George Soros, the international financier, and Robert L. Johnson, the former owner of Black Entertainment Network. Moreover, as the first female head of state in Africa, she has attracted a great deal of goodwill from women around the world as well as from other prominent individuals. More countries are opening or reopening foreign missions in Liberia; bilateral trade is increasing; grants and donations are beginning to flow into the country; and debt waivers have been actualized. Examples of FDI to Liberia include these: A joint effort among Robert L. Johnson Company, U.S. Oversea Private Investment, and CHF has established a US$30 million investment fund; the U.S. Oversea Private Investment Corporation has earmarked $100 million for economic development in Liberia; and Arcelor Mittal has entered into a $1.5 billion mining concession.[26]

Third, capacity building has taken hold. The Senior Executive Service (SES) is a national capacity-building program implemented through the Civil Service Agency (CSA) and supported jointly by the UNDP, USAID, the World Bank, Humanity United, the German and Greek governments, and TOKEN (Transfer of Knowledge Through Expatriate Nationals). TOKEN is a UNDP program that mobilizes qualified expatriates from developing countries, who for a specified time return to their countries of origin to share their skills and experience and to perform tasks that might otherwise have to be performed by international consultants. TOKEN, however, is only a partial solution. At present, the Liberian government is advertising for more than one hundred government positions. Other human-resource challenges include establishing standards, instituting internal controls, and developing a performance-evaluation program.

Capacity building requires both skilled workers and viable systems in which they can do their work. The entire system of governance in Liberia[27] will need to be reviewed and revamped. The only framework for this that currently exists is GEMAP, but GEMAP focuses more on the inflow and outflow of resources. What is needed is a means for mapping systems, reviewing functions, and implementing controls. This sort of framework will enable replication and scalable integration across ministries and agencies.

Besides GEMAP, the government has implemented interventions such as the Liberia Extractive Industries Transparency Initiative (LEITI), a Governance Commission (GC), a General Auditing Commission (GAC), a Public Procurement and Concession Commission (PPCC), a Truth and Reconciliation Commission (TRC), and the Liberia Better Business Forum (LBBF).[28]

GEMAP[29] is a partnership between the Government of Liberia and the international community. Its goals are to improve governance, enhance transparency and accountability, and lay a solid foundation for stability. GEMAP has six interlocking components: securing Liberia's revenue base; improving budgeting and expenditure management; improving procurement practices and granting concessions; establishing processes to control corruption; supporting key institutions of government; and building capacity. GEMAP has already enjoyed a number of successes: it has helped the government of Liberia more than triple government revenues by reforming the tax system (from US$81 million in 2005 to $290 million in 2008); it has instituted continuous financial controls and practices as per Executive Order no. 1; and it has streamlined the concession and procurement process by instituting PPCC.[30] The legislative act that established the PPCC calls for the standardization of the government's processes for granting concessions; it also ensures better coordination between the Bureau of Budget, and the Ministry of Finance.

In spite of GEMAP's successes, political commentators[31] in Liberia have questioned its relevance. They argue that GEMAP staff understand neither the country's cultural dynamics nor the intricacies of Liberian governance and that its activities can thus have only a limited impact on Liberia. Most professionals would disagree, pointing out that GEMAP's relevance cannot be judged solely in political terms. It is necessary, rather, to compare past practices with present-day ones within the institutions affected by GEMAP. Indeed, many Liberians would argue that GEMAP is highly relevant and that all Liberians have a vested interest in its success. Simply put, the purpose of GEMAP is to restore sound financial reporting to Liberian governance so that international donors will be assured that their donations (as well as internally generated resources) will be used for their intended purposes.

That said, GEMAP needs to be enhanced, refined, and complemented. The program focuses strongly on revenue generation, disbursement control, and integrity in procurement and concession-granting activities. Because Liberian institutions are prone to weak control, a complementary program is needed to work in tandem with GEMAP—Enhanced GEMAP,[32] whose purpose is to document, streamline, and automate institutions' operational and technical controls. This will facilitate knowledge and skill transfer; it will also generate a framework that can then be implemented at other ministries and agencies.

LEITI[33] is a private–public partnership involving the government of Liberia, the private sector, and civil society. This initiative, too, is supported by Liberia's development partners. It seeks to ensure transparency regarding payments to and revenues received by the Government of Liberia in connection with the operations of all oil, mining, and logging companies. LEITI work consists mainly of regular disclosures and audit reconciliations. All of the documentation of all material payments made by companies to the government is published; so are all materials about revenues received by the government from the companies.

At first glance, LEITI seems convoluted in both its mandate and its structure. For example, companies are required to report to civil society. However, there are guidelines for how this is to be done, and LEITI has the technical proficiency to streamline the necessary processes in terms both of other countries' laws and of the principles of the international Extractive Industries Transparency Initiative (EITI). So far, LEITI seems to be providing the needed "checks and balances" between the government and civil society with regard to keeping track of revenues generated and how those revenues are utilized. But because LEITI has just been implemented (as of May 7, 2007), it is too early to judge it a success or a failure.

The GC,[34] another creature of the CPA, is a reformed version of the now defunct Government Reform Commission (GRC). Its mandate is to develop a national framework for political and legal reforms, public-sector reforms, civic education, and national identity. It is intended to develop and instill a system of national integrity, monitoring, and evaluation. In its mandate it seems to have usurped some functions of the three branches[35] of the Liberian government. However its role is more facilitating.

One of the GC's most important tasks will be to reform the judiciary as well as landholding practices. In May and June 2008, as a result of land disputes, fifteen Liberians died in three of the country's counties. For its part, the judiciary lacks sufficient capacity to handle Liberia's post-conflict legal challenges. It also suffers, among other things, from inadequate capacity, manpower shortages, a lack of courthouses, a disconnect between common law and customary law, lack of jury protections, and poor salaries for legal professionals. Liberians are still suffering from the trauma of civil wars and are more prone to resort to violence as a means of redress. There are, though, grounds for hope; the GC is well led, the Liberian government is strongly committed to its success, and the international community seems resolved to make Liberia a shining example of conflict resolution.

The GAC[36] is Liberia's independent auditor—that is, the external auditor of the government. Its role is similar to the one played by public-accounting firms for the private sector in developed countries. (By contrast, GEMAP and LEITI have been established to ensure the government's transparency.) The GAC views itself as the defender of the Liberian people's interests and as the shock troops of government integrity. The legislative act that established the GAC was later amended to enhance its independence. The GAC is headed by John Morlu II, who was hired through an international vetting process sponsored by the EU. The GAC is currently conducting audits of all government ministries and agencies. The GAC's mandate is to conduct audits and inspect all government transactions. It is also expected to work in consert with other programs, the overall goal being to restore integrity to the government's stewardship of the nation resources.

Unfortunately, this goal seems far from achievable, since most ministries and agencies are not co-operating fully with the GAC in terms of providing documentation; often, this is simply because they don't have a paper trail to show him. Still, Morlu seems genuinely committed to the commission's goal. It remains to be seen how his audits will affect Liberians' perceptions of their government and of agency officials with regard to accountability and transparency.

The PPCC,[37] whose independence is protected by law, has developed standardized procedures for awarding, regulating, and overseeing public-procurement contracts and concessions. There is no direct relationship between the PPCC and GEMAP. However, because it controls government disbursements, GEMAP is able to ensure that the PPCC is succeeding at its work. Change is always resisted by its targets, and that is the case with the PPCC with regard to government ministries and agencies. However, it is the author's assessment that as a result of GEMAP, as well as GAC's constant audit memos, ministries and agencies are now complying with the PPCC's policies on procurement and concessions.

The TRC[38] has one of the most important tasks in present-day Liberia, especially in terms of sustaining the peace. That in fact is its purpose: to promote national peace, security, unity, and reconciliation. The TRC's mandate covers the period January 1979 to October 2003.

The TRC has a huge mandate to carry out. It is expected to investigate gross rights violations and violations of international law, to provide a forum for dialogue between victims and perpetrators, to investigate the antecedents of the years of civil unrest, to conduct a critical review of Liberia's past, to adopt specific mechanisms to address issues affecting women and children, and to compile a comprehensive written account of its activities and findings.

One of the most daunting tasks facing the TRC is gaining the co-operation of all the key actors[39] in the civil conflict. Charles Taylor is incarcerated in The Hague; Samuel Doe is dead; Prince Johnson,[40] who refused to co-operate initially, has appeared; others have not come forward. Johnson-Sirleaf has indicated that she will be providing her account of the civil crisis in a book to be published. Many Liberians contend that the TRC's work would have been easier if the president had met with it to give her account of the crisis. Perhaps that would have motivated more key players to come forward. It could still happen.

Liberians have long debated the relevance of the TRC. Some say it should be abolished because it lacks the authority to act on its findings. And in this regard, it is true that the TRC grew out of a compromise among the warring factions during the CPA. Others argue that abolishing the TRC would be premature, given that no other alternative is in sight to address the issues that led to the conflict or the issues arising from the conflict. Moreover, because the TRC was a child of the CPA, aborting it would mean contravening the CPA. An alternative might be to channel relevant suggestions for enhancing the TRC's work into programs under the auspices of the TRC.

The TRC has held its ground in terms of executing its mandate. It has been conducting hearings both locally and abroad. Prominent figures have testified, such as Tolbert's vice-president and a former U.S. Assistant Secretary of State. Most Liberians view this as proof of the TRC's importance to the peace process. But to solidify these gains, more needs to be done to educate the Liberian public about the TRC's activities.

The LBBF[41] is a public–private initiative that grew out of the Liberia Public–Private Sector Dialogue (LPPD) in July 2007.[42] It operates independently, with support from the IFC.[43] Its mandate is to facilitate dialogue on investment issues for the explicit purpose of enhancing the environment for private-sector activities, thereby creating more jobs and alleviating poverty. The LBBF hopes to increase private-sector participation in Liberia's economic development; to engage the private sector more fully with the government; to develop issue-specific public–private working groups that will champion viable recommendations for reform; and to support the development of education, awareness, sensitization, and consensus-building programs aimed at making the public and private sectors accountable.

The LBBF has achieved a great deal in its short span of operations. With the Business Reform Commission (BRC)[44] and the National Investment

Commission (NIC),[45] it has reformed Liberia's business registration process by reducing the number of days it takes to incorporate and register a business from ninety days to ten.[46] Also, the LBBF in collaboration with the NIC and the Investment Climate Team for Africa (ICTA) is helping the government draft an investment code with regard to certain businesses (such as cinemas, petroleum retailing, restaurant operations, cement retailing, and rice marketing).

Based on direct discussions with the LBBF as articulated by its progressive coordinator,[47] one can visualize the direction that Liberia's investment climate is taking. Reforms are occurring in four areas: starting a business, trading across borders, dealing with licences, and registering properties.[48]

Before the civil war, Liberia was one of the few countries in Africa that had a vibrant middle class. There is nothing resembling a strong middle class in Liberia today. The president and many far-sighted Liberians see the private sector as the route out of poverty and as the quickest means to develop an empowered middle class in Liberia. Again, desire must be translated into reality. As the LBBF works with the BRC and other relevant agencies of government, the government must find innovative ways to raise capital and trigger equity participation.

One doesn't want to inhibit the flow of FDI by establishing unnecessary protective laws; that said, quotas need to be established that will allow Liberians to raise themselves from the informal sector to the middle and upper tiers of their economy. Moreover, the informal sector is a useful hive of activity. The commerce and labour ministries and the NIC are attempting to capture data on that sector. Having done so, they could find ways to enable more Liberians to participate in concessions, and/or privatized corporations or arrangements. I propose that these quotas could start at a mere 10 percent, with a cap of 30 percent. Moreover, the government must begin to develop programs to reduce the loan-to-value (LTV)[49] and collateral requirements of lenders and other financing agencies. The National Investment Commission (NIC) is pursuing something similar to this through its SME program, but more needs to be done.

Consolidating the Gains

According to the UNDP's common country assessment (CCA)[50] report on Liberia, for the government to sustain the gains made thus far, it will have to focus on nine areas: economic revitalization, food security, health care and nutrition, hygiene, water and sanitation, education, basic infrastructure, community revitalization, national security, and the natural environment.[51] These nine areas are all linked. They all require significant financial commitments, and the government must be willing to act urgently.

Donor fatigue could set in unless urgency replaces complacency. Further-more, all of the above-mentioned interventions must be made if Liberia is to deal with lawlessness, corruption, and incapacity. The government needs to develop a holistic program for privatization, equip its institutions of higher learning, and leverage regional organizations such as the Mano River Union (MRU)[52] and ECOWAS.[53] Liberia needs to play a stronger leadership role in those organizations. And it must spearhead the process of establishing regional standards within those organizations.

Furthermore, the government must communicate more often with ordinary Liberians—on the streets, in the market halls, on farms—including with those who are illiterate. In an informal street poll conducted by the author, five Liberians out of twenty were aware of what the government had achieved and was doing. For every ten Liberians over the age of fifty-five who were polled, seven indicated that government was acting too slowly with respect to progress. Among college students, half understood what the government was trying to achieve and how it could affect their lives (author's own independent survey).

The current government has achieved much in less than three years. It has succeeded in qualifying as an HIPC, which has been a big economic boost. Unfortunately, these achievements have been dampered by inflation, especially for everyday market commodities, and corruption.

The government needs to find ways to reach the minds and hearts of ordinary Liberians. This is not self-promotion; it is simply about informing the masses about the realities they face. Liberians want to know why the prices of rice, sugar, and gasoline are so high. They need to understand why the government cannot subsidize everything and why most government-owned assets must be privatized. And they want to understand how these sacrifices will benefit them down the road. The government should not think that these people ought to already know, or that they are aware of its achievements and are willing to be patient.

Ellen Johnson-Sirleaf's government is offering a new start for Liberians and their troubled country. Her people hope she will turn things around, end the general agony, and garner some respect for their beloved country without interference from old-school politicians. Social and political euphoria is rising in Liberia, with most Liberians optimistic about a government that will not be based on mere political inclusion and accommodation, but rather on practical qualifications, including education, skills, and experience—not to mention personal character.

The danger in this euphoria is that Liberians will expect too soon the provision of basic necessities, such as water, electricity, employment, and the opportunities for ordinary Liberian to better their lives. The question permeating Liberia today is whether the new government has the political will to decisively tackle corruption and institute realistic policies that will promote good governance.

Notes

1 Sunny Nyemah is currently the Country Director of George Edward Consulting in Liberia and an adjunct professor at Metropolitan State University in Minnesota.

2 The Comprehensive Peace Agreement (CPA) established an interim government in 2003. Under this framework, elections were held in 2005 that ushered in Ellen Johnson-Sirleaf's government in 2006.

3 Ellen factor: A term coined by the author in one his many articles on Liberia. It refers to the widely held perception that "Ellen" equals "Harvard-trained international financial banker and international developmental manager"—that is, someone in whom international partners and investors have confidence.

4 Charles Taylor was elected the twenty-first president of Liberia in 1997 after leading a brutal rebellion. He was pressured into exile after LURD and MODEL rebelled against his government and is now on trial in The Hague for war crimes he allegedly committed in Sierra Leone.

5 Samuel Doe had been elected in 1985 as Liberia's twentieth president. He was chairman of the People's Redemption Council, the group that led the coup against President William R. Tolbert in 1980. Doe was executed by Prince Y. Johnson of the INPFL after the NPFL incursion in 1989.

6 LURD was one of the two rebel groups, and was generally considered the more formidable of the two that led the rebellion against the Taylor government in what is often referred to as the second phase of the Liberian civil war.

7 MODEL was the second of the groups that led the rebellion against Taylor government.

8 "Indigenous Liberians" are the native people of Liberia—that is, those who were inhabiting the place before the settlers came.

9 Americo-Liberians are descendents of the settlers.

10 http://www.liberiapastandpresent.org/1926FirestoneCA.htm.

11 William V.S. Tubman was the eighteenth President of Liberia and the longest-serving president in the country's history. He served Liberia from 1944 until his death in 1971.

12 The True Whig Party monopolized politics in Liberia from 1877 to 1980.

13 The Open Door Policy was modelled after an earlier Open Door Policy, introduced by U.S. President William McKinley and his Secretary of State, John Haley, with respect to China at the end of the nineteenth century.

14 The Unification Policy was intended to address intra-communal conflict by breaking down barriers between the Americo-Liberians and Indigenous Liberians.

15 There was a misconception that all Americo-Liberians benefited directly or were at least better off because of elitist ruling-class policies. In fact, many settlements or townships belonging to the descendants of settlers had been abandoned, or were significantly underdeveloped, including some quite near to the capital city of Monrovia.

16 President William R. Tolbert, Jr., the nineteenth president of Liberia, was an ordained Baptist pastor and former president of the Baptist World Alliance. He was one of the country's most progressive presidents.

17 "Humanistic capitalism" seeks to merge the safety and health needs of people and the environment with market-based economics. "Banker to the Poor" Muhammad Yunus describes it as a socially conscious business world in which investors are content to recoup their investments but do not expect additional dividends.

18 Kpelle is spoken by the Kpelle tribe, which hails from Bong County in central Liberia.

19 The "progressives" were student activists in Liberia as well as opposition Liberian leaders who had returned home from abroad. Notable progressives included the late Baccus

Mathews, Togba Nah Tipoteh, H. Bioma Fahnbulleh, Jr., Chea Cheapo, Oscar Quiah, George Boley, and Dr. Amos Sawyer.

20 The "Old Guard" were influential members of the True Whig Party who were committed to the idea of a one-party state.

21 The instigators were progressives living in Liberia at the time of the 1979 rice riot. http://www.globalsecurity.org/military/library/report/1985/liberia_1_oppositionmovements.htm.

22 https://www.cia.gov/library/publications/the-world-factbook/geos/li.html.

23 http://unmil.org/1content.asp?ccat=history&zdoc=1.

24 http://www.analystliberia.com/ellen_commissions_24_aug29_08.html.

25 http://www.mofliberia.org/externaldebt.htm.

26 http://www.analystliberia.com/mittal_promises_half_a_billion_investment_increase_dec13_07.html.

27 "Governance systems" refers to processes by which those in authority are selected, monitored, and replaced.

28 http://www.mofliberia.org; http://www.gempliberia.org; http://www.trcliberia.org.

29 GEMAP was agreed to by all parties to the CPA as an approach to restoring integrity and accountability to the Liberian government.

30 http://www.ppcc.gov.lr.

31 "Political commentators" refers to individuals or institutions that opine on issues affecting Liberia and Liberians.

32 "Enhanced GEMAP" calls for complementary institutions to enhance GEMAP's work with respect to the technical and operational controls of institutions affected by GEMAP programs.

33 LEITI is the Liberian version of the Extractive Industries Transparency Initiative (EITI), an international program that seeks to restore transparency and accountability in "resource-cursed" countries. It is a voluntary initiative supported by a coalition of companies, governments, investors, and civil-society groups.

34 The GC was established by an Act of Legislature of the Government of Liberia on October 9, 2007. http://libgovernance.org.

35 The Liberian government has three branches: the Executive, headed by the president; the Legislature, headed by the Speaker of the House; and the Judiciary, headed by the Chief Justice of the Supreme Court of Liberia.

36 The GAC is Liberia's independent auditor and its chief watchdog for accountability and transparency.

37 The PPCC is another child of the CPA. With the help of the EU and the World Bank, interim public-procurement policies and procedures, as well as guidelines for concessions, were endorsed by the World Bank and approved by the now defunct NTGL.

38 The TRC was enacted on May 12, 2005, by the interim legislative branch, also referred to as the National Transitional Legislative Assembly.

39 "Key actor" refers to an individual or institution that played a direct or indirect leadership role in a warring faction.

40 Prince Y. Johnson was a leader of the breakaway faction of the NPFL.

41 The LBBF is a public–private initiative funded by the IFC.

42 http://www.lbbf.org.

43 The LPPD was the working arrangement that was modified to become the LBBF.

44 The BRC is a committee established by the Liberian president to build consensus and consolidate economic, investment, and financing activities across agencies and ministries.

45 The NIC is headed by a former Wall Street executive who happens to be a Liberian (the

Honorable Richard Tolbert). He has at Liberia's disposal his expertise in facilitating the flow of foreign direct investment into Liberia.

46 http://www.nic.gov.lr.

47 The LBBF coordinator is a committed and qualified Liberian who has decided to return home and play a part in the redevelopment of Liberia.

48 http://www.moci.gov.lr.

49 LTV is an underwriting indicator that lenders use to determine the maximum amount to lend a particular project or client.

50 CCA, "common country assessment," is a report that provides an overview of the activities of the united system in Liberia with regard to developmental challenges.

51 http://www.undg.org/archive_docs/3131-Liberia_-_Common_Country_Assessment__CCA__-_CCA.pdf.

52 The Mano River Union (MRU) is a sub-regional group comprising Liberia, Sierra Leone, Guinea, and Ivory Coast.

53 ECOWAS is a regional group of West African countries. Liberia is a member. ECOWAS was instrumental in securing peace in Liberia.

Security-Sector Reform in Liberia

Mark Malan

10

Introduction

The concept of security-sector reform (SSR) was first put forward to a broader public in a speech made by Clare Short, the first minister of the UK Department for International Development (DFID), in 1998. However, several scholars and analysts have been wary of using the term "reform" and have suggested others, such as "security-sector transition" or "security-sector transformation." OECD DAC has settled on the term "security system reform."[1]

The OECD DAC Guidelines on Security System Reform and Governance agreed to by ministers in 2004 define the security system as including the following: core security actors (e.g., armed forces, police, gendarmerie, border guards, customs and immigration officials, intelligence and security services); security management and oversight bodies (e.g., ministries of defence and internal affairs, financial management bodies, public-complaints commissions); justice and law-enforcement institutions (e.g., the judiciary, the correctional system, prosecution services, traditional justice systems); and non-statutory security forces (e.g., private-security companies, guerrilla armies, private militias).

However SSR is defined,[2] the reform and democratic control of security agencies and the merging of security and development has become a strong focus of international intervention in post-conflict societies. Effective security structures under civilian and democratic control may not guarantee economic development, but they are certainly viewed as a precondition. This thinking is reflected in Liberia's Interim Poverty Reduction Strategy (IPRS) of February 2007, in which the government has organized key development issues and challenges under these four rubrics:

- Enhancing national security
- Revitalizing economic growth
- Strengthening governance and the rule of law
- Rehabilitating infrastructure and delivering basic services.[3]

Significantly, national security is the first pillar. It is also viewed as a separate one from strengthening governance and the rule of law, which suggests a narrower definition of the security sector than the one embodied in current SSR theory.[4]

In theory, comprehensive SSR should arise from a comprehensive national security review. SSR involves, at its core, the transformation of country's military and police forces—but it also involves a comprehensive review and restructuring of intelligence services, penitentiaries, the judiciary, and other agencies charged in some way with preserving and promoting the safety and security of the state and its citizenry.

However, in real-life war-to-peace transitions, the processes of SSR—as supported by the international community and bilateral donors—are often far more rudimentary than the conceptual paradigm suggests. They are often aimed simply at the training and equipping of armed forces and police agencies, with little attention or resources devoted to the other components of the security system. This is certainly the case in Liberia. The country still lacks a national-security strategy, a promulgated defence policy, and effective security-sector oversight and management mechanisms. The judiciary remains in urgent need of a comprehensive overhaul, and the same with the correctional services. SSR has focused almost exclusively on UN efforts to build up the Liberian police and on the Americans' rather intermittent efforts to establish a new Liberian army.

This chapter highlights the need for concerted and sustained SSR in Liberia. An overview of the legal and conceptual framework for engaging in SSR in Liberia is provided as backdrop to a review of efforts to reform (or rebuild) the Armed Forces of Liberia (AFL) and the Liberia National Police.

The Need for SSR in Liberia

The need for comprehensive security-sector reform in Liberia is obvious. During the 1980s, then President Samuel Doe recruited soldiers from his own Krahn tribe into the armed forces and then used them to harass other ethnic groups. After helping oust Doe, Charles Taylor used various state-security agencies as his private militia after he was elected president in July 1997. The election had been monitored by ECOWAS, pursuant to the September 1995 Abuja Accord. Taylor was expected to restructure the army, the police, and the various security agencies to reflect the neutrality of the new administration. However, the warlord-turned-president resisted ECOWAS's efforts to oversee a process of security-sector reform. His position was that the Abuja Accord, which mandated ECOWAS forces to restructure the Liberian army, had expired on August 2, 1997, when he was inaugurated as head of state, and that the restructuring of the national army was now his responsibility under the country's constitution.[5]

Taylor proceeded to marginalize the national army, the AFL, because he questioned their loyalty (the Krahn still dominated the AFL). Instead of unifying and professionalizing the security sector, Taylor created a network of competing security units and militias, headed by long-standing supporters, many of whom had been child soldiers who fought with him when he was a rebel leader. Most prominent among these was the Anti-Terrorism Unit (ATU), headed by Taylor's son, "Chucky."[6] Similarly, former National Patriotic Front of Liberia (NPFL) officials within the police service wielded considerable power. Taylor's cousin, the national police chief Joe Tate, was accused of having led gangs of looters and a political death squad during the civil war.[7]

Members of the security forces in rural areas generally were paid and provisioned inadequately and often extorted money, food, and goods from citizens. It was common practice to compel local communities to provide food, shelter, and labour for members of the security forces stationed in their villages. The Special Security Services (SSS) and the Police Special Operations Division (SOD) both mobilized to combat Liberians United for Reconciliation and Democracy (LURD), a rebel group consisting mainly of former NPFL rebels, who were paid a one-time fee of $150 and were expected to loot and pillage thereafter to support themselves.[8]

In short, a key feature of security institutions in Liberia has been the gross abuse of human rights (often with impunity) by security personnel through torture, arbitrary arrests and killings, and the use of official powers for private gain. Not surprisingly, by the time of the August 2003 Comprehensive Peace Agreement (CPA), both the population and the transitional government were deeply mistrustful of military and law-enforcement officials. Police and military officers were not regarded as sources of protection, but rather as entities to be feared. The steady degradation of professional standards in the face of political interference and manipulation left Liberia with a postwar security architecture characterized by redundancy, inadequate control, and incoherence. The present government inherited no fewer than fifteen separate agencies and structures tasked with a variety of security functions, some discrete and some overlapping.

It is not just the number of agencies that is cause for concern, but the redundancy and ambiguity concerning their functions and roles. For example, a number of agencies have the authority to arrest and detain individuals. Moreover, the National Security Agency (NSA), the Liberia National Police (LNP), the National Bureau of Investigation (NBI), and the Special Security Service (SSS), as well as the Ministry of Defense, all collect intelligence, including criminal intelligence, political intelligence, and—in the case of the NSA—foreign and national-security intelligence. The Ministry of National Security (MNS), established on September 6, 1979, also has a special responsibility for intelligence, as well as a role in coordinating the entire gamut of security services.[9] The notorious ATU was demobilized under the terms of the CPA, and there are strong arguments for abolishing a number of the other remaining security agencies, such as the Drug Enforcement Agency (because its mandate overlaps with that of the police and the NSA) and the National Bureau of Investigation (whose duties overlap with those of the NSA, the LNP, and the Bureau of Immigration and Naturalization). There have also been calls to dissolve the MNS, because it performs overlapping functions with the NSA and the National Security Council.

Overarching responsibility for developing a national-security strategy and policies is supposed to be vested in the National Security Council (NSC). The NSC was created on March 12, 1999, by legislative act. Among other things it has the responsibility "to identify and define the National Security goals of the Republic in relation to national power."[10] This role is critical, because comprehensive rationalization of the security sector cannot really proceed until the Liberian government produces a national-security strategy and supplementary legislation and policy documents. This is why the RAND Corporation has recommended that the NSC begin functioning regularly and without delay, that it engage legal and substantive experts from Liberia and its partners to frame a new national-security law, and that it oversee the implementation of the security-sector transformation plans that result from this process.[11]

The legislature is recognized as a crucial actor in SSR theory and may indeed be so in established democracies—in other words, when Parliament is able to carry out its legislative, representative, and oversight functions. Unfortunately, the Liberian legislature at the present time is beset with problems, including lack of institutional support, domination by the executive, corruption, lack of integrity among individual legislators, and—not least—lack of capacity to perform its oversight functions. The legislature itself is obviously in need of reform, but this will take many years to accomplish and there is a need to concentrate on the art of the possible and on those areas of SSR that must be pursued as an urgent priority.

The Institutional Framework for SSR in Liberia

SSR is being pursued and implemented in Liberia within the convoluted legal framework provided by the 1986 Constitution of Liberia, the CPA of 2003, and UN Security Council (UNSC) Resolution 1509 (2003).

The conditions for implementing the SSR program in Liberia are captured by Articles VII and VIII of Part Four of the CPA. Article VII, Section 1(b), stipulates that "the AFL shall be restructured and will have a new command structure. The forces may be drawn from the ranks of the present GOL forces, the LURD and the MODEL, as well as from civilians with appropriate background and experience. The Parties request that ECOWAS, the UN, AU, and the ICGL provide advisory staff, equipment, logistics and experienced trainers for the security reform effort. The parties also request that the United States of America play a lead role in organizing this restructuring program."[12]

The CPA provides specific criteria for restructuring the AFL—in particular, it specifies that recruits are to be screened with respect to educational, professional, medical, and fitness qualifications as well as prior history of human-rights abuses. It also stresses that the restructured army should reflect regional balance within the country.[13]

The CPA makes specific references to the agencies that should be restructured. For example, Article VII refers to the LNP and other security services such as the Immigration Service, the SSS, customs security guards, and other statutory security units.[14] The agreement also calls for the disarmament and disbanding of the "Special Security Units including the Anti-Terrorist Unit, the Special Operations Division (SOD) of the Liberia National Police Service, and such paramilitary groups that operate within organizations such as the National Port Authority (NPA), the Liberian Telecommunications Corporation (LTC), the Liberian [Petroleum] Refining Corporation and the Airports."[15]

UNSC Resolution 1509 (September 19, 2003) stipulates clearly that the UN Mission in Liberia (UNMIL) shall support the reform of the security sector. Specifically, UNMIL has been tasked to:

- Assist the transitional government of Liberia in monitoring and restructuring the police force of Liberia, consistent with democratic policing, to develop a civilian police training program, and to otherwise assist in the training of civilian police, in cooperation with ECOWAS, international organizations, and interested states; and
- Assist the transitional government in the formation of a new and restructured Liberian military in cooperation with ECOWAS, international organizations, and interested States.[16]

Though the CPA is specific about the Americans' role in restructuring the army, Resolution 1509 refers simply to "interested States."

From August 2003 to January 2006 the CPA was the principal source of legal authority for SSR in Liberia.[17] Article XXXV, Section 1(b), of the CPA suspended parts of the Liberian constitution. The CPA states that "the provisions of the present Constitution of the Republic of Liberia, the Statutes and all other Liberian laws, which relate to the establishment, composition and powers of the Executive, the Legislative and Judicial branches of the Government, are hereby suspended."[18] However, the presidential election of 2005 and the subsequent inauguration of Ellen Johnson-Sirleaf in January 2006 have again made the Constitution of Liberia relevant to the process.[19] As commander-in-chief of the AFL under Article LIV(e), the president "appoints members of the military from the rank of lieutenant or its equivalence and above; and field marshals, deputy field marshals and sheriffs."[20]

The constitution also provides a broad remit for the national legislature on security issues. For example, Article XXXIV(b) reads that the legislature has the power to "provide for the security of the Republic"; and under Article XXXIV(c) the legislature also has the power "to provide for the common defense, to declare war and authorize the Executive to conclude peace; to raise and support the Armed Forces of the Republic, and to make appropriations therefore provided that no appropriation of money for that use shall be for a longer term than one year, and to make rules for the governance of the AFL."[21] However, as noted earlier, the role of the legislative branch in SSR has hitherto been passive and marginal.

Despite ambiguities in the legal framework, there has been little dispute over the legality of SSR per se.[22] However, there are strong differences of opinion within Liberian civil society—and some of the security agencies themselves—as to the nature and scope of reform as well as the rationale behind it. According to the IPRS, the government's medium-term approach is to "develop a national security strategy to guide security sector reform, extend national security actions to ensure national safety, security and peace as well as build national security capabilities." The Governance Reform Commission (GRC), the Ministry of Defense (MoD), and the Ministry of Justice (MoJ) are supposed to lead this process. The IPRS also commits the government to developing a "comprehensive longer-term operational and institutional security reform agenda ... in order to rationalize various security forces, facilitate a change in culture of the security forces, define clear missions and tasks and ensure there are no duplications, overlap or conflicts of interest between security agencies."[23] The delivery date set by the government for a "national security policy and architecture" to be endorsed by Cabinet was March 2007, and the target for delivery of a "national defense strategy and other institutional level security strategies in support of the national security policy" was April 2007. [24]

The GRC is supposed to lead the development of a national-security strategy, in collaboration with the MoD and MoJ, but it has not succeeded in moving the process to any kind of conclusion. The GRC's chairman, Dr. Amos Sawyer, is a professor at Indiana State University and is not in Monrovia full-time.[25] Moreover, the GRC is burdened with the overall agenda of governance reform, and even though SSR is regarded as the bedrock of all other reforms, it is also the most problematic. For example, while the CPA indeed provided for the United States to play a lead role in defence transformation", the GRC contends that the American SSR Team is "muscling out everybody else" in the area of defence-sector transformation—and that the American-driven process does not sufficiently take account of regional security realities. In particular, defence (re)structuring is proceeding in isolation from the ECOWAS security architecture and does not seem to be based on a thorough analysis of the security dynamics of the Mano River Basin. The AFL is thus being constituted according to an apparently threat-independent approach to defence planning and structuring.[26]

The Defense Act that was to frame Liberia's defence policy was extremely controversial and was withdrawn by President Johnson-Sirleaf. SSR program staff from the United States subsequently helped MoD staff draft a new Liberian National Defense Act, in coordination with and incorporating guidance from the defense minister, Brownie Samukai, and the justice minister, Frances Johnson-Morris. The draft act, which is similar to the U.S. Title X, had been completed by December 2006, but a year later it was still being debated and vetted by the Liberian legislature. According to Thomas Dempsey, the draft act "delineated the responsibilities and missions of the Liberian Defense sector and established a solid foundation for civilian control and oversight of the AFL."[27] However, the GRC contends that the new draft does not differ significantly from the old Defense Act and that there is a clear need to first develop a comprehensive security-sector policy as well as an authoritative defence policy that can then be enacted in specific legislation.[28]

In February 2007 the GRC produced a draft "National Security Policy Statement of Liberia"—a normative statement of principles and a guide to policy formulation, rather than a national-security policy.[29] However, the document has not been discussed by the government and it has no official status. In the absence of an authoritative and comprehensive national-security strategy, and attendant legislation and policies, the only clear guidance for pursuing SSR in Liberia remains the RAND Report, which is based on international "best practices" and clear, logical analysis rather than an in-depth understanding of Liberia and the West African region. The RAND Report's overarching recommendation is that Liberia's capabilities architecture respond to a security concept in such a way that (a) public safety and law enforcement are immediate concerns, (b) the appearance of organized armed internal opposition can be anticipated and prevented, and (c) future external threats that may arise without long warning can be countered.

Even with foreign assistance, Liberia's economy does not permit large forces.[30] For Liberia's security forces, cost-effectiveness will need to mean complementary capabilities that cover the forces' core security functions, possess the right qualities, and can be used flexibly. The RAND Report concludes:

> The largest and most crucial components of Liberia's security sector are the Liberian National Police (LNP) and the AFL. The former should be the country's main internal security force; the latter should embody the country's main capabilities for military combat. The size and capabilities of the LNP and AFL largely determine the effectiveness, cost, and thus the cost-effectiveness of Liberia's security sector. Their roles and

missions and the relationship between them will largely determine how the new state provides security. Lack of clarity on missions risks duplication or gaps in capabilities, political contention, and operational failure.[31]

Besides calling for reconstituted police services and armed forces, the RAND analysis suggests a need for an additional capability that would complete and tie together currently planned capabilities—specifically, a mobile LNP unit that can perform either in combat or in a law-enforcement mode. RAND has therefore recommended the creation of a police quick-response unit (QRU) to complement the regular police. Unlike the police support unit, which is meant to deal with civil unrest (e.g., riot control), the QRU would be capable of defeating organized armed threats—specifically in times when countering the formation of armed opposition forces would overreach the capabilities of regular police yet not warrant the domestic use of the army. [32]

Rebuilding the Armed Forces of Liberia

As previously noted, the CPA explicitly asked the United States to play a lead role in restructuring the Liberian armed forces. The United States has pledged $210 million and signed a Memorandum of Understanding with the Interim Transitional Government of Liberia, formalizing the American commitment— through the SSR Program—to assist in demobilizing the existing Liberian military, recruiting and vetting recruits for an entirely new force, and then training, equipping, and sustaining that force until it is operational. In the absence of a valid National Defense Act, the RAND Report provides the most credible approach to establishing a new army. According to a former member of the SSR Program staff, "the force must be postured so that it is strong enough to defend the integrity of the nation's borders but not so strong that it threatens neighbors with its force-projection capability. Its structure, equipment, and training must be appropriate to the force's mission (for example, Liberia does not require F-16 fighter jets). Perhaps most critically, the new security force must not be so large that the government cannot pay its salaries. Such a condition is a precipitant to civil war." [33]

The most controversial facet of the SSR program has been its employment of two private contractors for program delivery. DynCorp International has been contracted to provide basic training for the AFL, and Pacific Architects and Engineers (PAE) has been awarded the contract for forming and structuring the AFL and its component units, and for providing specialized and advanced training, including mentoring, to the AFL's fledgling officers and non-commissioned officers. DynCorp's job has been to "recruit and make soldiers"; PAE is employed to "mentor and develop" them into a fully operational force. In addition, the U.S. European Command (EUCOM) has sent eight active duty officers and non-commissioned officers to work alongside PAE in mentoring the AFL commanders.[34] Three military bases have been established under the SSR program: the Barclay Training Camp (BTC); the Sandee S. Ware Military Barracks (built on the old VOA transmitter facility at Careysburg, on the outskirts of Monrovia); and the Edward B. Kessely Military Barracks (formerly Camp Schiefflin). DynCorp has rehabilitated and managed BTC and Camp Ware, while PAE has built the facilities for and managed Edward B. Kessely Military Barracks.

The SSR program provides for the demobilization of 13,770 soldiers who served in the old AFL, allocating one-time payments of between US$285 and $4,300, depending on the seniority and length of service of the demobilized personnel. Also, the SSR program is supporting the demobilization of the Ministry of National Defense (MoD)—which had 400 to 450 personnel on its books—as well as the retraining of selected candidates. On March 20, 2007, 119 civilian employees of the MoD graduated after completing seventeen weeks' training under the U.S. Defense Department.[35]

The SSR program has since supported the MoD by recruiting and vetting 12,100 applicants for service in the new AFL. DynCorp has designed and managed the recruiting and vetting program.[36] In the wake of the long civil war, during which so many civilians suffered, and a multitude of atrocities were committed by all armed groups, the Government of Liberia and the SSR program have established a number of stages for screening recruits for the new Liberian army. As explained by former SSR program and DynCorp employee, Sean McFate: "The goal of the recruiting, vetting, and training components of security sector reform is to achieve a force that maintains a professional ethos, respects the rule of law, cultivates public service leadership, is apolitical, and accepts civilian control with transparent oversight mechanisms."[37] In addition, the MoD has ruled that all commissioned officers in the AFL must hold a recognized university qualification at the bachelor's degree level,[38] and efforts have been made to ensure that the AFL reflects a healthy regional and ethnic balance.[39] When recruitment began in January 2006, a vetting council, whose members were drawn from the MoD, Liberian civil society, and the U.S. Embassy, was established to assess each candidate's physical fitness, literacy level, health, and human-rights record.

The Government of Liberia has decided that the new AFL will be trained according to U.S. Army doctrine, because this was the basis for training the old AFL. Every soldier, whatever the final mustering, is first trained as an infantry rifleman during the Initial Entry Training (IET) course ("basic training"), which was eleven weeks long for the initial intake. The period has since been reduced to eight weeks by cutting three weeks devoted to human-rights training and to education in civics and civil–military relations in a democracy. These subjects were dropped from the curriculum because of the high cost of basic training. DynCorp instructors are former drill instructors from the U.S. Army or the U.S. Marine Corps or have served in their respective Corps Instruction Schools. They are the type of people who can command an excellent rate of remuneration in the private-security industry in places such as Iraq and Afghanistan. This has driven up the DynCorp salary bill. Training in civic awareness, human rights, and international humanitarian law is being planned for a later stage of training, once soldiers have been assigned to permanent units and DynCorp is no longer billing the U.S. government for training time. NGOs have offered to provide this training gratis, which adds to the cost savings but also raises significant concerns about the low priority accorded to human-rights issues.

The DynCorp training program is much like the basic training presented in most armies; it includes subjects such as personal hygiene, drill, weapons instruction, field craft, and land navigation. The facilities at Camp Ware are designed to accommodate intakes of a maximum of 550 recruits. They are functional but by no means luxurious or extravagant. The basic weaponry provided to the AFL is compatible with that of other ECOWAS countries— AK-47 assault rifles and RPG-7 rocket-propelled grenade launchers. These were donated the Romanian government.[40]

The end state for the AFL is a professional army "modeled on US Army doctrine, that will support the national objectives of the Government of Liberia."[41] The SSR program plans to deliver, by September 2010, an AFL that essentially will be composed of the 23rd Infantry Brigade. The total planned strength of this brigade is 2,000 men and women: 146 officers and 1,854 enlisted ranks. The brigade will be commanded by a colonel and will have a headquarters element with a staff of 113.[42] It is planned that the brigade will have the following constituent units, sub-units, and sub-sub-units:

- 1st Battalion. A light-infantry battalion composed of 680 soldiers, organized into a battalion headquarters, three rifle companies, and a combat support company (in turn composed of an 81-mm mortar platoon, a signals platoon, and a transport unit). Each rifle company will consist of a company headquarters (including a 60-mm mortar section) and three rifle platoons.
- 2nd Battalion. Also 680 strong, with the same organization as above.
- An engineering company with a strength of 220.
- A military police company with a strength of 105.
- A Brigade Training Unit (BTU) with a strength of 162.
- A band platoon with 40 members.[43]

While the basic and specialized training of enlisted ranks and junior officers is well under way, there is clearly a gap when it comes to senior command positions in the AFL. Ideally, the appointment of the brigade commander, battalion commander, and senior staff officers should have preceded the formation, activation, and operationalization of the 23rd Brigade. The brigade certainly cannot be declared operational until such posts are filled by competent officers. However, it generally takes twenty to thirty years of military training and experience to develop a good brigade commander, and the AFL is being built from scratch.

During the initial training phase, except for salaries, the SSR program is funding every aspect of the AFL, from bases and base maintenance to uniforms and food.[44] However, according to the Office of Defense Cooperation (ODC), the SSR program is not entirely an American "closed shop," as suggested by the GRC and some civil-society interlocutors. A Defense Support Group for Liberia comprising representatives of all interested donor governments meets quarterly in Monrovia. Assistance to the AFL is being provided by other partners, sometimes making up for shortfalls in essential areas where needs cannot be met by the American team owing to funding limitations.[45] For example, the UK has offered to train company-grade officers and has provided an adviser (a lieutenant colonel) to the program., and Nigeria has offered 220 training slots on courses with the Nigerian Army. To help meet the pressing need for general transport, ECOWAS has loaned the AFL six five-ton trucks from its logistics depot outside Freetown in Sierra Leone.

The DynCorp and PAE contracts are managed and accounted for by the U.S. government through three key officials: the Contracting Officer (State Department); the Contracting Officer's Representative (State Department, Africa Bureau); and the chief of the Office of Defense Cooperation (ODC) within the U.S. Embassy in Monrovia. The ODC chief is responsible for liaising with Liberia's MoD and for supervising the activities of DynCorp and PAE in Liberia. He reports to the Contracting Officer through the Contracting Officer's Representative in the Africa Bureau. Funding for the SSR program— including the DynCorp and PAE contracts—is provided through the PKO budget, as well as through the International Military Education and Training (IMET) program (eight of the nine AFL officers who graduated in May 2007, and two AFL NCOs, completed courses in the United States).

Much has been said about the high costs of developing the AFL. One problem is that funding for the SSR program has been authorized and disbursed in dribs and drabs owing to the nature of the Department of State budgetary process as well as the congressional authorization process. The resulting delays have driven up costs and increased the time it is taking DynCorp to fulfill its contract to provide basic training for all recruits. At the end of 2007, DynCorp employed 82 international staff in Liberia as well as 239 Liberian staff.[46] The thorough recruiting and vetting process—for which expert investigators have been employed—has been time consuming and very expensive. Like other

State Department contracts, the DynCorp contract is "cost plus [overhead]."
As a consequence, cost escalations for goods and services—including idle
personnel time as a result of tardy disbursements—have been passed on to
the U.S. Government. Furthermore, DynCorp has a fixed "burn rate" for every
month it is retained in Liberia. The combined expenses of DynCorp and PAE
were US$18 million for the first six months of 2007.[47]

The timelines as specified in the original contracts and agreed to with the
Liberian MoD have thus slipped badly, mainly because of weak and erratic
U.S. funding.[48] Only 5 percent of the force had completed the basic IET course
by August 2007.[49] With the graduation of the second intake on September 7,
2007, this figure increased to 32 percent. By the first week of February 2008,
57 percent of the force had completed basic training; by May 2008, it was 82
percent. The 1st Battalion should be operational[50] by September 2009, the 2nd
Battalion by March 2010.[51]

While international SSR guidelines (e.g., as promulgated by OECD DAC)
call for a consultative process, the Liberian authorities—including the MoD,
the MoJ, the president, and the Inspector-General of Police (IGP)—have been
strongly resisting a public dialogue on security. So for that matter has the
SSR program team. In the absence of information and dialogue, the image of
DynCorp creating an armed elite is disconcerting to many Liberians. Amos
Sawyer recalls that in 1980 the U.S. Government spent $500 million to train
and equip the army of then president Samuel Doe. He warns that "every armed
group that plundered Liberia over the past twenty-five years had its core in
these U.S.-trained AFL soldiers." [52] Liberians fear that when the United States
withdraws from the SSR program and stops funding the AFL, they will find
themselves sitting on a time bomb. That is, their country will be home to a
well-trained and well-armed force of elite soldiers who are used to good pay
and conditions of service and who may be impossible for the Government of
Liberia to sustain on its own.

The Liberia National Police (LNP)

During the civil wars, police in Liberia (like the other security services) abused
human rights and used their official powers for private gain. By 2003 the population and the transitional government were deeply mistrustful of the LNP.
UNMIL was thus mandated to assist "the transitional government of Liberia in
monitoring and restructuring the police force of Liberia, consistent with democratic policing, to develop a civilian police training program, and to otherwise
assist in the training of civilian police, in cooperation with ECOWAS, international organizations and interested States."[53] For its part, Article VII of the CPA
refers to the restructuring of the LNP and other security services such as the
Immigration Service, the SSS customs security guards, and other statutory security units.[54] According to the RAND Report, "the primary missions of the LNP

are (a) to prevent and fight crime and (b) to maintain public safety. These missions call for a light but sizable, community-friendly police force that can earn the confidence and cooperation of the Liberian people. Anticipating occasional civil disorder, the LNP should also have a branch capable of riot control—e.g., the police support unit (PSU)."[55]

In 2004, UN Police (UNPOL) began to reform the LNP from scratch. UNPOL was required to assist the LNP in maintaining law and order; at the same time, it was mandated to restructure, retrain, and re-equip the police service. UNPOL registered some five thousand people who claimed to be members of the LNP. Some had no uniforms, and none had been paid for the past few years. They had survived mainly by extracting bribes from members of the public whom they were supposed to serve and protect. There was no effective law enforcement at all, and mob justice was rampant. Only the traffic division had smart uniforms and could be seen on duty; they were in a better position to impose bogus fines on motorists and thereby sustain themselves than other patrol officers.[56]

UNPOL faced an extremely difficult task. It did not have an executive mandate that would have granted its officers powers of arrest. Those powers were reserved for the same police they were expected to reconstitute. The solution was to vet and recruit a few hundred LNP officers from those who had been registered and to work alongside them in an effort to maintain law and order. From their personal allowances, UNPOL officers bought black T-shirts with POLICE printed in white letters as a makeshift uniform for this small cadre of officers. They also purchased stationery and basic office supplies; there was simply no budget line or funding within UNMIL for setting up the LNP. UNPOL then began joint patrols with four hundred of these LNP "Interim Police."[57]

UNMIL began reintroducing the LNP to the public through a sensitization program, emphasizing that UNPOL was acting in support of the new LNP and not as an independent law-enforcement agency. Simultaneously, UNPOL was busy developing a comprehensive recruitment, selection, and training program. Policy guidelines for the latter were formulated in conjunction with the National Transitional Government of Liberia (NTGL) through a joint NTGL–UNMIL Rule of Law Implementation Committee. At this stage, "not a dime had been forthcoming" in support of UNPOL's mandate to restructure the LNP."[58] Once recruitment began, the United States provided US$500,000 for the program, and UNMIL provided tented accommodation for trainees at the Liberian National Police Academy. Other donors followed, providing assistance in a piecemeal fashion. In 2006, for example, Norway and the Netherlands provided a donation to build permanent barracks at the Police Academy, and Belgium provided sidearms as well as ammunition for firearms training for select LNP candidates.[59]

A goal of 3,500 trained LNP officers was arrived at with the interim government of Liberia. Liberia's elected government subsequently adjusted this figure upwards, to 6,000. The selection and vetting criteria agreed upon by UNMIL and the Government of Liberia are similar to those in most African countries. Candidates for selection must be Liberian citizens between eighteen and thirty-five years of age and must have a high-school education. They must also be physically fit and mentally competent, with no criminal record—including no criminal charges pending. Nor can they be subject to any investigation for war crimes, crimes against humanity, or any crime that violates international human-rights conventions. In addition, candidates must relinquish any positions they might have held in any political organization. Recruitment and vetting have been coordinated by UNPOL's Restructuring and Recruiting section. All members of the new LNP must serve a two-year period of probation before their appointments are confirmed.

The vetting process for the LNP has been vigorous, albeit not perfect. About 2,700 individuals who had registered as members of the former police did not meet the selection criteria for admission to the LNP for training at the Police Academy; however, UNMIL did not have the US$4 million that was needed to provide severance packages for them. This meant that they were on the streets, alongside the new LNP officers, until late in 2005, when Britain provided the funds for their deactivation.[60] The deactivation of 2,351 members of the old LNP and 870 SSS officers was finally completed in June 2007, with the dismissed members receiving a one-time payment of about US$1,200 each.[61]

As recommended by the RAND Report, an integral Police Support Unit (PSU) has been formed within the LNP. Specialized training in disorder control and tactical operations has been provided to three hundred vetted and trained Police Academy graduates in Nigeria. Fifty-eight LNP members, including some members of the PSU, have received firearms training to date and are now qualified to carry firearms.[62] The bulk of LNP training, however, is conducted at the Police Academy in Paynesville on the outskirts of Monrovia. The training program initially concentrated on meeting numerical targets; more recently, though, under new UNPOL and LNP leadership, its focus has been on addressing critical gaps in police performance. For example, even when arrests are made, successful prosecutions are rare. Crime-scene investigation and case preparation have been extremely poor—no surprise, given the poor state of Monrovia's forensics laboratory and the total absence of forensics laboratories and expertise in the rest of the country.

The AFL is regarded as having state-of-the art clothing and equipment; in contrast, logistical support for the LNP has been extremely weak. For example, except for the police academy, there are no police barracks for LNP members.[63] The police in vast Lofa County, in northwest Liberia, have exactly one motorcycle and one pick-up truck to cover their entire patch. The

Lofa police headquarters cum station at Voinjama has one typewriter and no computers.[64]

The implications of such resource scarcity for police performance are obvious and make it especially difficult to isolate poor training as a principal reason for underperformance. That said, UNPOL's training team has been criticized for being too multinational; too many countries with diverse policing traditions, cultures, and practices have been involved. This has been observable, for example, in the different ways in which different classes of recruits have learned to drill and salute, reflecting the differing customs of trainers from different countries. Far too few local and regional instructors have been employed, and the duration of basic training has been far too short— three months versus the six months previously ensured by the LNP.[65] Despite these challenges, UNPOL and its LNP counterparts have made remarkable progress with training development and delivery at the Police Academy.

UNPOL established the National Police Training Academy (NPTA) in 2004, with a mandate to provide basic police training for 3,500 law-enforcement personnel, and with a curriculum and instructional method emphasizing human rights, democratic policing principles, and modern policing techniques. This target was achieved by June 2007, by which time 3,522 LNP personnel (3,319 men, 203 women) had graduated from basic training at the NPTA. The academy is the only institution in Liberia capable of providing training to law-enforcement officers, including prison guards. In addition, 358 SSS members and 210 Liberia Seaport Police (LSP) personnel have graduated from the basic training program.[66]

Having met its mandated target for the basic training of 3,500 LNP officers, the handover of primary responsibility for the basic training program from UNPOL to the LNP began in June 2007. The handover included responsibility for administration, course planning and scheduling, and training delivery.[67] The basic training program includes nine weeks at the academy, sixteen weeks of in-service training under the supervision of a field training officer (FTO), and four more weeks at the academy prior to graduation as a LNP patrolman. The program for the LSP includes three weeks at the academy, one week with an FTO, and two weeks back at the academy. The course for the SSS requires only nine weeks of training at the academy. Corrections personnel undergo lengthier training: twelve weeks at the academy, thirty-two weeks under an FTO, and four weeks back at the academy. There are sixty-four LNP FTOs currently supervising probationary police officers (PPOs) in twenty-six police zones and depots in the greater Monrovia area, as well as at PSU headquarters. The trainer-to-student ratio is a fairly healthy 1:8.

Basic training begins with a basic academic training of nine weeks. The subjects include these: general policing; democratic policing principles; crime investigation; Liberian law; tactical training; and use of force (theory only).

Students are required to take eight examinations during this phase. Those who fail to achieve the required 70 percent pass mark are provided with two weeks of remedial training. Those who fail exams thereafter are dismissed from the LNP. Successful candidates become PPOs.

All PPOs undergo sixteen weeks of training at the PSU; this includes training in civil-disturbance containment, Joint Task Force patrolling, and Traffic Division duties. Subsequent field training for all PPOs in the seven zones and eighteen depots covers Charge of Quarter (police station procedures) as well as Criminal Investigation Division (CID), community policing, traffic, and patrol duties. On completion of field training, PPOs return to the academy for four weeks of competency-based training in practical aspects of police work.[68] The extant basic training program is far too short to produce the quality of police expected by those who live in Liberia; it is also of much shorter duration than comparable police-training programs in other African countries such as Ghana, Namibia, and Zambia, where a minimum of six months' basic training is provided. The UNMIL/UNPOL Training and Development Coordinator, Dag Dahlen of Norway, has therefore led a development process that has culminated in a new, fifty-two-week LNP basic training program that is designed to produce "qualified Probationary Police Officers capable of operating independently and ready for permanent assignment."

The curriculum provides for a progressive training regime that starts with a basic skills program and ends with the graduation of qualified patrolmen. The new program, which was approved in January 2008, comprises an initial twenty-six-week academic training course at the NPTA, followed by a twenty-six-week probationary period of field training. The pressing need for front-line supervisory capacity within the LNP has been recognized, and a new Career Development Plan has been approved to address this shortcoming and fill the current leadership and supervisory vacuum that exists between senior LNP management and patrol officers on the beat.[69]

All training programs have been based on research and training needs analyses in an attempt to ensure quality and sustainability in course design and delivery. Since 2007 there has been a deliberate process of local institutional capacity building—one that is integrating LNP training and development personnel at all levels of the academy, with a view to handover to full local ownership in the first half of 2008. With this aim in mind, UNPOL has downsized its presence at the NPTA, from seventy-five international police officers in January 2006 to twenty UNPOL officers in April 2007. The LNP is advising UNPOL on training compatibility and standardization and has taken over responsibility for graduation ceremonies and record keeping. In the process, LNP administrative and personnel routines have shown considerable improvement. The LNP has helped draft NPTA policies and procedures, analyzing current training needs and modifying programs to reinforce identified shortfalls. The LNP has also produced a plan and budget proposal for year 2007–2008, one that includes NPTA operational costs and salaries. Plans are well under way to create permanent facilities by constructing or renovating buildings capable of sustaining long-term training courses with a daily capacity of 250 students—180 of whom will be accommodated on campus in permanent structures.[70]

One of the major short-term challenges is to get the costs of running the academy and the planned training courses—including organization, maintenance, and personnel costs—incorporated into the LNP national budget and funded by the Government of Liberia. Other challenges relate to discipline—such as the poor attendance record of LNP members of NPTA, and of LNP instructors. There is also a lack of instructors with sufficient and appropriate police experience to provide credible instruction, and a perennial need to enhance the quality of recruits who are admitted to the basic training program.

Unlike the PSU, which is meant to deal with civil unrest, the QRU is supposed to be capable of countering organized armed threats. QRU recruits will be selected from members of the extant PSU who have already received some training in the use of force and firearms. [71] According to the U.S. State Department, the planned QRU will "be based on a US model, and grounded on law enforcement doctrine and concepts—rather than a gendarmerie force."[72] Training for the QRU should ideally be provided by a single country (most appropriately, the United States), because the extreme multinationalism that has characterized the UNPOL training team is ill suited to the requirements of the QRU. However, UNPOL insists that the Police Academy will have ultimate responsibility for all LNP training and that trainers from the LNP and UNPOL (such as Norway, Czech Republic, Sweden, Serbia, and Ghana as well as the United States) will be involved in setting up the QRU, along with five American trainers. Meanwhile, a first-draft training curriculum for the QRU has been revised by UNPOL and LNP trainers so that it includes human rights and democratic policing standards. Also, it excludes the paramilitary component that was in the first draft.

The basic QRU course will be three months long. In addition to outstanding LNP equipment requirements, the QRU will require sidearms, sub-machine guns, other specialist weapons, ammunition for training and deployment, uniforms, and at least twenty vehicles. Additional training and accommodation facilities (beyond those already under construction at the Police Academy) will have to be built. The $5 million allocated by the United States is clearly insufficient to meet such needs, and it is unclear where the rest of the money will come from. The aim is to have two hundred QRU members trained and operational by July 2009.[73]

The first intake of one hundred recruits began training in April 2008, and a second intake of one hundred commenced training at the end of June 2008.

Elements of the QRU will deploy to duty stations throughout the fifteen counties. UNPOL estimates that it will take approximately five years to build the QRU to its full complement of five hundred.[74]

Conclusion

The discrepancy between the conceptual framework for SSR and practical realities in Liberia is due in part to the framework's emphasis on security as a process of good governance rather than as a tangible outcome—that is, the arresting of insecurity and the provision of decent law enforcement. Outside of Europe, a multi-sectoral, whole-of-government approach to SSR may be conceptually valid but unworkable in practice. In Africa, donor countries have generally not had the fortitude to see comprehensive processes through, and recipient countries have not had the financial and human resources to implement or sustain ambitious, overarching SSR programs. Nevertheless, much more can be done to actually arrest insecurity within a conceptually and practically more modest program that focuses mainly on military and criminal justice reform. It is clear that both the UN and the United States have made a start with police and military reform, but they have not done nearly enough toward accomplishing the SSR goals laid out in Resolution 1509—namely, to assist the transitional government of Liberia in monitoring and restructuring the police force of Liberia, consistent with democratic policing; to develop a civilian police training program; to otherwise assist in the training of civilian police, in cooperation with ECOWAS, international organizations, and interested states; and to assist the transitional government in the formation of a new and restructured Liberian military in cooperation with ECOWAS, international organizations, and interested states.

Quite rightly, UNMIL and UNPOL point to the lack of resources as an inhibiting factor in the accomplishment of their policing mandate. Such resource starvation is unacceptable. Progress on development in Liberia will not be sustainable if there is no rule of law. UN peacekeeping operations are neither mandated nor resourced to engage in long-term peacebuilding activities, including SSR. Other actors, both within and outside the UN system, are expected to undertake the bulk of this work.[75] The result is that SSR slips into a systemic funding vacuum while the UNSC continues to mandate missions to do SSR work, in the hope that a "lead nation" will step up to the plate and provide both the leadership and the resources to carry out what has been described as an essential task of peacekeeping.

Unfortunately, there is no such lead nation for Liberia. The country is in many ways less fortunate than neighbouring Sierra Leone, which faced similar, if not much larger and more urgent, SSR challenges. Britain supported the enhancement of short- and longer-term security in Sierra Leone through a program aimed at training, equipping, and advising government security forces. This program involved integrating British military advisers—who were serving British officers—into Sierra Leone forces; close coordination with the UN Mission in Sierra Leone (UNAMSIL) and the Sierra Leone Police; and the enhancement of the combat effectiveness of the forces through ongoing advice and training. The British advisers made sure that before UNAMSIL withdrew, the armed forces were operationally proficient and capable of conducting effective joint patrols with UN forces. Britain also seconded a senior British police officer to take charge as IGP; it also created an effective Office of National Security and helped produce a comprehensive national-security strategy and defence policy.

Britain's efforts in Sierra Leone stand in stark contrast to the Americans' SSR program, which has amounted to little more than the processing of recruits through boot camp. The job is done by private contractors. The trainers are all former American soldiers who have opted out of their national military and chosen an occupation with a stronger cash/work nexus. While contractors may be good at providing basic and even advanced infantry training, they are certainly not the ideal role models to instill notions of duty to country and military ethics—including the democratic principle of civil supremacy over the military. Indeed, in a country and region where recent history has been shaped by warlords and mercenaries, the U.S. Department of State has shown remarkable insensitivity by sending in contractors to shape the new army.

The immediate priority for both the U.S. Government and the UN should be to help the Government of Liberia draft and adopt a comprehensive national-security strategy and policy as the essential framework for continued support of the SSR agenda. Looking ahead to new missions, it is also clear that the UN should provide guidance on how resources may be found to match future SSR mandates authorized by the UNSC.

In the short term, the UN should ensure that future benchmarks for the drawdown of UNMIL forces are determined by qualitative criteria and are not based on numbers trained. This will require, among other things, enhanced efforts to produce reliable crime statistics, including victimization surveys in Monrovia and rural areas. There is no quick fix; the UN and the United States, as well as other significant donor partners, need to stay the course with Liberia, as they have done in Kosovo. SSR is a long process, not an event, and the premature withdrawal of international-security support would be disastrous for Liberia.

Notes

1   OECD, "OECD DAC Handbook on Security System Reform: Supporting Security and Justice" (Paris: 2007). http://www.oecd.org/dataoecd/43/25/38406485.pdf.

2   The term "security sector reform" is used in this chapter for the sake of simplicity, as it is used by the UN in Liberia. It is also used (erroneously) as the name of the American-led defence transformation program.

3 "Liberia: Interim Poverty Reduction Strategy Paper," IMF Country Report no. 07/60, February 2007.

4 International Monetary Fund (IMF), "Liberia: Interim Poverty Reduction Strategy Paper," Country Report no. 07/60 (Washington: February 2007), 32. http://imf.org/external/pubs/ft/scr/2007/cr0760.pdf.

5 Nicole Itano, "Liberating Liberia: Charles Taylor and the Rebels Who Unseated Him," Institute of Social Studies (ISS) Occasional Paper no. 82 (The Hague: November 2003).

6 Ibid.

7 http://www.globalsecurity.org/military/world/liberia/lnp.htm.

8 Thomas Jaye, "An Assessment Report on Security Sector Reform in Liberia," Governance Reform Commission of Liberia, September 23, 2006. http://www.kaiptc.org/_upload/general/Lib_Assess_Rep_on_SSR.pdf.

9 Government of Liberia, An Act to Repeal Chapter 2, Sub-chapter B of the Executive Law Establishing the Office of National Security and to Amend The Executive Law to Create and Establish in the Executive Branch of Government a Ministry to be known as The Ministry of National Secretary, September 6, 1979.

10 Government of Liberia, An Act to establish the National Security Council of the Republic of Liberia, March 12, 1999.

11 David C. Gompert et al., "Making Liberia Safe: Transformation of the National Security Sector," report prepared for the Office of the U.S. Secretary of Defense, RAND Corporation, 2007, 78.

12 Article VII, s. 1(b), of Comprehensive Peace Agreement (CPA), 2003, 15.

13 Article VII, ss. 2 (a–d) and 3, of CPA, 2003, 16.

14 Article VIII, s. 1, of CPA, 2003, 16.

15 Article VIII, s. 2, of CPA, 2003, 16.

16 UN Security Council (UNSC), Resolution 1509, S/RES/1509 (2003), September 19, 2003, 4.

17 Jaye, "An Assessment Report," 2006.

18 Article XXXV, s. 1(b), of CPA, August 18, 2003, 27.

19 Article XXXV, s. 1(e), of the CPA states that "all suspended provisions of the Constitution, Statutes and other laws of Liberia, affected as a result of this Agreement, shall be deemed to be restored with the inauguration of the elected Government by January 2006."

20 Articles 51 and 54(e) of the Constitution of the Republic of Liberia, 1986.

21 Article 34, ss. (b) and (c) of the Constitution of the Republic of Liberia, 1986.

22 However, a meaningful, long-term process of security-sector reform must consider the extent to which the constitution must be reformed as well. The issue of overlapping responsibilities of security institutions highlights the need to provide constitutional backing and clarification for all statutory security institutions. Moreover, the present constitution encourages abuses of power, especially by the president, who appoints virtually all the leaders of the security apparatus.

23 IMF, Country Report no. 07/60, 32.

24 Ibid., 34.

25 Amos Sawyer was president of the Interim Government of National Unity in Liberia from November 22, 1990, to March 2, 1994. He left Liberia in 2001 after Taylor's militia attempted to murder him and his colleague, Conmany Wesseh of the Center for Democratic Empowerment.

26 Amos Sawyer, Chairman of the Liberia Governance Reform Commission, Monrovia, August 21, 2007.

27 Thomas A. Dempsey, "Security Sector Reform in Liberia: Restructuring the Ministry of National Defense," unpublished information paper, June 17, 2007. Dempsey, a retired

U.S. Army colonel, served on the SSR team as Director of Ministry of Defense Reform and Training.

28 Amos Sawyer, see note 23.

29 Ibid.

30 The national budget for 2006 was a paltry US$123 million; for 2007 it was $199 million. Even if Liberia were to attain and sustain an economic growth rate of 10 percent, the baseline is so low that it would take twenty-five years for the economy to return to 1990s levels.

31 Gompert et al., "Making Liberia Safe," 25–26.

32 Ibid., 26–28.

33 Sean McFate, "The Art and Aggravation of Vetting in Post-Conflict Environments," *Military Review*, July–August 2007, 82.

34 Briefing by Lieutenant Colonel William Wyatt, Monrovia, August 28, 2007.

35 Mark Malan, "Security Sector Reform in Liberia: Mixed Results from Humble Beginnings," Strategic Studies Institute, U.S. Army War College, March 2008.

36 Sean McFate, "The Art and Aggravation," 82.

37 Ibid.

38 According to the *CIA World Factbook* estimates for 2003, only 57 percent of Liberians over fifteen can read and write. The literacy rate for men is 73.3 percent; for women it is 41.6 percent. In 2004 the interim government of Liberia estimated the literacy rate at a scant 28 percent.

39 At present no single ethnic group makes up more than 15 percent of the AFL.

40 Sergeant Major Spike Roberts (USMC, retired), Director of Training, Camp Ware, Monrovia, August 30, 2007.

41 Briefing by Lieutenant-Colonel William Wyatt, Monrovia, August 28, 2007.

42 Malan, "Security Sector Reform in Liberia."

43 Ibid.

44 The Government of Liberia (Ministry of Defense) is responsible for paying the monthly salaries of all members of the AFL according to an agreed salary scale. Those salaries range from US$90 for a private up to $170 for a sergeant major. This compares well to the basic monthly salary for civil servants, which is $50 per month. It is interesting that all members of the Band are paid at a rate of $140 per month, regardless of rank. Recruits undergoing basic training receive a salary of $40 until such time as they graduate as riflemen.

45 Wyatt, see note 36.

46 Malan, "Security Sector Reform in Liberia."

47 Ibid.

48 According to DynCorp, delays in the program launch were caused by certain actions of the national government, including the slow pace of voluntary relocation of civilians living at Camp Scheifflin.

49 DynCorp took up assignment in Liberia in August 2005.

50 Once soldiers have completed their training, they are formed into units by PAE; this is an administrative procedure that takes about a month to complete. Units are activated when they are joined by commanders under PAE mentorship. The first three companies of the 1st Battalion will be activated in December 2007. Battalions become operational after they are activated and have successfully completed an eighteen-month collective training cycle, which, for the 1st Battalion, began on March 12, 2008. At the end of this cycle (September 2009) the battalion will be evaluated for combat readiness. If it passes muster it will be declared operational.

51 Wyatt, see note 36.

52 Amos Sawyer, see note 23.

53 UNSC Resolution 1509 (2003), S/RES/1509, September 19, 2003, 4.

54 Article VIII, s. 1 of CPA, 2003, p. 16. UNMIL concluded the registration of statutory security agencies in April 2005—including the Liberia National Police, SSS, DEA, MNS, NBI, FDA, BIN, LPRC, MCP, RIA, LTC, LSP, and NSA.

55 Gompert et al., "Making Liberia Safe: 25–26.

56 Mohammed Al Hassan, Police Commissioner, UNMIL, Monrovia, August 30, 2007.

57 Joint patrols continue; the LNP still lacks the vehicles and capacity to patrol independently in mobile units. According to Al Hassan, the Government of Liberia allocated only US$269,000 for police vehicles in the 2006 national budget (last year's total national budget was a mere US$129 million).

58 Al Hassan, see note 58.

59 Dag R. Dahlen, Training and Development Coordinator, UNMIL/UNPOL, Monrovia, 02 September 2007.

60 Al Hassan, see note 58.

61 Ibid.

62 Dahlen, see note 61.

63 Cecil Griffiths, Executive Director, Liberian National Law Enforcement Agency (LINLEA), Monrovia, August 21, 2007.

64 Interview with Chief Inspector Koli, General Commander LNP, Lofa County, Voinjama, August 25, 2007.

65 Ibid.

66 Members of the SSS also received three months' training in the United States. Al Hassan, see note 46.

67 Dahlen, see note 61.

68 Ibid.

69 The process of developing standard operating procedures (SOPs) and a duty manual for the LNP is now complete. This task should have begun in earnest during 2004, and should have been completed long ago. This oversight by UNPOL and by the LNP's senior management is largely to blame for the lack of supervisory training to date and for the resulting "crisis in command" in LNP zones, depots, and police stations countrywide.

70 Dahlen, see note 61.

71 Owing to attrition, 256 members remain in the PSU. The extant vacancies, in addition to those arising from envisaged QRU recruiting and selection, will be "backfilled" by serving and recruited LNP general duty officers.

72 Interview with Deborah S. Hart, Active Response Corps, S/CRS, Monrovia, August 28, 2007.

73 Ibid.

74 Al Hassan, see note 58.

75 UN Department of Peacekeeping Operations, "UN Peacekeeping Operations: Principles and Guidelines" (New York: June 2007), para. 54.

State Building in a Post-Conflict Context

The Liberian Framework for Donor Aid and Private Investments

Caroline Khoubesserian

11

State building in a fragile context is an intricate process that requires a strong set of coordinated resources. This means that a comprehensive framework must exist to direct and absorb the efforts; conversely, several large unguided inputs can easily upset emerging stability and development results. In the absence of predetermined formulas, it is the intuition, analysis, and willingness of the leaders and major investors that determine the correct mix of donor aid and private investment for this process. With a post-conflict fragile state, the task is all the more arduous—the coordinated efforts must, in addition, take into account the origins of the conflict and the impact of the violence on the society. And all of this will typically need to happen in the context of a newly formed government and a weakened civil society. Despite such difficulties, there seem to be grounds for optimism with the Liberian state-building process now under way. The current government has formulated a framework—namely, the Poverty Reduction Strategy (PRS)—that includes a response to the causes and consequences of the conflict.

Liberia ended fourteen years of conflict in 2003, elected a new president—Madame Ellen Johnson-Sirleaf—in October 2005, and launched a rebuilding effort by jointly (with donors) establishing the Liberian Reconstruction and Development Committee[1] (LRDC) in March 2006. As part of its state-building process, the country must address a number of serious problems, including corruption, a violent past, mismanagement of resources, and a collapsed economy that has left it with close to 80 percent unemployment in the formal sector.[2] In response to these challenges, Johnson-Sirleaf and the LRDC have embraced the World Bank PRS process as a tool for managing state-building inputs, which mainly take the form of donor aid (and little private investment). A PRS process is not unique to post-conflict states, nor is it always viewed positively, but in Liberia's case it seems that the government and its partners have so far made it work while remaining sensitive to the causes and consequences of the conflict so as to incorporate adequate responses into the strategy. This all-important consideration of the conflict's causes and consequences is most visible in the national consultation process and the corresponding incorporation of its results into the 2008–11 PRS; in the devolution of power to county administrations; which have taken ownership of the PRS; in governance more generally; and in a rebalancing of the power that foreign investors have over natural resources in the country.

This chapter details the ongoing state-building effort in Liberia. It is based on observations made by the author during 2007, which she spent working with the UN peacekeeping mission in Liberia (UNMIL).[3] The chapter begins by outlining the causes and consequences of the conflict. Then it describes the state-building process, with a focus on the PRS, the national consultations, and the devolution of power. Third, it offers a case study of Lofa County (in Liberia's northwest) to help illustrate the conflict's impact on the country's people and its infrastructure as well as the corresponding needs that the state-building process is trying to address. Fourth, it examines donor-aid and private-investment contributions to the state-building framework. As the complex process of state building has only just commenced in Liberia (since 2006) and will require many years, the chapter's conclusions do not go too far. More time is needed for all the trends to settle into place before an in-depth understanding can be offered.

The chapter discusses what the author feels is the principal tool in state building for Liberia—the PRS. However, readers should recognize that other factors are at work, both positive and negative. Ongoing regional instability, steep increases in world food prices, and changes in the social dynamics of the country will certainly play a role. More directly linked to the discussed PRS process are the commitment and experience of Johnson-Sirleaf, the presence of UNMIL, the Liberian people's acceptance of UNMIL's presence, and the active presence of large international donors such as the United States. These elements should be considered positive and integral to the state-building process. Without this constellation of powerful actors and their accompanying resources the potential results will be unlikely to succeed.

The Causes and Consequences of the Conflict

Liberia is a West African country with a population of about 3.5 million,[4] most of which is concentrated near the coast around the capital, Monrovia. It is a heavily forested country known for its raw materials such as rubber, timber, iron ore, and diamonds. Like other African countries, it has few navigable rivers, which makes transportation expensive and development difficult.

Liberia has a unique history for its region. During colonial times, Sierra Leone was a British colony and Côte d'Ivoire and Guinea were French colonies, whereas Liberia was a destination for freed American slaves. To understand Liberia's more recent violent history (1989–2003), one must return to the time when freed slaves began arriving from the United States, for that is when underlying tensions that led to Liberia's recent civil conflicts began to develop.

In 1822 the American Colonization Society (ACS)[5] began sending freed black slaves to what is now Liberia. The goal was to have them leave the United States, on the reasoning that they would never be able to integrate into American society.[6] Over the next two decades about 15,000 former American slaves were sent to Liberia through the ACS and similar schemes.[7] White Americans were also sent to the colony, as governors. However, in 1847 the freed slaves—known by then as Americo-Liberians—declared independence for Liberia. Thus Liberia became the first independent nation in sub-Saharan Africa.

The Americo-Liberians were only about 5 percent of Liberia's population.[8] At the time they began arriving from America, sixteen African ethnic groups already inhabited the territory. There was little communication between the Americo-Liberians on the coast and the indigenous groups in the country's interior. Despite their minority position, the Americo-Liberians took over the country politically and economically. They dominated national politics, importing American concepts and forming the True Whig Party, which would govern in Liberia until the conflicts began in 1980. Also, Americo-Liberians were more adept at developing the economy as they had connections with the United States and more experience with the market economy.[9] As the Americo-Liberians developed their institutions of governance, they largely ignored the indigenous Liberians and did little to spread the new country's wealth. Gains from the economy were invested in Monrovia, leaving the rest of the country poor. Over time, relations between Americo-Liberians and the original inhabitants became defined by dependence (a result of economic disparity) and tensions (over the distribution of resources). This fostered resentment as well as sharp cleavages between the two groups. The fact that a handful of Americo-Liberian families constituted a governing elite only exacerbated this trend. It also encouraged widespread corruption within more and more repressive governments.

On April 12, 1980, Samuel Doe (a member of the Krahn ethnic group) led a successful coup, in the course of which President Tolbert and key members of his administration were executed. As leader of the People's Redemption Council (PRC), Doe pledged to end inequality and political oppression and to bring about democratic reforms. But as it turned out, his regime blocked constitutional and electoral reforms, and his development initiatives turned out to heavily favour the Krahn. On top of this, he imprisoned opposition leaders who challenged his rule, including the current president, Johnson-Sirleaf. As a result of all this, dissatisfaction and unrest continued to grow throughout Liberia.

In 1989 two groups attempted to end the Doe regime: the National Patriotic Front of Liberia (NPFL), led by Charles Taylor, and the Independent National

Patriotic Front (INPFL), a splinter group of the NPFL, led by Prince Johnson.[10] The INPFL soldiers captured and killed Doe in September 1990. A full-out conflict then ensued, during which groups divided by ethnicity looted the country and fought for control of its natural resources. The Economic Community of West African States (ECOWAS) attempted, in an unprecedented regional effort, to bring peace by sending three thousand African troops (ECOMOG) to Liberia shortly after Doe's murder. The success of this mission is very much open to debate. In 1997, Taylor was elected president; in 1998, the ECOMOG forces left Liberia. Taylor's rule turned out to be no improvement over Doe's; indeed, it was an especially violent and brutal time, during which the president involved himself in the smuggling of arms and diamonds throughout the region—especially in Sierra Leone, where serious atrocities were being committed during that country's own civil unrest. In 2000 a rebel group supported by neighbouring Guinea—Liberians United for Reconciliation and Development (LURD)—began launching attacks into Liberia through Lofa County. Intense fighting continued for several years until strong international pressure in 2003 brought the conflict to an end. At this time a peace accord was signed, Taylor was offered asylum in Nigeria, and UNMIL entered Liberia to maintain security and support peacebuilding efforts.

In humanitarian terms, the years 1989 to 2003 were a time of death, mass displacement, and destruction of basic services and infrastructure in Liberia. The warlords looted and vandalized as they willed. About 270,000 Liberians were killed during the two civil conflicts.[11] UNHCR registered around 560,000 internally displaced persons (IDPs) and refugees. The 2006 Comprehensive Food Security and Nutrition Survey (CFSNS) found that at one time or another during the fourteen years of conflict, 80 percent of Liberians had been displaced.[12] As people fled their homes, all activities—including agriculture, basic services, and economic and social programs—were abandoned. "Today there are only 51 Liberian physicians to cover the nation's public health needs, approximately one for every 70,000 Liberians. About 70 percent of school buildings are partially or wholly destroyed, and over half of Liberian children and youth are estimated to be out of school. A whole generation of Liberians has spent more time at war than in the classroom."[13] On top of all this, the country's social fabric was under tremendous stress; the warring factions often recruited children to fight, and the conflict exacerbated the country's ethnic divisions.

In economic terms, the World Bank described the Liberian case as follows:

> Historically, Liberia's economy has been predominantly commodities based. Prior to the war, the rubber industry generated over US$100 million in export earnings annually. The discovery of significant iron ore deposits attracted substantial foreign investment in the 1960s and 1970s,

with the export-oriented concession sector as a whole generating about one-third of government revenue ... By the end of fighting in 1997, most foreign businesses had left the country. Depletion of iron ore deposits, damage to mines, and the impact of the war on rubber production meant recorded exports fell from US$440 million in 1988 to US$25 million in 1997... Real income per capita remained about one-third that of pre-war levels.[14]

In 2007 the country's external debt was about US$4.5 billion[15] and the internal debt was about $900 million.[16] "The economy completely collapsed. GDP fell a catastrophic 90% between 1987 and 1995, one of the largest economic collapses ever recorded in the world."[17] The good news is that in December 2007, Liberia had its arrears cleared to the World Bank and African Development Bank (AfDB) and since March 2008 has qualified for debt relief under the Heavily Indebted Poor Country (HIPC) initiative.[18] Its internal debt of US$300 million has been evaluated as still valid, however.[19]

Post-conflict state building absolutely requires that a country identify the issues that brought it to turmoil. As the above account illustrates, the causes and consequences of the fourteen years of conflict in Liberia are complex and far-reaching. They extend over 140 years of perceived inequality and have strongly affected the entire population. Further, some of the key personalities throughout the conflict are still important actors in the country's political life. For Liberians to come to full terms with the conflict and its impact will take a great deal of time. One initiative already under way is the Truth and Reconciliation Commission (TRC), an independent body that has been tasked with providing a detailed assessment of the events based on Liberians' witness testimony.[20] This commission is marred by logistical and conceptual problems and has not yet completed its work; as an alternative, an account of the causes and consequences can be found in the government analysis provided in the PRS documents. That account serves as a starting point for the country.[21] For the purposes of this chapter, the key causes and consequences can be summarized as follows:

- Causes: profiteering from natural resources, government corruption, perceived and actual poor distribution of wealth, the arms trade, inappropriate justice and conflict resolution mechanisms.
- Consequences: mass displacement, lack of basic services (for some non-existence), halt to individual and national economic activities, poverty, destruction of infrastructure, fear and mistrust among population (especially of former child soldiers), lawlessness, a dysfunctional justice system.

State Building in Liberia—the PRS Consultations

The above summary amounts to a starting point for state-building in Liberia. Clearly, the government and its international partners—and, of course, the Liberian people—face an enormous amount of work in a great many sectors. So far, Johnson-Sirleaf and her government have developed policies and made reforms to encourage ongoing state building. Significant initiatives include these: financial management reforms; the removal of seven thousand "ghost employees" from the civil-service pay list;[22] changes to concession agreements in the logging, mining, and rubber sectors;[23] the appointment of county and assistant superintendents in all fifteen counties to enforce decentralization of governance; the rebuilding of schools and the elimination of school fees; and the rebuilding of major roads.[24] Crucially, the PRS has provided a comprehensive framework to guide these initiatives that the administration and major donors can work within.

The 2008–2011 Liberian PRS[25] has four pillars, which are the same as the LRDC subcommittees: Security, Economic Revitalization, Governance and the Rule of Law, and Infrastructure and Basic Services. The PRS document provides guidelines for the entire government and population of Liberia regarding the country's future direction. It also provides a road map for the principal donors in the state-building process. What makes this PRS especially important is that it has incorporated countrywide consultations that were conducted in 2007 to discuss development priorities, specifically with regard to infrastructure and basic services.

The district and county development consultations were launched in 2007. Lofa County served as a "test county" in March 2007. The plan was for county administrations—a relatively new development, strengthened by UNMIL and UNDP country support teams—to lead the process and in that way take own-ership for development and governance in their areas. To that end, meetings were organized in all six of Lofa's districts[26]—a rarity in the past, partially for logistical reasons—so as to ensure the participation of a cross-section of civil society, including clan leaders and women's groups. After the Lofa meetings were judged a success, similar consultations were held in all fifteen counties in late 2007.

These local consultations were an important step toward improved governance throughout Liberia. They forced the county administrations to consider the needs of their people and to lead them by consensus. This sort of local governance is a new concept in Liberia. If it is used effectively, long-standing divides and tensions among ethnic groups can become dynamic interactions. The hope is that local-level governance will be more responsive to the needs of the population and, it follows, to the underlying causes of the conflict. Power in previous Liberian administrations had been concentrated in Monrovia, and wealth distribution had been highly unequal. An inclusive consultation process, if the results take hold, would serve to mobilize and satisfy the different groups in the country.

The local consultations were used to identify basic demographic information and the specific resources available to the people, and to establish development priorities by sector. From all of this, a matrix of development projects was constructed. In all counties, the overwhelming majority of attendees identified their most pressing needs as health, education, and better roads.[27] The representatives of civil society who were consulted believe that if the state improves these, they will be better able to climb out of poverty. For example, they pointed out that their ability to grow crops depended on their being healthy enough to work, and that they then needed to be able to ship their produce by road.

That the priorities were similar across the country does not in itself mean that the consultations were a success. But it does, in the Liberia case, signal clearly what state building must involve and that Liberia as a whole is sorely lacking in key basic services. This should be no surprise, given that years of civil unrest largely destroyed the infrastructure, drove out much of the population (including its teachers and nurses), and ended all skills-development programs for children and youth. Furthermore, poverty and social marginalization can be directly related to the lack of these basic services. Incorporating into the PRS the priorities that emerged during the consultations, and acting on them, will be essential to reconstruction.

Roads are especially important to Liberian reconstruction. The lack of them and their poor condition (many were destroyed from a combination of the unrest and lack of maintenance) poses an incredible challenge to Liberians, donor agencies, and private investors. Even in Monrovia and the nearby economic zones, most highways are no better than potholed lanes. The inter-county roads are mostly dirt tracks pocked with small craters and dangerous log bridges. The tracks turn to mud during the rainy season; cars and trucks stay stuck in holes that are sometimes several metres deep for days, even weeks. Better roads will allow industry to develop outside of the capital; they will also enable people to get their products to market and to access services. However, the investment required to improve roads (as well as other infrastructure) will be enormous, and the time required will be long. In Liberia, a multi-donor approach is being used to begin roadwork in both rural and urban zones.

According to the World Bank: "Working in collaboration with UNMIL and UNDP, the [World] Bank has embarked upon a unique and innovative solution to emergency infrastructure repairs within a post-conflict environment: the Bank provides the funding; UNMIL engineering battalions provide the heavy equipment, and UNDP administrative support."[28] An important component of the road project is that it is labour intensive. Roads require maintenance, and local people are paid (albeit not much) to do it. This local employment in turn is helping Liberia to stabilize and its nascent economy to grow. This necessary first step to rebuilding a country will provide work for years to come.

Liberia faces a serious shortage of health and education services as well as roads. Efforts to address these shortfalls are very capital-intensive; the estimate for the infrastructure/basic-services pillar in 2008–9 alone is US$320.8 million.[29] This is 58 percent of the overall cost of the PRS for the year and is a huge amount for a country with a shattered economy and a small budget. Those leading Liberia's PRS so far have attracted $250 million in pledges from the World Bank and other donors such as the EU, the United States, and Japan. The money will go to implementing the PRS in 2008–9. The PRS will have to continue lobbying donors for many years, as other large sources of income (from taxes and private investments) are still not available to Liberia and will take much time to develop.

Private investment in Liberia has long focused on natural-resource extraction. The profits generated by such activities were what fuelled the years of civil conflict. Because of poor governance, even profits that did not go to buy arms mostly left the country without improving the lives of Liberians. Private investment can be so attractive to a poor country like Liberia that the temptation is to accept all offers to invest, but it must be ensured that both the investor and the country get a fair deal. In this regard, several international bans (e.g., on diamonds and timber) were placed on Liberian products during the conflict and were only lifted in 2007. Now that those bans have been lifted, the government does not appear to be falling into a dependency pattern with foreign investors; rather, it is seeking fair arrangements. It is renegotiating long-standing concessions with rubber companies and has established a competitive process in the mining and other industries to award contracts to the most satisfactory bidders .

Ideally, private investment in Liberia will move beyond extraction of natural resources into the processing of raw materials. Initial opportunities include the processing of Liberian coffee (a previously missed opportunity) and the rebuilding of pre-existing factories (e.g., palm-oil refineries) that were destroyed during the conflict.

Lofa County: State-Building Needs and Activities

The above has been a general view of Liberia's present condition. The next section focuses on state building as it relates to Lofa County.

Lofa County is the far northwestern corner of Liberia, bordering on both Guinea and Sierra Leone. Lofa is a forest and agricultural zone that was considered Liberia's breadbasket prior to the conflict. It has seven districts and a population of 270,144 representing several ethnic groups.[30] During the years of civil unrest, especially between 1999 and 2004, much of the fighting in Liberia took place in Lofa. LURD moved in and made it their base. In a countermovement, almost the entire population fled for its own safety.

Since 2004 a joint effort of the government and UNMIL has re-established security in the county. UNMIL soldiers patrol its borders and the main towns, as the Liberian Army has been dismantled[31] and the Liberian National Police has only recently been reconstituted. The government and UNMIL, again working in concert, undertook the disarmament of the rebel groups in 2005 and continue to develop programs for reintegrating into society those who were involved in the fighting. As an indication that security conditions in the county have improved, most of Lofa's people returned in 2006–7, through UNHCR-assisted programs, to begin rebuilding. As well, more and more humanitarian and development organizations have been setting up project offices in the county.

Current security problems include local petty crime as well as more organized high-stakes robberies from across the Guinea border. Also, sporadic disputes can develop along religious lines; these ultimately superimpose a contest over resources or rather a struggle for livelihoods. Most of the people in Lofa County are Kissi, Lorma, or Mandingo. Most are Christian, but a significant minority (mainly the Mandingos) are Muslim. Generally, religious and ethnic tolerance does exist and is publicly encouraged. For example, all official meetings and ceremonies in the area commence with a Christian prayer and close with a Muslim prayer. Yet there are simmering tensions, which sometimes threaten to boil over. For example, in September 2007 there were protests against the building of a mosque in Vezela (the Lofa district capital). The scenes during this protest—chants, threats, the carrying of machetes—were remnants of the past conflicts, but quickly dissipated through dialogue led by the county administration. To maintain the calm, ongoing peacebuilding efforts that benefit all communities should be sustained, as should equitable governance .practices and savvy political management.

The return to Lofa for the population is a hard process that requires much work for little gain. The returnees typically must rebuild their destroyed homes and clear their overgrown fields for planting. It can take several years of this work just to get to a subsistence level of living. Consequently, the farming population does not at present produce enough food to last through the year. In 2006 and 2007 it was deemed necessary to provide the people of the region with subsidized rice (which is the country's staple) to ensure an adequate food supply. Though food production has increased each year since peace was restored, the world food crisis has made life harder for local farmers because seed prices have risen. Those farmers will continue to need help, as the little income they are beginning to earn cannot cover the rising costs.[32] Farming in 2008 remains largely subsistence based, though some NGOs and private initiatives are helping farmers band together into collectives to produce cash crops. In Lofa there is a great deal of potential for co-operatives. Potential agricultural projects in Lofa include a palm-oil refinery and agro-processing businesses. It is not yet clear whether the government will be able to attract private investment for agro-business and provide incentives for co-operative farming.

Over the past two years, while the people have worked to rehabilitate their farms and homes, other local projects have been ongoing. First, and most important, small businesses are opening. Most of these are bottle shops and restaurants; however small, they offer the local people direct incomes and suggest directions that entrepreneurs can take. Another important source of income in the county is the multi-donor road project (mentioned in the previous section), which has been providing employment since 2006 to several hundred people. Other sources of income in Lofa are NGO projects for income generation and skills training, including programs that offer micro-lending. Finally, some local people are employed directly by NGOs and international agencies.

"Official" government in the area almost vanished during the conflict but is now returning. The court and administrative buildings endured attacks during the fighting and are still in a dismal state. Plans were made to renovate these structures in late 2008 with USAID and UN funding. Other actions to restore the government's presence include hiring competent staff; ensuring the availability of materials such as vehicles, furniture, computers, and electricity; and making sure that government employees are paid regularly. The pay issue is a serious challenge, as only the county seat, Voinjama, has a bank. That is where state funds physically arrive each month; from that one spot, pay packets must reach all civil servants in the county, which means resources for the transportation and ensuring up-to-date lists of employees. Despite these and other challenges—such as low salaries and understaffing—the county administration is taking the state-building process quite seriously.

Taking on development planning, as Lofa county did in early 2007, was a big step for the returning administration as well as for the struggling people it hoped to serve. Despite all obstacles, the county officials with the assistance of the UN support team and their national counterparts underwent the process twice in the same year (the second time when the national process was launched). During both rounds, strong efforts were made to include all parts of civil society in all districts as well as have government listen. Success was the result of co-operation between Monrovia and the local people. It is hoped that the dialogue this process launched will continue indefinitely.

NGOs and other donors in Lofa County have focused their projects on re-building schools and clinics.[33] Most of this infrastructure had been destroyed during the conflict, so the work mainly involves rebuilding facilities that existed before. The biggest project is being handled by the Swiss Agency for Development and Cooperation (SDC), which is rebuilding the Tellowayn hospital (150 beds) in Voinjama. This should be completed in late 2008 at a cost of US$2 million. Once staffing obstacles are overcome, this effort will greatly improve the breadth and quality of health services available in the county. This, along with continued building of health centres across Lofa to serve remote communities, will improve primary health care in the region. However, the question of costs (e.g., user fees) is a major factor and must be kept in mind to ensure access to health care for such a poor population.

Basic services in Lofa County require great improvement. The quality and availability of water, health, and education across the county is very low, and not just because infrastructure is lacking; personnel are also in short supply. Often a single teacher is assigned a grade-school class of seventy to one hundred children. There are only three Liberian doctors in the entire county, and there is no government engineer to oversee water infrastructure and quality. NGOs and the sponsoring donors are doing a great deal of work in these areas. Some examples: the International Refugee Council (IRC) has started a teacher training program; several medical humanitarian agencies (including the International Medical Corps and the International Committee of the Red Cross [ICRC]) are providing additional doctors and medical staff for health facilities; and agencies involved in water and sanitation projects (including Action Contre la Faim and ICRC) are building or rehabilitating water-collection points for the most vulnerable communities. The existing network of water sources depends wholly on these agencies and on the local water committees created to manage them.

Private-investment activities in Lofa are minimal to non-existent at the moment. Prospectors began surveying the county in 2008 once the ban on Liberian diamonds was lifted. Government activities to encourage private investment in the area are not yet developed, as providing basic services and infrastructure remains the absolute priority. Questionable stability, unskilled labour, and poor roads are all impediments to having large private investment in the region.

Overall, the people of Lofa County are undertaking their own rebuilding process, centred on restoring livelihoods such as farming and on rebuilding homes. The reintroduction of basic services and infrastructure, with the assistance of NGOs and donors, accompanies this process. The local and national governments are facilitating the process but are not managing it entirely on their own. The administration is working to identify people's needs and have them matched appropriately to the resources available from the donor community. Continuing to develop the capacity of local governance structures and injecting resources into the process is key for Lofa development. That work will require advances in education, governance tools, ongoing peacebuilding initiatives, and the rebuilding of all pre-existing infrastructure (including electricity and waste-management systems). Finally, more qualified staff will have to be attracted to the county. Improved infrastructure and basic services will continue to be the priority for the people of Lofa County, as was identified during the consultation process. To achieve these goals, government must continue forming partnerships with international donors to ensure that these services eventually return to the people.

Donor Assistance for Liberia

A basic question for state building is whether the resources exist to achieve that daunting goal. The Liberian government and donor partners have identified Liberia's needs and established a framework to guide political stabilization and economic growth. But where is the money to pay for it? This is where donor assistance is vital, especially in terms of infrastructure and basic services, both of which require cash injections immediately.

The president has the confidence of the international community, which is extremely important for a post-conflict country and which has facilitated access to funds for the agreed-upon priorities. In 2007 and 2008, funds were forthcoming, and were coordinated by various mechanisms such as the Liberia Trust Fund and the World Bank PRS funds.

Among the donor agencies, the World Bank is Liberia's biggest source of funds (approximately US$140 million in 2008–9). Other UN agencies and bilateral donors made pledges during the Liberian Poverty Reduction Forum and are channeling their funds into the Liberian Reconstruction Trust Fund (approximately $115 million in 2008–9).[34] For a country with 3.8 million people and a GDP of $730 million in 2007, these are very important sums.[35]

Liberia also receives funding through the Peacebuilding Fund (PBF) for post-conflict state building. The PBF is a new UN initiative, created during the reform process in 2005, meant to assist countries from the post-conflict to the development stage.[36] PBF funds are currently available to a very small number of countries. Of the entire US$260 million the fund has, Liberia receives $15 million.[37] Sierra Leone and Burundi were the first two countries to receive assistance through this fund (see Table 11.1). They have been deemed further along in the post-conflict period and thus eligible for more money. Population size has an impact on the amount of funding a country is allocated.

In comparing several post-conflict countries currently in a peacebuilding phase, with regard to available World Bank and PBF funds, Liberia seems to be on par and not particularly favoured. For all the countries, World Bank funds are clearly a more important source of assistance. This points to coherence in terms of the dedication and time put into the PRS as a primary tool for state building in Liberia, as it is a World Bank initiative. Also, the PBF funds are not especially directed at basic services and infrastructure projects. In Liberia they tend to have a more social nature to encourage activities that bring together conflicting communities. In the current situation, with smaller

Table 11.1
World Bank and PBF donations

Country	Population	Date of full PRSP	World Bank Funds 2008/2009[a]	Peacebuilding Funds[b]
Liberia	3.8 million	June 2008	US $140 million	US $15 million, February 2008
Sierra Leone	5.7 million	Mid-2005	US $244.6 million	US $35 million, March 2007
Burundi	7.2 million	September 2006	US $347 million	US $35 million, March 2007
Ivory Coast	18.9 million	Commenced December 2005	US $110 million (in 2007)	US $0.7 million, June 2008
Guinea	9.2 million	2002	US $216 million (in 2007)	Eligible for funds, since June 2008

Sources: For columns 2 to 4 the World Bank Country Brief of the individual countries; for column 5 the UN Peacebuilding briefs for the individual countries.

[a] World Bank, "Country Briefs." http://go.worldbank.org/SYO399CG10. For Sierra Leone, http://go.worldbank.org/COWMCN2VS0; for Burundi, http://go.worldbank.org/X3R55Z5AU0; for Côte d'Ivoire, http://go.worldbank.org/SN2JJO8PI0.
[b] UN Peacebuilding Fund, "Approved Projects and Progress Updates": for Liberia, http://www.unpbf.org/liberia/liberia-projects.shtml; for Sierra Leone, http://www.unpbf.org/sierraleone/sierraleone-projects.shtml; for Burundi, http://www.unpbf.org/burundi/burundi-projects.shtml; for Côte d'Ivoire, http://www.unpbf.org/Cote-dIvoire/Cote-dIvoire-projects.shtml; for Guinea, http://www.unpbf.org/Guinea/Guinea-projects.shtml.

resources at hand, one cannot imagine that the PBF would be the source of a coherent framework for a post-conflict state building, nor has it suggested it intends to play that role.

The key for Liberia will be to ensure that the major donors, along with other sources of funds, continue over the long term so as to support the undertaken initiatives in the necessary sectors. Much will depend on the ability of the current government to continue the positive governance process as well as on the ability of the major donors to participate in coordinated efforts in state building.

In particular, for coordination purposes, the large UN family will need to continue its common country assessments (CCAs) or a similar mechanism. Not only their funds, but also human resources and daily activities on the ground, should have a similar direction in order to provide coherence to the state-building effort. The UNMIL/UNDP development of and contribution to country administrations should persist, especially with regard to expanding their dialogue with the national level. Although auditing procedures should be considered, the country administration is a clear governance structure that can absorb resources and direct a state-building process while remaining close to the needs of the population. As well, INGOs, which are often funded by the big donor agencies, will need to keep their projects relevant to the evolving situation and continue to draw attention to the needs of the Liberian people. INGO projects often contribute directly to basic services and peacebuilding projects, so their activities will be crucial to Liberian state building for the next few years.

Liberia will not always be able to count on assistance funds. Eventually that aid will peter out as new world crises develop and draw off those funds. So the Liberian government must develop other sources of revenue for ongoing state building. This is where private investment becomes crucial.

Private Investment in Liberia

The Liberian president is well aware of the role that private investment can play in a poor country that needs to grow its economy.[38] This awareness brings with it an openness combined with caution, in that Liberia has sometimes in the past been too generous to foreign investors. For example, the government is encouraging Firestone Rubber Plantation and the Liberian Agriculture Company (LAC) to stay in the country; but it has also insisted on renegotiating their concessions, with the aim of ensuring that the country benefits from their activities. Specifically, the government has negotiated new rent and taxation schemes.

Private investment can be tricky and uncertain business in Liberia. There have been violent protests over the past few years centred on plantations, which are the symbol of foreign private business in the country. The robbery/murder in November 2007 of Bruno Michiel, the Belgian manager of the Grand Bassa rubber plantation, is likely linked to LAC's expansion plans.[39] This demonstrates that a certain degree of unhappiness exists among Liberians with foreign companies. From experience, Liberians understand that private investment generates revenue and creates jobs; but there is a trend appearing that demands transparency and a good deal for the people when the country's natural resources are involved.

Besides natural resources, Liberia has other benefits to offer private investors. The most likely investors include the African business community and the Liberian diaspora, which is based mainly in the United States. Tourism and light industry may one day prove to be options. For either to take hold, stability will have to continue and so will growth, and the government will have to establish appropriate taxation schemes that will benefit both investors and the Liberian people.

At this point, the state-building process depends almost entirely on donor aid. Private capital is welcome, but the government is not yet in full swing to attract such funds, and caution may be an underlying reason. In a weak post-conflict economy, too large an injection of private funds outside the state-building framework could dampen the real progress that Liberia is making. For their part, private investors are probably not prepared to risk too much in a post-conflict state such as Liberia at a time when rebuilding is just under way.

Overview and Future

At the present time, donor assistance is the driving force behind the costly state-building process in Liberia. Progress is only possible under good governance, and at present, so far, Liberia seems to be blessed with that. The PRS process is guiding both government and international donors through agreed-upon priorities for Liberia. Sticking to these priorities, in part identified through the consultative process in 2007, is essential to support Liberians as they struggle to regain their lives after years of conflict. Though Liberia should eventually benefit from private investment, there is little of it so far and thus it does not have a strong influence on the country's direction at this time.

To build on the achievements in the past few years a coherent framework and accompanying funds are key, Yet many twists and turns lay ahead for Liberian state building. How long will UNMIL stay in the country? What will result from the 2010 national elections? Will the region as a whole remain stable? Will the Liberian people remain engaged in their own governance? And most important, will the donor community remain actively involved in the country? The provision of aid in ways that address the causes and consequences of the past civil unrest will be decisive. At the same time, the continuation of aid will become a more troubling question in the coming years, and more diverse sources of funding will have to be found.

Notes

1 This committee is comprised of ministers from the Liberian government as well as major partners, including the UN, the United States, China, the World Bank Group, the EC, the IMF, the AU, and ECOWAS. It was created after a 2004 initiative that was more complicated, with a two-track monitoring system, failed. The LRDC has a steering committee and four working committees: Security, Economic Revitalization, Governance and the Rule of Law, and Infrastructure and Basic Services. It is responsible for implementing the PRS. For more information, see http://www.emansion.gov.lr/content.php?sub=Background&related=LRDC.

2 Republic of Liberia, "Liberia Poverty Reduction Strategy 2008–2011" (Monrovia: April 2008), 14–17. http://www.emansion.gov.lr/doc/Final%20PRS.pdf.

3 This chapter is the author's personal research and should not be interpreted as an official representation of the UN presence in Liberia.

4 Liberia Institute of Statistics and Geo-Information Services (LISGIS), "2008 National Population and Housing Census: Preliminary Results" (Monrovia: June 2008), 2. http://www.emansion.gov.lr/doc/census_2008provisionalresults.pdf.

5 The ACS was founded in 1816 to help freed black slaves leave the United States—that is, as a means to address the divisive debate in the United States over what to do with them. Opinion in the country ranged widely: some Americans did not want blacks to stay in the country; others wanted them to return to their "homeland"; and still others wanted to fight for the Black right to citizenship. Some ACS members were racists; others believed that freed

black slaves would be better off back in Africa. For more information, see http://personal
.denison.edu/~waite/liberia/history/acs.htm,http://www.loc.gov/exhibits/african/afam002.
html, and http://www.pbs.org/wgbh/aia/part3/3p1521.html.

6 The members of the society all held this view. However, their reasons varied. Some held rac-
ist views, others had paternalistic motives.

7 Public Broadcasting Service (PBS) website, "Resource Bank: American Colonization Society: 1816–1865" (2008). http://www.pbs.org/wgbh/aia/part3/3p1521.html.

8 Comfort Ero, "ECOWAS and the Subregional Peacekeeping in Liberia," UN Association
Conference, September 1995, n3. http://www.jha.ac/articles/a005.htm.

9 Harold Nelson, "Liberia: A Country Study—Americo Liberians and the Indigenes." http://
www.globalsecurity.org/military/library/report/1985/liberia_2_americoliberians.htm.

10 Taylor had already been politically active, a dissenter against Tolbert and, later, a member
of the Doe administration. But then he was accused of embezzling US$1 million. He was
imprisoned in the United States in May 1984, but escaped in September 1985 and fled to
Libya to plan a coup in Liberia. Prince Johnson was a member of Taylor's NPFL, but formed
his own rebel group after an internal struggle with Taylor's supporters. Prince was elected
senator in the 2005 national elections and still plays a role in Liberian politics.

11 Republic of Liberia, "Liberia Poverty Reduction Strategy 2008–2011," 14.

12 UN, "Liberia: 2007 Common Humanitarian Action Plan" (New York: February 2007), 8.
http://ochadms.unog.ch/quickplace/cap/main.nsf/h_Index/CHAP_2007_Liberia/$FILE/
CHAP_2007_Liberia_SCREEN.pdf?OpenElement. See also "Global IDP Database: Profile of
Internal Displacement—Liberia" (Oslo: Norwegian Refugee Council, August 2005). http://
www.humanitarianinfo.org/liberia/mediacentre/press/doc/Liberia%20-August%202005.pdf.

13 Republic of Liberia, "Liberia Poverty Reduction Strategy 2008–2011," 16.

14 Ibid., 14–17.

15 World Bank, press release, "World Bank & IMF Support Liberia's Decision Point Under the
Enhanced HIPC Initiative," March 18, 2008. http://go.worldbank.org/IH5FT051G0.

16 Republic of Liberia, "Liberia Poverty Reduction Strategy 2008–2011," 17.

17 Ibid., 15.

18 World Bank, press release.

19 Republic of Liberia, "Liberia Poverty Reduction Strategy 2008–2011," 17.

20 Truth and Reconciliation Commission of Liberia. https://www.trcofliberia.org.

21 Republic of Liberia, "Liberia Poverty Reduction Strategy 2008–2011," 14–17.

22 UN, "Liberia President Orders Ministers to Oust Corrupt Staff," April 28, 2008. http://www
.afrol.com/articles/18996.

23 For example, the Firestone concession was reduced by fifty years in 2008. For a comparison
of the old and new agreements, see http://www.emansion.gov.lr/doc/FirestoneAgreement-
Comparison20052008.pdf.

24 These reforms and others can be found and tracked through the LRDC pillar scorecards.
See http://www.emansion.gov.lr/content.php?sub=Pillar%20Scorecards&related=LRDC.
See also World Bank, press release, in "Note to the Editors."

25 Government of Liberia, "LRDC Structure." http://www.emansion.gov.lr/content.php?sub=
Structure&related=LRDC.

26 In mid-2007 a seventh district was created in Lofa.

27 Republic of Liberia, "Liberia Poverty Reduction Strategy 2008–2011," esp. Chapter 9, "Rehabilitating Infrastructure and Delivering Basic Social Services," 97–123.

28 "World Bank Liberia Country Brief: Donor Coordination." http://go.worldbank.org/
SYO399CG10.

29 Republic of Liberia, "Liberia Poverty Reduction Strategy 2008–2011," 136.
30 Liberia Institute of Statistics and Geo-Information Services, p. 5. N.B.: Estimates in 2007 ranged between 300,000 and 400,000.
31 New forces are undergoing training. About 1,000 have already been trained. The goal is 2,000 troops by 2010. See Government of Liberia, Ministry of National Defense, "Building a Trained and Disciplined Army Through a Rigorous Vetting Process" (April 21, 2008). http://www.mod.gov.lr/press.php?news_id=2.
32 For example, a change in diet from the traditional rice to spaghetti (which is cheaper) was noted in 2008. See Kate Thomas, "Liberians Drop Rice for Spaghetti." http://news.bbc.co.uk/2/hi/africa/7360649.stm.
33 Specifically ICRC, IMC, IRC, and UNICEF for health centres; and IRC, UNHCR, PWJ, UNDP, UNICEF and ARC for schools.
34 For a breakdown of the donor agencies and committed funds in education, health, and agriculture, see "Donor Aid Flows Database Portal." http://www.emansion.gov.lr/lrdcpublicusers/tbldonorfunds_list.php.
35 See World Bank, "Liberia Statistics." http://devdata.worldbank.org/AAG/lbr_aag.pdf.
36 UN Peacebuilding Fund, "United Nations Peacebuilding Fund—Bridging the Gap Between Conflict and Recovery." http://www.unpbf.org/index.shtml.
37 http://www.unpbf.org/index.shtml.
38 Consider the Liberia Private Sector Investment Forum, held in February 2007 in Washington; for its agenda, see http://www.africacncl.org/Events/Liberia_Investment_Forum.asp. Also consider the significant improvements in the corruption indicator for Liberia, a change of seventy-two positions in two years according to the World Bank; see http://www.emansion.gov.lr/doc/Liberia_Corruption.pdf. See also "Liberian President Happy with EcoBank." http://allafrica.com/stories/200901120637.html; Star Radio Liberia, "LRDC Wants to Seek Foreign Investment." http://www.starradio.org.lr/content/view/3764/59.
39 See "LAC Perpetrators Will Be Rounded Up: Global Bank Funds Seized in Robbery," http://www.analystliberia.com/lac_perpetrators_will_be_rounded_up_nov19_07.html; and "Body of Slain LAC Manager Off to Belgium," http://www.frontpageafrica.com/newsmanager/anmviewer.asp?a=5463.

Liberia
Building Peace Through Investment-Climate Reform[1]
David Bridgman and Robert Krech[2]

12

Introduction

Motives for participating in armed conflict are complex and not easily categorized, but in the late 1990s a key distinction was made regarding the nature of economic causes of conflict. Political scientists argued that exclusion from economic opportunities, popularized by the term "grievance," is an important cause of conflict. Horizontal inequalities such as differences in access to resources, assets, employment, or other commercial opportunities among regional, social, or ethnic groups were identified as examples of causes or drivers of conflict.[3] In contrast, economists identified economic resources as important drivers to the duration and intensity of a conflict. In this explanation, financial opportunities for economic actors and their incentives to end or prolong a conflict are linked to the occurrence of natural resources (e.g., timber or diamonds) as well as to the ability to divert them into the global trading system. Here, resources are used as sources of personal profit and as a means to sustain conflict.[4] Conflict can be recognized as a means to profit for some, as much as it destroys profit for others.[5] Current discussions in this debate recognize a more nuanced blend of both exclusion and profit in both explaining and responding to armed conflict, and extend the analysis to include questions of governance and institutions.[6] Extending the logic of Collier's research on the economic causes of conflict, practitioners have come to regard private-sector development needs as of greater priority and as worthy of early attention during reconstruction. Given that the private sector does not cease functioning during civil conflicts, and has been implicated in the causes of (especially) resource-based conflicts, private-sector development can no longer be ignored.

The rise in the intensity of civil conflicts since the end of the Cold War[7] was matched by an increase in postwar reconstruction of conflict-affected countries. The collective response of the international community to these countries developed during this period into a sophisticated and complex industry, as noted as by Roland Paris more than ten years ago.[8] The aid industry in conflict-affected countries is no less sophisticated, and it could be argued that it has become even more developed. The contemporary "menu" of reconstruction assistance (separate from humanitarian assistance) through UN, bilateral, multilateral, NGO, and reconstituted national-government activities includes reforming the security sector (e.g., DDR processes; reforming and training the military, police, and intelligence services; restoring and training the judicial branch); reforming the political system (e.g., drafting a new constitution; drafting new laws; supporting elections; strengthening parliaments; supporting civil society and the media as facets of a functioning democracy); and rebuilding economies (e.g., restoring the macroeconomic and public-finance systems, retraining their practitioners, and supporting the resumption of private-sector and market activity); to name but a few.[9] Liberia's experience of the past five years is consistent with this description.

While the above description accurately captures the scope of reconstruction interventions common to conflict-affected countries, within the past two years practitioners among the donor community have begun to re-examine the role of private-sector development (PSD) in post-conflict reconstruction. Early policy responses to the role of the private sector in conflict-affected countries did not immediately recognize the positive role the private sector could play in conflict-affected countries. Policies on the private sector started with the assumption that international companies need to improve their behaviour, given their role in conflicts. Policy options for the private sector from this perspective have ranged from UN Security Council (UNSC) sanctions, to voluntary codes of conduct (e.g., EITI++ compliance or the Kimberley diamond certification scheme), to domestic lobbying or even lawsuits to force behavioural change.[10] While these policy responses all represent "stick" options, few policy options for the private sector have employed "carrot" responses that seek to enhance the private sector as part of the peacebuilding process. The NGO International Alert was among the first to envision a positive role for the private sector in conflicts.[11] As this perspective gained acceptance among practitioners, the private sector came to be increasingly viewed as a source of investment and badly needed employment following civil conflict.

This chapter uses Liberia as a case to illustrate the emergence of a higher priority for private-sector development in post-conflict reconstruction, drawing on lessons learned from the investment-climate reform work of the International Finance Corporation (IFC) in that country. Following an initial brief background on Liberia's civil conflict, the chapter discusses Liberia's experience with post-conflict reconstruction. Two waves of economic reform are described, with specific reference to the importance of the Governance and Economic Management Assistance Program (GEMAP) as a set of economic reforms that have opened space for private-sector reforms. The chapter concludes with lessons drawn from private-sector reforms supported by the IFC.

Liberia's Civil Conflict

Liberia was founded as a republic by freed American slaves in 1847. Its government was dominated by Americo-Liberian descendents of the original settlers through the True Whig Party. In 1980, Samuel Doe staged a successful coup d'état that ended 133 years of de facto one-party rule by Americo-Liberians. In the decades prior to the coup, Liberia had not developed significantly outside of Monrovia, the capital. Under the Doe regime of the 1980s, conditions in the country deteriorated. His administration favoured the Krahn ethnic group. That, and human-rights abuses and worsening corruption, led to growing dissatisfaction among most Liberians. Liberia's civil war, which brought Charles Taylor to power, began in 1989 as a purportedly revolutionary war but soon degenerated into a brutal conflict marked by extremes of predation, violence, and economic warlordism. In these chaotic conditions, multiple factions emerged. Not content to appropriate the Liberian state's revenues for his own purposes, Taylor and his supporters fought Liberians United for Reconstruction and Democracy (LURD) and Movement for Democracy in Liberia (MODEL) rebels for control of the country's timber and rubber—and to a lesser extent, its diamonds and gold. Much of income generated went to buy arms. In addition, Taylor supported the Revolutionary United Front (RUF), a rebel group in neighbouring Sierra Leone that was waging an equally brutal war. Taylor supplied the RUF with weapons and fighters in exchange for diamonds looted from Sierra Leone's rich Kono District. Clearly, Liberia's—and Sierra Leone's—natural resources were being exploited to perpetuate violence. UNSC sanctions were eventually imposed on Liberia in an attempt to halt round-log and diamond exports from that country. Though a brief peace prevailed after the 1997 special elections that returned Charles Taylor to power, fighting eventually resumed, and continued into 2003, when Taylor left Liberia under international pressure.

The years of fighting devastated Liberia. About 450,000 Liberians became refugees or internally displaced persons (IDPs). An additional 103,019 Liberians would later register with the UN as combatants—and 11,282 of these were child combatants.[12] The war destroyed the country's health and education sectors, leaving facilities wrecked, their staff killed or displaced. By the time the war ended the under-five infant mortality rate was among the highest in the world, at 205 per 1000.[13] Maternal mortality was likewise among the world's highest, estimated at 578 per 100,000. The national literacy rate was thought to be 37 percent, and net primary enrolment was around 35 percent.[14] The widespread destruction of homes and public facilities meant that electricity and water utilities were essentially non-functioning throughout the country. GDP fell by 90 percent between 1987 and 1995;[15] per capita GDP in 2004 was approximately US$116; outstanding combined public and private debt stood at $4.5 billion.[16] Over 85 percent of Liberia's estimated 3 million people were unemployed. Equally devastating was the history of mismanagement of government services and exploitation of the country's natural resources. Systemic reform would be required to improve performance and restore public trust.

The private sector, too, was negatively affected in many ways by Liberia's conflict. Before the war, Liberia had been exporting iron ore, rubber, logs, coffee, cocoa, diamonds, and gold, extracted mainly through large international concessions. Despite a large debt, Liberia's official exports stood at $486 million in 1978;[17] the country's trade surplus in 1986 was $149.4 million.[18] With much of the country under the control of three different fighting forces and much of the population displaced, international investors left and domestic market activity fragmented. Trade in retail goods dominated urban centres near the border; agricultural production was limited. Coffee and cocoa production dropped by 91 and 79 percent respectively.[19] Key infrastructure, such as roads and the port, was damaged. The formal credit market collapsed by 93 percent with the closing of commercial banks,[20] and laws and policies were weakened, along with the country's institutions and human capacity. All of this was severely debilitating for the private sector as well as for the investment climate.

After the conflict ended, the international community launched a large peacekeeping and reconstruction program, which will likely continue for a number of years. To maintain security, Liberia hosted the UN Mission in Liberia (UNMIL), a peacekeeping mission that was 15,000 strong at its peak.[21] The international community spent about US$1.1 billion on Liberia's reconstruction between 2004 and 2006,[22] implemented in part by about 130 INGOs and 390 NGOs[23] in nearly all sectors. Central to Liberian reconstruction efforts over the past five years have been economic reforms that address (a) the failures of public institutions to stem corruption and (b) the involvement of Liberia's resources in its conflict.

Liberia's Reconstruction: First Economic Reforms—GEMAP[24]

When Liberia's reconstruction began in 2003, the inclusion of economic factors to explain the conflict was widely accepted by academics and practitioners alike. In part, this was because of the international community's experience in Sierra Leone's reconstruction,[25] which later influenced Liberia's program. The post-conflict focus in Sierra Leone had been on reintegrating child and youth combatants; corruption, poor governance, and private-sector reform were addressed only later, to the regret of some in the international community. Sierra Leone's experience with reconstruction was closely watched in Liberia, where economic-governance issues came to the fore as a result of Charles Taylor's flagrant pillaging of Liberia's resources and revenues for his own purposes. Though youth were similarly both victims and combatants in Liberia's civil conflict, Taylor's dismantling of the state and his use of war for his own profit—

and the subsequent misrule of the transitional government—made economic governance a priority for peace.

Liberia's war ended when Taylor left Liberia in August 11, 2003. After a brief administration by Vice-President Moses Blah, rule was turned over to the National Transitional Government of Liberia (NTGL) on October 14, 2003. Under the terms of the Accra Comprehensive Peace Accord (ACPA), each of the factions—the Government of Liberia, LURD, and MODEL—was allocated a share of the leadership positions in ministries, agencies, and state-owned enterprises (SOEs), as well as in the National Transitional Legislative Assembly. Civil society was also allocated a small number of positions. This power-sharing arrangement ensured broad representation of all factions across the government.

The NTGL took over a deeply troubled governance system. Decades of mis-management of public resources even prior to Taylor's presidency had eroded most institutional controls. Taylor's kleptocratic rule had further disabled gov-ernment institutions. The war economy that had consumed Liberia's resources only added to the problems. In a condition of such decay, the public service was demoralized, low in capacity, and riddled with corruption. As rebel factions gained ground, Taylor's government had increasingly directed expenditures to-ward military ends at the cost of civil servants' salaries. Liberia's civil servants had increased their rent-seeking activities in government processes in order to extract a living wage. As a matter of entitlement, key officials in revenue-generating entities became wealthy through graft and revenue theft. As a re-sult, the national budget had contracted from US$240 million in 1988 to $72 million in 2003.[26] Relations with international financial institutions were poor and deteriorating. Liberia was under UN sanctions on diamond and timber ex-ports because those revenues had been instrumental in promoting conflict in the region. Given these challenges and the grave humanitarian crisis, the im-mediate focus of the NTGL and the international community was on stabilizing the country, delivering emergency humanitarian assistance, empowering the NTGL, and mobilizing the UN peacekeeping mission. Broad capacity within the government to execute responsible governance simply did not exist.

The NTGL demonstrated promising performance on economic governance during its first months in office. The IMF initially reported substantially im-proved relations after the NTGL took power in October 2003; its 2004 Article IV consultation report was promising.[27] The NTGL took key first steps to boost revenue, restore an orderly budget process, and address key governance issues. In November 2003, Chairman Gyude Bryant issued Executive Order no. 2, which designated the Ministry of Finance the central revenue authority, with all revenue to be deposited in the Central Bank. Bryant also supported the previous request by the IMF to allow audits of the Central Bank of Liberia, as well as key state-owned revenue-generating enterprises (the National Port

Authority, Roberts International Airport, the Bureau of Maritime Affairs, the Liberia Petroleum Refining Company, and the Forestry Development Authority). The European Commission (EC) agreed to finance these audits, which were not intended to be forensic audits, but rather to focus on operational and accounting systems and procedures. In addition to all of this, the Economic Community of West Africa (ECOWAS) dispatched a corruption-investigation team to undertake its own study.

The EC audits revealed a composite picture of gross systemic, procedural, and human-resource incapacity in a context of irregular operating conditions arising from the conflict. Owing to a lack of information and documentation prior to October 2003, the EC audits were forced to focus on the period from October 2003 onwards, which only highlighted an alarming degree of large-scale mismanagement and abuses of financial resources during the NTGL period itself. While considerable progress had been made on the security and humanitarian fronts, the economic situation was stagnant or even regressive. Liberia was failing at economic governance. Contracts and concessions were a primary concern: a number of contracts had been signed that did not seem to be in the national interest. One example was a contract signed with a Chinese company for the disposal of state assets, most notably abandoned extracted iron ore, at excessively lopsided prices. A further example was a contract with a company called the West African Mining Company (WAMCO) that granted the company the exclusive right to all minerals from roughly one-third of the country (with an option for the remainder). The NTGL initially denied that this contract had been signed, but this proved not to be the case, and the contract was eventually annulled. The climate of governance had created a ripe opportunity for massive systemic mismanagement and corruption; the result was institutional deficiencies that made it difficult for auditors to render opinions on the country's financial records.

At a one-day meeting in Copenhagen at the tail end of a scheduled donor coordination conference, the international partners agreed (a) that Liberia's deficiencies in economic governance had been a key contributor to the fourteen-year civil war, and (b) that continued inattention to the issue posed a long-term risk to the peace process and ongoing or planned donor assistance. After intense debate and resistance from the NTGL, and much redrafting,[28] GEMAP was signed. GEMAP's provisions target key points along the length of the revenue stream, from revenue capture to auditing, in an attempt to bring greater control over the country's public finances. The six GEMAP components, supported by the World Bank, the U.S. government, the EC, the IMF, and other UN agencies as well as West African bilateral partners, are as follows:

- *Secure Liberia's revenue base.* This involves protecting the funds flowing into government accounts from key revenue-generating institutions, as well as customs charges, fees, and taxes, by building capacity, reinforcing transparency, and establishing transparent and accountable financial systems and procedures, with internationally recruited technical assistance and oversight. Basically, this means installing financial controllers at Liberia's state-owned enterprises and in Liberia's Central Bank to provide oversight of revenue, introduce improved accounting systems, and train staff.

- *Improving budgeting and expenditure management.* This involves strengthening and clarifying procedures for formulating and executing both budgets and financial-management processes. It requires building the capacity of the Ministry of Finance, putting clear and robust procedures and systems in place, and making information on the budget and spending publicly available. This has been accomplished by providing resident technical assistance to improve the functions of the Bureau of the Budget and the Ministry of Finance Cash Management Committee; by establishing a Resource Management Unit and Integrated Financial Management Information System platform at the Ministry of Finance; by embedding technical advisers in key revenue and expenditure departments; and by computerizing government accounts.
- *Improving procurement practices and concession-granting procedures.* This involves ensuring that all government procurements, concessions, contracts, and licensing procedures are undertaken openly, transparently, and according to international standards, so that the people of Liberia get the best value for their resources. To this end, a new procurement law for Liberia has been passed and a Public Procurement and Concession Commission (PPCC) has been created to support compliance with that law. Also, a review of the contracts and concessions signed by the NTGL has been conducted, with a view to annulling or renegotiating signed contracts as necessary.
- *Controlling corruption.* This involves putting mechanisms in place to detect and prevent corruption in both the public and the private sector. This effort has focused mainly on establishing a Anti-Corruption Commission.
- *Supporting key institutions of government.* This involves strengthening those institutions that are key to promoting and sustaining accountable government and good financial management, such as the General Auditing Commission (GAC), the General Services Agency (GSA), the Governance Reform Commission (GRC), and the PPCC.
- *Building capacity.* This involves building the capacity of Liberian institutions and professionals so that good-governance reforms are sustainable.

The institutional elements of GEMAP have been structured as a steering committee called the Economic Governance Steering Committee (EGSC), with a corresponding technical team. The EGSC is chaired by the Liberian president and is comprised of representatives of related government ministries and agencies, as well as the principal members of the international community engaged in the GEMAP program.

President Ellen Johnson-Sirleaf has strongly supported the program from her first days in office. In her inaugural speech in January 2006 she emphasized her commitment to governance reform and improved fiduciary management, but she also promised to "render GEMAP non-applicable in a reasonable period of time." Johnson-Sirleaf and others in her administration have defended the program as consistent with the present government's reform agenda, noting that Liberia's particular situation—especially its severe capacity limitations—has made the program a short-term necessity. GEMAP as a program has focused only indirectly on the private sector (i.e., through its review of government contracts and concessions, including the Arcelor Mittal and Firestone contracts). Concerted attention to private-sector reforms did not begin until February 2006.

Liberia's Reconstruction:
Second Economic Reforms—Investment-Climate Reforms

Despite the experience of the international community in Sierra Leone, and the experience of GEMAP in Liberia, private-sector reforms are still viewed as third-generation interventions for conflict-affected countries—that is, as coming third to humanitarian assistance and reforms to public financial management. The emphasis on economic governance initially hindered a focus on private-sector development, given that GEMAP tilted donor and government discourse strongly toward macroeconomic reform. However, this greater emphasis on GEMAP eventually forced attention onto the private sector. Put another way, attention to issues of economic governance in post-conflict Liberia led to a recognition that private-sector activities in Liberia needed to be uprooted from the war economy. It was widely acknowledged that to close the book on the country's recent conflict, the government would have to create jobs for Liberians and encourage investment, which in turn meant prioritizing private-sector reform.[29]

Investment Climate Assessment

In February 2006 the Foreign Investment Advisory Services (FIAS)—a multidonor service of the World Bank Group—came to Liberia to conduct a quick assessment of the country's investment-climate needs. Up to that point, few donors were engaged in the country with private-sector reforms. The initial assessment was an abbreviated 'mini-diagnostic' version of FIAS's Administrative Barriers Report, which reviews a range of investment-climate issues to identify constraints on the business-enabling environment. The mini-diagnostic was conducted in one week by a five-person team in co-operation with the World Bank office in Monrovia. Its key findings were that the commercial and investment legal framework was discriminatory as well as inconsistent with international best practices; that there were uncoordinated and excessive inspections of businesses; that customs procedures were excessive and uneven; that the tax system was highly discretionary; and that there was a high degree of mistrust between public- and private-sector actors. Also, most businesses were found to be operating informally. To varying degrees these findings were consistent with what FIAS had found with respect to private-sector needs in other conflict-affected countries, such as Rwanda and Sierra Leone. Moreover, these findings added to the already existing awareness (through GEMAP) of the low capacity and petty corruption that typified the governance of Liberia's institutions.

Phase I (September 2006–June 2007)

On the basis of the above assessment, FIAS opened an office in the World Bank country office and hired a coordinator to support the project-visiting expert teams. The country program was designed to roll out in phases, with the first phase consisting of the following: an "informality survey" that selected a sample of small and medium-sized firms that were operating informally (i.e., were not registered) in order to ascertain why they had not registered; a technical legal review, with assistance provided to draft a new investment code and incentives regime; the review and drafting of an institutional strategy and capacity-building program for the National Investment Commission (NIC); and the formation of Liberia's only public–private dialogue network, called the Liberia Better Business Forum (LBBF). The latter task involved defining the framework and mandates of the network and holding consultations on its objectives and outcomes. The informality survey, the review of the investment code and incentives regime, and the strategy/capacity-building program were completed during or just after the allotted timeframe of Phase I.

Phase II (July 2007–June 2009)

The second phase of the program extended the work of Phase I and added new activities. Following the "informality survey," work began on creating a new-business registry, complete with start-up procedures. This work involved reviewing the legal technicalities of business creation; designing a new registry and IT processes for it; designing new start-up procedures; and providing new equipment and training for staff. Work also began on developing the investor-outreach capacity of the NIC. New work was commenced in the area of trade-logistics reform; this involved redesigning and computerizing import and export procedures. Related to this, the government has asked for assistance in establishing a special economic zone at the Port of Buchanan, where Arcelor

Mittal loads iron ore. One innovative program has involved helping the Ministry of Agriculture to draft a model concession agreement for international bids for Liberia's oil-palm production. Liberia was included in the Doing Business annual rankings for the first time for the period covering the year to June 2007. Meanwhile, the public–private dialogue network is scaling up, with multiple foci: enhancing the legal and regulatory framework for commerce generally; finding a greater role for the private sector in the development of infrastructure; and supporting the work activities described above. The Doing Business data provide useful benchmarks for the public–private dialogue network, which the team is supporting as a means to achieve investment-climate reforms. Equally important, the program had added a robust communications stream that is integrated with the public–private dialogue network. This project goes beyond PR work and is training journalists on how to report on economic issues.

In response to Liberia's initial ranking in the Doing Business index, the president immediately convened a meeting of cabinet members and major donors to put in place a structure to improve the country's investment climate. A cabinet committee comprising the leading ministries involved in the economy was established that met weekly—at times daily—to put in place measures to improve the investment climate. Within nine months, no fewer than twenty-one regulatory improvements were made. The following year's edition of Doing Business showed that Liberia had improved in the index by ten places—an outstanding performance for a new entrant, especially a post-conflict country.

During the year, Liberia had made huge progress in other investment-related areas besides. An operating public–private dialogue is fuelling the development dialogue, a number of private-sector–supporting infrastructure developments are under way, huge private-sector investments are being considered, and progress has been made in a number of facets of the investment climate, beyond those captured by *Doing Business*.

Lessons Learned

The IFC's experience in investment-climate reform work yields a number of important lessons for private-sector development. Two of those lessons are discussed here.

Operational Innovation

The IFC piloted operational practices in Liberia that are increasingly being adopted elsewhere. It leveraged the resources and staff of the World Bank's Liberia office by co-locating its program on the World Bank site. This sharing of resources allowed the IFC to quickly introduce program elements in response to the government's interests and the country's challenges. This kind of rapid shift from analytical work to program implementation was viewed as critical to demonstrating commitment to reform in a fragile environment. As part of its efforts to respond quickly, the IFC placed staff on the ground early in the program to build stronger relationships with counterparts in both government and the private sector. This move was partly in response to the recognition that sensitive and technically complex reforms would demand additional efforts to build capacity.

Structuring Reform: Large Versus Small Businesses

There is no formula for sequencing private-sector reforms in conflict-affected countries, but from the phasing practised by the team a three-part structure has emerged. The first part centres on the public–private dialogue network, together with communications support. The Doing Business ranking has provided a tangible measure of progress in achieving reforms. As implementation issues arise, thematic working groups within the network bring government and leading private-sector actors together to find workable solutions. Solving implementation challenges has built trust and sometimes prevented stalling. In tandem with the public–private dialogue network activities is the second part, where the team works with relevant government officials to simplify regulations in the areas of business registration and trade logistics. In tandem with regulatory simplification is the third part of the structure, in the course of which the team has supported general investment promotion and agricultural-sector investment by supporting the performance of the NIC, as well as by helping the Ministry of Agriculture develop the oil-palm sector by developing model concession structures. This three-part structure is reflected in the phasing and suggests a useful strategy.

Structured in this way, the IFC team was able to target its products toward different types of businesses whose needs are different. The simplifying of regulations benefits all businesses entering and operating in Liberia, but especially small and medium-sized domestic enterprises (SMEs). As most SMEs operate informally, their growth is constrained by limited access to credit, to new partnerships, and to new cross-border trading opportunities. Larger firms, which are often more international than domestic, benefit more from support along sectoral lines; extractive industries are an example. This approach is not unique to IFC, which is helping draft a model concession agreement in the rubber sector. USAID is providing similar assistance to the mining sector with work on a new mining code, a mining cadastre, and concessioning procedures. Similarly, a multi-donor effort has assisted the Government of Liberia in the forestry sector by helping it draft a new forestry law and build the capacity of the Forestry Development Agency (FDA). The same effort has helped guide the tendering of concession opportunities for both domestic and international investors.

This tripartite structure makes it possible to align IFC investment-climate reform products with businesses in conflict-affected country programs, as in Table 12.1.

Table 12.1

Public–private dialogue

Small and Medium Enterprises	Large Companies
• Business registration	• Investment code
• Business licenses	• Industry specific reforms
• Taxation	• Investment promotion and generation
• Secured lending	• Special economic zones
• Trade	

Experience suggests that larger companies, especially international ones, possess enough resources to address regulatory constraints within the investment climate themselves (e.g., by hiring local law firms to deal with registrations and licences, or by negotiating regulatory issues when closing a deal), though it is true that a murky investment climate does severely reduce the number of firms interested in seeking investment. It makes sense, then, to separate SME reform products from SME products for larger companies. Public–private dialogue cuts across this division, but corporate social responsibility interventions could do the same, as could supply-chain-linking efforts between SMEs and larger companies.

Reform versus Investment

Another lesson from Liberia relates to the pace at which reform processes move relative to investment. Three sectors provide a useful comparison: forestry, mining, and tree crops. In the forestry sector, UNSC sanctions imposed an embargo on round-log exports and called for a new forestry law and a chain-of-custody system to track logs from origin to point of export for revenue-collection purposes, as well as to certify their legal origins and conflict-free status. This imposed halt to the forestry industry bought time to draft a new forestry law and regulations, to build some capacity in the FDA, to establish a chain-of-custody system, and to design and manage the concession process. In other words, the policy dialogue preceded all new investments.

The mining and rubber sectors did not have the same time and space as the forestry sector. In the mining sector, Arcelor Mittal had signed a US$1 billion, twenty-five-year concession with the NTGL before Johnson-Sirleaf ascended to the presidency and before any reforms to the commercial or mining regulatory regime. The social and environmental terms of the concession agreement were heavily criticized by Global Witness,[30] and concerns were raised by the donor community regarding the return on the deal for Liberia. Arcelor Mittal wanted to retain its concession, so, with governmental commitment to reduce corruption—not to mention resources from international partners to

---

Table 12.2

Legal, policy, and regulatory reform and the pace of investment
in forestry, mining, and tree-crop sectors

Forestry	Mining	Tree Crops
• Legal and regulatory reforms first, then investment • Structured concession-bidding process developed and carefully managed • Chain-of-custody system in place prior	• Arcelor Mittal concession agreement renegotiated pror to new legal framework • Off-shore oil-exploration contracts cancelled prior to new legal framework • New legal framework completed before current discussions on three new mines	• Firestone concession agreement renegotiated prior to new laws and regulations • New rubber and new oil-palm concessions signed prior to new laws and regulations • Other plantations out for bid while new law and regulations in draft

help with the renegotiation—Liberia was able to renegotiate the concession. In other words, a sovereign state violated the sancitiy of a contract, which slowed down an investor's entry into the sector, so that legal and regulatory reforms could take place.[31] In this instance the policy-reform work caught up with the sector.

In the tree-crop sector, investments have gone ahead of reforms, with reforms struggling to catch up. This has happened for two reasons. First, while most rubber plantations were under concession agreements that predated the conflict, a number of rubber plantations were abandoned by their concession holders during the fighting and subsequently occupied for years by ex-combatants during and after the civil conflict. These plantations were eventually cleared of ex-combatants by a UNMIL military operation that disarmed them and pushed them out. The Ministry of Agriculture placed these rubber plantations cleared by UNMIL under the commercial management of the Liberia Rubber Planters' Association; it also sent a clear message to international partners that the rubber plantations were off limits to GEMAP. Second, donor resources were already committed elsewhere. Except for the renegotiations relating to the Firestone rubber plantation, the plantations slipped off the radar of government and international-partner dialogue. Donors became re-engaged with the sector only when it became known that the Ministry of Agriculture was putting vacant rubber plantations out for international tender; international-development partners wanted to support policy reforms before the tendering was concluded. Realizing that the tendering could not be halted and that interested investors could not be held at bay, the donor partners began mobilizing support for policy reform in the sector (including the IFC's draft concession agreement). At the same time, the Ministry of Agriculture obtained pro bono legal aid from a large American law firm, which helped with the negotiations. The result has been a mix of legal and regulatory reforms in parallel with concession tendering, with pro bono legal aid attempting policy reform during the actual negotiations.

The three sectors tell a tale of optimal, acceptable, and suboptimal investment-climate reforms. A few observations from these experiences suggest a number of lessons. All of Liberia's resources were implicated in its conflict, but the forestry sector most of all. Unique to that sector, forestry benefited from UNSC sanctions that gave it sufficient space and time for reforms. Mining and rubber were not as implicated or under sanctions, but both benefited from concession reviews under GEMAP. The high-profile review of Arcelor Mittal and the cancellation of oil-exploration contracts likely delayed investor entry, which similarly gave space and time for reforms in the mining sector. The imperative to gain control of diamond and gold mining perhaps also provided an impetus to introduce reforms sooner. The rubber sector is similar to the mining sector in that a large, high-profile concession was renegotiated; but in contrast to the mining sector, no rubber concessions were cancelled. Significant for the rubber sector, the combination of governmental resistance to international partners' involvement in that sector and donor-funding commitments elsewhere resulted in a gap that is only now being filled. In some measure, reforms commenced through better-coordinated dialogue between donor partners and the government. While the optimal scenario—that of the forestry sector—is not likely to be repeated often, the middle acceptable scenario suggests that a coordinated approach by donor partners toward the government is crucial if the third, sub-optimal scenario is to be avoided.

Conclusion

As some observers have noted, Liberia "arguably more than anywhere in the world, is a darkly resplendent example of the resource curse."[32] As much as Liberia's resources drove its conflict, its resources offer the country an opportunity to recover and grow. The economic nature of the conflict generated the first generation of economic reforms, which centred on the GEMAP program. These reforms contributed to the conceptual space that enabled work on the private sector earlier than in other contemporary conflicts.

With hindsight, it would have been more appropriate for recovery efforts to target Liberia's economy earlier in the reconstruction effort. In light of the awareness that inequitable access to economic resources had contributed strongly to the conflict, it would have been appropriate to have immediately begun work on restructuring access to those resources so that as the society recovered, previous access patterns were not replicated. This conclusion probably holds for other post-conflict countries, given that access to resources (or economic access) often contributes to conflict.

It is curious that countries emerging from conflict are often in a better position to fundamentally reform their investment climate. Possibly the awareness that "the system is broken" reduces the power of vested interests. Whatever the case, aggressive reformers with a strong political mandate seem to make fast progress. A lesson from Liberia and other post-conflict countries is that it is both necessary and relatively easy to seek early changes in the economic rules. Reconstruction efforts should build on this opportunity for early economic reconstruction.

In a quickly evolving country context that can often be highly politically charged, trade-offs abound. There remain fundamental challenges with which the IFC continues to struggle. The first important trade-off for the IFC is between addressing the needs of large investors and addressing those of small businesses. On the one hand, reigniting the private sector could arguably best occur in sectors of Liberia's comparative advantage. On the other hand, private-sector support might best be addressed to the needs of the numerically greater businesses that employ a larger number of people in urban areas. The second important trade-off is between getting investors in-country and getting policies right. The urgent need to welcome investors who generate jobs is undeniable, but the risk of not altering the faulty dynamics of the war economy is equally compelling.

By quickly implementing its programs with innovative operational practices, the IFC was able to bring a more coordinated response to the full scope of commercial needs. In this manner, it managed the first trade-off by increasing its resources and ground presence to bring simultaneous support. The second trade-off remains an ongoing challenge. In future reconstruction efforts, the IFC would seek to undertake policy reforms to critical sectors even earlier, both in anticipation of investor interest, but also to support the government's wish to attract new investment even earlier.

Notes

1 Portions of the beginning of this chapter were drawn from an unpublished paper by Matt Chessen and Robert Krech, "Post-War Reconstruction in Liberia: The Governance and Economic Management Assistance Program (GEMAP)," presented at the International Workshop on Peacebuilding and Corruption, hosted by the Department of Politics and International Relations at Oxford University, March 22–23, 2007.

2 "This publication is a product of the staff of the World Bank Group. The findings, interpretations and conclusions expressed in this publication do not necessarily reflect the views of the Executive Directors of the World Bank Group or the governments they represent."

3 Frances Stewart, *Horizontal Inequality: A Neglected Dimension of Development* (Helsinki: Wider, 2001).

4 Paul Collier and Anke Hoeffler, "Greed and Grievance in Civil War," Oxford Economic Papers 56, no. 4 (2001): 563–95; Andrew Rosser, *The Political Economy of the Resource Curse: A Literature Survey* (London: Institute of Development Studies, 2006).

5 David Keen, "The Economic Functions of Violence in Civil Wars," Adelphi Paper no. 320 (Oxford: Oxford University Press, 1998); Phillipe Le Billon, "The Political Ecology of War: Natural Resources and Armed Conflicts." *Political Geography* 20 (2001): 561–84.

6 David Malone and Heiko Nitzschke, "Economic Agendas in Civil Wars: What We Know, What We Need to Know," Discussion Paper no. 2005/07 (Helsinki: Wider, 2005).

7 SIPRI (Stockholm International Peace Research Institute), *SIPRI Yearbook 2008: Armaments, Disarmament, and International Security* (Oxford: Oxford University Press, 2008).

8 Roland Paris, "Peacebuilding and the Limits to International Liberalism," *International Security* 22, no. 2 (1997): 54–89. Paris refers to some of the substantial literature on postwar reconstruction that had already been developed by the late 1990s. This literature has not diminished since his article ten years ago.

9 Marina Ottaway, "Rebuilding State Institutions in Collapsed States." *Development and Change* 35, no. 5 (2002): 1001–23.

10 International Alert, "Local Business, Local Peace: The Peacebuilding Potential of the Domestic Private Sector" (London: 2006); Macartan Humphreys, "Natural Resources and Armed Conflicts: Issues and Options," in *Profiting from Peace: Managing the Resource Dimensions of Civil War*, ed. Karen Ballentine and Heiko Nitzschke (London: Lynne Rienner, 2005).

11 International Alert, "Local Business, Local Peace: The Peacebuilding Potential of the Domestic Private Sector" (London: 2006).

12 National Commission on Disarmament, Demobilization, Rehabilitation, and Reintegration (NCDDRR) and UNMIL, "Fortnightly DDRR Consolidated Report for Phases 1, 2 & 3," Status of Disarmament and Demobilization Activities as at January 16, 2005.

13 http://www.unicef.org/infobycountry/liberia_statistics.html.

14 UNDP, Ministry of Planning, Ministry of Health and Social Welfare, Liberia Institute of Statistics, and Geo-Information Systems (LISGIS), "Liberia Human Development Report 2006: Mobilizing Capacity for Reconstruction and Development," Monrovia.

15 Steve Radlet, "Reviving Economic Growth in Liberia," Working Paper no. 132 (Washington: Center for Global Development, 2007).

16 IMF (International Monetary Fund), "Liberia: 2005 Article IV Consultation—Staff Report; Public Information Notice on the Executive Board Discussion; and Statement by the Executive Director for Liberia," IMF Country Report no. 05/166 (Washington: 2005).

17 Radlet, "Reviving Economic Growth in Liberia."

18 Randolph Fleitman, "Apparent Bottoming Out of the Economic Decline and Fall in Dollar Open New Trading Opportunities," *Business America*, March 14, 1988.

19 Radlet, "Reviving Economic Growth in Liberia."

20 Ibid.

21 http://unmil.org/content.asp?ccat=history.

22 Author's calculation based on bilateral and multilateral agency survey conducted in September 2006.

23 Information obtained March 13, 2007, from http://www.humanitarianinfo.org/Liberia/coordination/contacts/docs/Contact%20List_20060606_Today.pdf.

24 Governance and Economic Management Assistance Program (GEMAP) Agreement, Final Version, signed by International Contact Group for Liberia and National Transitional Government of Liberia, September 9, 2005. http://www.gemapliberia.org/files/GEMAP_Final_and_signed_by_NTGL.pdf.

25 As it turned out, a number of people who worked for the UN, NGOs, or bilateral aid agencies in Sierra Leone subsequently worked in Liberia (including one of the authors of this paper), bringing with them lessons learned from their Sierra Leone experience.

26 James Brooke, "International Report: Mission to Liberia Evidently Fails," *New York Times*, December 5, 1988; IMF, "Liberia: 2002 Article IV Consultation, Overdue Financial Obligations to the Fund—Review Following Declaration of Ineligibility, and Decision on Suspension of Voting and Related Rights—Staff Report; Staff Statement; Public Information Notice and Press Release on the Executive Board Discussion; and Statement by the Executive Director for Liberia," IMF Country Report no. 03/74 (Washington: 2003). According to an article by President Ellen Johnson-Sirleaf, Liberia's budget in 1980 was US$900 million ("Underwriting Liberian Rebirth Political Reform and Economic Progress," *Ethnic Conflict* 28, no. 4 (2007).

27 IMF, "Liberia: Report on Post-Conflict Economic Situation and Prospects for January–June 2004—Staff Report; Staff Statement; Public Information Notice on the Executive Board Discussion; and Statement by the Executive Director for Liberia," IMF Country Report no. 04/84 (Washington: 2004).

28 Renata Dwan and Laura Bailey, "Liberia's Governance and Economic Management Assistance Program," joint review by the Department of Peacekeeping Operations' Peacekeeping Best Practices Section and the World Bank's Fragile States Group (Washington and New York: May 2006).

29 Existing programs paid attention to the private sector before this conceptual space for private-sector reform opened up. GEMAP involved a contract and concession review, and a multi-donor forestry reform program involving legal, policy, and administrative reforms, as well as forest-concession bidding support to revive the sector with clean investors. But these activities were integrated into programs without explicit "private sector" labels.

30 Global Witness, "A State within a State: The Inequitable Mineral Development Agreement Between the Government of Liberia and Mittal Steel Holdings NV," report by Global Witness (September 2006).

31 Investor entry was slowed also because controversial offshore oil-exploration concession blocks were reviewed and bitterly contested under GEMAP, but eventually cancelled.

32 Partnership Africa Canada and Association of Environmental Lawyers of Liberia/Green Advocates, "Land Grabbing and Land Reform Diamonds, Rubber, and Forests in the New Liberia," Occasional Paper no. 17, Diamonds and Human Security Project (Ottawa: Partnership Africa Canada, 2007), 2.

Afterword

Eddy Maloka[1]

Ending violent conflicts in Africa and overcoming the traumas and challenges of post-conflict transitions are top priorities if the continent is to claim the twenty-first century or, at the very least, meet the 2015 deadline for achieving the UN's millennium development goals. Indeed, the objective of the Policy Framework on Post-Conflict Reconstruction and Development (PCRD), which the African Union adopted at its January 2006 Summit, was "to improve timeliness, effectiveness and coordination of activities in post conflict countries and to lay the foundation for social justice and sustainable peace, in line with Africa's vision of renewal and growth."[2] The PCRD "is conceived as a tool to consolidate peace and prevent re-lapse of violence; help address the root causes conflict; encourage fast-track planning and implementation of reconstruction activities; and enhance complementarities and coordination between and among diverse actors engaged in PCRD processes."[3] The PCRD also identifies six areas around which post-conflict and reconstruction interventions can be organized: security; political governance and transition; human rights, justice, and reconciliation; humanitarian assistance; reconstruction and socio-economic development; and gender mainstreaming in all interventions.[4]

The PCRD is anchored in five core principles: African leadership; national and local ownership; inclusiveness,equity, and non-discrimination; co-operation and coherence; and capacity building for sustainability. It is the first two principles—ownership and leadership—that are singled out in the paragraphs that follow.

The Accra Conference "From Civil Strive to Peace-Building: Examining Private Sector Involvement in West African Reconstruction" was a timely intervention whose recommendations will feed into ongoing efforts aimed at strengthening Africa's resolve to bury, once and for all, the misery of wars whose cost to the continent is well recorded. One challenge with post-conflict transitions in Africa relates to the extent to which they can avoid the consequences described in Naomi Klein's The Shock Doctrine: The Rise of Disaster Capitalism (New York: Metropolitan, 2007). According to Klein, post-disaster situations, like the aftermath of a war, are sometimes exploited to impose a political-economy agenda on a country that its citizens, and sometimes even its elite, would ordinarily have opposed.

One effective and reliable measure to safeguard post-conflict countries from the imposition of a "shock doctrine" by external actors is African ownership and leadership as espoused particularly in the NEPAD philosophy and program. African ownership and leadership depend on two sets of variables. One relates to context and setting, the other to actors. By context and setting, it is meant that whatever measures are put in place or solutions are implemented, these must be consistent with African reality, history, and experience and with those of the country itself. Actors must have a profound familiarity with the same things; and ideally, they should be African themselves. In addition, African ownership and leadership should be given effect in the domain of resources and technical expertise required for the situation at hand.

Sadly, most post-conflict transitions on the continent are owned and led by non-Africans. There are a number of reasons why. First, the national elite in a post-conflict situation tend to be highly fractured, held together by some peace accord in such a way that they cannot present a united front to determine the agenda, content, pace, and direction of the political economy of the transition. Second, in most cases, national institutions, including the state machinery, are in utter disarray and therefore at the mercy of multitudes of initiatives being introduced into the country by external actors targeting, for example, the public service, the armed forces, the police, and local government. Third, the economy is likely to be in no better condition, and like the national institutions is likely to be subjected to all sorts of therapy by external actors. Fourth and finally, the national civil society has certainly been weakened by war and its consequences, with many citizens in exile and many more among the internally displaced or in the ranks of the armed groups that are being demobilized and reintegrated into society. In that sort of situation, civil society is in no position to seriously contest the agenda being set. Indeed, many civil-society formations in the country will be NGOs funded by non-African donors.

So, what one has in the scenario above is, on the one hand, a post-conflict transition that is usually very fragile, with a fractured elite at the helm of weak institutions and a weak economy, and a civil society trying to get a footing in the direction of a normal life. And on the other hand, one has a host of actors, most of whom are non-African, with resources, geopolitical muscle, and technical expertise to intervene in the transition, especially in the areas of security, demobilization and disarmament, political governance, human rights, justice and reconciliation, humanitarian assistance, gender mainstreaming, economic reconstruction and socio-economic development, and the rehabilitation of infrastructure.

Clearly, Africa needs to build its own capacity to own and lead the post-conflict transition at the level of affected countries, the sub-region, and the African Union. This capacity has to be, first and foremost, political: the continent must be in a position to manage this host of actors flooding into post-conflict countries, and more than anything, it needs to be able to set the agenda and determine the political-economy outcome of the transition. For this, speeches and concept papers will not suffice; the continent has to have its own resources and technical expertise to intervene at least in the six areas of post-conflict transition that are identified in the AU's PCRD policy framework.

For example, the AU's PCRD framework envisages the following interventions in the area of political governance and transition:[5]

- (Re)establish consensus of governance by developing mechanisms and processes that guarantee broad-based participation and leadership, allow for collective determination of needs and priorities, and guarantee local ownership of the process.
- Commence a process—one that is fair and inclusive—at national, regional, and local levels for all sectors of the society, including displaced populations and the diaspora, to determine the national vision and to design strategies for its attainment; to engage in dialogue that defines the national identity; and to establish and reinforce a legitimate state.
- Facilitate the establishment and/or restoration of inclusive democratic public institutions and civil authorities, as well as legislative oversight capacity.
- Establish constitutional governance (democracy), including periodic political competition with opportunity for choice, as well as the rule of law.
- Adopt policies and legislation to address the challenges of corruption at the national, regional, continental, and global levels.
- Create credible, transparent, and accountable transitional public institutions that are able to ensure the rule of law and deliver basic public services.
- Create mechanisms to ensure accountable, efficient, and effective public office holders and civil servants.
- Establish rules and realistic timetables for interim government/ authorities.
- Initiate processes that fast-track comprehensive capacity building at the state/institutional and non-state levels; this should include encouraging members of the Ddiaspora with leadership and other relevant skills to return to the country.
- Promote the involvement of local civil-society organizations in governance processes at all levels.

- Engage in rebuilding political/process skills, such as mediation, negotiation, and consensus building, that are key to transformation of society but that are often destroyed during the conflict.
- Establish processes that encourage ongoing impact assessment to ensure corrective activities and alignment of reconstruction programs with evolving needs.
- Address and deal with the root causes of conflict, by ensuring administrative justice, among other things.
- Facilitate the creation of mechanisms that encourage decentralization of power, and of resource management, to all levels of governance from the national to the grassroots.
- Integrate continental frameworks of governance into PCRD strategies.
- Establish a secure civic space that is not dominated by spoilers.
- Facilitate societal transformation in ways that reflect the interests of women, address their needs and aspirations, and consolidate any gains associated with the conflict, to improve their lives.
- Ensure the participation of women in the entire public sphere.
- Establish civic education and other public campaigns to raise awareness and understanding of the new political structure and vision, especially among the youth.

This agenda for the governance aspects of post-conflict transitions is massive and requires resources, capacity, and political will to implement. The African Ministers of Public Service and Administration have been meeting as a forum of the African Union since 1994 on a biennial basis to address challenges facing the African public service continentwide, and have since identified the governance dimension of post-conflict transitions as one of the areas that require their engagement. With a forum of this nature, Africa should be in a better position to act collectively to contest the ownership and leadership of the agenda being shaped in post-conflict countries.

However, notwithstanding the efforts of these ministers, the continent has still a long way to go with respect to ownership and leadership in post-conflict transitions. As noted earlier, the dominant actors in this area are non-African, and furthermore, the solutions and political-economy models that are being packaged and implemented in some post-conflict countries on the continent have been conceived outside the African context and setting. Regarding resources and required technical expertise, these are also sourced from outside the continent. This is one big challenge—perhaps one of the biggest of this century—and one that Africa is profoundly determined to overcome.

Where and how can the private sector contribute to successful post-conflict transitions? This question was addressed carefully by the participants at the Accra seminar. The involvement of the private sector can, without doubt, strengthen the capacity of a country to own and lead its post-conflict transition. Thus the recommendations that came out of the conference should be considered for possible action on the policy front.

Notes

1 Eddy Maloka is the Adviser on Governance, Public Administration, and Post-Conflict Reconstruction at the NEPAD Secretariat. Previously, he headed the African Legacy Program at the 2010 FIFA World Cup Organising Committee. Between 1999 and 2006 he was the CEO of the Africa Institute of South Africa (AISA).
2 African Union, Policy Framework on Post-Conflict Reconstruction and Development, p. 3.
3 Ibid.
4 See ibid., p. 8.
5 See ibid., pp. 8–13.

Recommended Reading

Addison, Tony, Philippe Le Billon, and Mansoob S. Murshed. 2001. "Finance in Conflict and Reconstruction." Discussion Paper No. 2001/44. August. Helsinki, Finland, United Nations University, World Institute for Development Economics Research. http://www.unepfi.org/fileadmin/documents/conflict/addison_lebillon_murshed_2001.pdf.

African Press Organization (2008). "Sierra Leone / Peace Building Fund (PBF) approves seven new projects to enhance peace in Sierra Leone," *African Press Organization*, http://appablog .wordpress.com/2008/07/17/sierra-leone-peace-building-fund-pbf-approves-seven-new -projects-to-enhance-peace-in-sierra-leone, accessed 12 February 2009.

Campbell, Kelly, and Adams Fusheini (2006). "Creating a More Inclusive Peace in Côte d'Ivoire," *USIPeace Briefing*, http://www.usip.org/resources/creating-more-inclusive-peace-c-te-divoire.

Curran, David, and Tom Woodhouse (2007). "Cosmopolitan Peacekeeping and Peacebuilding in Sierra Leone: What Can Africa Contribute?" *International Affairs* 83, no. 6: 1055–70.

Government of Sierra Leone (2005). "Poverty Reduction Strategy Paper 2005–2007." http://planipolis.iiep.unesco.org/upload/Sierra%20Leone/PRSP/Sierra%20Leone%20PRSP2005 .pdf.

Government of Sweden (2009). Ministry of Foreign Affairs. Strategy for Swedish Development Cooperation in Sierra Leone for the Period Ending in December 2013. http://www.regeringen .se/content/1/c6/12/33/46/8ebb8523.pdf.

Grey-Johnson, Crispin (2006). "Beyond Peacekeeping: The Challenge of Post-Conflict Reconstruction and Peacebuilding in Africa." *The UN Chronicle Online Edition*, http://www .un.org/Pubs/chronicle/2006/issue1/0106p08.htm, accessed 12 February 2009.

Labonte, Melissa (2004). "Frustration or Facilitation? Peacebuilding 'Ownership' in Sierra Leone and the Reproduction of Social Inequalities." Paper prepared for the American Political Science Association (APSA) Conference, Chicago, September 1–4, 2004.

OECD (Organization for Economic Cooperation and Development). 2008. *African Economic Outlook 2008*. Paris: AfDB/OECD.

Public International Law and Policy Group (2006). "Economic Reconstruction: Targeted Development Mechanisms. Quick Guide." New York: Public International Law and Policy Group.

UNDP/UNFPA, UNICEF, and WFP (2007). Report on the Joint Field Visit to Liberia of the Executive Boards of UNDP/UNFPA, UNICEF, and the World Food Program. February 25–March 5. New York.

United Nations (2008). UN PBF Bulletin 4 August. Update 01 August 2008. http://www.un.org/peace/peacebuilding/PBCFastFacts/PBFBulletin1August2008.pdf.

——. "Gaining Momentum on the Ground." *UN PBF Bulletin* No 2. Update 28 January 2008. http://www.un.org/peace/peacebuilding/PBCFastFacts/PBF%20Bulletin%2028%20 Jan%202008.pdf, accessed 12 February 2009.

UNPF (United Nations Peacebuilding Fund) (2008). *Priority Plan for Peacebuilding Fund (PBF)*. Liberia 2008. New York: UNPF.

Von Gienanth, Tobias, and Thomas Jaye (2007). "Post-Conflict Peacebuilding in Liberia: Much Remains to Be Done." Report to the Third Annual KAIPTC/ZIF Seminar, Accra, Ghana, November 1–3.

World Bank Report No. 32564: "Implementation Completion Report on a Credit to the Amount of US$79.66 million to the Republic of Côte d'Ivoire for a Private Sector Energy Project." June 27. Washington: World Bank.

——. Sierra Leone Country Brief. World Bank, Washington. Updated March 2009. http://web. worldbank.org/WBSITE/EXTERNAL/COUNTRIES/AFRICAEXT/SIERRALEONEEXTN/0,, menuPK:367833~pagePK:141132~piPK:141107~theSitePK:367809,00.html/.

Contributors

Siham Abdulmelik is a consultant working with the NEPAD Support Section at the UN Economic Commission for Africa. Previously, she worked in Sudan in the field of parliamentary development with the Canadian Parliamentary Centre. She was involved in developing the peacebuilding program designed to enhance the capacity of the National Assembly and the Southern Sudan Legislative Assembly to support the peace agreements signed and to strengthen the democratic process under way. Her background is in economics and public policy. Her research interests are in African governance mechanisms, institutional capacity building, and post-conflict recovery.

Chrysantus (Chris) Ayangafac is a senior researcher at the Institute for Security Studies, Addis Ababa office. His research interest is conflict prevention, management, and resolution in Africa. He is currently researching regional security mechanisms in Africa with a specific interest in the African Peace and Security Architecture. He has published widely on conflict and integration in Africa. His latest publication, as editor, is *The Political Economy of Regionalization in Central Africa.* He is also a reviewer for the *International Journal of Transitional Justice* and has done extensive radio and television interviews on conflicts on the continent with radio stations such as SADC Africa, Channel Africa, and Radio Netherlands. Currently he is a Ph.D. student at the University of Witwatersrand, Department of International Relations. His proposed Ph.D. thesis is titled "The Natural Resources Conflict Nexus: Bringing Back Politics."

Hany Besada is the Senior Researcher and Program Leader of the Health and Social Governance Program at the Centre for International Governance Innovation. Mr. Besada's research interests include African economic and political development, Middle East studies, international diplomacy, fragile/failed states, private-sector development, and conflict resolution. He holds his M.A. and B.A. in International Relations from Alliant International University in San Diego, where he specialized in peace and security studies. Before joining CIGI, he worked as the Business in Africa Researcher at the South African Institute of International Affairs (SAIIA) in Johannesburg, South Africa. Prior to that, he worked as a research manager at Africa Business Direct, a trade and investment consulting firm in Johannesburg. He also worked at a number of non-governmental and governmental research institutes and offices. These included Amnesty International, the Office of U.S. Senator Dianne Feinstein, United Nations Associations, and the Joan Kroc Institute of Peace and Justice.

Lydie Boka-Mene's background is in international economics and finance (Diplomatische Akademie, Vienna, Austria). She has twenty years' experience in project finance (including agricultural commodities) and management as well as risk analysis. Her employers include USAID, the International Finance Corporation, the African Development Bank, and other financial institutions in Africa, Europe, and the Middle East. She is the founder and manager of StrategiCo. (http://www. strategico.org), which specializes in risk analysis in Africa and the Middle East using a methodology designed to capture developing countries' risk. Ms. Boka is a dual citizen of France and Côte d'Ivoire. StrategiCo. clients includes corporate and financial institutions, as well as decision makers from Africa and the Middle East.

David Bridgman is the lead expert in private-sector development in the World Bank Group Investment Climate Team for Africa. He leads the team's work on investment institutions in Africa and holds specific responsibility for leading the team's advisory program in Liberia. Previously, he managed MIGA's Sub-Saharan Africa Program. Before that he established and managed MIGA's global investment promotion capacity-building program. A South African national, he holds degrees from South African and American universities, finishing with a Ph.D. in International Development from Cornell University. During his career he has served on numerous public and public–private sector boards and has held teaching and research positions at universities in South Africa and the United States. Prior to joining MIGA, he established an economic development agency in South Africa and was actively involved in development matters during and after South Africa's political transformation.

Jonathan Coppel is the executive program manager of the NEPAD-OECD Africa Investment Initiative and senior economist developing user guidelines for the Policy Framework for Investment with the OECD Investment Division. Since joining the OECD he has held a range of positions, including Deputy Counsellor to the Chief Economist, head of the EU and UK Desks, and energy market analyst. Mr. Coppel has also held senior management positions in the Reserve Bank of Australia. He started his career at the Australian Commonwealth Treasury. He was educated at the Australian National University and at Columbia University in New York.

Vadim Ermakov is an associate at PricewaterhouseCoopers in Porto, Portugal. He holds a B.A. in international economic relations from the University of World Economy and Diplomacy in Tashkent, an M.Sc. in technology and innovation management from Sussex University in Brighton, and an M.P.P. in public policy from the Hertie School of Governance in Berlin. Prior to joining PwC he completed an internship at CIGI in Waterloo, Ontario, where he worked with Hany Besada, a senior researcher and program leader in the Health and Social Governance Program. While studying in the United Kingdom, he was a policy consultant at the South East of England Development Agency and successfully completed the project Nurturing Innovation in the South-East Region: Assessment of the Innovation Advisory Service. He also worked on several development projects in Uzbekistan, supervised by the European Bank for Reconstruction and Development.

Andrew Goodwin majored in political science at the University of British Columbia and pursued a graduate degree in international relations at the Institut d'Études Politiques de Lille. He interned at the West African Network for Peacebuilding in Ghana and the International Crisis Group in Senegal, where this chapter was co-authored. He is currently a junior consultant at the UN Office on Drugs and Crime.

Willene A. Johnson is currently president of Komaza, Inc., an economic consulting firm specializing in the role of finance in development and reconstruction. Focusing on Africa, Dr. Johnson conducts research and offers instruction in various subjects, including microfinance and security-sector resource management. From January 2000 to September 2001, she served in Abidjan, Côte d'Ivoire, as the U.S. Executive Director of the African Development Bank, overseeing AfDB policies and development activities throughout Africa. She also serves as a member of the UN Committee for Development Policy and as the Vice-Chair of the Grameen Foundation African Advisory Council. Until recently, she was Chair of the Sub-Saharan African Advisory Committee of the U.S. Export-Import Bank and an adjunct professor of applied economics and management at Cornell University. Her work in finance and development builds on insights gained during nearly twenty years in the Federal Reserve System, where her career included economic research, foreign exchange, international financial markets, international affairs, and equal employment opportunity. Her education includes an A.B. in social studies from Radcliffe College, Harvard University, an M.A. in African history from Saint John's University, and a Ph.D. in economics from Columbia University.

Andrew Keili, a mining engineer by profession, is managing director of CEM-MATS Group Ltd., a leading multidisciplinary engineering and project management consulting practice in Sierra Leone. Mr. Keili worked for a substantial period in the diamond and rutile mines in Sierra Leone before embarking on consultancy work. Over the past thirty years he has held positions of increasing responsibility in the private mining industry, in parastatals, and in consultancy work in Sierra Leone. He has an extensive background in the formulation and review of government policies, particularly in the mining, environmental, and infrastructure sectors, and has written extensively on the Sierra Leone mining industry. He has done consultancy work for several companies in the United States, Ukraine, and various countries in Africa. He is a member of the National Policy Advisory Committee to the president of Sierra Leone and has substantial experience in the Sierra Leone business sector. Mr. Keili is also chairman of the board of trustees of the National Social Security and Insurance Trust in Sierra Leone and a council member of the Sierra Leone Chamber of Commerce, Industry, and Agriculture and the Sierra Leone Institution of Engineers.

Caroline Khoubesserian has been working as a humanitarian aid worker since 2006 in Darfur, Liberia, and currently in Haiti. From 2003 to 2006 she was the senior research officer with the Centre for International Governance Innovation, where she coordinated several projects on multilateral governance, including global health governance and the L20 project. She has also worked in Lesotho with the Ministry of Justice to compile a UN Human Rights Report on Economic, Social, and Cultural Rights. She holds an M.A. in international politics from Dalhousie University and a B.Sc. in political science from the University of Ottawa.

Robert Krech has worked on conflict-affected countries for the past ten years, including Cambodia, Laos, Nepal, Sierra Leone, Liberia, the Democratic Republic of Congo, Haiti, and Somalia. He completed his graduate work in political science at the University of Toronto, where he focused on post-conflict reconstruction and conducted field research in Sierra Leone. He has published on postwar reconstruction and presented widely on the topic. He has worked for the World Bank for the past six years and lived in Liberia for two years, where he worked in the World Bank country office. Currently he works for the Foreign Investment Advisory Services in the World Bank Group as an operations specialist for Fragile and Conflict-Affected Countries.

Mark Malan is an analyst with the New Zealand Centre for Army Lessons. From May 2007 to July 2008 he served with Refugees International as Peacebuilding Program Officer and Executive Coordinator for the Partnership for Effective Peacekeeping. From 2004 to 2006 he established and headed the Conflict Prevention, Management, and Resolution Department of the Kofi Annan International Peacekeeping Training Centre. From 1996 to 2003, he served as a senior researcher and head of the Peace Missions Program at the Institute for Security Studies. Before joining the ISS, he served for twenty years with the South African Army, attaining the rank of lieutenant colonel and holding a variety of posts, including senior lecturer in political science at the SA Military Academy. Malan has developed a number of regional peacekeeping training courses and manuals and has published extensively on regional security and peacekeeping in Africa. He has been an active participant in the African and global policy debate on peace support operations. He drafted the White Paper on South African participation in peace missions and was a contributing author to the supplementary volume of the ICISS report, *The Responsibility to Protect.*

Eddy Maloka is currently the Adviser, Governance, Public Administration, and Post-Conflict Reconstruction, at the NEPAD Secretariat. Previously he was responsible for the African Legacy Program at the 2010 FIFA World Cup Local Organizing Committee. For seven years he was CEO of the Africa Institute of South Africa. Before joining the AISA, Maloka was a lecturer at the University of the Western Cape and the University of Cape Town; for about two years after that he was a political adviser in the Office of the Premier in South Africa's provinces of Gauteng and Mpumalanga. Maloka writes widely on development issues on the African continent. He researches extensively on political and developmental issues in Africa, including the history of the liberation struggle in South Africa, and writes a weekly column for the Sowetan. Maloka has delivered lectures at the world's premier universities, including Oxford and Princeton. He is Vice-President for Southern Africa of the Association of African Political Science and President of the SA Association of Political Studies.

Emmanuel Nnadozie is senior economist and chief of the UN Coordination Unit for AU/NEPAD Support at the UN Economic Commission for Africa (ECA). At one time he was focal point for the African Peer Review Mechanism at ECA. Before joining ECA in June 2004 he was an economics professor at Truman State University (1989–2004), visiting professor at the University of North Carolina (1996–97), and research fellow at Oxford University (1994). He is also the former chief planning officer at the World Bank's Agricultural Development Program in northern Nigeria. His scholarly works have appeared in academic and non-academic journals all over the world, and he is general editor of *African Economic Development*. An award-winning educator, he was recognized as the Most Outstanding Black Missourian of the Year in 2003. He has served as president of the African Finance and Economics Association of North America (1999–2001) and editor of the *Journal of African Finance and Economic Development* (1998–2002).

Sunny Nyemah is managing consultant at George Edward Consulting, where he directs the assurance and compliance operations. He is also an adjunct faculty member at Metropolitan State University, Minnesota. In addition, he sits on the board of African American Family Services, the Pan African Chamber of Commerce, and Liberia Environmental Watch. He is a member of the Minnesota Society of Certified Public Accountants, the National Association of Corporate Directors, the International Compliance Association, and the Anti-Money Laundering Compliance Association, and is a Certified Internal Auditor, a Certified Investment and Derivative Auditor, a Certified International Project Manager, a fellow of the American Academy of Project Management, and a graduate of the Real Estate Institute (GRI). He holds Series 6 and 63 Licensures of the National Association of Securities Dealers. Prior to joining George Edward Consulting, Mr. Nyemah was a senior director at Global Equity Lending, an emerging lender with more than $500 million in revenue, based in Suwannee, Georgia, where he was responsible for building a $5 million monthly pipeline of residential loans and for supervising more than 200 associates. In addition to his investment and financing background, Mr. Nyemah has worked at Robert Half International (RHI) as a management consultant, providing financial management consultancy to such companies as Norwest Bank (Wells Fargo), Aegon-USA, CIMA Labs, and Renewal by Anderson (Anderson Windows). Mr. Nyemah holds a master's degree from the University of St. Thomas graduate program in software engineering, in Minnesota, and is a prospective graduate of the Thomas Jefferson School of Law, California (LL.M. program in international public law and finance).

Sunday Abogonye Ochoche holds a B.A. (1977) in philosophy from the University of Ibadan, Nigeria, and M.A. (1981) and Ph.D. (1983) degrees in peace studies from the University of Bradford. Dr. Ochoche was SSRC-MacArthur Foundation Visiting Individual Fellow to the Institute of Development Studies, University of Sussex. He was also post-doctoral fellow of the SSRC-MacArthur Foundation in International Peace and Security Studies at the Matthew B. Ridgway Center for International Security Studies, University of Pittsburgh, and before that taught political science at the University of Jos, Nigeria. Subsequently, he joined the Nigerian War College as Deputy Director, Military Strategy. Later he became director of research. He was appointed the first Director General/CEO of the Institute for Peace and Conflict Resolution, the Presidency, Abuja, Nigeria, in which capacity he also served as adviser to the president on conflict management in Africa. He is currently Senior Political Affairs Officer, UN Integrated Office, in Sierra Leone. Dr. Ochoche was a member of the national committee that drafted Nigeria's Defence Policy in 1997. In September 2002 he headed a four-nation ECOWAS committee to investigate the matter between Guinea-Bissau and Gambia. He was also a member of several Nigerian delegations to the UN General Assembly and AU summits. He is a fellow of War College, Nigeria.

Ozonnia Ojielo is Senior Peace and Development Advisor to the UN Resident and Humanitarian Coordinator in Kenya, as well as Chief, Peace Building and Conflict Prevention, UNDP Kenya. In his prior position, he was senior governance adviser and head of the Governance Program at UNDP, Ghana. Previously, he was chief of operations and subsequently officer-in-charge at the Sierra Leone Truth and Reconciliation Commission, during which period he supervised the statement taking, research, investigations, and report-writing work of the commission. Prior to that, he was a human-rights lawyer (1990–2002), academic (at the Enugu State University of Science and Technology, Enugu, Nigeria, 1997–20001), and president of the research and advocacy NGO, Centre for Peace in Africa, in Lagos, Nigeria (1993–2002). He was a technical adviser to the Malawi Human Rights Commission (1999–2001), adviser on alternative dispute resolution to the maritime industry in Nigeria, and president and fellow of the Institute of Chartered Mediators and Conciliators of Nigeria (2000–2005). He is also a fellow of the Society for Peace Studies and Practice, Nigeria, and of the 21st Century Trust, London. He is the author of two books—*Alter-*

native Dispute Resolution (Lagos: CPA Books, 2001), and *Managing Organizational Disputes* (Lagos: CPA Books, 2002)—and editor of a third, *Rethinking Peace and Security in Africa* (Lagos: CPA Books, 2002). Ozonnia holds a Ph.D. in peace and conflict studies from the University of Ibadan; a B.A. and M.A. in history from the University of Nigeria, Nsukka; an LL.B. from the Anambra State University of Science and Technology, Awka, Nigeria; and an M.B.A. in strategic management from the Paris Graduate School of Management, Paris. He has also attended professional courses in conflict transformation (Eastern Mennonite University, Virginia), conflict research (University of Uppsala, Sweden), international conflict resolution (Austrian Study Centre for Conflict Resolution/European Peace University, Stadschlaining), and conflict management and election observation (Scuola Superiore Sant' Anna, Pisa, Italy).

H.E. Darren Schemmer, High Commissioner of Canada to Ghana and Ambassador to Togo (BW.Ed. [Social Sciences], University of Alberta, 1982; M.B.A., Royal Roads University, 2002), joined the Canadian International Development Agency in 1989 as a development officer with the Andes Program, Americas Branch. He has since served abroad in Tegucigalpa, Washington, and Cairo. At CIDA headquarters he has served as Senior Departmental Assistant to the Minister for International Cooperation; Director General, Policy, Planning and Management; and Director General, Haiti, Cuba, and Dominican Republic.

Miran G. Ternamian is a former research officer at the Centre for International Governance Innovation in Waterloo, Ontario. Mr. Ternamian's interests include Africa's economic, political, and security development, social justice as a means to peacebuilding, and environmentally sustainable economic development policies. He holds an honours B.A. from McMaster University and an M.B.A. in strategic management from Wilfrid Laurier University in Waterloo, Ontario. Prior to joining CIGI, he worked in Ottawa with the Bilateral Market Access Division of the Department of Foreign Affairs and International Trade. As a trade policy officer, Mr. Ternamian assessed Canadian industry interests, export opportunities, and import sensitivities with key trading partners.

Oren E. Whyche-Shaw has over the past twenty years held senior positions in the private sector, the not-for-profit sectors, and the public sector. She has worked in developing and emerging-market environments and in North and Sub-Saharan African countries advising on strategies to stimulate the growth of African capital markets and the private sector. Ms. Whyche has held positions at J.P. Morgan, Citibank, R.J. Reynolds Industries, Owens Corning, the African Development Bank, Technosesrve, Inc., and the U.S. Treasury. She has served on the boards of the Planned Parenthood Federation, the African Venture Capital Association, the African Export-Import Bank, and Plan USA. She received a B.Sc. in mathematics and French from Capital University (Columbus, Ohio) and an M.B.A. from the Columbia University School of Business.

Gilles Olakounle Yabi is a senior analyst of the West Africa Project (Dakar) with the International Crisis Group at the time of writing. He joined the International Crisis Group's West Africa office in September 2004 and conducts research on francophone West Africa. Dr. Yabi is responsible for the research and writing of the policy reports and briefings published by the International Crisis Group on the conflicts and political crises in Côte d'Ivoire and Guinea. He also con- tributed to the West Africa Project's research activities on other countries and issues in West Africa. Prior to joining Crisis Group, he completed a doctoral thesis in economics on the determinants of foreign direct investments and their impact on the economic growth in developing countries. He holds his Ph.D. and a postgraduate degree in development economics from the Centre of Studies and Research on International Development of the University of Clermont-Ferrand and a master's degree in international economics from Sorbonne University in Paris. He has also worked as a journalist for the Paris-based newsmagazine *Jeune Afrique*.

Index

Books in the Studies in International Governance Series

Alan S. Alexandroff, editor
Can the World Be Governed? Possibilities for Effective Multilateralism / 2008 / vi + 438 pp. / ISBN: 978-1-55458-041-5

Hany Besada, editor
From Civil Strife to Peace Building: Expanding Private Sector Involvment in West African Reconstruction / 2009 / xxiv + 288 pp. / ISBN: 978-55458-052-1

Jennifer Clapp and Marc J. Cohen, editors
The Global Food Crisis: Governance Challenges and Opportunities / 2009 / xviii + 270 pp. / ISBN: 978-1-55458-192-4

Andrew F. Cooper and Agata Antkiewicz, editors
Emerging Powers in Global Governance: Lessons from the Heiligendamm Process / 2008 / xxii + 370 pp. / ISBN: 978-1-55458-057-6

Jeremy de Beer, editor
Implementing WIPO's Development Agenda / 2009 / xvi + 188 pp. / ISBN: 978-1-55458-154-2

Geoffrey Hayes and Mark Sedra, editors
Afghanistan: Transition under Threat / 2008 / xxxiv + 314 pp. / ISBN-13: 978-55458-011-8 / ISBN-10: 1-55458-011-1

Paul Heinbecker and Patricia Goff, editors
Irrelevant or Indispensable? The United Nations in the 21st Century / 2005 / xii + 196 pp. / ISBN: 0-88920-493-4

Paul Heinbecker and Bessma Momani, editors
Canada and the Middle East: In Theory and Practice / 2007 / ix +232 pp. / ISBN-13: 978-55458-024-8 / ISBN-10: 1-55458-024-2

Yasmine Shamsie and Andrew S. Thompson, editors
Haiti: Hope for a Fragile State / 2006 / xvi + 131 pp. / ISBN-13: 978-0-88920-510-9 / ISBN-10: 0-88920-510-8

Debra P. Steger, editor
Redesigning the World Trade Organization for the Twenty-first Century / forthcoming 2009 / ISBN: 978-1-55458-156-6

James W. St.G. Walker and Andrew S. Thompson, editors
Critical Mass: The Emergence of Global Civil Society / 2008 / xxviii + 302 pp. / ISBN-13: 978-1-55458-022-4 / ISBN-10: 1-55458-022-6

Jennifer Welsh and Ngaire Woods, editors
Exporting Good Governance: Temptations and Challenges in Canada's Aid Program / 2007 / xx + 343 pp. / ISBN-13: 978-1-55458-029-3 / ISBN-10: 1-55458-029-3